S0-AHS-562

The Lorette Wilmot Library
Nazareth College of Rochester

DEMCO

VILLA-LOBOS
COLLECTED STUDIES BY L.M. PEPPERCORN

Villa-Lobos

COLLECTED STUDIES BY
L. M. PEPPERCORN

Scolar Press

WITHDRAWN
LORETTE WILMOT LIBRARY
NAZARETH COLLEGE

© L.M. Peppercorn, 1992.

All rights reserved. No part of this publication may be reproduced, stored in a retrieval system, or transmitted in any form or by any means, electronic, mechanical, photocopying, recording, or otherwise without the prior permission of the publisher.

Published by
SCOLAR PRESS
Gower House
Croft Road
Aldershot
Hants GU11 3HR
England

Ashgate Publishing Company
Old Post Road
Brookfield
Vermont 05036
USA

British Library Cataloguing-in-Publication Data.
A Catalogue record for this book is available from the British Library.

ISBN 0 85967 906 3

Printed in Great Britain at the University Press, Cambridge

Contents

Introduction

Researchers, musiciologists, university faculty members, scholars, students, musicians and music lovers need the latest research findings of others in order to continue their work. Looking for such information and locating publications is often arduous and laborious, time-consuming and frequently futile and unsuccessful because international reference works, music dictionaries and encyclopedias fail to list the latest bibliographies; in addition, entries in international bibliographies are ordinarily many years behind schedule due to most unfortunate delays in classifying, indexing and computerizing the urgently needed information.

Over the years the author was many times invited by various people to gather together her studies on H. Villa-Lobos and make them available as a collection in book form, to facilitate access to the widely dispersed material, published in several languages, in several European countries, and in the United States and Brazil. Even bibliographical information of these studies was sometimes hard to find, since dictionaries and other reference works only sparingly listed an insufficient number of the author's Villa-Lobos bibliographies, for reasons mentioned above and also for lack of space.

As a tribute to the centenary of Villa-Lobos's birth in 1987, the *Staden-Jahrbuch* in São Paulo, Brazil, published (Nos 34/35, 1986, pp. 225–229) the author's Villa-Lobos bibliography up to that time as an initial contribution to meeting the demands of Villa-Lobos researchers and devotees. Yet, the dissemination of the *Staden-Jahrbuch* is limited: it may not reach all those who require more information and knowledge. The author therefore decided to reprint in book form all her studies on Villa-Lobos. They range over a period of fifty-one years, begun in 1940 shortly after she met the composer in the late 1930s when she was Rio de Janeiro music correspondent for *The New York Times* and *Musical America*; they conclude with her journalistic contribution in 1991.

Many of the studies are presented in their original format, but illustrations have been omitted in some cases. The facsimile reproductions may add to readers' enjoyment in enabling them to see how the original studies appeared. To offset directly from previously published material reduced production costs, editorial work and proof-reading and thus allowed prompt publication of this volume in the year following the appearance of the last study of the composer.

Inevitably typographical errors creep into printed texts. The author found it useful, therefore, to add an 'Errors and Omissions' list and to include, occasionally, a few informative items discovered after the original studies were published. The *Errata* are added after each study. She also considered it valuable to append a Chronology of Villa-Lobos's life.

In closing, the author wishes to thank the numerous editors and publishers for their permissions to reprint her studies in this volume. Due acknowledgement is made in a listing at the end of the book.

L.M.P.

Chronology

Only a selection from Villa-Lobos's major works is listed here under the date they were composed.

1859	25 February: the composer's mother is born in Rio de Janeiro: Noêmia Umbelina Villa-Lobos, daughter of Antônio Santos Monteiro and Domitildes Costa Santos Monteiro.
1862	7th January: The composer's father is born: Raúl Villa-Lobos, son of Spanish parents: Francisco da Silveira Villa-Lobos and Maria Carolina Serzedelo Villa-Lobos.
1884	Marriage of the composer's parents.
1885	3rd November: Birth of their first child, Bertha – nicknamed Lulucha – who dies in 1976 as Mrs Romeu Augusto Borman de Borges; she leaves three children: Clélia (b. 11 Sept. 1908), Haygara (b. 10 May 1917) and Paulo Emygidio (b. 10 Oct. 1922).
1887	5 March: Heitor Villa-Lobos is born.
1888	13 May: Princess Isabel, daughter of Emperor Pedro II, signs – in her father's absence – the 'Golden Law' which abolishes slavery in Brazil.
	10 October: the composer's sister, Carmen – nicknamed Bilita – is born. She dies on 20 April 1970 as Mrs Danton Condorcet da Silva Jardim; she leaves one daughter: Haygara Yacyra.
1889	17 January: the composer and his sister, Carmen, are baptized at São José Church in Rio de Janeiro.
	15 November: Proclamation of the Republic in Brazil.
	Villa-Lobos's father, Raúl, publishes the first of a series of scholarly books.
1890	16 October: Raúl Villa-Lobos finds work at the National Library in Rio de Janeiro. He gives up medical study for lack of funds; two years later, on 6 October, he is promoted to librarian and, in 1896, entrusted to reorganize the Senate's Library.
1897	23 June: The composer's brother, Othon, is born who dies prematurely, at age 21 in 1918; electrician, married to Octavia.
1899	18 July: Raúl Villa-Lobos, at age 37, dies of malaria in Rio.
1899/1900	Heitor Villa-Lobos's first compositions: *Os Sedutores*, *Dime Perché* for voice and piano.
1901	3 April: Villa-Lobos enters Pedro II College.
1904–07	Villa-Lobos composes short songs and piano pieces and sketches small chamber work; *Comédia Lírica*.
1905	Villa-Lobos moves in bohemian circles and mixes with popular composers and interpreters including Ernesto Júlio Nazaré, Joaquim Francisco dos Santos (Quincas Laranjeiras), Eduardo das Neves, Anacleto Augusto de Medeiros,

	Irineu de Almeida, Francisca (Chiquinha) Hedwiges Gonzaga, Catulo da Paixão Cearense.
1906–07	Villa-Lobos attends sporadically courses at Rio de Janeiro's Instituto Nacional de Música (now: Escola de Música da Universidade Federal do Rio de Janeiro).
ca 1910	Villa-Lobos takes private harmony lessons with Agnelo França and advice from composer Antônio Francisco Braga.
1911	*Piano Trio No. 1 op. 25*
ca 1911/12	Travels to Paranaguá, state of Paraná, where, for a short time, he works in a match factory, then to Belém, state of Pará, Bahia and Manaus.
1912	1 November: meets Lucília Guimarães (b. 26 May 1886 in Paraíba do Sul), a pianist, teacher and, later, interpreter of his music. *Suite Infantil No. 1* for piano.
1912/13	*Sonata Fantasia No. 1* (Désespérance) for violin and piano. Villa-Lobos moves to Rua Souza Neves 15 in the Tijuca area. In the afternoons he plays cello in a small ensemble to entertain guests at the Confeitaria Colombo in Rua Gonçalves Dias, and in the evenings in the Assírio Restaurant in the Opera House's basement.
1913	September: The Ballets Russes, on its first visit to Rio de Janeiro, perform part of Borodin's *Prince Igor*, *Scheherezade*, *L'Après-midi d'un Faune*. Music of the Russians and French Impressionists influence Villa-Lobos who plays cello in the Theatre's orchestra.
	12 November: Villa-Lobos marries Lucília Guimarães; they move into the home of his wife and her brothers at Rua Fonseca Teles 7 in São Cristóvão area.
1914–15	*Danças Características Africanas* for piano solo.
1915	29 January: A concert, given by the composer, Lucília and a friend in the nearby mountain village, Nova Friburgo, includes, for the first time, some of the composer's music. The concert takes place at Teatro D. Eugênia.
	March–June: *Violoncello Concerto No. 1, op. 50.*
	31 July: For the first time, some of Villa-Lobos's music – *Suite Característica* for strings – appears in a concert program in Rio de Janeiro, given by the Sociedade de Concêrtos Sinfônicos, conducted by Villa-Lobos's former teacher A.F. Braga.
	13 November: Villa-Lobos organizes in Rio de Janeiro the first concert entirely with his own music.
1915/16	*String Quartet No. 2 op. 56.*
1916	February: *Sonata No. 2 op. 66* for cello and piano; *String Quartet No. 3*; *Symphony No. 1 op. 112 (Ascenção).*
1917	Finishes *Miniaturas* for voice and piano. Villa-Lobos plays cello in the Odeon Movie House. He begins serious auto-didactical studies of theoretical treaties by Berlioz and Vincent d'Indy to school himself in instrumentation.
	3 February: Villa-Lobos organizes the second concert with his own music.

	July: Villa-Lobos's first acquaintance with the music of Stravinsky and Ravel performed by Diaghilev's visiting Ballets Russes in Rio. September: Alexander Smallens conducts Tristan and Isolde. Orchestral works: *Amazonas, Uirapuru, Naufrágio de Kleônikos.* 17 November: Villa-Lobos organizes the third concert with his own works.
1917/18	*Piano Trio No. 3.*
1918	Villa-Lobos, his wife and in-laws move to Rua Visconde de Paranaguá 11. He writes the fourth act of his opera *Izaht.* After meeting Artur Rubinstein in Rio de Janeiro, he composes *A Prole do Bebê No. 1* for piano. 15 August: Villa-Lobos organizes, and partly conducts, the first concert with his orchestral works.
1919	May–June: He writes *Symphony No. 3 (A Guerra)*, as one of three composers who are each commissioned by the Director of the Instituto Nacional de Música to compose a symphony on the occasion of the Peace Treaty Commemoration. October: Villa-Lobos sketches *Symphony No. 4 (A Vitória)* and plans his *Symphony No. 5 (A Paz)*; the latter is eventually finished in 1950. Villa-Lobos leaves the home of his in-laws and, together with his wife, moves to the Rua Didimo 10 in the Tijuca area, the couple's home until May 1936. Beginning of public recognition: occasionally conductors and soloists include his music in their concert programs. To these interpreters the composer dedicates his subsequent compositions.
1919/20	*Carnaval des Crianças Brasileiras.*
1920, 1922	Felix Weingartner conducts in Rio de Janeiro music by Wagner and includes *Naufrágio de Kleônikos* and *Dança Frenética* in one of his programs.
1920, 1923	Richard Strauss conducts his compositions in Rio de Janeiro.
1921	Boris Godunow and other Russian music is performed in Rio de Janeiro. Vera Janacópulos sings three songs from *Miniaturas* in Paris, the first time that Villa-Lobos's music is heard there. *Quatuor, Epigramas Irônicos e Sentimentais, A Prole do Bebê No. 2.*
1922	During a 'Week of Modern Art' in São Paulo Brazilian contemporary and avant-garde writers, poets, painters and composers organize lectures, recitals and exhibitions – including three recitals (13, 15 and 17 February) of Villa-Lobos's music – to promote Brazilian art and music. Villa-Lobos obtains a grant from the Brazilian government for a one-year sojourn in Paris.
1923	*Poème de l'enfant et de sa mère, Nonetto.* 30 June: Villa-Lobos embarks for Europe on the S.S. Croix.
1924	In Paris, 15 February, Villa-Lobos conducts music of Latin American composers but none of his own. 9 and 16 March: Villa-Lobos conducts Brazilian music, including his own, with the Orquestra Sinfônica Portuguêsa at the Teatro São Luiz in Lisbon. 28 March: Villa-Lobos conducts Brazilian music in Paris' Musée Galliéra. 3 April: He gives a concert in Brussels.

4 April and 11 April: During the Exposition d'Art Américain Latin in Paris' Musée Galliéra Villa-Lobos's music is played.

9 April: The Sixth Jean Wiéner Concert includes a chamber music piece by Villa-Lobos (Trio for oboe, clarinet and bassoon, comp. 1921).

30 May: Villa-Lobos conducts his works and premiers his *Nonetto* in Paris' Salle des Agriculteurs. This was his most important concert in Paris at that time.

In the summer Villa-Lobos returns to Rio de Janeiro. Here, the great breakthrough happens: he creates his own musical style. *Chôros No. 2* and *No. 7*.

8 October: Villa-Lobos signs his first contract with the Paris publishing house Éditions Max Eschig. Previous works were mainly published by Arthur Napoleão in Rio de Janeiro.

1925   In January and February Villa-Lobos conducts Brazilian and French music in São Paulo and on 18 and 20 February a concert with his own works which met with success. *Chôros No. 3*.

On 1 and 17 June Villa-Lobos attends two chamber music concerts of his works in Buenos Aires. Upon his return to Rio de Janeiro he writes *Chôros No. 5* and *No. 8*.

On 30 November and 5 December he presents his new compositions in São Paulo.

1926   In Rio de Janeiro arranges concert of his music. He persistently organizes, all the time, concerts to present his latest works as others are not inclined to include his music in their programs. He gives three more concerts, 31 October, 15 and 19 November. The fertile composing period continues throughout that year: *Chansons Typiques Brésiliennes*, *Três Poemas Indígenas*, *Serestas*, *Cirandas*, *Chôros No. 4* and *No. 10*.

December: He embarks for Paris with his wife, Lucília, financially sponsored by Arnaldo and Carlos Guinle, two Brazilian industrialists, to spend three-and-a half years in France.

1927   January: Villa-Lobos settles at Place St. Michel 11. Begins to arrange and edit the Guinle brothers' collection of folk- and children's songs. Publication, financed by the Guinle brothers, is foreseen. But no publisher is found. The collection is never returned to its owners, the Guinle brothers; the whereabouts of the collection has since remained unknown.

Villa-Lobos signs a further contract with Éditions Max Eschig. The composer meets internationally renowned artists: Stokowsky, Albert Wolff, Edgard Varèse and Florent Schmitt, *Le Temps*'s music critic, who becomes a great admirer of his music.

24 October and 5 December: Villa-Lobos presents his latest compositions with the Orchestre Colonne at the Maison Gaveau.

1928   *Quinteto em forma de Chôros, Twelve Études and Suite Populaire* for guitar.

23 and 24 November: Stokowsky and the Philadelphia Orchestra perform Villa-Lobos's *Danças Características Africanas* in Philadelphia and, on

	27 November, at Carnegie Hall in New York. This is presumably the first time that American audiences hear a work by the Brazilian composer.
1929	21 January: Villa-Lobos signs a further contract with Éditions Max Eschig. 2/3 February: Albert Wolff and the Concerts Lamoureux perform *Chôros No. 8*. The composer writes *Deux Chôros (Bis)*, *Suite Suggestive*. During the summer Villa-Lobos vacations in Brazil and conducts a series of concerts in Rio de Janeiro and São Paulo. *Mômoprecóce*. In early October Villa-Lobos embarks for Barcelona to conduct, on 18 October, Brazilian music including his own; then he travels to Paris.
1930	25 January and 21 March: Further contracts with Éditions Max Eschig. 23 February: Villa-Lobos's *Mômoprecóce* is premiered in Paris' Salle Pleyel with the Brazilian soloist Magda Tagliaferro. 1 April: Villa-Lobos attends a chamber music concert in Liège. 3 April and 7 May: In Paris' Maison Gaveau, Villa-Lobos presents his newest compositions. At the end of May, he and his wife, Lucília, leave Paris for Brazil. He is not to return to France until after World War II. During the second half of the year Villa-Lobos gives a series of concerts in São Paulo including his own works, interrupted only by Brazil's October Revolution with its forebodings of nationalistic tendencies. The composer begins his *Bachianas Brasileiras* series.
1931	Villa-Lobos with a group of musicians undertakes a musical pilgrimage into São Paulo's hinterland, organized in conjunction with the respective Municipalities, offering music in places otherwise deprived of cultural events. 24 May: at the Campo São Bento in São Paulo Villa-Lobos conducts his first mass chorus with unexpected success. This marks the beginning of the composer's interest in choral singing and choral arrangements of folk- and children's songs. Villa-Lobos with his group of musicians visits São Paulo's hinterland twice more. On his return to the city of São Paulo, he conducts two more concerts on 6 and 21 October which include his newest choral arrangements. At year's end he finally settles in Rio de Janeiro. *String Quartet No. 5*.
1932	18 April: SEMA (Superintendência de Educação Musical e Artística do Departamento del Educação da Prefeitura do [então] Distrito Federal) is decreed, to make choral singing in municipal schools mandatory. Villa-Lobos is nominated head of SEMA, a post specifically created for him. For the first time in his life, Villa-Lobos, age 45, has a secure monthly income. He forms his music teachers' chorus, called Orfeão de Professores. *Caixinha de Boas Festas*.
1933	The composer creates the Villa-Lobos Orchestra, dismantled the following year for lack of funds, and conducts unorthodox programs.
1934	On the occasion of the South American Theosophical Congress Villa-Lobos conducts two concerts on 18 and 20 June.
1935	In connection with his SEMA activities, Villa-Lobos organizes a number of concerts between August and December.

1936	25 April: Villa-Lobos attends the First International Congress for Musical Education in Prague and returns via Berlin and Barcelona to Rio de Janeiro. 28 May: Villa-Lobos decides to separate from his wife Lucília and leaves their home. *Ciclo Brasileiro.*
1937	*Descobrimento do Brasil, Missa São Sebastião.*
1938	Villa-Lobos composes the first movement of his *Bachianas Brasileiras No. 5* which was to become his most internationally celebrated piece. The second movement is composed seven years later.
1939	4–9 May: New York's World Fair Villa-Lobos's music is heard during a Festival of Brazilian music. *As Três Marias.*
1940	16–20 October: At a further Festival of Brazilian music, held at New York's Museum of Modern Art, Villa-Lobos's music is performed. The composer gives concerts in Montevideo, Uruguay.
1942	July: First performance of *Chôros No. 6, No. 9* and *No. 11* in Rio de Janeiro. Villa-Lobos launches the Conservatório Nacional de Canto Orfeônico in Rio de Janeiro which is decreed on 26 November. *Bachianas Brasileiras No. 7.*
1944	26 November: Villa-Lobos's American debut in Los Angeles with the Werner Janssen Symphony Orchestra has little success. Five days previously he receives an honorary doctorate in law from Occidental College. *Bachianas Brasileiras No. 8, String Quartet No. 8.*
1945	*Fantasia for violoncello and orchestra, Bachianas Brasileiras No. 9, Piano Concerto No. 1, Symphony No. 7, Madona.* 28 January: The League of Composers offers a chamber music concert of Villa-Lobos's music at New York's Museum of Modern Art. 8 and 9 February: Villa-Lobos's first New York appearance with the Philharmonic Orchestra is followed by appearances in Boston and Chicago. 14 July: Villa-Lobos launches the Brazilian Academy of Music in Rio.
1946	13 March: Villa-Lobos's mother, Noêmia, dies.
1947	After a visit to Rome, Villa-Lobos travels to New York to receive from Edwin Lester, President of the Los Angeles Civic Light Opera Association, a commission to write the operetta *Magdalena.* From now on until the end of his life, the composer lives part of every year in the USA, Europe and Brazil, and guest conducts in other Latin American countries.
1948	9 July: Villa-Lobos enters New York's Memorial Hospital for a cancer operation of the bladder.
1950	*String Quartet No. 12.*
1951	*Concerto for Guitar.*
1952	Villa-Lobos chooses the Bedford Hotel in Paris for his European headquarters. 17–19 June: Villa-Lobos conducts the Israel Philharmonic Orchestra. *Symphony No. 10, Concerto No. 4 for piano.*
1953	*Odisséia de uma Reça, Fantasia Concertante, Concerto for Harp, Alvorada da Floresta Tropical, String Quartet No. 14, Concerto No. 2 for violoncello.*
1954	*Concerto No. 5 for piano, String Quartet No. 15*
1955	*Symphony No. 11, Concerto for Harmonica*

1955/56   Basil Langton commissions Villa-Lobos to compose music for a ballet, based on Eugene O'Neill's *The Emperor Jones*, and John Blankenship commissions the composer to set Federico García Lorca's play *Yerma* to music.

1957   *Symphony No. 12, Quinteto Instrumental, String Quartet No. 17.* On the occasion of his 70th birthday, Villa-Lobos is made an honorary citizen of São Paulo and in this city a festival takes place with his music during a 'Villa-Lobos Week' in September. The Brazilian government declares 1957 the 'Villa-Lobos Year'.

1958   *A Menina das Nuvens*; M.G.M. commission Villa-Lobos to write the music for the film *Green Mansions*, based on the novel by W.H. Hudson; *Bendita Sabedoria, Magnificat Aleluia*.
           3 December: The University of New York confers on Villa-Lobos an honorary doctorate.

1959   12 July: In Bear Mountains, USA, Villa-Lobos conducts the last concert of his life.
           14 July: In Rio de Janeiro, Villa-Lobos receives the Carlos Gomes Medal.
           11 August: Villa-Lobos, hospitalized for uraemia and kidney congestion, makes his will, in Rio de Janeiro.
           7 September: Villa-Lobos attends the last concert of his life at the Municipal Theatre to hear his *Magnificat Aleluia*.
           17 November: Villa-Lobos dies, at his home, in the Rua Araújo Pôrto Alegre 56, Apt. 54, in Rio de Janeiro.

1960   From February through April, the New York Public Library holds an exhibit in Villa-Lobos's memory with photographs, recordings, scores and books.

1961   20 January: The Museum Villa-Lobos in Rio de Janeiro – decreed on 22 June 1960 – opens its doors under the direction of Arminda Villa-Lobos, the composer's companion during his last twenty-three years. Since then, the Museum holds yearly festivals and competitions and publishes books and recordings.

1966   25 May: Villa-Lobos's wife, Lucília, dies.

1971   5 March: On the occasion of the 84th anniversary of Villa-Lobos's birth, a memorial plate is affixed at Paris's Bedford Hotel.
           12 August: Première of *Yerma* at Santa Fe Opera, Santa Fe, New Mexico, USA.

1985   5 August: Arminda d'Almeida Villa-Lobos, the composer's companion, dies aged seventy-three in Rio de Janeiro (b. 26 July 1912)

A VILLA-LOBOS OPERA

RIO DE JANEIRO.

THE four-act opera "Izaht," by Villa-Lobos, the Brazilian composer, was given its first performance at the Municipal Theatre in Rio de Janeiro on April 6 and executed as a private presentation for musicians and the st ff of the music-educational department of the municipality. The house was packed and the composer, who conducted, had a great success. This event took place shortly before the actual music season began in South America. The almost thirty-year-old work was heard in its entirety for the first time in Brazil, although not staged, but given as oratorio; the overture and occasionally the last two acts have been played before. Outside this country "Izaht" has remained unknown.

Only in his youth did Villa-Lobos confine himself to opera writing (he wrote five altogether). In later years he abandoned the idea of dramatic composition entirely and turned to other forms. Nevertheless, "Izaht" (the only opera of the five which is completely orchestrated) belongs to his favorite works, as he has realized herein his idea of being original. The music, written during 1912 and 1914 (the first and third acts being orchestrated in 1918 and the two others in 1920) when the composer was in his middle twenties, is a typical product of his youth.

* * *

In spite of a strong Puccini influence, one of his models at the time, "Izaht" indicates willful characteristics of Villa-Lobos's more mature style and reminiscences of Brazilian folk motives. The music of the third and fourth acts is more dramatic, contrasting and more elaborate than the first two, in which the lyric tendency prevails. In the final act various combinations of instrumental colors are already typically his own, a special characteristic which comes to perfection in his later works.

For the flute as well as for the 'cello—the latter used elaborately, for instance, in the "Bacchianas Brasileiras," played in New York last year—he seems to have had a predilection in those early days. The flute, a favorite and much used instrument among the Brazilian natives, must have attracted his attention during his extended stay in the interior which had preceded the conception of "Izaht." And the 'cello he likes best of all the instruments he plays himself.

On the whole, the music of "Izaht" keeps pace with the romantic and complicated plot and reflects the composer's idea of and attitude toward opera writing: to omit dullness and boredom. This may be the reason for the quickly changing motives, the brisk transitions and the rapid alterations of arias, ensembles and chorus. However, the chorus plays a prominent role, and the fine and expressive setting of the voices clearly shows Villa-Lobos's outstanding ability in this direction, of which he has taken full advantage in the choral works written during the last ten years.

The libretto of "Izaht," signed by Azevedo Junior and E. Villalba, is actually by the composer himself; the subject and layout are so typically Villa-Lobos that they leave no doubt as to the originality of its text-writer. In the decidedly romantic plot with castles and taverns turn up viscounts and other nobility, gypsies, gangsters and Parisian apaches. Villa-Lobos says the opera is of an "essentially psychological character" and gives full and detailed descriptions of each character. This explanation brought about considerable controversies when parts of "Izaht" came to light many years ago, as it was maintained that every dramatic work necessarily has a psychological basis.

The unusual story is as follows: Izaht, a depraved gypsy girl, belongs to a gangster band in the suburbs of Paris and has to entice rich people. For the first time in her life she falls in love, with a viscount who rescues her from the slaps of her father. In the meantime, the gangsters plan to rob the house of the viscount's fiancée, and later on that of the viscount. Izaht rescues him from the gangsters. Izaht dies when the gangsters are about to kidnap the count's fiancée. Finally the leader of the band, a decayed nobleman, recognizes in the viscount's fiancée his own natural daughter.

Unlike many other stage composers Villa-Lobos approaches opera writing with an idée fixe: For him it is the lowest class of serious music, a music essentially meant for the great public and the masses which want to be entertained. In his opinion one has, therefore, to meet the public's taste and sacrifice one's own ideals even to such an extent that tuneful and almost vulgar melodies should take the place of proper ones. This makes the extraordinary plot understandable.

New York Times, 28 April 1940, IX, 8

Corrigenda/addenda

Second paragraph (English text), and fourth paragraph (Portuguese text) line 1–3:
The other four operas were only projected. They are: *Femina, Jesus, Zoé, Malazarte.*
In later years Villa-Lobos wrote three more stage works:
  1. *Magdalena* (comp. 1947, perf. 26 July 1948), Philharmonic Hall, Los Angeles,
       cond. A. Kay.
  2. *Yerma* (comp. 1955/56, perf. 12 August 1971), Santa Fe Opera, Santa Fe, New
       Mexico, cond. Christopher Keene.
       Brazilian performance: 26 May 1983, Teatro Municipal, Rio de Janeiro, cond.
       Mário Tavares.

European performances: 12 and 13 July 1989 (concert performance), Queen Elizabeth Hall, London, cond. Odaline de la Martinez. Bielefeld, Germany, 9 December 1990 (First European stage performance)

3. *A Menina das Nuvens* (comp. 1967–1958), perf. 29 Nov. 1960), Teatro Municipal, Rio de Janeiro, cond. Edoardo di Guarnieri.

Second paragraph (English text), line 12 ff and *second column, first paragraph (Portuguese text)*, line 1 ff.

Izaht: Ouverture (conceived Sept. 1915, perf. 15 May 1917), during a benefit concert for the Patronage of Minors, Rio de Janeiro, conductor: Villa-Lobos.

Act III (conceived 1914, perf. 13 June 1921), as a concert performance, Teatro São Pedro, Rio de Janeiro, conductor: Villa-Lobos.

Act IV (completed 1918, perf. 15 August 1918) as a concert performance, Teatro Municipal, Rio de Janeiro, conductor: Villa-Lobos.

Act I & II (likely composition dates: shortly before the concert performance of the complete opera, on 6 April 1940) Teatro Municipal, Rio de Janeiro, cond. Villa-Lobos.

Stage performance of complete opera: 13 December 1958, Teatro Municipal, Rio de Janeiro, conductor: Edoardo di Guarnieri.

Uma Ópera
de H. Villa-Lobos

O grande diário norte-americano "The New York Times", publicou na edição de 27 de Abril um artigo·da sua colaboradora musical no Rio de Janeiro sobre a realisação da ópera "Izaht" de Heitor Villas-Lobos. Aqui o reproduzimos :

A ópera em quatro atos "Izaht" de Villa-Lobos, o compositor brasileiro, foi representada pela primeira vez no Teatro Municipal do Rio de Janeiro no dia 6 de Abril e realizada como apresentação particular ·para músicos e os colaboradores do Serviço de Educação Musical da Prefeitura do Distrito Federal. O teatro esteve cheio, obtendo um sucesso enorme o compositor regente.

Realizou-se a representação um pouco antes da abertura da temporada atual na América do Sul. Pela primeira vez a obra de quasi 30 anos foi completamente ouvida no Brasil, embora não representada em cena, mas realizada em forma de oratória. A "ouverture" e, raramente, os dois últimos atos, já foram apresentadas antes. Fora do Brasil, "Izaht" ficou desconhecida até agora.

Somente quando joven, Villa-Lobos dedicou-se a escrever óperas (escrevendo cinco). Nos anos posteriores abandonou completamente a idéia de composição dramática, orientando-se para outras formas musicais. "Izaht", a única ópera das cinco que se acha completamente orquestrada é uma das suas obras de predileção, porque nela realizou o seu ideal de originalidade. A música

escrita entre 1912 e 1914 (o primeiro e o terceiro atos foram orquestrados em 1918 e os dois outros em 1920) é um produto típico da mocidade do compositor, que nesse tempo vivia no meio de seu terceiro decênio.

Apesar da influência de Puccini, que foi um dos seus modelos neste tempo, "Izaht" já indica singularidades especiais do estilo maduro de Villas-Lobos e recordações de motivos de folclore brasileiro. A música do terceiro e quarto atos é mais dramática, contrastada e desenvolvida do que a dos dois primeiros atos, onde prevalece a tendência lírica, No último ato varias combinações de côres instrumentais são típicas de Villa-Lobos, aperfeiçoadas nas obras posteriores.

Já nesses primeiros tempos Villa-Lobos parece ter tido uma predileção pela flauta e o violoncelo, que ulteriormente, por exemplo, foi especialmente usado na "Bachianas Brasileiras", apresentadas em Nova York no ano passado. Parece que a flauta, instrumento favorito e muito usado entre os indígenas do Brasil, atraíu o seu interesse durante suas longas viagens pelo interior do Brasil, antes da concepção de "Izaht". E o violoncelo é o instrumento que ele próprio prefere entre todos os instrumentos que toca.

De um modo geral a música de "Izaht" corresponde a uma ação romântica e complicada e reflete as idéias atitudes do compositor em relação a composição de óperas: evitar tédio e monotonia. Essa pode ser a razão da mudança rápida dos motivos, das passagens velozes e das alterações imprevistas das árias, conjuntos e cores. A parte do coro é saliente e a composição fina e expressiva das vozes mostra claramente o talento notavel do maestro revelado por completo nas obras de coros escritas nos últimos 10 anos.

O "libretto" de "Izaht", assignado por Azevedo Junior e E. Villalba foi escrito verdadeiramente pelo próprio compositor: o assunto e a construção são tão tipicamente Villa-Lobos que não deixam alguma dúvida sobre a originalidade do compositor do texto. Na ação expressivamente romântica com castelos e tabernas aparecem viscondes e outros nobres, ciganos, bandidos e apaches de Paris. Villa-Lobos diz que a ópera é "de caráter essencialmente psicológico e dá descrições completas e pormenores de cada caráter. Esses esclarecimentos provocaram controvérsias importantes quando partes de "Izaht" apareceram muitos anos atrás, porque foi declarado que toda obra dramática necessariamente tem uma base psicológica.

A ação pouco comum é a seguinte: Izaht, uma moço cigana depravada, pertence a um grupo de bandidos dos subúrbios de Paris e deve seduzir homens de fortuna. Pela primeira vez na sua vida ela apaixonou-se por um visconde que a salva do chicote de seu próprio pae. Entretanto os bandidos planejam roubar a casa da noiva do visconde, e depois o próprio visconde. Izaht salva-o das mãos dos bandidos. Izaht morre, quando os bandidos tentam raptar a noiva do visconde. Por fim o chefe dos bandidos, um fidalgo arruinado, reconhece na noiva do visconde a sua filha natural.

Diferente de muitos outros compositores do palco, Villa-Lobos tem uma "idéia fixa" escrevendo óperas. Para êle é a categoria mais inferior da música que influe essencialmente sobre o grande público e as multidões que querem ser divertidas. Na opinião dêle, então, é preciso, ir de encontro ao gosto do público e sacrificar os próprios ideais a tal ponto que melodias acessiveis e quasi vulgares devem substituir as próprias.

Musica Viva, 1(3), July 1940, 6–7

Musical Education in Brazil

SHORTLY after Getulio Vargas became head of the Brazilian government in 1930, all educational problems were given greater attention and decisive changes took place. One of the most weighty modifications of the curriculum was the introduction of music into the schools.

It is unique, perhaps, as well as significant that in 1932 the Director General of Education invited the country's most prominent composer, Heitor Villa-Lobos, to take charge of musical education in the public schools. Without the indefatigable efforts, the splendid initiative and the brilliant ideas of this man, Brazil would not be able to boast of such rapid development and sound achievement during the short period of eight years.

Villa-Lobos recognized immediately the primary material on which he could build. He had, first of all, a people with excellent vocal ability. He perceived, too, which foreign systems, already proven beneficial, could be applied and which would have to be modified. His most far-reaching accomplishment was the creation of a special scheme suitable for pupils who had not yet reached the same educational level musically as those in other countries but who could be brought to an equally high standard. Villa-Lobos' principle has been that music teaching in the schools is not an end in itself, but the medium for discipline, civic training, and artistic education. It is significant that he puts artistic education in the final place. This is because, in his opinion, the Brazilians will be able to appreciate serious music to the full only if their attitude toward art is definite and well grounded, if they are disciplined enough

to listen with attention and understanding, and also if they have learned to value and respect the music of their own country.

From the outset Villa-Lobos realized that the only way to create in Brazil an intelligent concert-going public—which is his ultimate goal—was to concentrate on the musical education of boys and girls, because they form the coming generation which, if properly and rightly trained, will raise the artistic and cultural level and support musical life in general. Although the obstacles, especially considering the tremendous mixture of races in Brazil, might have appeared insurmountable, Villa-Lobos has solved the problem splendidly. By training the ear and having short musical phrases sung correctly with the help of a manisolfa system[1] especially invented for this purpose, while the classes were divided into performers and listeners, he began to develop individual self-control and group discipline. All this was by no means an easy task, although it seems the most natural thing to any outsider.

The next step was to teach the children the difficult national anthem and nursery, folk, and national songs. This, too, may at first appear unnecessary, but if these songs were sung at all they were likely to be roared and much disfigured. Having improved the children's discipline, Villa-Lobos could be sure that with great patience and endless perseverance he would succeed in having the songs performed correctly and musically. But self-control alone has not been his aim, since on the

[1] *Villa-Lobos' manisolfa method is built on the Tonic Solfa system; however, it uses fewer syllables and more hand signs and can thus serve for any key and any chromatic notes.*

whole music and music teaching mean to him not art for art's sake, but a means to foster the good in mankind. Thus instruction in folk and national songs should evoke a patriotic but not nationalistic feeling and perception in Brazilian youth, an understanding of the vast country and its divergent inhabitants, appreciation and respect for their countrymen and, finally, regard and esteem for people in the world at large. This is what he understands by civics. When this has been achieved he can proceed to make the school children acquainted with the art music of all periods and all countries—this, in Villa-Lobos' mind, is musical education. But in Brazil it would have been impossible to start with the latter, because the basis for an intelligent comprehension of it would have been entirely lacking.

The principal plans for education in Brazil are made by the Ministry of Education and Public Health. However, each of the twenty States and the Federal District, which have autonomous administration, carry out these plans according to local conditions; the work is supervised by the Federal authorities. Because of the vast area of Brazil and the different cultural levels of the various States, this is the only possible way to achieve educational progress. School attendance is compulsory, but because of various obstacles, including a shortage of teachers and an insufficiency of adequate schools, it has not yet been generally enforced.

The supervision and control of all musical education in the public schools of Rio de Janeiro is centralized in the S. E. M. A. (Musical and Artistic Education Service, Department of Education of the Federal District), whose initiator and musical director is Villa-Lobos. The Service is composed of a council, consisting of the director, a technical assistant, a head of instrumental music, and an assistant,

and its work is divided into five sections, each of which has its own staff working out plans and administering various divisions. Attached to the S. E. M. A. is a special radio station that broadcasts solely to schools, except for post-graduate courses to teachers and municipal employees. The S. E. M. A. also supervises the local theaters and those artistic societies which are subsidized by the municipality; furthermore it furnishes appropriate music for the Section of Physical Education and does research work in national music to be adopted by the schools later on.

The S. E. M. A. plans to extend its work to all the States in the country, but as the movement is new and the lack of suitable teachers is still serious, many years will no doubt pass before a nationwide program can be put into effect.

Music teaching in Rio de Janeiro and the rest of the Federal District is given in four kindergarten, 207 elementary, twelve intermediate, five experimental, one prevocational and two technical secondary schools. This does not mean, however, that all these schools have regular music lessons; the shortage of trained music teachers has prevented it so far. Once or twice a week 60 schools have regular music lessons from 25 to 45 minutes in length. Forty teachers are in charge of these lessons. This means that one teacher must often instruct classes in various schools, which involves much waste of time in travelling from one place to another. The music lessons in the remaining schools are given at irregular intervals by teachers of other subjects, as far as their schedules permit. To prepare and train the latter, at least to some extent, the S. E. M. A. has a special adviser to give the necessary help and some sort of guidance.

For the training of music teachers, Rio de Janeiro has a special institute, so far the only one in the country. The establishment of similar institutions throughout the nation is forecast in the regulations of an education law which have been drafted but not yet signed by the President. The course in music education for teachers in Rio de Janeiro extends over four years, and musical training at the National School of Music must either precede or be taken simultaneously. Usually six to eight teachers specializing in music pass examinations each year; however, at the start of the movement and also this year, a far greater number completed the course. Seventy trained music teachers who have passed their examinations and hold a certificate are waiting to be engaged by the municipality. Apart from the usual musical subjects the teachers are taught gymnastics to develop their sense of rhythm, proper breathing as preparation for *a capella* singing, and the manisolfa system. The principal thing, however, is to instill into them the right idea of teaching music to school children—namely, that music is not a fancy subject or a luxury, but a means to the end outlined at the beginning of this article. There is also a special teachers' chorus called *Orfeão dos Professores*, in which certified teachers as well as aspirants have to take part once a week and which from a purely artistic point of view has obtained unusual results.

In the grade schools usually two classes with forty pupils each are taught together. It should be the rule to have music lessons given from the first school year onward, but as a sufficient number of teachers has not yet been employed, only the last three of the five elementary school years include music.

The music course for the five years of elementary school is very well thought out, and it is interesting to see how beneficial it is under a practical musician such

as Villa-Lobos. The pupils start in the first year by learning the G-clef and the manisolfa singing of five-note phrases, and in the second proceed to singing longer phrases taught by ear, the first verse of the National Anthem and that of the Hymn to the Flag, as well as one or two easy songs. In the course of the next three years they learn to sing part-songs, taught by the special manisolfa system, so as to train their ear. The old custom of learning songs from printed music is discarded. Instead of a piano, the tuning-fork is used throughout. This is perhaps the most remarkable feature of Villa-Lobos' method, and the results have been surprisingly good. Also the teachers are trained to invent four-part songs, which they teach to the classes by the ten-finger system. A number of other national songs, easy melodies from dictation, sight reading of light tunes, part-singing of folksongs and marches, as well as some knowledge of instruments and a few dates in the history of music are taught during the remaining years in elementary school. Already the results prove that Villa-Lobos' program is wisely planned and will lead to his goal of making the pupils acquainted with music itself and not merely with its theoretical background.

The music course in the secondary schools is more elaborate. Besides the manisolfa training, which is the basis of all school music-teaching and is included in each lesson up to the most advanced, the students learn songs of various styles and periods, but especially those of Brazilian composers. As mentioned above, the latter is one of the main points in Villa-Lobos' scheme since, in his opinion, students must first of all be trained to know and understand the music of their own country before they can appreciate foreign music. To encourage this study the teachers have to give short lectures on

Brazilian composers and their works, and on African, Indian, Spanish and Portuguese music insofar as they have influenced Brazilian music. National folklore as it is linked with music and art in general is likewise discussed. Short surveys of musical history and of the development of the orchestra and its instruments are given too.

Another interesting feature is that harmony, the use of the metronome, and other theoretical matters are not taught separately, but applied to actual music performed by the pupils during their lessons. Thus these subjects appear natural to them; they seem something integral, not boring and useless stuff.

It is astonishing to see how well all the boys and girls are trained, and above all to observe the joy they exhibit during music lessons. Having improved their musical consciousness, Villa-Lobos can unhesitatingly ask the teachers to inform them about the importance of concerts, opera performances, musical expression in general, and the significance of building up an understanding concert-going-public. The results of the last-mentioned point cannot yet be observed; some years must pass before the youth of today is mature enough to support the musical life of the community.

School orchestras do not yet exist, but in two of the three technical secondary schools for boys, bands have been organized as an extra-curricular activity, and the pre-vocational school even has a professional band to train the boys for public, military or municipal groups. Instrumental lessons, given individually, extend over a period of six years and consist of two courses in the technical secondary schools. Those in the pre-vocational school run through three years. Theory, choral singing, breathing, and the playing of woodwind and brass instruments are taught.

Here again the students' intelligence is developed and his thinking power stimulated, because after a time the teacher has brought his pupil to a point where further training can be left to the boy himself. The student is still supervised and given lessons now and then, but the point is to educate him to be self-critical and to have enough energy and perseverance to study and practice by himself.

The use of phonographs in schools is not greatly favored by Villa-Lobos, who rightly claims that the children's musical consciousness has not as yet improved sufficiently to benefit by the use of records. Only about 30 percent would be interested in listening to recorded music which, as he says, is not enough to warrant the installation of apparatus and records, even apart from the cost involved.

Included in Villa-Lobos' scheme is also the teaching of music in the ten municipal Adult Schools, but the same obstacle—the shortage of sufficient and adequate teachers—has so far prevented the execution of this plan. Only for the celebration of national holidays are the adults of these schools trained, in order to participate in the mass choral demonstrations that take place each year on Independence Day or the Day of the Proclamation of the Republic. These mass choirs consist chiefly of school children; last year there were 30,000.

Concerts for children, three of which were given in 1932, did not prove very successful and therefore had to be abandoned. For one thing, the children's listening capacity was not mature enough and besides the Municipal Theater, with its eighteen hundred seats—the only suitable place for these concerts—was too small. Consequently during 1934 and 1935 another plan was tried which seems to have been more successful, but this too was not continued. It provided for so-called "educational concerts" given by bands that visited various schools once or twice a year.

It is hard to tell what will be the actual results of this new movement and of Villa-Lobos' educational project, because its eight years of existence are too short a period to permit any definite conclusions to be drawn. But one thing, perhaps the most decisive in the whole scheme, has proved to be appropriate and right—that is, the method. Villa-Lobos has emphasized more than once that he is not working to see the final results of his endeavors during his lifetime, but rather that he is establishing a permanent basis for the future.

Bulletin of the Pan American Union, **74**(10), October 1940, 689–93

VIOLIN CONCERTO BY VILLA-LOBOS

By LISA M. PEPPERCORN
RIO DE JANEIRO.

PERFORMANCES of a Villa-Lobos orchestral work are a rarity in Brazil. His music is more popular abroad than in his native country. True, almost all his major works were played in Brazil at least once. However, this dates back to the middle of the Twenties when the composer himself organized and conducted his newly written music. Since that time his countrymen have shown little enterprise to give representations of Villa-Lobos's compositions.

Last season, Stokowski conducted the "Momoprecoce" for piano and orchestra. The success of this score did not stimulate the musicians here to perform others of Villa-Lobos's comprehensive output.

* * *

One had to wait for the French conductor Albert Wolff to see a Villa-Lobos orchestral work reappear in the concert programs. Wolff, an old friend of Villa-Lobos from the time the latter lived in Paris at the end of the Twenties, is familiar with the style of the composer's work. It is not surprising that Villa-Lobos has entrusted Wolff with a first performance of his violin concerto last month at the Municipal Theatre.

Villa-Lobos has written several works for solo instrument and orchestra, but only for one has he applied the traditional term "con-

First Complete Hearing Of Score Takes Place In Brazil

certo," namely, for the 'cello concerto written in 1915. The three piano concertos—suite for piano and orchestra (1913), Momoprecoce (1929), Chôros No. 12 and the unfinished Chôros No. 11—show his endeavor to employ uncommon titles and forms at all stages of his artistic career. For the piece for violin and orchestra, Villa-Lobos has chosen the name "Fantasia de Movimentos Mixtos (Fantasy of mixed movements) written in three parts." The external form of a classical concerto for solo instrument and orchestra is still retained. He calls the three movements "Alma Convulsa," 1921 (Torment), "Serenidade," 1920 (Serenity), and "Contentamento," 1921 (Contentment). Perhaps we may assume that personal experiences have preceded the conception of this work. When the Fantasy was given for the first time on Dec. 15, 1922, at the Municipal Theatre in Rio it consisted of another form. The slow second movement took the place of the first and was followed by another quick one, called A Mariposa na Luz" (The Butterfly in the Light), written in 1917. Then the composer separated the latter. When the Fantasy was played again in Paris in May, 1930, it was heard in its present form, without the last movement.

* * *

Last year, when the composer conducted its performances in Montevideo and Buenos Aires, the last part remained again unheard. In December, 1940, and January of this year Villa-Lobos took to the rewriting of this movement. The composer says that the third movement was lost in Paris after his return to Brazil in 1930. We think

we are not wrong to presume that the last part was conceived roughly, but never worked out and given its final form. Our assumption may be supported by the fact that its make-up and style have little affinity with the first two movements. It is, undoubtedly, more mature in form, clearer in the treatment of the subject-matter and, above all, more detached in the layout of the actual themes.

The first movement uses a number of themes, partly of Indian flavor, which appear only once or are repeated several times, without receiving symphonic handling. This is typical of Villa-Lobos's writing. His abundance of ideas leaves him little opportunity for development. On the other hand, the thematical material is conceived in such a way that it is less suited for the usual working-out technique.

* * *

Peculiarities in Brazilian melodies, harmonic and instrumental devices to characterize the country's ambiance and rhythmic patterns occurring in Brazil's folklore are employed, although the composer says that it contains "no influence or suggestion of folklore." This movement contains elements which appear interesting on paper, but seem to get lost at the actual hearing. This complexity is not unusual for Villa-Lobos's music written in this epoch.

The second movement also contains characteristics of his style of twenty years ago. Quasi ostinato-like patterns in the orchestra accompany expressivelike themes in the violin. By far the best is the last movement with its outspoken virtuoso solo part.

Under the baton of Albert Wolff the work received a happy representation. The success was shared by the excellent young Brazilian violinist, Oscar Borgerth, whose technical command and understanding interpretation were much applauded.

New York Times, 8 June 1941, IX, 5

Corrigenda/addenda

First column, third paragraph, last line, add:
on 23 April 1941. American première: 15 April 1973 in a concert given by the Music
Department of the Carnegie-Mellon University in the Carnegy Music Hall in Pittsburgh.
Soloist: Sidney Harth, conductor: Chauncey Kelley. European first performance: 26 April
1975, Berlin State Academy for Music. Soloist: Götz Bernau, conductor: Alvaro Cassuto.

First column, fourth paragraph, line 4:
Since the article was published, Villa-Lobos wrote nine more works for solo instrument
and orchestra which he called Concerto:

I.   *Five Piano Concertos*:
      No. 1 (comp. 1945, perf. 11 Oct. 1946) Teatro Municipal, Rio de Janeiro, soloist:
      Ellen Ballon, conductor: Villa-Lobos.
      No. 2 (comp. 1948, perf. 21 April 1950), Teatro Municipal, Rio de Janeiro, soloist:
      Jo ão de Souza Lima, conductor: Villa-Lobos.
      No. 3 (comp. 1952/57, perf. 24 August 1957), Teatro Municipal, Rio de Janeiro,
      soloist: Arnaldo Estrella, conductor: Eleazar de Carvalho.
      No. 4 (comp. 1952, perf. 9 January 1953), Pittsburgh Symphony Orchestra, soloist:
      Bernardo Segáll, conductor: Villa-Lobos.
      No. 5 (comp. 1954, perf. 8 May 1955), London Philharmonic Orchestra, soloist:
      Felicja Blumental, conductor: Jean Martinon.
II.   *Concerto for Guitar and Orchestra*
      (comp. 1951, perf. 6 Feb. 1956) Houston Symphony Orchestra, soloist: Andres
      Segovia, conductor: Villa-Lobos.
III. *Concerto for Harp and Orchestra*
      (comp. 1953, perf. 14 January 1955), Philadelphia Symphony Orchestra, soloist:
      Nicanor Zabaleta, conductor: Villa-Lobos.
IV.   *Concerto No. 2 for Cello and Orchestra*
      (comp. 1953, perf. 5 Feb. 1955), New York Philharmonic Orchestra, soloist: Aldo
      Parisot, conductor: Walter Hendl.
V.   *Concerto for Harmonica and Orchestra*
      (comp. 1955/56, perf. 27 Oct. 1959), Kol Israel Orchestra, Edison Hall, Jerusalem,
      Israel, soloist: John Sebastian, conductor: George Singer.

Second column, line 5:
delete: *Chôros No. 12* and add after *Chôros No. 11* for Piano and Orchestra (comp. 1928,
according to *Villa-Lobos – Sua Obra*, MEC/DAC/MVL, Rio de Janeiro, 1972, p.39)
though likely sketched in that year but only completed for the first performance on 18
July 1942 at the Teatro Municipal, Rio de Janeiro. Soloist: José Vieira Brandão, conductor:
Villa-Lobos.

Second column, third paragraph, line 12:
For May 1930 read 7 May 1930

Second column, fourth paragraph, line 3:
Add date after Buenos Aires: 31 October 1940

NEW VILLA-LOBOS WORKS

RIO DE JANEIRO.

A NUMBER of orchestral works by Villa-Lobos were recently presented for the first time, directed by the composer, at the Rio Municipal Theatre this Summer. The programs consisted of two orchestrations of piano works (Rudepoêma and Bachianas Brasileiras, No. 4), the Third Suite of the Descobrimento do Brasil (the First Suite was given in New York last year), Chôros, Nos. 6 and 9, and Chôros No. 11 for piano and orchestra. According to the programs the three Chôros were composed between 1926-29, but the musical style of Chôros Nos. 6 and 11, like the first number of the Third Suite, suggests that if these works were conceived at that time the actual writing must have been done recently.

The greatest success was achieved by Chôros No. 6, a piece that lasts thirty minutes. Despite polyrhythms, percussion and brass effects and other elements that have always prevailed in the Villa-Lobos music in which the Brazilian tendency dominates, Chôros No. 6 is conceived on a more universal basis. The work is inspired, profound and one of his best compositions to date. In the lyrical passages, which are very impressive, Villa-Lobos continues the style of some of the Bachianas Brasileiras. The structure is clear and tight, the treatment of the subject-matter interesting and the orchestra, which includes some little known percussion instruments, said to be of Indian origin, is less overloaded than in other works of that kind.

Chôros No. 11, a work which takes more than an hour to perform, is not a piano concerto in the usual sense. The difficult piano part, played by the Brazilian pianist, José Vieira Brandão, is treated rather like an orchestral solo voice. Stylistically, the work is not unlike Chôros No. 6, but less balanced and very long. However, Chôros No. 11 is quite dramatic and impressive and has some highly inspired passages, including those where the piano is accompanied by the string section.

New York Times, 11 October 1942, VIII, 6

Corrigenda/addenda

First Paragraph, add first performance dates of Rudepoêma:
15 July 1942: *Chôros No. 9, Rudepoêma, Bachianas Brasileiras No. 4*
18 July 1942: *Chôros No. 6 and Chôros No. 11, Descobrimento do Brasil, third Suite.*

Some Aspects of Villa-Lobos' Principles of Composition

LITTLE was known of Villa-Lobos outside Brazil until the United States attributed a special significance to his name a few years ago. This man, whom they have sometimes called the most interesting modern composer of the Americas, is of small stature and untamed temperament. He is ignorant of the year of his birth, and says that there are only two great composers in the world, namely, "Bach and I". Moreover, he has told so many deviating stories of his life to all and sundry that it is difficult, at times, to discriminate between *Dichtung und Wahrheit*. Possessed by a strange ambition to be different from others in every way, he has embellished his rather uneventful and struggling life with fictitious happenings in which his belief is unshakable. Proud of being self-taught, except for some insufficient lessons in harmony, he has naturally adhered to this idea in his compositions.

Glancing at the comprehensive range of Villa-Lobos' works, works which include every type of music, one cannot fail to notice that certain compositions speak a personal language while others, though interesting as a reflection of his individuality, do not reveal the same strength and intensity. Villa-Lobos' special gift is his ability to absorb, coupled with an imaginative power and a skill for experimenting. As a rule, he conceives his music in two to four parts and sometimes only afterwards determines to which instrument or group of instruments they should be given. He solves this problem in various ways. If he has decided, for instance, upon a piece for violoncello and piano, he may later transcribe it for violin and piano,[1] probably because he is attracted by the other instrument's timbre. Another example is the transcription of a duet for flute and clarinet (*Chôros, No. 2*) into a piece for piano solo.

On yet another occasion Villa-Lobos used the same piece from a different angle. Stimulated by certain expressionistic ideas which were current some years ago he intended to write a ballet which he called *The Evolution of Aeroplanes*, to which he wrote the story. Yet, instead of providing a musical background that would fit such a singular idea, he indicated that the following pieces should be adapted:—*Inquieta, Valsa Mystica* and *A Maripoza na Luz*. Looking at this a little closer, one finds, however, that the first piece, *Inquieta*, is the last movement of the *Suite Caracteristica* for strings written in 1912 or 1913. The second, *Valsa Mystica*, was originally a piece for piano solo taken from a collection of three piano pieces called *Simples Collectanea*, which was composed in 1917, while the last, *A Maripoza na Luz*, has a particular story of its own. Written for violin and piano in 1917, it was intended to be the third

[1] These transcriptions include *Sonhar*, op. 14 (1914), *Berceuse*, op. 50 (1915), *Cappriccio*, op. 49 (1915), *Elegie* (1916), *O Canto do Cysne Negro* (1917).

number of a series called *Os Martyrios dos Insectos*. Later, Villa-Lobos orchestrated the piano part and, coupled with a slow movement called *Serenidade*, the two pieces came out as the *Fantasia de Movimentos Mixtos*.[2] And eventually, *A Maripoza na Luz* found its way into the above-mentioned ballet which has never actually taken shape as an entity.

This is not the only occasion that he has readapted compositions, and in so doing he has shown great skill in concealing what he has done by means of a different title or a seemingly convincing story attached to the composition. A case in point is the orchestral series *Discovery of Brazil* (1936–37), which consists of ten pieces grouped into four Suites. Examining this set in detail one finds only five original compositions (*Introduction* from the First Suite, *Impressão Moura* and *Festa nas Selvas* from the Third Suite, and *Procissão da Cruz* and *Primeira Missa no Brasil* from the Fourth Suite), whereas three items (*Alegria* from the First Suite, *Adagio Sentimental* and *Cascavel* from the Second Suite) are orchestrations of pieces[3] written about twenty years before the Suite was put into shape, and of the remaining two we have so far only the titles. To cover up what he has done and, at the same time, to make the series attractive to those who care for native matters, Villa-Lobos has written a long preface to the score. In this he explains that "the material for the symphonic series came from historical documents dating from the period of Brazil's discovery" and that he was principally inspired by the letters of Pero Vaz de Caminha to King D. Manoel. Which letters he had in mind is not quite clear, since only one exists.

The fate of the *Bachianas Brasileiras* which, according to the composer, fuse the spirit of Bach with that of Brazil, is again different. *Bachianas Brasileiras, No. 1*, for eight violoncelli is said to have been written for the Brazilian composer-conductor, Walter Burle Marx, and the Rio de Janeiro Philharmonic Orchestra in 1932 at the special request of the conductor to whom (together with the orchestra) the work was dedicated. The manuscript copy of the composition contains, however, the indication "written in São Paulo in 1930" without any dedication whatsoever.[4] *Bachianas Brasileiras, No. 2*, for chamber orchestra is only an orchestration of three pieces for violoncello and one piece for piano solo.[5] Yet, to fit his Bach scheme, Villa-Lobos simply added *Prelude, Aria, Dansa* and *Toccata* to the titles of the original compositions.

---

[2] In 1941 *A Fantasia de Movimentos Mixtos* was performed for the first time in its final form, the movements being *Alma Convulsa, Serenidade* and *Contentamento*.

[3] *Alegria* is an orchestration of a piece for piano solo called *Alegria na Horta* (1918), taken from the collection entitled *Suite Floral*. *Adagio Sentimental*, in its original form, is a song called *A Virgem* (1913) and *Cascavel* is an orchestration of a song of the same name written in 1917.

[4] I believe that the first movement was written only between 1936 and 1938, because until 1936 only the last two movements were ever performed. The first performance of the complete work was given in 1938.

[5] The three pieces for violoncello are *O Canto do Capadocio, O Canto da Nossa Terra* and *O Trenzinho do Caipira*. *Lembrança do Sertão* was originally written for piano solo.

Bachianas Brasileiras, No. 3, has yet to be written. But why not write a fourth one in the meantime? In 1941 the titles were ready, composed as usual of a neo-classical heading and a Brazilian title in brackets. Pieces for piano solo, written during the last decade, were combined, and a Prelude, composed in 1941, was added for the publication of this heterogeneous set.

In a way, one feels inclined to presume that a certain inconsistency exists between some of the musical works as they stand and the intellectual conception of the composer. On the one hand are the compositions and on the other a bunch of explanatory notes written many years afterwards. It is difficult to say whether Villa-Lobos wrote these works with a programmatic idea in mind which he merely put into words on a later occasion, or whether he felt that a prefatory text would make his music better understood. I tend, however, to the conclusion that in a number of cases a preconceived plan must have existed, otherwise the many explanations would be irrelevant, since the music intended for them has still to be written.

Villa-Lobos' procedure of composing in the case of some large-scale works has been unusual too. In Paris in 1928 for example, he planned to write a piece for piano and orchestra which he called *Chôros, No.* 11. A few sketches were about all he jotted down. Yet, twelve years later when his friend Arthur Rubinstein happened to be in Rio de Janeiro and asked the composer to write him a piece for piano and orchestra, Villa-Lobos set to work, saying that he had only to rewrite *Chôros, No.* 11, since the complete score had been lost after his return from Europe. The fact is, however, that the composition had probably taken shape in his mind in Paris that year, but for some reason only a few sketches were actually put on paper. This is sufficient for him to say that the composition was written, because he feels he can rely on his memory, no matter how much time may pass between the spiritual conception and the writing down of his idea. Villa-Lobos calls this 're-writing a work'. It is interesting, too, that such compositions are dated from the year they were conceived spiritually and not when they were written down. The last movement of the *Fantasia de Movimentos Mixtos* originated in a similar way, as I have described elsewhere.[6]

Needless to say, these instances cannot be generalized to define Villa-Lobos' process of composing. Nevertheless, they are typical of a man who needs neither mood nor inner readiness, but creates a composition whenever the occasion demands. This may perhaps explain the irregular development of his artistic career. His works, as a whole, do not show that continuous thread that is so obvious in the music of other composers. Of course, every single piece bears the mark of his individuality, just as his works as a whole reflect his musical personality. Yet it is difficult to discover the artist's development in the tremendous range of his compositions. There is no continuous line, and

---

[6] "Violin Concerto by Villa-Lobos" in *The New York Times*, 8th June, 1941.

so one cannot predict his next work.   He may, for a time, adhere to a certain style, he may suddenly jump back to a form of expressing himself which he seemed to have dropped years ago, or he may take up an entirely new line. He appears to enjoy doing the unexpected, though it may actually be his restlessness that prevents him from being attached to one special style or type for a long time.   Should any occasion call for a new work, he would write it, even if it meant changing over to quite a new form or leaving a work unfinished. What a student of his compositions may regard as the typical style of Villa-Lobos, seems almost to have come about by coincidence.   There are many promises without fulfilment and there are many blossoms without previous buds.   Interesting and fascinating as many of his compositions may be, there is a strange absence of natural growth; they do not ripen as man does in life. His finest works are not built up on his earlier music.   They are not peaks of a mountain range, but rather single columns standing out against a background of less individual compositions.   Though they may be regarded as the culmination of his artistic strife, they remain isolated and not interlocked like links of a chain.   Hence, if we take just his work as it presents itself at present, regardless of what the artist may still create, it is almost impossible to point to one special period and to label it as the zenith of the composer Villa-Lobos.

Essential however is the fact that he has created compositions which differ widely from those written previously in Brazil.   It is probably true to say that Villa-Lobos has taken into account all the wealth original Brazilian music could offer him.   He has freely quoted popular melodies current among the people, and especially among the children, of his country.   He has done so in the sets, for piano solo, such as the *Cirandas* (1926), *Cirandinhas* and *Brinquedo de Roda*. They are used again in the Fifth String Quartet (1931) and in *Momoprecoce* (1929) for piano and orchestra, a piece which is based on a collection of piano solos called *Carnaval das Crianças Brasileiras* (1919).

The songs *Tres Poemas Indigenas* (1926), on the other hand, are based on original folk melodies as the title already indicates.   Yet the *Chansons Typiques Brésiliennes* are merely harmonizations of folk-tunes and popular themes. If he has borrowed liberally from the fascinating treasure collected by others in the songs mentioned, he has also created pseudo-folk-melodies as, for instance, in the twelve *Serestas* (1926) for voice and piano.   He has absorbed the melodic and rhythmical traits characteristic of the original musical language and has made them part and parcel of his own nature in order to create a genuine composition based on the rhythmical and melodic *données* of folk material. This is obvious, too, in the orchestral works *Chôros, No.* 8 (1925) and *Chôros, No.* 10 (1926), in the wind and string ensemble *Chôros, No.* 7 (1924) and in the superb little piano piece *Alma Brasileira* (*Chôros, No.* 5), written in 1925.   In none of these, as with those works which bear no indication to the contrary either in the title or at the outset of the composition, has Villa-Lobos ever quoted folk-melodies.   The tune to the words *Rasga o Coração*, by Catullo

Cearense, which is used in the *Chôros, No.* 10 is no "savage Indian chant",[7] nor is it derived from folk material. It is a popular song picked up from Anacleto de Medeiros, a friend of Villa Lobos' early years. This applies likewise to the lyrical melody which appears in the *Chôros, No.* 4 (1926), which is no folk song, but a popular tune that Villa-Lobos remembered from the time when he frequented Bohemian circles. It is interesting that Villa-Lobos has made use of many possibilities in his treatment of folk material. He has liberally borrowed folk-melodies and harmonized them. He has achieved genuine compositions on a folk-song basis, and has also concocted synthetic wholes of folk-elements and rhythmical and melodic fragments of this stuff. He has deliberately quoted popular themes in otherwise original compositions, or arranged these tunes for part-singing.

Not only this. Presumably on the suggestion of Roquette Pinto, the Brazilian anthropologist, Villa-Lobos has made other experiments. In the *Procissão da Cruz* (1937) from the Fourth Suite of the *Discovery of Brazil* he uses an original Indian folk-melody against an Ambrosian chant, sung by a double chorus and accompanied by an ever-repeated one-bar rhythm played by a bassoon and double bassoon. His handling is again different in the *Primeira Missa no Brasil* (1936) from the same work. A classical *Kyrie* of the Gregorian missal counterpoints a pseudo-Indian folk-tune. The tune was written in collaboration with Roquette Pinto to ensure the authentic flavour, and the text, based on the original Tupy-Guarani language, is also the result of their combined work.

The works of Villa-Lobos which are connected with folk material are his most personal compositions. The others, though reflecting his individuality in other ways, lack much of his characteristic intensity and vigour. They seem to give evidence of a man wanting to prove his ability in all fields, in spite of the fact that only certain spheres really put him at ease and exhibit his personality at its best. To the first group belong the symphonies, the violoncello concerto, the trios, some of the quartets, and in a way, the *Suite Suggestive* (1929) and the opera *Izaht*. Throughout the symphonic works one seeks in vain for dynamic structure, and all one is confronted with is patchy and episodic. They show disconnected motives, dressed up snippets following one another, virtuosic showmanship in disjointed sections, but a complete lack of fusion into one organic whole. It is difficult to say what the reason is for Villa-Lobos' inability to think in organic wholes. Folk-melodies and popular tunes, necessarily conceived on a small scale, have not been without influence on him in this respect, as has much of the music of the Russians; one notes in particular his indebtedness to Tchaikovsky. Villa-Lobos has unquestionably become aware of some sort of difficulty in conceiving formal structure. This may be the reason why he has constantly said that the *Chôros* and *Serestas*

---

[7] Olin Downes in *The New York Times,* 14th May, 1939, calls it "an Indian chant of the savages".

are a "novel form of musical composition" (which they are not since they make a virtue of a weakness in constructing organic forms).

Much of Villa-Lobos' music is an accumulation of ideas. His rich phantasy and ready imagination, an imagination working, however, in episodes and sensations and not in conceiving elaborate plans, may perhaps explain a certain clumsiness in the structure. Yet, in one instance, an interesting free organic form was achieved, namely in the *Chôros, No.* 10.

If lack of structural perfection in symphonic works may appear as a weakness, it passes almost unnoticed in smaller forms, because of the interesting texture. Here Villa-Lobos has ample opportunity to exhibit his special gift of versatility of expression. The orchestration, though in part emphasizing unmixed registers, is often too heavily loaded. Villa-Lobos' intimate knowledge of the orchestra impels him frequently to give all the instruments something to do. He does so, not necessarily because the structure of the work asks for a full orchestra, but simply to keep all the players occupied. The horizontal conception and linear treatment of the parts, the thinking in melodic lines and timbre effects, and not in terms of thematic development, may account for this peculiarity.

On the other hand, Villa-Lobos' striking sense of colour effects and orchestral timbre has induced him to use the instruments in a new way. Accordingly, in certain passages for violins, chords and arpeggios in harmonics are to be played above the bridge. Sometimes his imagination misfires when it comes to practical details. A case in point is the *Chôros, No.* 8, where he prescribes (page 109 of the miniature score) that paper should be placed between the strings of the piano. This might be startling and peculiar if the listener could perceive it; yet, a full orchestra and a second ordinary piano are used at the same time, and the effect is completely covered. Besides, the player has only four bars to prepare the piano, which makes it almost impossible to put the paper between the strings. All he can do is to place the paper on top of them, though it makes little difference.

Villa-Lobos' special love of colossal orchestras (Third and Fourth Symphonies) has never entirely abated. He augmented a full-sized instrumental body in early years by adding unfamiliar instruments. Hence, an augmented percussion ensemble was apparently all there remained for him to lay his hands on. Many rarely used instruments, not necessarily percussion ones, such as the violinophone, have perhaps enlarged the timbre scale of the orchestra. There are nevertheless others which may in a way emphasize the authenticity of original Brazilian music, yet their use appears in some cases to be a symptom of Villa-Lobos' deliberate striving to be unusual. Moreover, the use of these instruments must hinder frequent performance.

Villa-Lobos' feeling for orchestral colours and his love of experiment impelled him to combine instruments in an unfamiliar manner. In small groups such as in the *Chôros, No.* 4 (1926) for three horns and one trombone, the *Chôros bis* (1929) for violin and violoncello, the *Chôros, No. 2* (1924) for flute and clarinet and the *Bachianas Brasileiras, No. 1* for eight violoncelli, he shows an astounding capability in exploiting the resources of the respective instruments.   Even if such small-scale works are extended to voice ensembles with instrumental accompaniment, the original scheme remains the same, as in the case of the *Primeira Missa no Brasil* from the *Discovery of Brazil.*   In this an assortment of wind instruments (clarinet without mouthpiece, two ordinary clarinets, one bass clarinet, one bassoon and one double-bassoon) supported by three Brazilian percussion ones (Xucalha de côco, Réco-Réco and Trocano) strikes one as bold and daring, considering the effect produced by the ever-repeated rhythm of the instruments set against a double chorus.

Miniature forms, as a rule, give Villa-Lobos ample scope to display his knack of deriving unusual expressions and colours from a minimum of material. This applies not only to instrumental but to vocal compositions.   Words have not always inspired Villa-Lobos' musical ideas, unless they were written specially for him as in the case of the *Epigrammas Ironicos e Sentimentaes* (1921 and 1923).   Should the spoken language be a deliberate part of the musical composition, however, he knows where to draw his examples.   Gramophone records and collections of folk melodies have, undoubtedly, pushed his imagination in this direction and made him compose such fascinating vocal passages as we find in the *Nonetto* (1923) and the *Chôros, No. 10.*   He has used fragments of the original Indian idiom or formed syllables based on African sources to produce ingenuous onomatopoeic effects, matched with the instrumental background.   The attraction of mixing unfamiliar-sounding words with musical tones has inspired Villa-Lobos to go even a step further and create his own words to emphasize his musical ideas.[8]   Clever as this may be, the danger of abuse is very real.   Vocal and instrumental *glissandi*, though effective on rare occasions, lose much of their original sparkle when exaggerated.

The effective brilliance of Villa-Lobos' individual works results primarily from timbre effects and linear conception.   All the rest is, in Villa-Lobos' case, of secondary importance.   Flexibility of key was probably suggested to him by the music of the Russians.   Whole-tone, pentatonic and modal scales, though perhaps piquant, have seldom become living tissue in his work. They are part of Villa-Lobos' stock-in-trade, as little and as much as are the harmonic devices.   The working to death of the chord of the seventh, side-slipping (originally borrowed from Italian opera composers), the perpetual pedal points and the unceasing *ostinati* are an obvious element in his music, a commonplace rather than a technical pecularity.   Unresolved seconds for percussion effects, passages built on fourths instead of thirds or even in one instance (*Amazonas*, 1917) chords of the fourth are more accidental

---

[8] *Cf.* the vocal interjections in Delius' *Eventyr.*—[ED.]

than deliberate. What appears to be harsh and daring in the harmonic texture is the outcome of horizontal writing. Harmony itself has little attraction for Villa-Lobos; he prefers rather to exploit other fields nearer his heart. Colour, timbre and sound are all that matter to him; harmony is a mere necessary support, formal structure an inevitable foundation.

The Music Review, **4**(1), February 1943, 28–34

THE HISTORY OF VILLA-LOBOS'S BIRTH-DATE

ON March 5, 1947, Heitor Villa-Lobos, the Brazilian composer, was sixty years old. The date went unnoticed in the musical world. No special celebrations, as would only be natural for a composer of Villa-Lobos's reputation both in Brazil and elsewhere, took place. It was not modesty on the part of the composer that he impeded the celebration of Brazil's most outstanding living composer, and it was no negligence of his friends and admirers either to omit such a date, in spite of the fact that Villa-Lobos himself was, at that time, absent from his home in Rio de Janeiro, fulfilling engagements in the United States. The crux of the matter is that the precise year in which Villa-Lobos was born was only discovered a few days *after* Villa-Lobos's sixtieth birthday.

The year of his birth was always a puzzle to everyone interested in the composer's art and the happenings of his life. It seems natural that Villa-Lobos himself ought to have known in which year he was born. However, he did not. Not that he ignored it entirely, but his statements as to the exact date varied according to the circumstances ; possibly he did not even care at all in which year he was born. Lexicographers, musicologists and others looking for facts, however, thought differently. Most, if not all of them, naturally turned to Villa-Lobos himself in the first place. Once such a date appeared in one or the other of the publications recognized in the musical world as reliable standard works, the date went on being quoted by others, with reference to the source of publication. It so happens that Grove's ' Dictionary of Music and Musicians ' (Supplementary Volume) (London, 1940), and Baker's ' Biographical Dictionary of Musicians ' (Fourth edition, revised and enlarged, New York, 1940), both carry the date 1881. Renato Almeida, the Brazilian musicologist, must have been reluctant to accept this, for he chose his own sources and gave 1890 as the date of Villa-Lobos's year of birth in his ' História da Música Brasileira ' (Second edition, Rio de Janeiro, 1942), the standard book on Brazilian musical history. We had seen the same date in two publications that appeared in France about twenty years ago ; a book entitled ' Kings, Jazz and David ' by Irving Schwerké (Paris, 1927) and an article in the French periodical *Musique* (No. 4,

January 15, 1929) by Suzanne Demarquez. Both writers were in touch with Villa-Lobos during the composer's stay in France at that time which leads to the assumption that it was Villa-Lobos himself who furnished the information. Andrade Muricy, a music critic of Rio de Janeiro's leading morning newspaper *Journal do Commercio* who belongs to a group intimately connected with the composer's art and choral singing and teaching, gives 1885 in a publication entitled *Musique Brésilienne Moderne* (Rio de Janeiro, 1937). And Prof. Luiz Heitor Corrêa de Azevedo, who holds the chair of folklore at the National School of Music at the University of Brazil in Rio de Janeiro and is well known both in Brazil and the United States for his reliable research work, agreed to 1885 in his ' Relação das Operas de autores Brasileiros ' (Rio de Janeiro, 1938). All these writers accepted the date, from whatever sources they got it, in good faith.

Villa-Lobos's identity papers contain almost as great a variety of birth-dates as he has documents. His French *carte d'identité*, issued on December 15, 1927, bears the year 1891 ; his former voting paper, dated October 6, 1934, mentions 1883. In order to be safe from any further bother and, at the same time, to satisfy all those who were approaching him to clear up, once and for all, the mystery about the year of his birth, Villa-Lobos, in 1941, asked the editor of the then existing musical periodical in Rio de Janeiro, *Musica Viva*, to include in a special issue dedicated to him (Ano I, No. 7/8, Jan./Feb., 1941) a ' summarized authentic biography ' which he himself supplied. He decided on this occasion to have been born in 1888. A few months later in the same year (1941) Nicolas Slonimsky was in Rio de Janeiro on his tour through South America. Not trusting anyone or anything that was said or published with regard to Villa-Lobos's birth-date, he heard from the composer (as the present writer, too, and doubtless many others had done) that Villa-Lobos remembered to have been baptized in the Church of Sao José at the Rua Misericordia in Rio de Janeiro. However, Slonimsky says (in his book ' Music of Latin America ', New York, 1945) that ' my diligent search through birth registries of that church revealed no entry on Villa-Lobos '.

It would certainly be useless to undertake a search through birth registers, because during the period of the alleged years of Villa-Lobos's birth, that is from 1881 till 1891, birth registration was not compulsory in Brazil. When Villa-Lobos was married at the registrar's office on November 12, 1913, a birth certificate or anything stating the year of his birth was apparently not available, for the present writer found at the registrar's office that Villa-Lobos's mother made a statement (dated October 24, 1913) which was attached to the marriage documents, to be found at the Eighth Civil Registrar in Rio de Janeiro, in which she declares that her son was born in the Federal Capital in 1886. (The marriage registration, however, says that Villa-Lobos was twenty-eight years old.) Yet even Villa-Lobos's mother was wrong as has now been proved. Vasco Mariz, who is working in the Brazilian Ministry of Foreign Affairs and preparing a little book on Villa-Lobos which will soon be published, may or may not have known about Slonimsky's pilgrimage to the Sao José Church. Be that as it may, he paid a call to the same church and found Villa-Lobos's baptismal entry in 1889 which states that Heitor Villa-Lobos was born on March 5, 1887. On the same day was also baptized Villa-Lobos's sister, Carmen, his junior by approximately one year and a half (born October 10, 1888).

The Monthly Musical Record, **78**(898), July/August 1948, 153–5

Villa-Lobos's Brazilian excursions

Heitor Villa-Lobos—the 85th anniversary of whose birth falls on 5 March 1972—arrived in Paris for the second time in 1927; he had the financial backing of rich Brazilian philanthropes to enable him to stay in the French capital for several years. He was soon introduced and welcomed in Parisian cultural and intellectual circles, and he moved happily among the celebrities of the time. Keen to make a name for himself, to be original and different from others, the self-assured Villa-Lobos sought to catch his hosts' attention with a series of fantastic stories about his experiences with indigenous tribes in Brazil's interior.

> Captured by savages, he was for three days witness of funeral ceremonies which were celebrated in his honour because his hosts were preparing to eat him . . . .[1]
>
> More dead than alive, he remained meanwhile in a state of unconscious receptivity which allowed him to register accents of his officiates . . . Freed by whites, he came back from this terrible adventure with lots of rhythms and modulations with which he has since fed his compositions[2]

On another occasion he said:

> In the cause of one of my expeditions, I had brought with me a gramophone and some records. I had a diabolical idea: I wanted to see what effect the music of European patrimony had on the Indians. Having arrived at a certain tribe whereto, I am sure, the benefits of civilization had never penetrated, I installed my machine and let it play them something perfectly consonant. My Indians shouted and hit the mechanical divinity which I had all the trouble to protect against their furor. But no, you are mistaken: it was not my Pandora Box of which they were afraid, but the music itself. The proof? When calm was restored, I played a record of Indian music, collected among another tribe with which this one could not have had any contact. The good savages passed from one extreme to another and they began to shout, sing, dance and offer all signs of religious respect to the gramophone. When they were sufficiently exalted, I made an experiment: I again played the first record. There was a moment of astonishment, then, an instant later, the poor machine was nothing but a heap of timber and scrap iron . . . Like the savage in the fable, mine could not stand the idea that it was the same mouth that blew alternately the flame and the cool . . . I often repeated this experiment and the reactions which I had observed were almost always as conclusive if not as violent . . . This has cost me several gramophones and also some guitars (sometimes I used a guitar). Progressions of consonant chords played on my guitar had a discouraging reception but, on the other hand, my improvisations on indigenous rhythms excited the enthusiasm of the Indians.

[1] René Dumesnil, La Musique Contemporaine en France (Paris, 1930), i

[2] Le Monde Musical no.12 (Paris, 31 Dec 1927)

This was one of my most beautiful successes in my career as an instrumentalist.[3]

It is difficult to know whether these tales, which soon made the round, were accepted at face value or with a grain of salt (particularly the story that he had found his wife among some Indian tribes). At any rate, some of the musical press seemed to find them worth publishing. Villa-Lobos cannot have believed in them himself, but knew that no one in Paris was in a position to check the facts. Although speed within the communications media in the 1920s was not what it is today, Villa-Lobos's tales soon reached his home town's local press, and disgusted his countrymen; they felt that their compatriot in Paris had done a serious disservice to Brazil and had caused embarrassment to Brazilians. This did not make much impression on Villa-Lobos, in spite of the fact that in those years he was not yet recognized in Brazil as the country's leading composer—though he had aroused considerable attention with the Brazilian qualities of his works written a few years before his second departure to Europe.

Villa-Lobos's involvement in Paris with real or imagined travel stories was no isolated occurrence. The travel route which he supplied to a Brazilian music review[4] in Rio de Janeiro in 1941 for a 'summarized authentic biography' runs as follows: he went to the north of Brazil to visit Espirito Santo Bahia and Pernambuco; the following year his travels took him to the interior of the Brazilian states of Minas Gerais, Mato Grosso and Sao Paulo; from there he descended to Sao Paulo's harbour, Santos, and took a boat to Bahia in north-eastern Brazil; he claimed to have made Bahia his headquarters from where he visited all northern Brazilian states as well as 'several countries bordering on Brazil'.

That route is not identical with those published elsewhere and which presumably were also based on information given by the imaginative Villa-Lobos at some time or other. The revised and enlarged fourth edition of Baker's Biographical Dictionary of Musicians (1940) quotes Villa-Lobos to the effect that 'in 1912 he joined a scientific expedition into the interior of Brazil to study native customs and music'. During his stay in Paris, he gave a slightly different version to Suzanne Demarquez who states[5] that he had several opportunities to join scientific missions, among others, German missions.

After Villa-Lobos had returned to Brazil in 1930, and was nominated head of the Music Educational Department of Rio de Janeiro's municipality, he

[3] Guide du Concert, 6 June 1930; quoted in O Globo (Rio de Janeiro, 18 Oct 1930)

[4] Musica Viva, i, 7-8

[5] Musique, 4 (15 Jan 1929)

gave a version of his travels to the Brazilian music critic and writer, José de Andrade Muricy. That version was much closer to what he repeated in 1941. Muricy[6] declared that Villa-Lobos, laden with ophicleide and saxophone, went at the age of 19 to Espirito Santo, Bahia and Pernambuco, and two years later undertook a second journey which led him to Manaus, from where he travelled by land to the state of Minas Gerais, where he stayed a whole year.

By the start of World War II Villa-Lobos, aged 52, was approaching the zenith of his career both as a musical educator and as a composer. He was just about to catch—for the first time, in a more profound and lasting way—the attention of the United States musical world when, for the World's Fair in New York City in 1939, a number of records of his music (and that of other Brazilian composers) were prepared in Brazil; newspapers as important as the *New York Times*, and musical journals, began to occupy themselves with Villa-Lobos, publishing reviews of his works that were performed in Brazil and the USA.

It was at that time that I asked Villa-Lobos, in Brazil, to give me his own reading and interpretation of his travels into the country's interior. His account runs approximately as follows. He said that he made three trips. The first took him from Rio de Janeiro via Bahia, Sergipe, Recife, Fortaleza and Belém to Manaus (which so far represents nothing unusual). But from Manaus, Villa-Lobos said, he sailed some of the Amazon's left affluents, up and down, starting with the Rio Negro to the point

Musique Brésilienne Moderne (Rio de Janeiro, 1937)

where the Rio Branco branches off, and on that river he went as far as the town of Boa Vista. As Soon as he returned to Manaus, he embarked on another venture. This time he sailed some right affluents of the Amazon. He started with the Madeira river, next the Purus river until he reached Acre Territory, and finally he ventured out on the Solimoes river which led him to the town of Iquitos. After Villa-Lobos's return to Manaus, he went to Belém in the state of Pará, travelled the Tocantins river up to where the Araguaia river turns off, on which he sailed next. Having arrived at the island of Banan-al, Villa-Lobos transferred himself to the Rio das Mortes and went as far as Cuiabá in the state of Mato Grosso. He came back the same way until he again reached Tocantins river which he sailed up to the state of Goías. Here he disembarked and journeyed by land via Belo Horizonte, the capital of the state of Minas Gerais, back to Rio de Janeiro.

The second trip, according to Villa-Lobos, took him from Rio de Janeiro along the eastern coast of Brazil to Belém in the state of Pará. From there he sailed the Amazon river, transferred himself to the Tapajos, a right affluent of the Amazon, and returned the same way to Rio de Janeiro. On his third and final trip, he journeyed from Rio de Janeiro to Sergipe: he next embarked on the Sao Francisco river and sailed up to the state of Minas Gerais, where he disembarked to return by land home to Rio de Janeiro.

All through his life, Villa-Lobos embellished dates and facts concerning himself, though not, of course, with seriously deceptive motives. He just wanted to be original and unique, and perhaps he simply enjoyed getting involved with extraordinary happenings and adventures, creating a legend that at times became difficult to separate from the real facts of his life. Possibly, noticing that some of the people he encountered in Europe (and later foreign visitors who, more and more, came to call on him in Rio de Janeiro) were uninformed about Brazil. he simply delighted in playing on this ignorance and enjoyed seeing them believe in his impossible stories and descriptions. His own personal charm and his outgoing manner may have convinced many that what he said about himself was the truth. It is doubtful that Villa-Lobos, intelligent person as he was, ever came to believe in these stories himself.

I have tried in vain in Brazil to find anybody who could confirm or deny whether Villa-Lobos had made the trips of which he told, so it is unlikely that we will ever know the truth about these unusual journeys. He was a courageous man, enterprising, energetic and audacious, an indefatigable, venturesome person all through his life. It is not impossible that he undertook at least part of the trips about which he boasted. However, checking these itineraries on the map is bound to raise doubts as it seems almost impossible that Villa-Lobos could have made such journeys accompanied only by one or two friends. Travelling in these regions is a bold and daring undertaking even today; it was even more so at the beginning of the century.

The idea that Villa-Lobos did more than sail up and down the rivers he mentioned seems like a fairytale; what sounds even more like wishful thinking is the idea of his having penetrated the virgin forests for a solitary, one-man encounter with several tribes and indigenous groups and his musical experiments and experiences with the aborigines. It is possible that his meeting E. Roquette-Pinto in later years and his friendship with that eminent man had aroused his imagination. In 1912 Roquette-Pinto accompanied the expeditions of General Cândido Mariano da Silva Rondon into the interior of Brazil, and he described his observations and studies in his book called *Rondônia*. Roquette-Pinto also noted folk tunes of the Indians (his records are available at the National Museum in Rio de Janeiro with some of the tunes quoted in the book). Perhaps Villa-Lobos identified himself with Roquette-Pinto in his imagination, half believing himself to have made the journeys into the interior and to have come face to face with the aborigines whose tunes he recorded. Then he started to spread tales about those travels as though he, not Roquette-Pinto, had undertaken them; and gradually he may have come to believe in the travel stories himself and they became part of his own legend. How else could his claim that he visited 'several countries bordering on Brazil'—a statement he made for the 'authentic biography' published in *Musica Viva* when USA interest in him was increasing—be interpreted? Only because, in his imagination, he aspired even to outdo Roquette-Pinto.

It does Villa-Lobos no harm, nor does it prejudice his work, that he involved himself with such fanciful stories, which realistic people may always have taken with a grain of salt. The stories add to the charm and unpredictability with which Villa-Lobos liked to surround his person, and by which many who came in touch with him were amused and entertained but never bored.

Musical Times, **113**(1549), March 1972, 263–5

Corrigenda

p25 *second column, second paragraph, line 9*:
For Sao read São
line 10:
For Sao read São
p26, *second column, line 7*:
For Solimoes read Solimões
second column, line 17:
For Goías read Goiás
second paragraph, line 8:
For Sao read São

VILLA-LOBOS: FATHER AND SON

Heitor Villa-Lobos, the most famous Brazilian composer of this century, was born in Rio de Janeiro in March 1887 and died there in November 1959 at the age of seventy-two. He had returned to Rio only four months earlier from one of his frequent concert tours in the United States and Europe where he is appreciated largely because of the flavor and color of Brazil that is reflected in many of the more than a thousand compositions he wrote.

Few know that it was Heitor's father Raúl who awakened in him some interest, or at least some curiosity, in Brazil's land, people, and lore and who probably endowed him with his musical gift.

Heitor was the oldest of eight children, three of whom died at an early age. Though it is a matter of speculation what course Heitor's musical development might have taken had Raúl not died of malaria in July 1899 at the age of thirty-seven, it might well have evolved differently.

After Raúl's death the widowed mother had a hard time making ends meet, and the twelve-year-old Heitor was often left to himself. Economic hardship and lack of further encouragement from a musically interested parent may have been partly responsible for Heitor Villa-Lobos never receiving any formal musical training except for some rudimentary and rather sporadic harmony lessons from Agnello França at the National Institute (later called School) of Music in Rio de Janeiro, an institution that was later incorporated into the University of Brazil. Had he lived, it is more than likely that Raúl would have made it

possible for Heitor to receive some good musical
training during his adolescent years or even
before.

*Raúl Villa-
Lobos, who
awakened his
son's interest
in Brazil's land
and lore and
who probably
endowed him
with his
musical talent*

*Heitor at
eighteen during
his Bohemian
"wander-years"
when he played
in night clubs,
bars and movie
theaters*

Raúl, an educated and cultured person, interested in literature, geography, history, and
particularly in music, was twenty-five years old
when Heitor was born. He loved to spend time
with his eldest son, to whom he described Brazil's
rivers, mountains, towns, and cities, and the
people that lived in the far-off regions of the
Brazilian hinterland. He showed him maps and
pictures, and narrated some Brazilian legends and
myths as well. It is difficult to ascertain how
profoundly his father's tales and descriptions
impressed Heitor, but some of them must have left
traces in his mind, for the ballet called *Amazonas*,
which Villa-Lobos wrote in 1917, is based on a
tale that his father told him. Throughout his life
Heitor showed a marked interest in the people
of his country. It is true that in later years the
immediate impulse to write music about them
came from tendencies and trends of the time,
such as the recognition of native music and later
nationalistic thinking. It may have been his
father's stimuli that promoted Heitor to occupy
himself with folklore and folk music much before
many of his Brazilian contemporaries.

Heitor grew up in a musical atmosphere. Raúl's
musical interests were wide. He attended opera
performances, participated as cellist in amateur
chamber-music groups, and was a member of the
Symphonic Club. But above all, Raúl played music
at home, and gave his son his first cello lessons.
Whether Raúl taught him to play the guitar is
unknown, but the guitar, a popular instrument in
Brazil, attracted Heitor Villa-Lobos and he both
played it well and wrote for it.

Observing Heitor's enthusiasm for music, Raúl
introduced him to those European composers
whose music was in vogue. Among them were
Meyerbeer, Verdi, and Leoncavallo, and the two
composers whose music greatly influenced that of
his son: Wagner and Puccini. It was before the
turn of the century that Heitor first heard music
from Wagner's *Tannhäuser* and *Lohengrin* at his

home, to which Raúl often invited other musically
interested friends to discuss operas and to play
parts of them at the piano. Perhaps Raúl took
Heitor to the opera house, although no records are
available to prove that he did. *Bohème* was first
performed in Rio when his father was still alive
and he showed a special liking for it and surely
played parts of it to his son. Puccini's influence on
Heitor was not less than that of Wagner. He became better acquainted with the music of both
when, as a member of Rio de Janeiro's opera
orchestra, he performed their works. Some of
Heitor Villa-Lobos' music composed between his
twenty-sixth and thirtieth years was strongly
influenced by Puccini. Even very much later—
four years before his death—Villa-Lobos' opera
Yerma, which he wrote in 1955 to words of
Federico García Lorca, again showed strong
Puccini influences according to comments from
the press after the work's first performance on
August 12, 1971, during the summer opera season
at Santa Fe, New Mexico. This was despite the
fact that Heitor Villa-Lobos' musical style had
taken on a completely different flavor and color
between 1924 and 1955.

Music was not Raúl's only interest. Literature
was his other inclination. It led to his competing
for and winning the post of clerk in Rio de
Janeiro's National Library. At the age of twenty-
eight, in October 1890, Raúl took up his new post
with a small salary. Diligent and intelligent as
he was, he was promoted to library assistant two
years later. Yet Raúl did not find complete ful-
fillment in his work at the Library. His literary
interests had a wider range—one year prior to his
Library employment he had published his first
book, and now, living among books, he felt compelled to write some more.

He wrote on pedagogical and historical subjects
and, being apt at languages, translated the works
of others into Portuguese. Raúl occasionally
published his writings under the pseudonym
Epaminondas Villalba. Heitor apparently liked the

name and signed some of his early compositions
with it, merely adding the word *Filho* (Junior)
to it.

Such literary activity, zeal and interest naturally
influenced Heitor who as an adult also showed
considerable interest in books on many subjects,
though he had little leisure to read much of what
he bought for his own extensive private library.

Meanwhile Raúl had come to such high standing
at the Library that in 1896, three years before his
death, he was commissioned to reorganize the
Library of the Brazilian Senate, and according to
a report in Rio de Janeiro's *Gazeta de Notícias* of
July 20, 1899, his catalog was published.

During his lifetime Raúl had made a small
career for himself. The child of humble parents,
Raúl was sent to the Asylum for Impoverished
Children (later called the João Alfredo Boarding
School). Although he had no money for education,
he had the good fortune, through the recommen-
dation of a friend, to enter the Alberto Brandão
school. Talented and amiable, he immediately
made friends, joined others in playing music and
drew pencil portraits of his friends and colleagues.

Whatever made Raúl enter the University to
study medicine for two consecutive years is
unknown, because his interests lay in a completely
different direction. It was literature and music
that interested him in the first place. So when no
more money was available to pay for his studies,
he decided to become a school teacher.

Raúl's literary and musical gifts were inherited
from his mother who survived him by many years
and who was a cultured and educated person. It is
little known—if at all—that Heitor was partly of
Spanish descent, through his father who was the
child of Spanish parents. And while Spanish influences via Portugal had entered Brazil and
Brazilian music in centuries gone by, perhaps the
Spanish element Heitor inherited may also have
had some influence on his musical style, which had
become so typically Brazilian, just as the Hispano-
Portuguese influences had contributed their

respective parts in the formation and integration of Brazilian music in the past.

Portuguese ancestry was also shared by Heitor Villa-Lobos: his maternal grandfather, Antônio dos Santos Martis, a musician who played the piano and occasionally even composed some dance music of the type that was popular in those days, was of Portuguese descent. His daughter, Heitor's mother, Noemia, was a Brazilian and a completely different person. She was neither musically nor literarily inclined nor had she had any specific influence on Heitor as a musician, and her life was taken up with rearing her several children under difficult circumstances.

Américas, **24**(4), April 1972, 19–24, also published in Portuguese and Spanish.

Corrigenda

p 33 *line 5:*
For Martis read Martins

THE VILLA-LOBOS MUSEUM

IT DOES NOT happen often that a contemporary composer, shortly after his death, is honored by having a museum established to commemorate his name, life, and work. Now, after a dozen years of solid activity, the Villa-Lobos Museum in Rio de Janeiro has given ample proof of its *raison d'être;* it has become an institution well known both in and outside of Brazil. But it was not always that simple at first.

During Heitor Villa-Lobos' lifetime some people in Brazil had already hit upon the idea of founding the Villa-Lobos Museum. When the composer heard of it, he exclaimed, "A museum is something for the deceased, and I am of course still very much alive!"

"It seems they want to file me away," he commented in 1956 to Clóvis Salgado, the former Brazilian Minister of Education and Culture. "Perhaps they wish to believe me incapable of producing any more. Well, they have made a mistake: I am feeling stronger than ever, and find no lack of inspiration to continue producing my music. Creating music is my profession, my life, my joy. No museum."

Thus Villa-Lobos energetically opposed Project No. 1,588, which, in 1956, Amarylio de Albuquerque, then Director of the Secretariat of the Chamber of Deputies, had launched to establish a Villa-Lobos Museum to preserve the composer's works and personal memorabilia in order to do full justice to the greatest Brazilian composer of the first half of the twentieth century. Albuquer-

que said in an address in Rio de Janeiro, on November 4, 1970, that he and other Brazilians had felt pangs of guilt because of the "indifference that surrounded Villa-Lobos in Brazil," which had never paid him the tribute he deserved.

Paris, however, had already recognized Villa-Lobos' talents in the middle of the twenties, when he was in France on his second sojourn, sponsored by Brazilian philanthropists, from early 1927 to the middle of 1930. (Villa-Lobos' first stay in France, from the middle of 1923 until the middle of 1924, was on a Brazilian Government grant.) It was in those years of the late twenties that he was given a chance to present his most recent works, with their typical Brazilian flavor, to the Parisian public, and they were discussed and reviewed in the music periodicals and the daily press.

France and other European countries again welcomed Villa-Lobos after the end of World War II. This time it was the major orchestras and the radio stations that invited him to conduct his music, and the recording companies asked him to perform his works. Thereafter, he visited Europe almost every year until shortly before his death, fourteen years ago.

But it was primarily the United States that, since World War II, had really appreciated Villa-Lobos. On his first visit there, in late 1944 and the winter of 1945, he was invited to conduct in Los Angeles, Boston, and New York City, and was awarded an honorary doctorate, in addition to numerous other tributes in various cities. From then on he was engaged annually to conduct the great U. S. orchestras, to have his music published, his works performed and recorded. It was, in fact, the United States that propelled Villa-Lobos into international recognition as a major composer and helped him to fame. And it was in the United States that a foundation, various orchestras and individuals, and persons of other nationalities whom he had met there commissioned him to write a ballet, concertos, chamber music, and other works. These commissions added to an already tremendously prolific and productive, if not always very original, period of his artistic activity in those years. And it was again the United States that regarded Villa-Lobos as the most important contemporary Brazilian composer and honored him accordingly. He was sought after by orchestras, artists, recording companies, and universities alike.

So it was suddenly no longer necessary for Villa-Lobos to make efforts in his own behalf, or to get backing from Brazilian philanthropists to finance his work, as was the case in the twenties in France, nor was there any further need to organize concerts himself, as he had had to do at home, in his native Brazil, to get his music performed. It was now the United States that requested him to perform for its people, every year, until one fine summer evening, when Villa-Lobos conducted a concert at Bear Mountain, New York, on July 12, 1959, during the Empire State Music Festival: it was destined to be the last concert he would ever conduct.

But Brazil had fallen far behind. It was not until 1956 that Amarylio de Albuquerque had recognized the absolute necessity and urgency that something be done. But Villa-Lobos' own opposition, coupled with other adverse circumstances, made it impossible, at

the time, to make the Villa-Lobos Museum a reality. Not until several months after Villa-Lobos' death, on November 17, 1959, did the Museum materialize. On June 13, 1960, President Juscelino Kubitschek de Oliveira signed the decree that established the Museum. Clóvis Salgado signed the enactment on January 20, 1961, which arranged for the organization of the Museum.

The Museum was installed in the Palace of Culture in downtown Rio de Janeiro—only one block from where Villa-Lobos had lived—in a building that had housed the Ministry of Education and Culture before its transfer to Brasília. Arminda Villa-Lobos, the composer's wife and companion since the mid-thirties, was made the Director of the Museum. Intimately acquainted with his thoughts, life, and works, she made the Museum into a living monument to the composer. It is not a museum in the traditional sense. True, it holds Villa-Lobos' personal belongings, including published works, photos, recordings, several of his batons, and much that has been written and published about him. In this way, the Museum has preserved the past.

But the Museum's intention, right from the start, has been to live in the present as well. So, initially, 284 tapes were made, with music and comments on the composer, for weekly broadcasts over a Rio de Janeiro radio station. Next followed classification and indexing of the Museum's holdings for consultation by visitors, students, and scholars. With this spadework done, activities began in earnest in all possible fields.

Eight lecture cycles were arranged between 1966 and 1972 on specific subjects relating to the composer. At periodic intervals, close to twenty LP recordings of his music were issued. Six volumes have so far been published, entitled *Presença de Villa-Lobos* [Presence of Villa-Lobos] and containing re-prints of articles on him and lectures and recollections of those who had known him.

To encourage research on Villa-Lobos' music, the Museum has orga-nized essay contests to be written in Portuguese by university students of any nationality, on specific subjects such as his *Bachianas Brasileiras*, his string quartets, his piano music, and other top-ics, the winners receiving a cash prize, a silver medal with Villa-Lobos' effigy, a parchment certificate, and publication of the essay by the Museum.

Three international instrumental con-tests have also been held: for string quartets in 1966, for guitar in 1971, and for instrumental ensembles last year. These contests, open to all irrespective of age and nationality, are dedicated primarily to Villa-Lobos' music. The jury is international in composition. Three awards are given: a cash prize. gold, silver and bronze medals with Villa-Lobos' likeness, and a parchment certificate. The winners give a public concert or a radio and television recital, arranged by the Museum.

All of these activities have, over the years, taken place within the framework of the annual Villa-Lobos Festival, which is held in November to commem-orate the anniversary of the composer's death. It is also marked by a memorial Mass in the Candelária Church in Rio de Janeiro. and by concerts of his or-chestral works, chamber music. and solo pieces. The Festivals have been held every year since 1961 and have become an institution through which the Mu-seum endeavors to keep the flame aglow and to be not merely a shrine to the memory of the past but a place of lively activity.

Américas, **25**(11/12), November/December 1973, 18–23, also published in Spanish.

Corrigenda

p 35 *second column, line 5:*
For June 13, read June 22

Heitor Villa-Lobos

Festanlässe zum Todestag des brasilianischen Komponisten

Der 1887 in Rio de Janeiro geborene Komponist, dessen Todestag sich in diesem November zum fünfzehnten Mal jährt, stellt wohl die stärkste Potenz unter den südamerikanischen Komponisten dieses Jahrhunderts dar. Seine zahlreichen Konzerte, Sinfonien und Sinfonischen Dichtungen — unter ihnen die Sinfonische Dichtung «Erosão» (1950) —, seine «Bachianas Brasileiras», seine Ballette und Vokalwerke, aber auch einige Werke innerhalb seiner Kammermusik und seiner Lieder gehören zu den wertbeständigsten der neueren Komposition, liegen die geistigen und stilistischen Wurzeln des Brasilianers auch noch stark in den impressionistischen und nationalistischen Strömungen des 19. Jahrhunderts.

Der breit veranlagte Künstler, auf den auch die Gründung des brasilianischen Nationalkonservatoriums für orpheonischen Gesang im Jahre 1942 zurückgeht, gelangte allerdings in seinem Heimatland erst langsam zur Anerkennung. Paris hatte Villa-Lobos' großes Talent bereits in den zwanziger Jahren erkannt, als der Komponist während einiger Jahre in Frankreich weilte. Brasilianische Industrielle hatten dem Künstler einen mehrjährigen Aufenthalt in Paris ermöglicht, wo Villa-Lobos, nach einem kürzeren früheren Besuch, von Anfang 1927 bis Mitte 1930 lebte und mit dem kulturellen Leben und den bedeutendsten Künstlern des damaligen Paris in Berührung kam. Dieser Aufenthalt war für Villa-Lobos entscheidend, bot sich ihm jetzt doch auch die Gelegenheit, seine jüngsten Werke aufzuführen. Diese hatten, im Gegensatz zu den Kompositionen, die er beim ersten kurzen Pariser Aufenthalt mitbrachte, einen ausgesprochen brasilianischen Charakter, der das Publikum aufhorchen ließ und die Aufmerksamkeit der Presse erweckte. Seit dieser Zeit war Paris der Ausgangspunkt von Villa-Lobos' Ausstrahlung in Europa.

In erster Linie waren es aber die Vereinigten Staaten von Amerika, die seit dem Zweiten Weltkrieg Villa-Lobos' Bedeutung erkannten. Von 1944 an war er ein jährlicher Gast in den USA, wobei ihn die bedeutendsten Orchester als Dirigenten verpflichteten, um seine Werke selber den amerikanischen Publikum vorzustellen. In den Vereinigten Staaten gelangte Villa-Lobos zu Ruhm und Ehren; von allen Seiten kamen Kompositionsaufträge für Ballette, Solokonzerte, Kammermusik und Werke weiterer Gattungen. Diese Aufträge erfüllte er neben vielen zusätzlichen Anforderungen, vor allem als Dirigent. Es war eine ungeheuer fruchtbare und aktive Zeit, wenn auch aus diesen späten Jahren die Werke, von Ausnahmen abgesehen, nicht mehr die gleiche Originalität besitzen wie in früheren Jahren. Diese späte Aktivität währte bis zum letzten Konzert seines Lebens, das er am 12. Juli 1959, also vier Monate vor seinem Tod, dirigierte. Es fand im Rahmen des Empire State Music Festival in Bear Mountain im Staat New York statt.

In Brasilien galt der Prophet im eigenen Land noch immer eher wenig. Allerdings wurde, nachdem Villa-Lobos in Rio de Janeiro gestorben war, die Initiative zu einem *Villa-Lobos-Museum* ergriffen; am 22. Juni 1960 unterzeichnete der damalige Staatspräsident Juscelino Kubitschek de Oliveira eine Verordnung zu seiner Gründung. Sieben Monate später unterschrieb der Kultusminister Clóvis Salgado da Gama den Gesetzeserlaß mit besonderen Weisungen zur Organisation des Museums.

Das Museum wurde im Stadtzentrum von Rio de Janeiro, im Palácio da Cultura, untergebracht. In diesem Gebäude, das nahe bei Villa-Lobos' ehemaliger Wohnung liegt, befand sich früher das Ministerium für Bildungswesen und Kultur, ehe es nach der neuen Bundeshauptstadt Brasília verlegt wurde. Das Villa-Lobos-Museum untersteht der Abteilung für kulturelle Angelegenheiten des Ministeriums für Bildungswesen und Kultur. *Arminda Villa-Lobos*, die Lebensgefährtin des Komponisten seit der Mitte der dreißiger Jahre, wurde zur Direktorin des Museums ernannt. Mit Villa-Lobos' Werken und seinen Gedankengängen vertraut, sah sie ihre Aufgabe darin, das Museum zu einer lebendigen Gedenkstätte des Komponisten zu machen. Es gibt im Villa-Lobos-Museum persönliche Gebrauchsgegenstände des Komponisten wie einige seiner Taktstöcke, seinen Gaveau-Flügel, Drucke seiner Werke, Schallplatten, Photographien und vieles, das über ihn geschrieben und veröffentlicht worden ist. Das Villa-Lobos-Museum stellte 284 Tonbänder her mit Aufzeichnungen von Musik und Kommentaren des Komponisten; sie dienten bisher in erster Linie für Darbietungen einer Radiostation in Rio de Janeiro, die dem Ministerium unterstellt ist. Mehr als zwanzig Langspielplatten sind bis jetzt durch das Museum herausgebracht worden. Zwischen 1966 und 1973 fanden insgesamt zehn Vortragszyklen über die verschiedenartigsten Themen statt, die sich mit Villa-Lobos befassen; bis Ende letzten Jahres publizierte das Villa-Lobos-Museum ferner acht Bände «Presença de Villa-Lobos». 1965 wurde ein *Werkkatalog* veröffentlicht, der nun in zweiter Auflage in Vorbereitung ist.

Das Museum fördert wissenschaftliche Essays, die zwar in Portugiesisch verfaßt sein müssen, an denen sich aber Wissenschafter jeder Nationalität beteiligen können. So entstanden im Lauf der Jahre Studien vor allem über Villa-Lobos' «Bachianas Brasileiras», seine Streichquartette und seine Klaviermusik. Fünf internationale Instrumental- und Gesangswettbewerbe veranstaltete das Museum seit 1966: im ersten Jahr für Streichquartette, 1971 für Gitarre, 1972 für Instrumentalensemble, 1973 für Gesang und dieses Jahr für Klavier. Diese Wettspiele sind in erster Linie Villa-Lobos' Musik gewidmet, doch werden daneben auch Werke anderer brasilianischer Komponisten berücksichtigt. Alle diese Veranstaltungen, einschließlich der Preisverteilungen, werden im Rahmen eines jährlich wiederkehrenden *Villa-Lobos-Festivals* abgehalten. Es findet jeweilen im November statt, zum Andenken an den Todestag des Komponisten (17. November), der auch mit einer Kirchenmesse in Rio de Janeiro begangen wird. Zu diesen Festveranstaltungen gehören auch Orchester- und Kammermusikkonzerte sowie Solorezitals.

Dieses Jahr, zu Villa-Lobos' fünfzehntem Todestag, wählte das Museum als Essay-Thema *«Die Technik und thematische Analyse von Villa-Lobos' Gitarrenmusik»*. Anläßlich dieses Todestages fand gleichzeitig ein zweiter wissenschaftlicher Wettbewerb statt, bei dem die Bewerber ausschließlich Universitätsstudenten sein mußten. (Die Aufgabe war hier eine 20seitige Monographie über den Komponisten selber.) Zur Feier des fünfzehnten Todesjahres gehörte ein Interpretationskurs der Gitarrenmusik von Villa-Lobos unter der Leitung des brasilianischen Gitarristen *Turíbio Soares Santos,* der durch seine Schallplattenaufnahmen dieser Werke international bekannt geworden ist. Für den 9. September hatte Arminda Villa-Lobos zu einem Vortrag eingeladen über das Thema «Villa-Lobos fern von Brasilien — Villa-Lobos im Ausland». Der Dozent war Luiz Heitor Corrêa de Azevedo, der brasilianische Musikwissenschafter, der durch seine Tätigkeit beim Conseil international de musique der Unesco in Paris in Europa bekannt geworden ist. Diese Festveranstaltungen, die jedes Jahr seit 1961 wiederkehren, sind in Brasilien zu einer festen Einrichtung geworden, bei denen sich das Villa-Lobos-Museum bemüht, auch in die Zukunft zu wirken.

Heitor Villa-Lobos
(b. Rio de Janeiro, March 5, 1887—d. there, Nov. 17, 1959)

Heitor Villa-Lobos, the Brazilian composer, was the son of Noêmia Villa-Lobos, a Brazilian of Portuguese descent, and Raúl, a Brazilian of Spanish parents. The youth's first contacts with music, playing the cello and hearing some of Puccini's music, came through his father, a teacher, library clerk, and amateur musician, who died in 1899. In 1907 Villa-Lobos, aged twenty, was a pupil of Agnello França (harmony) and later of Benno Niederberger (cello); he was otherwise self-taught and had no formal musical education. As a teenager he earned a living by playing in bands that cultivated popular music and in theatre and film-house orchestras. In 1921 this activity took him to the northeast of Brazil (Bahia, Recife), to Manaus at the Amazon River, and to the southern town of Paranaguá in the state of Paraná, where he worked for a while as a commercial clerk in a match factory.

Yet, neither at that time, nor earlier or later in life, did Villa-Lobos join any scientific expeditions, nor did he travel on his own through Brazil's interior or to far-off territories to get to know the music of the aborigines or to study and collect folklore material. Folk songs that he harmonized (*Chansons Typiques Brésiliennes*) were collected by others, and folkloric tunes that he expanded and enlarged, such as *Três Poemas Indígenas*, were taken from phonograph recordings of other traveling researchers. In Villa-Lobos's entire musical output there is not a single folk tune or any folklore material that he had collected himself. His compositions are, however, full of pseudo-folklore melodies of his own creation.

In 1913 Villa-Lobos married Lucília Guimarães, from whom he separated in the 1930s. As a member of the Rio de Janeiro symphony and opera orchestra, he became well acquainted with Italian operas. Puccini left his mark on two of Villa-Lobos' operas, *Izaht*, an early work, and *Yerma*, written four years before his death. It was also in 1913 that Villa-Lobos came to know, through his orchestral playing, the music of the Russians and the Impressionists, which strongly influenced his compositions in the years that followed. Tchaikovsky's melodic pattern and those of other Russian composers are noticeable in his First Cello Concerto, op. 50, Second String Quartet, and some of the early symphonies. Impressionistic traces are already perceptible in his vocal music of that time and in some of the piano pieces, like *Simples Colletânea*, but more strikingly in such orchestral works as *Amazonas* and the chamber-music composition *Quatuor*.

In 1917 Villa-Lobos, still playing in the orchestra, heard Stravinsky's music; three years later he heard works of Richard Strauss, who conducted some of his own music in Rio de Janeiro. The huge orchestras of Strauss's *Elektra* and *Salome* left their marks on some of Villa-Lobos's orchestral music written at that time, such as the Third and Fourth Symphonies. In 1918 in Rio de Janeiro, Villa-Lobos met Darius Milhaud, who at that time was secretary to Paul Claudel, the French ambassador. He also met Artur Rubinstein, who three years later (1921) first performed the composer's piano music *A Prole do Bebê No. 1*, written shortly after their first encounter.

With a government grant, Villa-Lobos spent one year (beginning in the middle of 1923) in Paris, from where he made side trips to Lisbon and Brussels. In Europe he was made aware that music with local color was what Europeans expected of a Brazilian composer with hopes of becoming famous, rather than works in the traditional forms and style which he had written thus far. This experience was the decisive turning point in Villa-Lobos's musical development. Henceforth his compositions were to contain pseudo-folkloristic tunes and elements, and would be written in non-traditional forms of his own invention, like the *Chôros*, or conceived for unorthodox instrumental chamber-music ensembles with and without the human voice.

Soon after his return to Rio de Janeiro, Villa-Lobos used the word "folklore" for the first time in connection with the piano piece *Sul América*, commissioned by the Argentine newspaper *La Prensa*. It was during this Brazilian sojourn (1924–1927), between his two European stays in the 1920s, that Villa-Lobos wrote many of the compositions that made him famous in Paris upon his return to that city, and later in other parts of the world. To this period belong some of his *Chôros* and vocal music such as the *Três Poemas Indígenas* and the *Chansons Typiques Brésiliennes*.

The second stay in Paris, financed by wealthy Brazilian philanthropists, lasted from the beginning of 1927 until the middle of 1930. During that time, Villa-Lobos tried to interest the Paris publishing house, Max Eschig, in issuing some of his works. He also saw to it that he could conduct some of his music in Paris and in other cities: Brussels (in January, 1929), Barcelona (October 1929), and Liège (April, 1930). Paris again left its imprint on Villa-Lobos's compositions: The *Suite Suggestive No. 1*, written in 1929, a year before he left Paris, clearly reflects contemporary trends that were the craze in Europe during his second Parisian stay, when the grotesque and extravagant were popular with some composers and had found expression in a few works of Satie and Milhaud. Though the *Suite Suggestive* is not representative of Villa-Lobos's style and is rather an escapade within his musical output, it is a work by which Villa-Lobos intended to show that he, too, could write in the style of his time, if need be. Far more significant, however, is the fact that neoclassical trends, in vogue during his second period in Paris, inspired Villa-Lobos to combine what Paris offered him in that respect with a Brazilian idiom. The result was the series of works titled *Bachianas Brasileiras*, in which Bach's technique was applied to musical material with a Brazilian flavor. He started on the *Bachianas Brasileiras* right after he left Paris and as soon as he had set foot on Brazilian soil.

Though Villa-Lobos composed in every genre – operas, symphonies, traditional chamber music, vocal music, and concertos – the fruit of his sojourns in Paris in the 1920s was not that he became subdued by European influences then prevailing, nor was he overpowered by styles of his European contemporaries; rather, Paris awakened him to the possibility of creating his own, very personal musical idiom – to originate and compose music that, in form and content, was not only a novelty for non-Brazilians but for his own compatriots as well. To hoist the *chôro* from its popular significance to a form played in the concert hall was a stroke of genius (though it is debatable whether Villa-Lobos's *Chôros* are, after all, not merely works given a title he chose for various types of compositions in a free form). This was a novelty without precedent even for his native Brazil. And to combine Bach's polyphonic structure with Brazilian pseudo-folkloristic tunes and elements and to create yet another completely novel type of composition, the *Bachianas Brasileiras*, was again something without a forerunner either in Brazil or elsewhere.

These two extremely personal inventions and innovations would alone make Villa-Lobos an exceptional composer in any setting. Yet, his vast and versatile production of chamber music with its great variety of instrumental combinations is another manifestation of his creative power and musical imagination for ever-changing mixtures of instrumental color. Therein lies, next to the *Chôros* and the *Bachianas Brasileiras*, Villa-Lobos's exceptional significance as a composer.

After the 1930 revolution Villa-Lobos remained in Brazil until shortly before the end of World War II, a stay interrupted only by a few trips abroad (Prague, Germany, and Barcelona in 1936, and Montevideo and Buenos Aires in 1940). These were the years of his pedagogical activities. In 1931 he made four concert tours through the state of São Paulo to bring music to the hinterland. Villa-Lobos also gave his first mass chorus demonstration in that year. In 1932 he became director of the Music Education Department of Rio de Janeiro's Municipality. A decade later (1942) he supervised music education in the whole of Brazil and founded, in the same year, the Conservatório Nacional do Canto Orfeônico. In 1933 he presented, for the first time, his music teachers' chorus and conducted an orchestra that bore his name. From this pedagogical period date also his collections of choruses for unisono two, three, four, and five voices, called *Guia Prático, Canto Orfeônico*, and *Solfejos*, which are arrangements of nursery rhymes and children's and folk songs for chorus (subsequently some were arranged for piano solo).

The year 1939 brought the first contact with the United States. On the occasion of the New York World's Fair, Brazilian-made recordings of the composer's music were played, some of his works were performed, and reviews of his music appeared in the daily and musical press. Five years later, in 1944, he went to the United States for the first time. Upon his return to Brazil in 1945, he founded the Academia Brasileira de Música and conducted in Chile. In 1946 Villa-Lobos again conducted concerts in Rio de Janeiro and Argentina. The following year he made his second trip to the United States. In 1948 Villa-Lobos first conducted in Paris and then returned to New York for a successfully performed operation (for cancer) on his bladder.

From then until the end of his life in 1959, Villa-Lobos divided his time between the United States, Brazil, and Paris, with one side trip to Israel. He occupied himself in conducting his works, making recordings, and writing a vast number of compositions, many of them commissioned. During this last period of his life, he returned to traditional compositional forms, often employing a virtuoso style, particularly in the concertos for solo instruments and orchestra, the symphonies, and quartets. Some of the music of that period is very complex in style and some rather difficult to perform. It is part of a total musical output said to reach about one thousand works.

On the occasion of Villa-Lobos's seventieth birthday, Brazil proclaimed 1957 a "Villa-Lobos Year", and São Paulo, which had acknowledged his talents long before his native Rio de Janeiro did, and at a time when he was a struggling composer, programmed a "Villa-Lobos Week". The mayor of New York honored him, on that occasion, with a citation. Many honors were conferred on Villa-Lobos during his lifetime. Among them were the awards of Commander of the Order of Merit (Brazil) and Commander of the Legion of Honor (France). On June 22, 1960 the Museum Villa-Lobos was founded in Rio de Janeiro with Arminda Villa-Lobos as its director. On March 5, 1971 a memorial plate was unveiled at the Bedford Hotel in Paris, where he had resided during his frequent Parisian sojourns.

PRINCIPAL WORKS BY VILLA-LOBOS

Chôros:

No. 1 for guitar (1920).
No. 2 for flute and clarinet (1924).
No. 3 for clarinet, bassoon, sax., 3 horns, trombone, and male chorus (1925).
No. 4 for three horns and trombone (1926).
No. 5 for piano (1925).
No. 6 for orchestra (1941).
No. 7 for flute, oboe, clarinet, bassoon, sax., violin, and cello (1924).
No. 8 for 2 pianos and orchestra (1925).
No. 9 for orchestra (1942).
No. 10 for orchestra and chorus (1926).
No. 11 for piano and orchestra (1941).
No. 12 for orchestra (1944).
No. 13 for 2 orchestra bands (date unknown).
No. 14 for orchestra, band, and chorus (date unknown).
Two Chôros bis for violin and cello (1929).
All published by E, except Nos. 13 and 14 (MS) and No. 1 (A.N.)

Bachianas Brasileiras:

No. 1 for 8 cellos (1930–32 and 1936–38).
No. 2 for chamber orchestra (1930–31).
No. 3 for piano and orchestra (1938).
No. 4 for piano (1930–41), also orchestrated (1941).
No. 5 for voice and orchestra of cellos (1938 and 1945).
No. 6 for flute and bassoon (1938).
No. 7 for orchestra (1942).
No. 8 for orchestra (1944).
No. 9 for string orchestra or a capp. chorus (1945).
Published: 1, 5, 6, AMP; 2, 3, 4, R; 7, 8, 9, E.

Orchestra:

Ibericárabe (1914) A.N.
Danses Africaines (orchestrated 1916) E.
2 Sinfonietas (1916, 1946) SMPC.
12 Symphonies (1916–57). Nos 1, 8, 9, 10, 11, 12, E; 2, 3, 4, 5, 6, 7, R.
Naufrágio de Kleónikos (1917) MS.
Suite Suggestive No. 1 (1929) E.
Caixinha de Boas Festas (1932) R.
4 Suites *Descobrimento do Brasil* (1936–37 and 1942) E.
New York Skyline (1940) E.
Madona (1945) E.
Odisséia de uma Raça (1953) IMP.

2 Suites for chamber orchestra (both 1958) E.
Fantasia Concertante for orchestra of cellos (1958) AMP.
Green Mansion (1958) MS.

Solo Instrument and Orchestra:

2 Concertos for cello and orchestra (1915, 1953) E.
Fantasia de Movimentos Mistos for violin and orchestra (1920–21 and 1941) SMPC.
Momoprecoce for piano and orchestra (1929) E.
5 Concertos for piano and orchestra (1945–54) E.
Fantasia for saxophone and string orchestra (1948) SMPC.
Concerto for guitar and orchestra (1951) E.
Concerto for harp and orchestra (1953) E.
Concerto for harmonica and orchestra (1955) AMP.

Operas:

Izaht (1914–40), performed in Rio de Janeiro, Dec. 13, 1958. MS.
Madalena (1947), performed in Los Angeles, July 26, 1948. MS.
Yerma (1955–56), performed in Santa Fe, New Mex., Aug. 12, 1971. E.
A Menina das Nuvens (1957–58), performed in Rio de Janeiro on television, No. 29, 1960. MS.

Ballets:

Amazonas (1917) E.
Uirapuru (1917), orchestrated (1934) AMP.
Mandu-Çarará (1940) E.
Rudá (1951). E.
Gênesis (1954) E.
Emperor Jones (1955) E.

Religious Music:

Tantum Ergo (1908–10) MS.
Vidapura (1919) E.
Missa São Sebastião (1937) AMP.
Magnificat-Alleluia for orchestra mixed chorus and solos (1958) F.
Benedita Sabedoria for a capp. chorus (1958) E.

Piano:

Suite Infantil No. 1 (1912) A.N.
Suite Infantil No. 2 (1913) A.N.
Danças Características Africanas (1914–15) A.N.
A Prole do Bebê No. 1 (1918) E.
A Prole do Bebê No. 2 (1921) E.
Histórias da Carochinha (1919) A.N.
Carnaval das Crianças Brasileiras (1919–20) A.N.
Rudepoema (1912–26), also for piano and orchestra E.
Cirandas (1926) A.N.
Cirandinhas (undated) E.
Saudades das Selvas Brasileiras (1927) E.
Francette et Piá (undated) E.
Ciclo Brasileiro (1936) V.V.
As Três Marias (1939) F.

Vocal Music:

Miniaturas (1916–17) A.N.
Historietas (1920) A.N.
Epigramas Irônicos e Sentimentais (1921) A.N.
Serestas, Nos. 1–12 (1926), A.N. Nos. 13–14 (1943) E
Três Poemas Indígenas (1926) E.
Chansons Typiques Brésiliennes (undated), Nos. 1–10 (E) Nos. 11–13 (MS).

Chamber Music:

3 Piano Trios (1911, 1915, 1918) E.
4 Sonatas for violin and piano (1912–13, 1914–40, 1920, 1920–23) E.
Pieces for cello and piano (last four also arranged for violin and piano):
Little Suite (1913) A.N.
Prelude, op. 20, No. 2 (1913) A.N.
Sonhar, op. 14 (1914) A.N.
Capriccio, op. 49 (1914) A.N.
Berceuse, op. 50 (1915) A.N.
O Canto do Cisne Negro (1917) A.N.
17 String Quartets (1915–57). Nos. 1, 9, 10, 11, SMP; 2, 3, 13, 14, 15, 16, 17, E; 4, 5, 6, 7, 12, AMP; 8, R.
Sonata No. 2 for cello and piano (1916) E.
Trio for oboe, clarinet, and bassoon (1921) E.
Quatuor for harp, celesta, flute, sax., and women's chorus (1921) E.
Nonetto for flute, oboe, clarinet, bassoon, sax., celesta, harp, piano, percussion band, and mixed chorus (1923) E.
Suite for voice and violin (1923) E.
Poême de l'enfant et sa mère for voice, flute, clarinet, and cello (1923) E.
Quintet for wind instruments in form of *Chôros* for flute, oboe, clarinet, Engl. horn, and bassoon (1928) E.
Sexteto Místico for flute, oboe, sax., harp, celesta, guitar (1945) E.
Assobio a Jato (The Jet Whistle) for cello and flute (1950) SMP.
Fantasia Concertante for piano, clarinet, and bassoon (1953) E.
Duo for oboe and bassoon (1957) E.
Instrumental Quintet for flute, harp, violin, viola, and cello (1957) E.
Fantasy in three movements in the form of *Chôros* for wind orchestra (1959) P.

Music for Guitar:

Suite Populaire Brésilienne (1928) E.
12 Etudes (1928) E.
15 Préludes (1940) E.

Miscellaneous:

Guia Prático, collection of Brazilian nursery rhymes, children's and folk songs, arranged for chorus (2 volumes) and arranged for piano (10 volumes), both 1932.
Solfejos for chorus (2 volumes), 1940–46.
Canto Orfeônico (2 volumes), 1940–50.

ABBREVIATIONS OF PUBLISHERS

AMP: Associated Music Publishers, New York.
F: Carl Fischer, New York.
P: C.F. Peters, New York.

SMPC: Southern Music Publishing Co., New York.
E: Max Eschig, Paris.
R: Ricordi, Milan.
A.N.: Arthur Napoleão, Rio de Janeiro.
V.V.: Vicente Vitale, Rio de Janeiro.
MS: Manuscript.
IMP: Israel Music Publications, Tel Aviv.

Bibliography

(With the exception noted, all writings are in English.)

Burle-Marx, Walter: *Brazilian Portrait; Modern Music*, Vol. 17, No. 1, New York, 1939.

Druesdow, John: *The Chamber Works for Wind Instruments by Villa-Lobos* (typewritten copy); Latin American Music Center, Indiana University, Bloomington, Ind., 1963.

Johnson, Robert L.: *Villa-Lobos's Chôros No. 10, Analysis and Critical Survey* (typewritten copy); Latin American Music Center, Indiana University, Bloomington, Ind., 1963.

Mariz, Vasco: *Heitor Villa-Lobos* (English translation and abbreviated version of originally Portuguese book); Latin American Monographs Series, University of Florida, Gainsville, Fla., 1963. Second ed., Brazilian-American Cultural Institute, Washington, D.C., 1970.

Orrego Salas, Juan A.: *Heitor Villa-Lobos: Man, Work, Style; Inter-American Music Bulletin*, Pan American Union, No. 52, Washington, D.C., 1966.

Parks, Gordon: *The World of Villa-Lobos; Show Magazine*, Vol. 2 (11), 1962.

Peppercorn, Lisa M.: *Musical Education in Brazil; Bulletin* of the Pan-American Union, Washington, D.C., 1940.

A Villa-Lobos Opera; New York Times, April 28, 1940.

Violin Concerto by Villa-Lobos; New York Times, June 8, 1941.

New Villa-Lobos Works; New York Times, Oct. 11, 1942.

Some Aspects of Villa-Lobos's Principles of Composition; Music Review, Vol. 4, No. 1, Feb., 1943, Cambridge, Eng.

The History of Villa-Lobos's Birthday Date; MMR, No. 898, London, July–Aug., 1948.

Villa-Lobos's Brazilian Excursions; The Musical Times, Vol. 113, No. 1549, March, 1972.

Heitor Villa-Lobos: Life and Work of the Brazilian Composer; Atlantis, Zurich, 1972 (in German).

Villa-Lobos, Father and Son; Américas, Vol. 24, No. 4, Washington, D.C., April 1972.

Slonimsky, N.: *A Visit with Villa-Lobos; Musical America*, Vol. 61, No. 15, New York, 1941.

Music of Latin America; New York, 1946.

The Flamboyant Chanticleer, Villa-Lobos; Show Magazine, Vol. 2, 1962.

Smith, Carleton Sprague, and M. Roméro: *Heitor Villa-Lobos; Composers of the Americas*, Vol. 3, Washington, 1957 (with catalogue until 1957).

Weinstock, Herbert: *Villa-Lobos;* in *The Book of Modern Composers*, by D. Ewen, New York, 1942.

The International Cyclopedia of Music and Musicians, 1975 and 1985, 10th and 11th edns, 2368–71

LE INFLUENZE DEL FOLKLORE BRASILIANO
NELLA MUSICA DI VILLA-LOBOS

Heitor Villa-Lobos, massimo compositore brasiliano della prima metà di questo secolo, deve in gran parte la sua fama, in patria e all'estero, alle musiche tipicamente brasiliane da lui scritte. Della musica indigena del suo paese Villa-Lobos cominciò tuttavia ad occuparsi soltanto all'età di trentasette anni; e per quanto strano possa sembrare, non fu dal natio Brasile che egli trasse originariamente ispirazione a seguire una via diversa da quella tradizionale di composizioni come trii, quartetti, sonate, sinfonie e concerti per strumenti solistici e orchestra: fu l'Europa, e in particolare Parigi, a suscitare in lui il desiderio di ricercare e utilizzare le fonti brasiliane come elemento fondamentale della sua musica.

Nell'estate del 1923 una sovvenzione del governo brasiliano aveva consentito a Villa-Lobos di passare un anno a Parigi. Nella capitale francese egli aspirava, com'è naturale, a farsi un nome; ma la cosa non era facile per un nuovo venuto. Al tempo stesso Villa-Lobos dovette constatare, con sorpresa, che molti parigini si aspettavano da un compositore del suo paese qualcosa di originalmente brasiliano, e non della musica da camera o orchestrale tradizionale. Non una musica in tutto e per tutto esotica, ma che almeno si differenziasse da quella dell'Europa centrale più o meno come la musica russa o cèca si distingueva dallo stile francese e da quello italiano.

Ma in fatto di composizioni di ispirazione amerindiana Villa-Lobos non aveva nulla da mostrare, dato che a quel tempo la sua musica era ancora largamente influenzata da Debussy, Cajkovskij e altri compositori russi. Tuttavia, deciso a eccellere e a distinguersi dagli altri, Villa-Lobos non esitò ad attirare l'attenzione in altro modo, per soddisfare la curiosità dei parigini e il loro desiderio di qualcosa di tipicamente indigeno. Cominciò così a raccontare di essere venuto in contatto con tribù brasiliane nei suoi numerosi viaggi nell'interno del paese. Parlava dei suoi prolungati soggiorni nella regione amazzonica, dei contatti personali avuti con gli indigeni di quel territorio, della sua raccolta di materiale folkloristico, delle arie e dei ritmi indigeni di cui aveva preso appunto, e delle sue registrazioni fonografiche di canti e danze indiane.

La verità però è che Villa-Lobos non penetrò mai, in tutta la vita, nelle foreste vergini di quelle regioni, non entrò mai in contatto diretto con indiani e tribù di nessun genere, non ne annotò mai melodie o ritmi, e certo non fece mai registrazioni fonografiche né raccolse materiale folkloristico; e neppure scrisse né pubblicò mai nulla sul folklore.

Quando Villa-Lobos tornò in Brasile, verso la fine dell'estate 1924, lo stimolo avuto a Parigi a comporre musica che riflettesse le fonti originarie del suo paese non tardò a dare frutti: pochi mesi dopo, il 23 marzo 1925, Villa-Lobos usò per la prima volta il termine « folklore » in relazione a un'opera per piano solo commissionatagli dal giornale argentino « La Prensa ». Il pezzo, eseguito soltanto cinque anni dopo, il 6 giugno 1930, non spicca per pregi particolari nel quadro della vasta produzione di Villa-Lobos; ma il compositore sentì la necessità di metterne in risalto l'ispirazione sud-americana aggiungendo alla musica una breve nota in cui è detto che « la composizione è basata sul folklore tipico dei paesi sud-americani ». Anche il titolo *Sul América,* fu scelto per differenziare il pezzo dalla tradizionale musica pianistica europea.

Sul América, nonostante la sua modesta importanza, segna una svolta nella carriera di Villa-Lobos, in quanto tra la fine del 1924 e l'inizio del 1925 cominciò il periodo più fecondo della vita musicale del compositore, quello in cui furono scritte le sue opere più significative: significative per il loro carattere intrinsecamente brasiliano. Ed è interessante notare che Villa-Lobos non dovette visitare le regioni interne del Brasile, ma fu Rio de Janeiro, sua città natale, a offrirgli la possibilità di venire in contatto con il folklore del suo paese.

Va ricordata in primo luogo l'amicizia di Villa-Lobos con Edgard Roquette Pinto, che nel 1912 aveva accompagnato il generale Cândido Mariano da Silva Rondon nelle sue spedizioni in quelle che erano allora regioni parzialmente inesplorate, e sparsamente popolate da indiani, soprattutto negli stati del Mato Grosso, di Goías e dell'Amazonas. Roquette Pinto raccontò a Villa-Lobos molte cose sulle sue osservazioni, studi e ricerche folkloristiche, raccolte anche in un volume pubblicato col titolo di *Rondônia*.[1] In questo libro sono citati fra l'altro vari motivi musicali indiani, come la melodia *Nozani-ná,* che Roquette Pinto aveva raccolto fra gli indiani Parecés e che attrasse l'attenzione di Villa-Lobos. Il musicista si servì di quest'aria a due riprese: una volta nel suo *Chôros n. 3* per clarinetto, sassofono, fagotto, tre corni, trombone e coro maschile, composto nel 1925 ed eseguito la prima volta il 30 novembre 1925; in questa composizione, peraltro, il motivo in questione non ha una parte di grande rilievo. Più interessante è invece il trattamento che di quest'aria Villa-Lobos fece in un pezzo vocale con accompagnamento di pianoforte, che è la seconda di una serie di canzoni a cui egli diede il titolo di *Chansons Typiques Brésiliennes.* Qui la melodia *Nozani-ná* è armonizzata da Villa-Lobos. Ricorderemo per inciso che un altro compositore brasiliano, Oscar Lorenzo Fernândez, si servì di questa melodia nel poema sinfonico *Imbapara.*

(Esempio tratto dal volume *Rondônia* di E. Roquette-Pinto, V. Ed., Companhia Editoria Nacional São Paulo 1938)

L'amicizia di Villa-Lobos con Roquette Pinto fu feconda anche per altri riguardi. Senza dubbio Roquette Pinto parlò al compositore di opere pubblicate da altri scienziati viaggiatori in cui era possibile reperire materiale folkloristico. Si può dunque ragionevolmente supporre che grazie a Roquette Pinto Villa-Lobos venne a conoscenza del lavoro di Johann Baptist von Spix (1781-1826) e Carl Friedrich Philipp von Martius (1794-1868), *Brasilianische Volkslieder und Indianische Melodien,* appendice musicale al volume *Reise in Brasilien*

---

[1] E. Roquette Pinto, *Rondônia*, Companhia Editora Nacional, 4ª ed., São Paulo 1938.

(Monaco 1831), che offrì a Villa-Lobos una ricca fonte di materiale interessante. Non ci risulta che Villa-Lobos citasse mai nessuna di queste arie nella sua produzione musicale, ma lo studio che egli ne fece certamente lo portò a utilizzare gli elementi costitutivi delle melodie indigene.

Un'altra opera colpì la fantasia di Villa-Lobos, poiché sappiamo che egli ne menzionò l'autore in relazione alla sua composizione *Canide Ioune-Sabath*,[2] la prima di tre canzoni da lui raccolte nel ciclo intitolato *Três Poemas Indígenas,* ciclo composto nel 1926 ed eseguito per la prima volta il 5 dicembre 1927 con accompagnamento orchestrale. A differenza del trattamento da lui fatto della melodia *Nozani-ná* nelle *Chansons Typiques Brésiliennes* Villa-Lobos adesso rielaborò e ampliò l'originale, precisando che *Canide Ioune-Sabath* era « basata su una melodia indigena raccolta da Jean de Léry nel 1553 ». Il francese Jean de Léry viaggiò (non nel 1553 ma soltanto nel 1557) al seguito dell'ammiraglio Nicolas de Villegaignon, che intendeva fondare una colonia ugonotta in Brasile. Léry descrisse le sue osservazioni ed esperienze in un libro famoso, *Histoire d'un voyage faict en la terre du Brésil autrement dite Amérique,* che ebbe parecchie edizioni e traduzioni nel XVI e XVII secolo. La terza edizione, pubblicata nel 1585 da Antoine Chuppin a Ginevra, contiene — per la prima volta — cinque melodie degli indiani Tupinambà. Queste melodie mancano però nelle prime due edizioni, e nelle edizioni moderne le arie non sono sempre identiche, come ha dimostrato con accurate ricerche l'eminente musicologo brasiliano Luiz Heitor Corrêa de Azevedo. I risultati di tali ricerche, esposti al congresso annuale della American Musicological Society a Minneapolis, Minnesota, nel dicembre 1941, furono pubblicati da questa società nel 1946.[3]

I libri sul Brasile contenenti musica folkloristica non furono le sole fonti di cui Villa-Lobos poté disporre a Rio de Janeiro nei suoi studi sulla musica brasiliana. Presso il Museo Nazionale esistevano raccolte discografiche di melodie indigene; e Roquette Pinto, che in qualità di amministratore di quel museo nel periodo 1926-1935 vi

---

[2] « Canide Ioune » significa uccello giallo; « Sabath », canto elegiaco.
[3] *Tupynamba Melodies in Jean de Léry's Histoire d'un voyage faict en la terre du Brésil*, Atti della American Musicological Society, Congresso annuale 1941, Minneapolis, Minnesota. A cura di Gustave Reese; edito dalla Società, Virginia, Richmond 1956, pagg. 85-96.

aveva aggiunto nuove sezioni, fra l'altro di strumenti e di registrazioni
fonografiche per lo studio di quel tipo di musica, senza dubbio spinse
Villa-Lobos a venire ad ascoltare le arie che lui stesso aveva raccolto
e registrato. In questo museo, che Villa-Lobos visitò spesso insieme
alla moglie Lucília, egli ebbe la possibilità di ascoltare arie indigene
come la melodia *Nozani-ná* (numero di catalogo 14.597), e un'altra
(n. 14.598), detta *Teirù*. Quest'ultima melodia fu incorporata da
Villa-Lobos nella seconda di un ciclo di tre canzoni da lui intitolato
Três Poemas Indígenas, e poi rielaborata in modo analogo nella composizione intitolata *Canide Ioune-Sabath.*

A parte le registrazioni discografiche il Museo — che nel 1946
fu incorporato nell'Università del Brasile col decreto n. 8.689 del
16 gennaio — offrì a Villa-Lobos anche un'altra possibilità, grazie alla
sua bella raccolta di strumenti musicali conosciuti e usati fra gli indiani.
Questi strumenti dovettero affascinarlo, poiché egli ne incluse alcuni
in parecchie delle sue opere orchestrali.

Come abbiamo visto, Villa-Lobos armonizzò a volte arie folkloristiche (*Chanson Typiques Brésiliennes*), rielaborò ampliandole melodie
della sua terra (*Três Poemas Indígenas*), o in qualche caso incluse
un'aria popolare in una composizione (*Chôros n. 3*), e più tardi canzoni
popolari e infantili (in *Cirandas, Cirandinhas,* che sono due cicli per
pianoforte, o nel *Quinto Quartetto per archi*).

Non contento di questi elementi e dell'introduzione sporadica di
strumenti indigeni per dare alla sua musica un sapore tipicamente
brasiliano, Villa-Lobos si propose mete più ambiziose dopo il suo
ritorno dal primo viaggio in Europa. Volle essere unico e originale
anche in un altro modo: le sue composizioni dovevano abbandonare
le forme e i titoli tradizionali per qualcosa di insolito, qualcosa che
fosse una novità anche per gli ascoltatori di musica d'arte brasiliana
del suo stesso paese. Scelse quindi una forma libera anche meno orto-
dossa di quella del poema sinfonico. Musicista autodidatta, privo di
preparazione accademica, salvo per qualche lezione elementare di armo-
nia avuta in gioventù, egli sentiva di potersi esprimere meglio in questo
modo. Quanto ai titoli, scelse qualcosa di completamente diverso,
qualcosa che prima di lui non era mai stato usato né in Brasile né in
altri paesi: titoli come *Chôros, Seresta,* e più tardi altri ancora.

Soprattutto nei Chôros gli parve di trovare l'intelaiatura adatta
per ogni sorta di composizioni e di espressioni musicali, sicché comin-

ciò a chiamare Chôros composizioni di ogni tipo: un pezzo per pianoforte, uno per chitarra, duetti strumentali, musiche strumentali da
camera per piccoli complessi, opere orchestrali con o senza coro e composizioni per strumento solista e orchestra. Il titolo Chôros, a suo
giudizio, avrebbe ulteriormente accentuato il carattere brasiliano della
sua musica.

Il termine Chôros, e la musica relativa, non erano però invenzioni
di Villa-Lobos, anche se egli se ne servì in modo nuovo. Tale termine,
come spiega il folklorista e musicologo Renato Almeida nel suo libro
História da Música Brasileira,[4] in cui egli cita l'opera di Jacques Raimundo *O Negro Brasileiro*, « era giunto in Brasile dall'altra sponda
dell'Atlantico, dalla costa africana dove le tribù cafre praticavano una
sorta di concerto vocale con danze detto xôlo... I negri brasiliani
davano ai loro balli, organizzati nel giorno di San Giovanni o in altre
festività nelle grandi aziende agricole dove lavoravano, questo nome
di xôlos, che per una confusione con un paronimo portoghese si mutò
in xôro. Quando questo xôro passò nelle zone urbane, diventò
Chôro... ». « Chôros è una denominazione generica. Significa gruppo
di strumenti, uno dei quali assume funzione solistica. Lo stesso nome
indica anche la musica suonata da questo gruppo di strumenti. Si tratta
comunque di una sorta di musica strumentale popolare, suonata
all'aperto e paragonabile forse alla serenata ».[5]

Ma non sono né il nome né la forma del Chôros a rendere la musica
di Villa-Lobos così essenzialmente brasiliana; l'uno e l'altra sono soltanto un tocco molto personale che Villa-Lobos volle dare alle sue
opere. Il carattere brasiliano della musica di Villa-Lobos dipende
piuttosto dall'impiego deliberato di certi elementi e caratteristiche
tipici della musica indigena, elementi e caratteristiche che gli servi-
rono a creare arie, ritmi e combinazioni timbriche strumentali sue
proprie, in quanto gli offrivano per il pensiero musicale e i mezzi
espressivi una varietà molto maggiore delle arie folkloristiche o meglio
dell'impiego musicale delle medesime, che sono già qualcosa di com-
piuto di per sé. Ciò che dà alla musica di Villa-Lobos il carattere
brasiliano che le è proprio è l'impiego e l'applicazione di certi inter-

---

4 RENATO ALMEIDA, *História da Música Brasileira*, F. Briguiet & Cia, 2ª ed., Rio de
Janeiro 1942.

5 R. ALMEIDA, Op. cit.

valli, scale e ritmi, appartenenti alla musica indigena, elementi di cui si giovò l'ispirazione artistica del compositore, già di suo tanto ricca di creatività.

(*Traduzione di Franco Salvatorelli*)

Nuova Rivista Musicale Italiana, **X**(2), April/June 1976, 179–84

Corrigenda

p48 *line 2*:
For Goías read Goiás
p49 *line 15*:
For 1557 read 1556
FN 3 last line:
For Virginia, Richmond, 1956, read Richmond, Virginia, 1946

FOREIGN INFLUENCES IN VILLA-LOBOS's MUSIC

The Brazilian composer Heitor Villa-Lobos, famous at home and abroad, and hailed as the most important representative of his country, made a name for himself, principally because of the Brazilian character of his music. Yet, he was already in his late thirties when he turned his attention to Brazilian folklore. Odd as it may seem it was not Brazil that had inspired him to do so. In fact it was Paris which made him realize that a Brazilian composer, if he ever wanted to succeed in a world where competition was strong and others had made a reputation for themselves due to their particular style and ideas, he, too, had to show the world something that was not only outstanding but totally different from European music. So it was obvious that when he returned to Brazil after a one-year stay in Paris on a Brazilian government grant between the middle of 1923 and the middle of 1924 that Villa-Lobos began to turn his back on traditional forms and styles and switched to something native. This change was quite abrupt and sudden, it was less an inner urge but rather a desperate necessity trying to seek fame and fortune, be talked about and call attention.

It was the turning point in Villa-Lobos's life. He had made one of the most important decisions in his entire career. He renounced the past, took leave from traditions, broke almost completely with everything to which he had adhered previously. It was a vital decision, a tremendous resolution because his contemporaries, at that time, had not yet produced anything along the lines on which he now set his mind.

There were, it is true, certain movements in Brazil to break with the past and hail the future, but a future that was not defined precisely, just a call to sever off with traditions and seek new ways and means of expression in order to be modern and contemporary. There was — what today would be labeled a protest movement — a commotion in São Paulo in early 1922, called "The Week of Modern Art". It was staged in São Paulo because that city was already in those days perhaps more progressive than tropical Rio de Janeiro at Guanabara Bay with her more leisurely life. But what Brazilian intellectuals demanded and proclaimed during the famous Week was modernism in much the same fashion as modern movements were taking shape elsewhere in the world, particularly in Europe. The style was the same as was current in Central Europe.

LORETTE WILMOT LIBRARY
NAZARETH COLLEGE

Villa-Lobos played a central figure in this heated argumentation. But when his chance came to go to Europe the following year, those who had supported his being sent over there, either on the ground to learn or perform his works or conduct the music of his Brazilian contemporaries and elders, were convinced that he had really some novelties to present. But all he had to show were compositions in the usual traditional forms, styles and titles.

Because until the end of 1924 and early 1925 when Villa-Lobos was already 37 years old, his music was strongly under the influences of others. Right from the beginning, until he returned from his first Europe trip, Villa-Lobos was, musically speaking, a child of his time. His music had all the earmarks of Wagner, César Franck, Puccini, Debussy, Tchaikovsky and the Russian Five. Their works were performed in Rio de Janeiro. Villa-Lobos not only thus had an opportunity to hear their music, he also played those works himself when making a living as cellist in Rio de Janeiro's orchestra. There was no escaping from these composers, they were his masters from whom the self-taught composer, who never had any formal musical training, learned and took his music lessons.

Villa-Lobos had come in contact with Wagner and Puccini's music before that time, when he was still a small child. His father, Raúl, who played the cello, attended opera performances and joined others in amateur music making, had observed in Heitor, his oldest child, a keen interest in music. On occasions, he had played some of Wagner's music to his son at home. The real impact, however, came later when Heitor played in the orchestra, particularly under Alexander Smallens, in 1917, when "Tristan and IsoLde" was performed for the first time in Rio de Janeiro. But it was not so much Wagner's music that inspired Villa-Lobos. Wagner influenced him in quite a different way. What had impressed Villa-Lobos apparently much more was Wagner's expressing his ideological thoughts. This seemed to Villa-Lobos worth imitating: he, too, wanted to manifest his belief, ideas and philosophy. But since opera writing was not exactly his line – he wrote only three and not too original ones in his life – he, therefore, could not compete with Wagner in manifesting his philosophy in works for the stage, but tried to do it with symphonies and composed some *Weltanschauungsmusik.*

Already the First Symphony, op. 112, written in 1916, at the age of twenty-nine, and which was performed for the first time four years later, on August 30, 1920, is based on a text that dates from a time he was twenty years old. The words are signed with the borrowed pseudonym of his father, Epaminondas Villalba, to which Heitor added the word *Filho* (Son). In this text, he expressed his youthful philosophy about the artist's soul and fate in relation to the universe and subtitled the Symphony, "The Unforeseen". Originally, the words appeared only in the concert program, but later, they prefaced the Symphony's score.

It was not an isolated occurrance that Villa-Lobos eypressed his philosophy in this way. To continue along this line, he surely must have welcomed an opportunity that presented itself in 1919, when he was commissioned to write a symphony in commemoration of the Peace Treaty. He called the work "The War", and dashed it off in a remarkably short time, from May till June 12, 1919. Yet, not completely satisfied with what he had said musically, he again added his philosophical observations about the war. Not only that, he soon wrote another symphony, his Fourth, which he called "The Victory", in which he again gave vent to his idea on victory. He even had planned a Fifth Symphony, to be called "The Peace", again with an underlying text, of course, but did not finish it at that time.

If Wagner had inspired Villa-Lobos to express his ideologies in words, he had also influenced him to use a large instrumental body, something he had not done previously. Striving to be unique already at that age and stage of his career, Villa-Lobos intended not only to out-do Wagner but also Richard Strauss. Already Villa-Lobos's symphonic poem "Amazonas", written in 1917, that later was also performed as a ballet, and which is based on a story his father, Raúl, had told him, already makes use of Wagner's "Ring" orchestra and that of Richard Strauss's "Elektra" and "Salome" whose music had meanwhile been played in Rio de Janeiro. However, in his Third Symphony, "The War", composed two years after the "Amazonas", Villa-Lobos asked for 164 players, including 26 first violines, 24 second violines, 12 violas, 12 violoncelli and 12 basses. Not enough with this, he demanded, additionally, a 37-member Fanfar ensemble. The Fourth Symphony is by no means any more modest regarding the instrumentation. Quite the contrary. It is even more ambitious: apart from a similar Fanfar-ensemble as in the Third Symphony, Villa-Lobos requests a five-instrument internal ensemble.

Wagner seemingly was Villa-Lobos's godfather to make him express his own philosophy and use a gigantic orchestra. But in these symphonies, which musically speaking, are rather a hotchpotch of styles, there are also other influences apparent which were prevalent at the time Villa-Lobos composed these works. Because a much stronger impact than the music of Wagner had the music of Tchaikovsky and some of the Russian Five. This was quite understandable.

In September 1913, when Villa-Lobos was 26 years old, appeared in Rio de Janeiro the Russian Ballet under Fokine's direction with Nijinsky as soloist, and performed such works as Borodin's "Prince Igor", Rimsky-Korsakow's "Scheherazade", Balakirew's "Tamara",

as well as Debussy's "L'Après-midi d'un Faune". With these works,
as member of the orchestra, he became intimately acquainted. Prior
to that period, he had already heard smaller works from Glasonouw
and also Balakirew's "Ouverture on Three Russian Themes", when
these works were played in Rio de Janeiro between 1911 - 1913
though they probably did not impress him deeply.

Four years after its first appearance in Rio de Janeiro, the Russian
Ballet returned once more to Rio in 1917. This time it danced to the
music of Rimsky-Korsakow, Ravel and, above all, to Stravinsky's
"Petrouchka", "L'oiseau de feu" and "Feu d'artifice". This music
definitely opened an entirely new sphere of sound combinations,
textures, forms and rhythms to Villa-Lobos; musically speaking, it
was a complete novelty. He found himself suddenly under a powerful
impact of various influences in the years between 1913 and 1917:
Tchaikovsky, the Russian Five, Debussy and Stravinsky. This was a
great deal to digest for Villa-Lobos who, until that epoch, was mainly
schooled along the lines of Italian and French opera composers, Wagner and others of the romantic period. Now, the Russian Ballet introduced him to an absolutely new world.

Villa-Lobos, a self-taught musician, absorbed the music of Tchaikovsky and the Russian Five more easily than the refined and subtle
color and orchestral combinations of the French impressionist. Because form and texture of the Russians were much more akin to his
own talent. The affinity between the two even showed in some of
Villa-Lobos's musical thought or melodic lines which have a definite
likeness to those of the Russians. Finally, he felt at home. Because
the Russians also offered him something that was exactly to his
liking: a different technique to handle thematic material which was
nearer to his heart and better fitted to his skills than theme development in the classical style. For a self-taught composer this latter was
harder to come by, although he also experimented with the cyclic
form of César Franck in his own symphonies.

Villa-Lobos had always rejected the notion to have been influenced by the Russians. He even claimed that he disliked them.
Obviously, he reacted in this way because he refused to admit the
similarity in character between himself and the Russians as far as the
music is concerned.

Tchaikovsky's influence and that of the other Russians on Villa-
Lobos's music is already traceable in such an early work as the First
Great Violoncello Concerto, op. 50, written in 1915[1] and performed
for the first time on May 10, 1919. Here Tschaikovsky's influence is

---

1   The date is taken from the manuscript. The printed work, published by Max
    Eschig (Paris 1928), has the date 1913.

unmistakable, not so much in the conception of the Brazilian composer's first large-scale work but rather in the first movement's melodic downward trend as well as in the general structure. Prior to the Violoncello Concerto Villa-Lobos had tried to find his own style in such works as the "Suite Característica" for strings, written in 1913, and first performed on July 31, 1915, and the Suite for Piano and Orchestra, written in the same year, but performed for the first time only on December 15, 1922. But now the Russians' music clearly showed the way and indicated the right path. In his melodies, to some extent, also in the structure of his works, Villa-Lobos often followed in Tchaikovsky's steps.

The most obvious similarity, however, between Villa-Lobos and Tchaikovsky and the other Russians shows in the melodic structure. Villa-Lobos's Second Piano Trio which dates from the same year as the Violoncello Concerto and which was performed originally on November 12, 1919, is a good example. Here the thematic material is reminscent of Tchaikovsky. The main subject's first bars are seemingly a variation of the principal subject from the second movement of Anton Rubinstein's String Quartet, op. 90, No. 1, in g-minor. Still more interesting is the theme from the Second Piano Trio's third movement, the Scherzo, because quite a number of its variations appear in other of Villa-Lobos's many works. The most striking elements in this example are the five first notes which he loved so much that he used them over and over again in several smaller and larger works. To these belong the piano pieces "Valsa Scherzo", op. 17, "Petizada" and "A Lenda do Caboclo".

Curiously enough, a modified form of those five notes, a sort of forerunner, had already appeared in Villa-Lobos's First Sonata Fantasia for violin and piano, dated 1912. The melodic device occurs once more in "E o pastorzinho cantava" from the piano series called "Histórias da Carochinha", composed in 1919. This melodic pattern or formula had entered Villa-Lobos's music possible not through any study of Brazilian folklore music or some indigenous music. The device, odd as it may seem, appears in Rimsky-Korsakow's music. He, too, varied, modified and shaped it, and in variations, as Gerald Abraham pointed out in his book "Studies in Russian Music" (Freeport, N.Y., 1968), it appears in Rimsky-Korsakow's works. In its purest form it occurs in the "Snow Maiden" in Lel's third song "which follows the tumblers' dance in the festival in the Holy Wood", according to the English musicologist. The five notes are the exact reversal of this motiv. Abraham believes that Rimsky-Korsakow's motiv was in fact inspired by Tchaikovsky's Quartet in D-major. Naturally, it is impossible to determine how Villa-Lobos came by this pattern and why it occupied his mind so vividly. The fact remains that it appears again and again in some or the other form.

At any rate, it was not a mere coincidence. This is apparent from the fact that Villa-Lobos was inspired by yet another melody from "Snow Maiden", namely the Tsar theme which is but a variation of this same formula. It appears already in Villa-Lobos's First Sonata Fantasia for violin and piano, written in 1912, and first performed on November 13, 1915. Whenever the phrase turns up, it appears not as an isolated device but within a melodic pattern. Only once does it emerge in its purest form, namely in the Second Piano Trio's third movement. In other words, to Villa-Lobos the Russian-inspired-pattern is not an end in itself but rather a brick or an element he used to build his own melodies.

The Second Piano Trio also gives evidence that he was, at that time, in more than one way under the influence of others. The two themes of the *Finale,* the first of which is introduced by the violoncello, begins with a descending medody whose similarity with some such themes of Tchaikovsky is obvious. Also the Second String Quartet, op. 56, written in 1915 and performed for the first time on February 3, 1917, reminds occasionally of the Russians. Due to his own unacademic musical development which was similar to that of some of them, he felt their kindship. So when around 1920, he began to shape his own style, the more rhapsodic form of the Russians found some parallel in his own compositions.

Yet, the Russians' influence was not limited to Villa-Lobos's chamber music. Also smaller pieces, like the much played piano work "A Lenda do Caboclo", written in 1920 and given for the first time on March 13, 1927, could not quite escape this effect. Here an interesting phenomenon is perceptible. The main theme of this piece, in slightly modified form, is a device often found in the Brazilian *modinhas.* Yet, its affinity can also be linked with Rimsky-Korsakow who "probably [derived] it from the familiar 'Sidel Vanya', the chief melody of the *andante cantabile* of Tchaikovsky's D-major Quartet" as Gerald Abraham stated in his already quoted book and which is a melodic pattern which in Rimsky-Korsakow's music returns very often.

The interesting question now arises: how did all this happen? On the one hand are Villa-Lobos's melodies which might very well be derived from the Brazilian *modinhas.* On the other hand are the Russians' melodies which, too, were inspired by folk or popular music in their country. There is no question that Villa-Lobos knew the music of the Russians but whether it was their music or rather the Brazilian *modinhas* from which he borrowed the devices, may never be answered accurately. Maybe, he felt a certain similarity between the music of the Russians and that of the *modinhas* of his own country and conciously or unconciously concocted something of his own that obviously had traces of the two, since, after all, his own style, at that time – between 1915 and 1919 – was by no means clearly defined nor did it show any truly personal characteristics and features.

At any rate, the Russians left their mark on Villa-Lobos's symphonic works beyond any doubt, particularly the melodic structure which is clearly reminiscent of Tchaikovsky. A typical example is Villa-Lobos's Fourth Symphony: the first movement's first theme is but a variation of the main subject from the *Finale* of Tchaikovsky's Fifth Symphony. Tchaikovsky was not alone in leaving traces in this symphony. In the second movement appears a motiv which is similar to that of the "Polovetsian Girls' " chorus from Borodin's "Prince Igor". Villa-Lobos uses the same elements. How much Villa-Lobos's themes are linked with the ideas of the Russians is unmistakable from yet another theme in this symphony which reminds of the first eight bars of the main subject from the Scherzo of Borodin's First Symphony in E-flat major. The second part of the Villa-Lobos melody however seems to be a device from the last movement of Tchaikovsky's Second Symphony in C-major which, in turn, is borrowed from the popular Russian song "Der Kranich".

While the Russian traces can be observed in some of Villa-Lobos's larger works, like symphonies or other traditional compositions, such as trios and quartets, Debussy's more delicate impressionistic music had quite a different effect on the Brazilian composer. Debussy probably ignited Villa-Lobos to turn his thoughts towards France and French subject. This was not too difficult for him because French cultural values played a vital part in Brazil before the Fall of France during the Second World War. The educated spoke French, they went to France for periodic stays at regular intervals. French culture, art and philosophy contributed considerably to Brazil's way of thinking.

From his father, Raúl, who was apt at languages, Villa-Lobos perhaps inherited this gift and knew that language, and maybe, something about France before he departed for Paris. But the subtle impressionistic music of Debussy was certainly foreign to him.

Thus, while Villa-Lobos did not, or felt he could not, compose music with a French touch immediately after his acquaintance with Debussy's works, he wanted at least to give his music a French flavor in other ways. So he selected French titles and composed songs to French texts, particularly those written soon after "L'Après-midi d'un faune's" performance in Rio de Janeiro for the first time in September 1913. The first such piece, called "L'Oiseau", op. 10, was composed in May 1913, a few months before the *Ballet Russe* arrived in town. But the Ballet's programs were already rehearsed and smaller works of Debussy had previously been played in Rio de Janeiro. "Fleur Fannée", op. 18, written one month after (October 1913) the Ballet was in Rio de Janeiro, definitely shows Villa-Lobos's inclination towards the French. "Les Mères", op. 45, written the following year (August 1914) did, too. Villa-Lobos's first experiments to go French were rather external for the time being.

Yet, three years later, he began to go a step further. In a three-part-piano series, called "Simples Colletânea", which he began in 1917 but only finished two years later, Villa-Lobos added not only French translations to the Portuguese titles. He also added, in French, such indications as "très lent et très expressif", or "misterieux", or "joyeux et animé". Villa-Lobos also let himself be influenced by such poets as Victor Hugo and La Fontaine. Poems of the first he set to music. The latter, however, made him hit on another idea: he composed a piano series which he entitled "Fábulas Características". To "O Gato e o Rato", written in 1914, the third and only of the three pieces of this work which was ever performed (February 3, 1917), Villa-Lobos added an explanatory text, published in the concert program of the first performance and which says that "the third piece is part of a descriptive collection of musical pieces about the 'impressions' of fables by La Fontaine and other Fabulists". Additionally, he used some impressionistic elements such as whole-tone scales, accumulations of seconds and occasionally extreme registers.

Next Villa-Lobos borrowed from Debussy something entirely different: he had observed that Debussy's subject matter came from a completely different sphere of ideas, something he had never before encountered in the compositions of others. This unusual ambiance tempted him to try something unusual, too. So he turned to a completely different subject matter, something his own country offered him, and conceived the "Danças Características Africanas" which were written between 1914 and 1915 and in parts performed between 1915 and 1919. Except for the name, the music bears rather earmarks of impressionistic music with borrowings from Tchaikovsky and reminds hardly of anything "characteristically African".

But now Villa-Lobos started to use impressionistic devices less sparingly. Perceptible are these elements already in the Third Piano Trio, written in 1918, (though the first movement was already composed in August 1917) and first performed on October 21, 1921. Here Villa-Lobos uses patterns which he had occasionally applied in some songs and piano works in earlier years but now they appear more frequently and more regularly. Far more important, however, is that Villa-Lobos, for the first time, experiments with some new effects of his own invention and indicates at one point "frappant bien avec l'ivoire du bôut de l'archet".

Neither compositions for the piano nor songs not even larger orchestral works gave Villa-Lobos the right possibilities to employ impressionistic devices in quite the way he visualized. So he felt he had to combine instruments in a new fashion to achieve the kind of color and sound he wanted. Selecting hitherto unusual instrumental ensembles for chamber music compositions was something he never again gave up during his whole life.

With this medium he produced exceptionally beautiful music at all times. Instruments of all sorts of combinations really exalted his intuition and creative genius for ever new color combinations, something in which he was unexcelled. Debussy's subtle music must have guided him on to this path though it was probably not Debussy's music alone. Other events in his life were contributing factors such as his acquaintance with Darius Milhaud who, in 1919 was Secretary to Paul Claude, who was French Ambassador in Rio de Janeiro at that time. Villa-Lobos's meeting with Artur Rubinstein in 1918 also helped. Four years later, on July 8, 1922, he played Villa-Lobos's piano series "A Prole do Bébé", No. 1 — written shortly after his encounter with Rubinstein — though without the last number "Bruxa" which was composed later. Milhaud and Rubinstein surely opened him new horizons, spoke about new trends and tendencies current outside of Brazil and perhaps familiarized him with the music of other impressionistic and post-impressionistic composers.

Because Villa-Lobos's "Quatuor", composed in 1921 and performed originally in the same year, on October 21, reflects quite clearly impressionistic thoughts and not French indebtedness merely in the selection of titles and selection of poets or the occasional use of impressionistic elements. The Quatuor's ensemble, conceived for harp, celesta, flute, alt-saxophone and women's chorus, offered Villa-Lobos completely new possibilities for color combinations. How strong Debussy's influence was at that time also shows in the work's sub-title "symbolic quartet" which, however was eliminated when the work was published nine years later. Because meanwhile Villa-Lobos had considerably changed his style and taste and so had general trends. He also removed an explanatory text, a feature he liked in those years between 1916 and 1921 but which was later abandoned, a few exceptions excluded.

The text, at any rate, should underscore his intent that the "Quatuor" reflects a French impressionistic style. He felt compelled to emphasize this for yet another reason. Uncertain if his music really conveyed impressionism to those he meant to reach with this work, he believed this purpose should be stressed additionally in a text.

Because it was during those early years that Villa-Lobos sought and obtained support from Brazil's moneyed society in Rio de Janeiro and São Paulo. These circles, as mentioned before, were French oriented. And the "Quatuor" should, in some way, remind his sponsors of France. With this he hoped to make them more inclined to assist him in his career — which indeed they did. They really helped him to get some of his music performed in Brazil and, in later years, also backed him materially to live comfortably for several years in Paris. To these sponsors also belonged Madam Laurinda Santos Lobo, a patron of the arts, to whom Villa-Lobos not only dedicated the "Quatuor" but also the concert at which the work was first performed.

The "Quatuor's" original text speaks eloquently of the "conventions and the mundane life" — some yielding to his backers — while the music is definitely indebted to Debussy which is perceptible in still another way: The choice of a small and unusual instrumental combination assisted by women's voices can be traced to Debussy's Sonata for flute, viola and harp, as well as to "Sirènes" from the "Nocturnes" for orchestra and chorus. With both works Villa-Lobos was acquainted. The "Nocturnes" were played in Rio de Janeiro the previous year he conceived his "Quatuor" in September 1921 during a series of six symphony concerts conducted by Richard Strauss who also performed some of his own works. This was a time when Felix Weingartner and Richard Strauss alternated their yearly Rio de Janeiro appearances between 1920 and 1923 included. Their concert and opera performances included works by Wagner, Richard Strauss, Mahler, Debussy, Korngold and even a small work by Villa-Lobos himself.

During rehearsals, as orchestral member, Villa-Lobos became acquainted with Debussy's "Nocturnes". And with his facilities to compose, Villa-Lobos wrote the "Quatuor" in a relatively short time to get it ready for the São Paulo performance towards the end of October. Irrespective of impressionistic tendencies in this work, the "Quatuor" clearly manifests the path on which Villa-Lobos would proceed from now on, such as his rich treasure of ideas and his uncanny talent to handle human voices, in a way hitherto new in Brazil. True, the chorus from the "Sirènes" had inspired him but he used his ideas in his own personal way.

In other words, his personality was emerging; he did not merely adopt devices borrowed from others, but modified and shaped them with his own ingenuity. This is particularly perceptible in his treatment of voices and words. Because words were important to Villa-Lobos not because of what they expressed but rather what they could do to contribute and enhance the musical sound-effect he had in mind. Such examples in the "Quatuor" are numerous, i.e. a motiv to which Villa-Lobos remarked: "battez légèrement la bouche avec la pointe des doigts de façon à bien marquer chaque croche. On peut aussi prononcer sur chaque croche la syllabe 'lou' sans battre."

If the "Quatuor's" impressionistic character manifests itself in the choice of instrumental and vocal ensemble, the symphonic poem and ballet "Amazonas", written four years earlier and performed for the first time on May 30, 1919, is impressionistic in other respects. Here an entire impressionistic technique is perceptible, such as tremoli and flageolet notes or the oftentimes devided and muted string ensemble, or glissandi chords in the harp or harp flageolet or introducing themes solo-like by wood-wind instruments. Additionally, Villa-Lobos applies, over and over again, whole-tone scales and quite a few sixth and forth progressions. Interestingly, already at this early stage of his musical career Villa-Lobos used progressions of chords of forths in the brass, piano and devided first violins with chromatic second progressions in the second violins and chromatic sixth progressions in the violas. Everything rests on a pedal point, played by timpani and double basses. With this material, Villa-Lobos tempted to create a impressionistic atmosphere, although the "Amazonas's" subject matter is purely Brazilian. Still, he must have felt that the impressionistic palette was suitable to underscore the indigenous legend his father had told him when he was a child.

Irrespective of impressionistic elements, the orchestral range surely is not. It rather follows Wagner's "Ring" orchestra, as mentioned before, and requests additionally such special instruments as Sarrusophone, Violinophone and Viola d'Amore, probably with no intention to out-do Wagner this time but to achieve special instrumental colors. This strive to attain new sound effects, though not yet always successful in this work, nevertheless, shows that impressionistic conceptions worked unconciously in his mind and were gradually taken shape. Because occasionally, he invented really something new regarding instrumental color effects for which an orchestral work gave him far greater possibilities than those for the piano or even songs.

In an entirely different way influenced Puccini the Brazilian composer's music and — way of thinking. His first contact with the Italian composer dates from the time his father, an amateur cello player, frequented opera performances and joined others in amateur music making. During Raúl's short life — he died at the age 37 of malaria in 1899 — Puccini's "Bohème" was performed in Rio de Janeiro, and had impressed Raúl to such an extent that he delighted in playing some parts from it at home to his son Heitor. He loved the kid and was fascinated by the child's early musical inclinations. On the grown-up Heitor Villa-Lobos, Puccini's effect was quite different:

there was an epoch — though no records of the period are available — when Villa-Lobos wrote music criticisms. The clippings are undated and the name of publication not mentioned. The reviews are signed with the borrowed pseudonym of his father, Raúl, who had occasionally published some of his numerous books with the pen-name Epaminondas Villalba. Heitor added the word *Filho,* as he had done on other occasions. Villa-Lobos reviewed only opera performances. This is the more surprising as this type of music never really appealed nor fascinated him much in life.

Among the reviews is one about "Traviata" and another one about "Butterfly". He found that "we get accustomed to 'Traviata's' banality". Yet "Butterfly" impressed him in two different ways and both are extremely characteristic for Villa-Lobos. One reflects his way of thinking, the other the powerful impact on his musical creativity. Villa-Lobos said in the review that Puccini "only made concessions to the public to make a lot of money with his operas" and at another point he says "the audience likes the chorus's improvised singing with the mouth shut". This last observation is particularly revealing for Villa-Lobos as he was to use similar devices in some of his later works, i.e. the "Quatuor" and, extremely beautiful, in the "Bachianas Brasileiras", No. 5, for voice and violoncelli.

As to the concessions which Puccini, in Villa-Lobos's opinion, had made to the public's taste, this reverberated on Villa-Lobos's own operas. He did not write more than three operas in his life. "Izaht", a work that was composed over many years with numerous interruptions until it was finished shortly before its first performance (yet not on the stage but in the concert hall) on April 6, 1940, though begun already in 1914, reminds occasionally of Puccini. But by far the most perceptible evidence of Villa-Lobos's belief that a Puccini-style opera would earn a lot of money, is his opera "Yerma", written in 1955/56, four years before his death and performed for the first time on August 12, 1971 by the Santa Fe Opera in New Mexico, in the United States.

When Villa-Lobos composed this opera, he was already a pretty sick man. After a successfully performed cancer operation of the bladder in New York's Memorial Hospital in July 1948, he was forthwith constantly under medical treatment in America and elsewhere to check a progresively declining state of health, consequences of the bladder extraction among other organs. So he was obliged, during the last eleven years of his life, to accept quite a number of commissioned works in order to pay doctors' bills, medicine and treatment. The comissions were not far between. Additionally, his uncommissioned musical output was tremendous in those years, it was a prolific time, yet not one of his most original and personal as far as ideas and

ingenuity were concerned compared to years gone by. This was partly due to his failing health, partly due to the fact that, at the time of
the operation, he was entering the seventh decade of his life and
partly the result of a declining creativity after an enormous production in his first sixty years of his life which has few parallels.

The fact that he really had to make money in addition to regular
incomes from his position as head of the Music Educational Department at Rio de Janeiro's Municipality and from royalties of his
works and recordings, possibly made him remember Puccini. He still
appraised Puccini in the same way as in those early youthful years,
hoping that with a Puccini flavored opera he just would hit the
jack-pot.

When he wrote his opera "Yerma" to words by Federico García
Lorca, commissioned by Hugh Ross and John Blankenship, Puccini
was his musical model. Whether Villa-Lobos was right that a Puccini
styled opera appeals to the public or whether it was García Lorca's
plot or both, the fact remains that the work played to a sell-out
audience at the Santa Fe Opera House in New Mexico where the
world's premiere was staged. "It's a piece much like 'Turandot' –
polytonal Puccini", was one press comment.[2] "The conservative music is partly oriented on Puccini ... At any rate, the work appeals to
the audience, judging from the heavy applaus ... Another advantage is
its relatively easy staging without scenic changes. This may well help
the opera to be represented in other places as well", according to
another review.[3]

Villa-Lobos apparently had the right feeling what would help his
opera to success. For him right means and style were determined
factors, irrespective of whether this was truly Villa-Lobos. In all
fairness to the ingenious and versatile composer that Villa-Lobos was,
of course, some elements of Puccini's music were indeed much akin
to his own. To these belong certain lyrical melodies, perceptible even
in such an entirely different piece as his "Bachianas Brasileiras",
No. 5. Moreover, Puccini's choice of oriental and exotic subjects influenced Villa-Lobos, at the beginning of his career, to the effect that
he believed that something outlandish was what the public wanted.
Thus, to capture the audience's attention in this respect, Villa-Lobos
chose in 1914 a title for a piano piece which would exactly do that.
He called it "Ibericárabe". First performed on January 29, 1915, this
unassuming little piece is from an orchestral work called "Suite
Oriental". The word oriental was borrowed from Puccini probably.
"Ibericárabe", a concoction of Iberic and Arabic was derived from

2 Newsweek, New York City, August 23, 1971.
3 Neue Zürcher Zeitung, Zürich, September 4 1971.

the Spanish Peninsula, something loosely connected with his own Brazil. Yet, the title was incomprehensible to the concert audience. It had to be changed into "Canção Ibérica" for the first performance, according to the concert program. Apart from these outward features his music contains Puccinian characteristics such as melodic lines consisting sometimes of broken seventh chords, supported by *faux-bourdons* or sometimes *ostinato tremoli* in the basses and the like.

To make concessions to the public's taste by writing a Puccini styled opera as in the case of "Yerma", select compositions titles to appeal to his audience, compose music with a Brazilian touch and angle as in practically everything he wrote after his return from his first trip to Paris, as Europeans expected something native from a Brazilian composer, were not isolated incidents and phenoemena. All through his life, Villa-Lobos who charmed and captivated many who came in contact with him by his pleasing and unassuming personality, was, nevertheless, a man who desperately sought to be unique, and original, to attract attention, to be different from others, and, at the same time, to prove to himself and others that he, too, could write exactly in the same style as they did and – if need be – cope with any eccentricities that were fashionable in Europe in the twenties.

The "Suite Suggestive", No. 1, written in 1929 and performed for the first time on August 26, 1929, did exactly that. Within his total musical output, it represents an escapade and yet it proves how much he let himself affect by contemporary trends around him while living in Paris. It delighted him to demonstrate that he, too, could write in the style of that time though when he actually did so, it was already a little *déjà vu.* Sati's "Parade" in which are used typewriters or Milhaud's "Machines Agricoles" and "Catalogue de Fleurs" belonged to an epoch in which the grotesque and extravagant were popular. Though perhaps a little belated, Villa-Lobos contributed his part with his "Suite Suggestive", No. 1.

For instance, the third piece, called "Cloche-pied au flic", consists only of thirteen bars, but the ensemble is elaborate in as much as it requires three metronomes, violine, viola, cello, bass, bassoon, key-bugle and percussion band to accompany a vocal duet. How much he was affected by current trends and particularly by expressionism is reflected in the eccentricity to use different instrumental ensembles plus voices for each of the Suite's seven little pieces, written to texts by the Brazilian poets Oswald de Andrade and Manuel Bandeira and the Frenchman René Chalupt. But he was not satisfied with the use of odd instrumental ensembles and brief pieces with pompous titles. He wanted more. In one piece, the fifth, called "Charlot Aviatuer" *(comique),* he showed off his knowledge in matters American, perceptible in the accompanying text which refers to the motion picture, "The Kid" with Charlie Chaplin and Jackie Coogan, and other current topical events such as the prohibition, Ice-Cream Soda Parlors, drugstores, as well as Lindbergh's flight across the Atlantic in his plane "The Spirit of St. Louis".

He really seemed to enjoy the thought that he — a Brazilian in Paris — could not only write works with native elements and indigenous subjects, but was completely up-todate in current musical and other topics of his time. And yet, Villa-Lobos remained true to himself despite occasional escapades or, at times, writing with an eye to public success. Many of the influences under which he was at the beginning of his career, were beneficial to his musical development. They stimulated and animated him, he took from them what suited him, they were a sort of launching pad from which to take off to some place where he was no longer indebted to anyone but himself, after having emerged as the truly original and ingenious composer whose music reflected the Brazilian character for which he became famous at home and abroad.

RESUMO

Varios músicos europeos influenciaram o caminho musical do compositor brasileiro Heitor Villa-Lobos. Muito cedo, Richard Wagner o inspirou a exprimir seu pensamento ideológico e a usar uma orquestra bastante grande. Evidentemente, Villa-Lobos foi impresionado pelas estruturas melódicas de Stravinsky, Tchaikovsky e Rimsky-Korsakow. Sentindo uma certa afinidade com os russos, ele chegou a descobrir seu estilo proprio. De Claude Debussy vêm os vestigios impressionistas e a preocupação com a cor do som. E Puccini o estimulou a usar temas orientais e exóticos, e melodias líricas. Só depois de absorver estes pensamentos e estilos estrangeiros, Villa-Lobos conseguiu tornar-se um compositor verdadeiramente brasileiro.

Ibero-Amerikanisches Archiv, **3**(1), 1977, 37–51

Corrigenda

p54 *third paragraph line 8*:
For IsoLde read Isolde

line 12 from bottom:
For opera read stage works
line 11 from bottom:
for three read four
p55 *second paragraph first line*:
For eypressed read expressed
p60 *line 3*:
For Fannée read Fanée
second paragraph line 5:
For misterieux read mystérieux
p61 *line 2*:
For bôut read bout
third paragraph line 8:
For Claude read Claudel
third paragraph line 9:
For Artur read Arthur
p64 *third paragraph line 3*:
For three operas read four stage works
p66 *second paragraph line 6*:
for phenoemena read phenomena
third paragraph line 2:
For August 26, 1929 read June 29, 1929

THE FIFTEEN-YEAR-PERIODS
IN VILLA-LOBOS's LIFE

The life of Heitor Villa-Lobos, the Brazilian composer, divides itself into clearly defined fifteen-year-periods. Each differs from the previous ones. The interesting phenomenon is that the changes which occurred were brought about by outside happenings. Partly responsible for these abrupt shifts is the fact that Villa-Lobos's life-span fell into an epoch of important historical events in Brazil as well as in the world.

Villa-Lobos was born (March 5, 1887) at a time when Brazil was still an Empire on the British model under Emperor Dom Pedro II. Villa-Lobos died (November 17, 1959) only five months before the United States of Brazil, long since a Republic, moved her capital from seashore Rio de Janeiro at Guanabara Bay to land-locked, man-made Brasília on the high plateau in the state of Goías, on April 21, 1960[1].

Villa-Lobos was barely one year old, when, on May 13, 1888, slavery was abolished in Brazil by Princess Isabel[2], heiress to the one and, at that time, regent during the temporary absence of her Father, Dom Pedro II[3]. She signed the Golden Law *(Lei Aurea)*

1 Brazil's first capital was the city of São Salvador (1549 - 1763) in the North-Eastern state of Bahia. She was transferred to the City of São Sebastião of Rio de Janeiro (1763 - 1960) at a time when the political and economic center of the colony shifted to the South. Each city was the capital for close to two hundred years.

2 Isabel, the Imperial Princess of Orléans and Bragança, daughter of Emperor Dom Pedro II and Empress Teresa Cristina Maria de Bourbon, married Prince Luís Felipe Maria Fernando Gastão de Orléans, Conte d'Eu, on October 15, 1864. They had three children. During her father's absence in Europe, she represented the Emperor as regent. During her first regency she signed the law (September 28, 1871) which would free future children of the slaves. During her third and last regeny she signed the Golden Law. After the proclamation of the Republic on November 15, 1889 she went to Europe. She died at the Châuteau d'Eu in France.

3 Dom Pedro II de Alcântara from the House of Bragança (1825 - 1891), son of Emperor Dom Pedro I of Brazil and Maria Leopoldina Josefa Carolina of Habsburg, Archduchess of Austria and Empress of Brazil (1797 - 1826) reigned from April 1, 1831 until the proclamation of the Republic on November 15, 1889. During his reign occurred the war against Paraguay. He further-ed European immigration, stimulated Brazil's economy and showed great interest in the Arts and Sciences. Under his regency the first railroads and telegraph lines were built.

which abolished slavery. This affected the coffee planters' economy and the farmers turned against the Emperor. A military coup under Marshall Manuel Deodoro da Fonseca (1827 - 1892) was followed by a bloodless overthrow of the monarchy and the proclamation of the Republic on November 15, 1889 when Villa-Lobos was two and a half years old. Two years later (1891) Brazil had her first republican constitution, based on that of the United States of America, on which Brazil was uninterruptedly governed until the 1930 world economic crisis.

After his deposition Dom Pedro II and his family went into exile. They lived modestly in Paris at the Bedford Hotel, Rue de l'Arcade 17, 8th Arrondissement, near the Madeleine where Dom Pedro II died two years later (1891). A memorial plate at the Hotel's façade reminds of Dom Pedro's stay. In 1952, sixty-one years after the Emperor's death, Villa-Lobos, then at the prime of his international fame as composer, also settled at the Bedford Hotel which he made his European headquarters until his death seven years later. The fact that Villa-Lobos had chosen this same hotel, where a plate to his memory was unveiled below that of Dom Pedro II on the occasion of the composer's 84th birthday in 1971, was probably no coincidence. With a sense of his own place in the history of music, Villa-Lobos must have selected this same hotel. The hotel management offered him the use of the same chambers which Dom Pedro II had once occupied as well as the use of the Emperor's writing desk which was placed into Villa-Lobos's living room[4]. Villa-Lobos who was a child of the Empire chose to live and dwell during his final years of his life in the same hotel ambiance as had his great Brazilian compatriot once done.

Villa-Lobos's first fifteen years — his childhood — were not different from those of other kids his age or those of other sons of a public servant who was a librarian at Rio de Janeiro's National Library. Villa-Lobos grew up in a modest, but cultural and intellectual home. His father, Raúl (1862 - 1899)[5] was, in addition to his library work, a prolific writer and translator, amateur cellist and portrait painter. He dedicated much of his spare time to his son Heitor — one of several children[6] — because he sensed the boy's musical talent and curiosity for literature and geography which the youngster displayed already at an early age.

Raúl had planned a good education for his son Heitor. He entered Pedro II College in Rio de Janeiro on April 3, 1901, two years after

---

4 After Villa-Lobos's death the Bedford Hotel agreed to transfer this writing desk to Brazil. It is now at the Villa-Lobos Museum in Rio de Janeiro.
5 Raúl was the son of Spanish parents: Francisco da Silveira Villa-Lobos and

his father's death, at the age of fourteen. Nevertheless, the sudden death of his father, who succumbed to malaria at the age of thirty-seven, brought this well paved course to an end around the turn of the century. Villa-Lobos's mother, Noêmia,[7] who survived her husband by forty-seven years, had a hard time to make ends meet to support herself and her children on a small widow's pension. Any formal education or even higher education which the intellectual Raúl (it may be assumed) might have conceived for his talented son, Heitor, was out of the question under the prevailing financial circumstances of the Villa-Lobos family. The changed economic situation determined Villa-Lobos's next fifteen years (1900 - 1915); it was up to him to choose his own path economically and professionally. This determined his forming and adolescent years.

To begin with, he had to make a living. This was not too difficult. As violoncellist, he found work in coffee houses, vaudeville and traveling theater companies, which, in later years, took him as far as Bahia and Manaus at the Amazon River. His work, particularly, in Rio de Janeiro, brought him in touch with composers of Brazilian popular music who wrote chôro[8], lundu[9] and maxixe,[10] tango and

... Maria Carolina Serzedelo Villa-Lobos. He came from modest background. Lack of financial funds prevented him to pursue his medical studies after the second year. He became a teacher instead. In 1890 he found work at Rio de Janeiro's National Library. In 1896 he was commissioned to reorganize the Senate's library. He is the author and translator of several books, some of them published under the pseudonym Epaminondas Vilalba, a pseudonym which his son Heitor occasionally used, adding the world *Filho* (Son).

6 Heitor Villa-Lobos's sister Bertha (1885 - 1976), a housewife, was married to Romeu Augusto Borman de Borges. They had three children: Clélia (born September 11, 1908), Haygara (born May 10, 1917) and Paulo Emygidio (born October 10, 1922). Sister Carmen (1888 - April 20, 1970), a teacher, was married to the late Danton Condorcet da Silva Jardim. They had one daughter: Haygara Yacyra. Brother Othon (1897 - 1918), an electrician, was married to the late Octavia.

7 Noêmia Umbelina Villa-Lobos (February 25, 1859 - March 13, 1946) who married Raúl in 1884 was the daughter of Antônio Santos Monteiro and Domitildes Costa Santos Monteiro.

8 Chôro, as the folklore specialist and musicologist Renato Almeida explains in his book "História da Música Brasileira" (second Edition, Rio de Janeiro, 1942), in which he quotes Jacques Raimundo's work "O Negro Brasileiro", was something "that had come to Brazil from the other side of the Atlantic, from the African coast where the Kaffir tribes practiced a sort of vocal concert with dances, calles xôlo ... The Brazilian negroes called their balls which they staged at St. John's Day or on other holidays on the big country estates where they were employed, xôlos which through some confusion with a Portuguese paronyn turned into xôro. When this xôro moved to urban regions it became Chôro" ... "Chôro is a generic name. It signifies a group of instruments, one of which takes a solo part. Chôro is also called a piece of music played by that group of instruments. At any rate, it is a sort of popular

polka which were en vogue in those days and cultivated in those circles to which Villa-Lobos soon belonged and where he often played, instead of the violoncello, the guitar. Prominent amongst his companions were Ernesto Júlio de Nazaré[11], Joaquim Francisco dos Santos[12], Eduardo das Neves[13], Anacleto Augusto de Medeiros[14], Irineu de Almeida[15], Francisca (Chiquinha) Hedwiges Gonzaga[16] and Catulo da Paixão Cearense.[17] Villa-Lobos contributed his share to the merry music making of his pals and wrote a chôro and a mazurka. Yet he must have felt his lack of technical training and that some kind of formal musical education would be helpful. So he decided, around 1906/07, at the age of twenty, to seek some instruc-

> instrumental music played in the open air and perhaps comparable with a serenade."

9 Lundu of Bantu origin was popular in Portugal in the 16th century and came to Brazil in the 18th century. In the 19th century the dance was replaced by a song of cheerful character. In Portugal it was accompanied by guitar, bandolim or viola, in Brazil by viola or guitar. The choreography is illustrated in two engravings by Moritz Rugendas (1802 - 1858) in "Malerische Reise in Brasilien", published by Engelmann & Cie (Paris, 1835) in the Sections "Europäerleben" (3rd Div., Pl. 18) and "Sitten und Gebräuche der Neger" (4th Div., Pl. 17).

10 Maxixe is an urban Brazilian dance which appeared around 1870.

11 Ernesto Júlio de Nazaré (1863 - 1934), a Brazilian self-taught composer and pianist. Played the piano in cinemas, music stores and in public in the state of São Paulo and the south of Brazil. Was famous for his Brazilian tangos (he wrote about 120), also composed waltzes and polkas. An ear ailment since his childhood led to deafness in old age. In his last years he was psychically disturbed and ended his life tragically.

12 Joaquim Francisco dos Santos ("Quincas Laranjeiras", 1873 - 1935), Brazilian composer of popular music and guitarist. Son of a carpenter, he came to Rio de Janeiro from his native town Olinda in the northern state of Pernambuco at the age of six months. At eleven he worked in a garment factory called "Alliança" in the Laranjeiras district. This probably got him his nickmane "Quincas Laranjeiras". In later years he was public servant in the Inspectorate for Hygiene and Assistance, the later Municipal Assistance Department. He also played the flute.

13 Eduardo das Neves (1874 - 1919), Brazilian singer and composer of popular music. One of the most popular artists at the beginning of the 20th century. Appeared at horse circuses, in Cafés and other entertainement centers in Rio de Janeiro and other parts of Brazil. Played the guitar and is author of satirical poems.

14 Anacleto Augusto de Medeiros (1866 - 1907). Brazilian composer of popular music. Studied at the *Conservatório Imperial de Música* (today *Escola de Música da Universidade Federal do Rio de Janeiro*) played many instruments, especially the saxophon. Founded (November 15, 1896) the Fire Fighting Band. He was its first conductor. He set to music poems of Catulo da Paixão Cearense, a contemporary bard, especially the poem "Rasga o Coração" (Break the heart). Villa-Lobos subtitled his composition for orchestra and chorus, called "Chôros" No. 10 "Rasga o Coração" (composed 1926) in memorary of Cearense's poem.

tions at the *Instituto Nacional de Música*[18] which, however, he frequented only sporadically. A few years later, he supplemented his fragmentary musical education and took harmony lessons with Agnelo França[19] and sought the advice of the Brazilian composer Antônio Francisco Braga[20] at a time when he turned from a composer of popular to serious music.

Decisive during Villa-Lobos's crucial forming years were events between 1910 and 1913: He married Lucília Guimarães (on November 12, 1913),[21] an accomplished pianist in her own right. She was a helpful mate at this early stage of Villa-Lobos's endeavors to write serious music. She guided him technically in many ways. Marriage

15 Irineu de Almeida (1873 - 1916) Brazilian composer of popular music and ophicleid player. Around the turn of the century he was known under the name of Irineu Batina (batina means soutane) because he always wore a cassack. He was founding member of the Fire Fighting Band together with Anacleto Augusto de Medeiros. There he played the ophicleid and trombone (1896 - 1916). Between 1904 - 1905 he frequented the saloon *Cavaquinho de Ouro* (Gold Fiddle), a meeting place for Villa-Lobos, Quincas Laranjeiras and others. Since 1907 he was often a guest of Alfredo da Rocha Vianna's father in the Rua Vista Alegre in the Catumbi district, where, since 1911, he instructed his son who later became a well-known composer of popular music under the pseudonym of Pixinguinha (1898 - 1973).

16 Francisca (Chiquinha) Hedwiges Gonzaga (1847 - 1935) Brazilian composer of popular music and pianist. Descended from a well-to-do family. Obtained a good education. Pupil of Arthur Napoleão (1843 - 1925) with whom she gave concerts. Visited Europe (1902, 1904, 1906). She was an emancipated lady, piano teacher and member of a dance band by the Brazilian flutist and composer Joaquim Antônio da Silva Calado (1848 - 1880). Composed since her childhood, wrote about two-thousand dances, about seventy-seven scores for burlesque, operettas and revues which were successful in her time.

17 Catulo da Paixão Cearense (1866 - 1945) Brazilian bard. In 1880 he came to Rio de Janeiro from his native São Luís in the state of Maranhao. His poems were set to music by many of his contemporaries of popular music.

18 Its original name was *Conservatório Imperial de Música* founded by Francisco Manuel da Silva (1795 - 1865), composer of the National Anthem of Brazil. It was opened on August 13, 1848 in Rio de Janeiro. On January 12, 1890 it took the name of *Instituto Nacional de Música* and on July 5, 1937 the name of *Escola Nacional de Música da Universidade do Brasil* and on November 18, 1966 it was again renamed *Escola de Música da Universidade Federal do Rio de Janeiro*.

19 Agnelo França (1875 - 1964) Brazilian music teacher and composer. After some studies at his home town Valença in the state of Rio de Janeiro, he continued his studies in Rio de Janeiro at the *Instituto Nacional de Música* (today *Escola de Música da Universidade Federal do Rio de Janeiro*). Was professor for harmony at this institute for forty years (1904 - 1943). His compositions were played by Brazilian orchestras. His book "A Arte de Modular" (The art to modulate) was also translated into French.

20 Antônio Francisco Braga (1868 - 1945), Brazilian composer, conductor and teacher. Studied at the *Conservatório Imperial de Música* (today *Escola de*

also contributed to a less bohemian life which the Villa-Lobos couple
now set up, first at the Rua Souza Neves 12 and than at the Rua
Didimo 10 in the Tijuca district. Decisive, too, was Villa-Lobos's
entry into the orchestra of Rio de Janeiro's Municipal Theatre[22]
inaugurated on July 14, 1909. This made Villa-Lobos, as soon as he
joined this orchestra, acquainted with classical symphonic music and
operas. Operas, symphony concerts and ballets, all on a high international standard and patronized by the Municipality, were given
every year. They included first performances of "Salome" (July 15,
1910), Pietro Mascagni's first visit to Rio de Janeiro and his conducting his "Isabeau" (July 21, 1911), and "Rosenkavalier" (1915).
Under Walter Mocchi's management (1913 - 1926) were heard not
only "Walküre" and "Parsifal" but he brought to Rio de Janeiro in
1913 the Russian Ballet under Michael Fokine with W. F. Nijinskij.
They presented "Prince Igor", "Scheherezade", "Tamara", "l'Après-
Midi d'un Faune". The music of the Russians and that of the French
impressionists, each in its own way, influenced Villa-Lobos's thinking, the choice of his composition titles and text poets and gradually
also his instrumentation and musical style. Thus, the second fifteen-
year-period of Villa-Lobos's life consisted of his learning music the
practical way: first through his close contact with popular music and
its composers, and then his intimate contact with serious music as
orchestral member. He absorbed the richness of these offerings intellectually, an amalgamating approach to which he adhered all his life.
As a result Villa-Lobos composed now more intensely and tried his
hand on all genre: chamber music, songs, works for piano, violin and

... *Música da Universidade Federal do Rio de Janeiro*). With a government grant
   he went to Europe in 1890. In Paris he was a pupil of Mascagni. In 1896 he
   went to Germany (Dresden and Bayreuth), came under Wagner's influence
   and then lived for some time in Italy. After a ten-years' absence he returned
   to Brazil in 1900. 1902 - 1938 professor at the *Instituto Nacional de Música*
   (now *Escola de Música da Universidade Federal do Rio de Janeiro*); 1913 -
   1933 conductor of the orchestra of the *Sociedade de Concêrtos Sinfônicos* in
   Rio de Janeiro.

21 Lucília Guimarães Villa-Lobos (May 26, 1886 - May 25, 1966) studied piano
   and solfège at the *Escola Nacional de Música* (today *Escola de Música da
   Universidade Federal do Rio de Janeiro*). Met Heitor Villa-Lobos on November 1, 1912 whom she married a year later. Interpretor of his music. They
   separated on May 28, 1936. They had no children. Subsequently Lucília
   continued her musical activities as pianist, choral conductor.

22 The *Teatro Municipal*, modelled, en miniature, after the Paris Opera, was part
   of a grandiose urbanization project with parks and beautiful buildings on
   tree-lined avenues and streets, including the Avenida Rio Branco. The Municipal Theatre was opened in the presence of Nilo Peçanha (1867 - 1924) who,
   as Vice-President of Brazil (1906 - 1910), became temporary President
   (June 14, 1909 - November 15, 1910) due to the death of President Afonso
   Augusto Moreira Pena.

violoncello, even began to compose an opera ("Izaht"), also smaller orchestral works and those for solo instrument and orchestra. All of a sudden, an outside event occurred: It should shape his next fifteen years: the opportunity to have his music performed in public. He was almost twenty-eight years old by then. The year was 1915. It was really a memorable year in Villa-Lobos's life and for his career. It was a watershed, a divide. He was to leave his forming years behind and began to consider himself a composer of serious music who sought public recognition.

The year 1915 gave Villa-Lobos five chances to present himself to an audience. At first, during a vacation, in the mountain village of Nova Friburgo, near Rio de Janeiro, in the *Teatro D. Eugênia* (January 29, 1915) where he also introduced himself, together with his wife Lucília, as interpretors. A second concert (February 9) and a third one (February 28) followed at the Cinéma Odeon in the same village. The three concerts were preparatory public appearances. The real test came on July 31, when Antônio Francisco Braga included Villa-Lobos's "Suite Característica" for strings (written in 1913) in one of his subscription concerts given by the *Sociedade de Concêrtos Sinfônicos* at the Municipal Theatre in Rio de Janeiro. Encouraged, Villa-Lobos undertook to organize himself a concert exclusively with own works at the *Associação dos Empregados de Comércio* in Rio de Janeiro on November 13, 1915). The press reviews were not uniform in their opinion but recognized a special talent. These first public appearances in 1915 made Villa-Lobos decide to dedicate himself exclusively to a career as a composer and seek ways and means to have his works performed.

The ensuing years between 1915 and 1930 were Villa-Lobos's most important creative years. He formed and found his personal style that became his trade mark. He tested himself and the public's reaction. So he organized practically every year his own concerts. Until 1917 all were chamber music concerts. Since 1918 he presented himself as composer of orchestral works, some conducted by himself, some by others.[23] These opportunities animated him to pour out an avalanche of works of all types though his musical style was still turned towards internationalism under the influence of the music he experienced as orchestral member. During the second appearance of the Russian ballet under Serge P. Diaghilew in 1917 were performed. "Petruschka", "L'Oiseau de Feu", "Feu d'artifice".

23 In 1920 Felix Weingartner included – as the only Brazilian piece – Villa-Lobos's "Naufrágio de Kleônikos" when guest conducting at Rio de Janeiro's Municipal Theatre. In 1924 Vera Janacopulos Staal, a Brazilian singer, presented in Paris three pieces – "Cromo", "Sino da Aldeia" and "Viola" (Colored Engraving, Village Bell and Violet) – from the song cycle "Miniaturas" (Miniatures), composed between 1912 and 1917.

"Daphnis et Chloé" and works by Rimsky-Korsakow. The orchestra also played "Tristan und Isolde", "l'Apprenti Sorcier", Vicent d'Indy and Italian music, Mahlers' First Symphony and Korngold's "Viel Lärm um Nichts". All this broadened Villa-Lobos's musical horizon with repercussions on his instrumentation and musical thinking.

An event took place halfway through this fifteen-year period which indicated the path that eventually should lead him away from his present internationally attached style. Villa-Lobos was invited to participate at the Week of Modern Art in São Paulo in 1922 where a group of modern painters, writers, musicologists and composers declared themselves avantgardists and independent from European influences. The group consisted of prominent intellectual, cultural and artistic Brazilians, as Anita Malfatti[24], Mário Raúl de Morais Andrade[25], Ronald de Carvalho[26], Renato Costa Almeida[27], José Oswald de Souza Andrade[28], Paulo da Silva Prado[29], Guilherme de Andrade Almeida[30] and José Pereira da Graça Aranha[31]. His contacts and experiences in São Paulo most likely nurtured his desire to go abroad like his predecessors[32] had done before him. He yearned to pass some time not in Italy but Paris, the intellectual center in the

24 Anita Malfatti (1896 - 1964), Brazilian painter, studied in São Paulo, Berlin and the U.S. Her exhibitions prepared the way for the Week of Modern Art in 1922 in São Paulo at which she participated. Her paintings were included at the São Paulo Bienale (1951 and 1963). She had shows in Argentina, Chile, Peru.

25 Mário Raúl de Morais Andrade (1893 - 1945), Brazilian poet, critic, musicologist and public servant. Studied at *Conservatório Dramático e Musical* in São Paulo. He taught piano and history of music at the Conservatoire in later years. Played a prominent part in the São Paulo Week of Modern Art (1922). From 1934 - 1938 was head of the Cultural Division of São Paulo's Municipality. Organized the foundation of a chorus and quartet, founded lending libraries, children's libraries and a public discoteque, furthered admission-free concerts, plans for a new library, the organization of expeditions to collect Brazilian folklore and the convocation of the *Congresso da Lígua Nacional Cantada* (1937). Lived in Rio de Janeiro (1938 - 1940) as literary critic and taught esthetics at the University of the Federal Distric. He was the most influencial, most versatile, cultured and intellectual personality of the modern movement of his time and influenced the younger generation of poets, composers and intellectuals. Author of scholarly books on music and Brazilian folklore, wrote poems and essays.

26 Ronald de Carvalho (1893 - 1935) Brazilian poet and critic. Studied law (1912), represented his country as diplomat in various South American countries, Paris, Holland, Mexico and the U.S. Began his literary career in 1910, participated at São Paulo's Week of Modern Art (1922). Victim of automobile accident. To his works belong "Pequena História da Literatura Brasileira" and "Epigramas Irônicos e Sentimentais" which were set to music by Heitor Villa-Lobos.

27 Renato Costa Almeida (born 1895) Brazilian teacher, writer and musicologist.

twenties. A government grant in 1922 helped him to realize his dream. He spent twelve months in Paris from the summer of 1923[33] until the summer 1924.

The Paris stay was a transition period from the first half to the second half of this fifteen-year-period. During this transition he came to the conclusion that he would have to turn his back on internationalism and express the 'soul' of Brazil in his music, as folklore and national elements were the fashionable trends in Europe in those days. They helped to make their composers successful. Villa-Lobos approached this problem intellectually. It became his turning point as a composer.

He returned to Brazil determined to embark on a new musical style in texture, substance, title and instrumentation. He went about it intellectually probably an inherited quality from his father. Villa-Lobos now began to study books, three principally: "Rondônia" by Edgar Roquette Pinto[3,4], "Brasilianische Volkslieder und Indianische

... Director of the *Colégio Franco-Brasileiro*, professor at the *Conservatório Brasileiro de Música*, Secretary of the National Commission of Folklore, member of numerous institutions. Author of several works, including "História da Música Brasileira" (History of Brazilian Music; Rio de Janeiro, 1926, 1942).

28 José Oswald de Souza Andrade (1890 - 1954), Brazilian poet, writer and journalist. Studied law, founded (1911) humoristic periodical, met (1917) Mário Raúl de Morais Andrade. They advocated and championed the modernistic movement in Brazil, which led to the convocation of the Week of Modern Art (1922) in São Paulo. Launched (1924) the literary movement *Pau Brasil* (Brazil Wood). Sojourn in Europe where he met the avantgardists. Lectured at the University of São Paulo (1945). Fought for an authentic Brazilian literature.

29 Paulo da Silva Prado (1869 - 1943) Brazilian historian and sociologist, participated at the Week of Modern Art in São Paulo (1922). Was the greatest analyst of Brazil's social life during the pre-revolutionary period. Studied law, was President of the National Coffee Council (1931/32).

30 Guilherme de Andrade Almeida (1890 - 1969), Brazilian poet and journalist. Studied law in São Paulo, worked with various publications. Member of the Brazilian Academy of Letters and other Institutions. Supported the modern movement of his time. Wrote poems and essays.

31 José Pereira da Graça Aranha (1868 - 1931) Brazilian writer and diplomat. Descended from a patriarchal family from Brazil's North. Studied law in Recife in the state of Pernambuco. Was founding member of the Brazilian Academy of Letters. His book "Canaã" (1902) was epoch-making. He wrote his play "Malazarte" (1911) in Portuguese and French. It was played in Paris. At the beginning of the twenties, he turned towards the modern movement which led to the Week of Modern Art in São Paulo (1922).

32 Antônio Carlos Gomes (1836 - 1896), Henrique Oswald (1852 - 1931), Alexander Levy (1864 - 1892), Alberto Nepomuceno (1864 - 1920) and Antônio Francisco Braga (1868 - 1945).

33 He left Brazil on June 30, 1923 on the French steamer "Croix".

Weisen", *Musikbeilage zu "Reise in Brasilien"* by Johann Baptist von Spix and Carl Friedrich Philipp von Martius[35] and "Histoire d'un voyage faict en la terre du Brésil autrement dite Amérique" by Jean de Léry[36]. He also visited Rio de Janeiro's National Museum[37], listened there to recordings of indigenous music and studied native instruments. He read voraciously. His curiosity in these matters became insatiable. His was a renewed period of forming years on a higher level than in his youth. He not only learned from practice, but this time from scientific and learned sources and authentic melodies

34 E. Roquete Pinto (1884 - 1954), Brazilian anthropologist, studied medicine in Rio de Janeiro. Participated at the 1907/08 mission of Cândido Mariano da Silva Rondon (1865 - 1958) in the Northeast of Mato Grosso state. In 1912 he went to Goías and the Amazon through scarcely populated indian regions where he collected material about the Parecís indians and made recordings and photos, described in the ethnological work "Rondônia". He founded (1937) and directed (until 1947) the National Institute of Educational Cinema where he orientated, in 1937, the historical part of the film "Descobrimento do Brasil" (Discovery of Brazil) filmed by Brazil's Cacao Institute of Bahia with music by Heitor Villa-Lobos. He was a member of the Brazilian Academy of Letters and the Brazilian Institute of History and Geography and Director (1926 - 1935) of Rio de Janeiro's National Museum.

35 Two Germans, the zoologist Johann Baptist von Spix (1781 - 1826) and the botanist Carl Friedrich Philipp von Martius (1794 - 1868) described the fauna and flora of Brazil as experienced during a two years and eleven months expeditions (1817 - 1920). Spix died during the publication of the book.

36 The Frenchman Jean de Léry went to Brazil in 1557 when he accompanied Admiral Nicolas Durand de Villegaignon (1510 - 1570) who tried to establish a Huguenot colony in Brazil. Léry described his observations and experiences of ten months' stay in Brazil in his now famous book "Histoire d'un voyage faict en la terre du Brésil autrement dite Amérique" which appeared in several editions and translations in the 16th and 17th centuries. The third edition, published in 1585 by Antoine Chuppin in Geneva, contains, for the first time, five melodies of the Tupinambá indians. These melodies are, however, missing in the first two editions, and in modern editions the tunes are not always identical. Villa-Lobos's "Canide-Ioune Sabath" (canide means yellow bird, sabath means elegiac song), the first of three songs from the cycle "Três Poemas Indígenas" (Three Indigenous Poems, composed 1926) is based on an indigenous song which was collected by Léry. Villa-Lobos again studied Léry's book in his preparation for the score of his composition "Descobrimento do Brasil" (Discovery of Brazil), composed between 1936 and 1942 (Cf. Lisa M. Peppercorn, *Heitor Villa-Lobos, Leben und Werk des brasilianischen Komponisten*, Zurich, 1972, pp. 215 - 216).

37 The National Museum was founded on June 6, 1808. Since 1892 it is installed in the old Imperial Palace at Quinta da Boa Vista in Rio de Janeiro. Villa-Lobos frequently visited this Museum with his wife Lucília. There he heard the Nozani-ná melody, registered under No. 14,597 which he used in his "Chôrus" No. 3 for clarinet, saxophone, bassoon, three horns and trombone and male chorus (composed 1925) and as second number in his song cycle "Chansons Typiques Brésiliennes". He also heard at the Museum the indigenous tune Teiru registered under No. 14,598. This melody Villa-Lobos incor-

from old chronicles. It suited him well. His interests were hightened, he felt hilarious, ecstatic. During the heights of these blissful moments, he let himself tempt to shake off tradition and internationalism, substituted by his own inventive creation regarding form, title and style. He dared to give his works names hitherto unknown in serious music like "Chôros", "Serestas", "Cirandas". And he came to use unusual instrumental chamber ensembles with extraordinary harmony and sound devices and colors in which he was to excel throughout the rest of his life and used pseudo-folkloric devices which gave his music a specific flavor. During the two and a half years in Brazil (1924/27), spent in São Paulo and Rio de Janeiro where he also presented to the public most of his latest creations, Villa-Lobos had found himself and shaped his style bearing characteristics which made him the most outstanding representative of his generation in Brazil. So he yearned to return to Paris to show what he had done. And with his customary energy and will power he succeeded to interest two Brazilian industrialists and philanthropists, the brothers Arnaldo (1884 - 1964) and Carlos Guinle (1883 - 1969) who sponsored a three and a half year sojourn in France from January, 1927 until June 1, 1930. Settled with his wife Lucília at the Place St. Michèle 11 in Paris and financially unpreoccupied, these were happy and delightful years filled with composing and performing his works in public, getting his music published by Editions Max Eschig in Paris and rubbing elbow with the musical and cultural world in Paris. It was exactly the life he had envisaged for himself. These years were tremendously productive and fertile though he was, by no means, at that time, an accepted nor much played composer either in Europe or Brazil. He was discussed, no doubt, in the general and the musical press on both sides of the ocean but a controversial figure, rather than a recognized composer. He still had to fight to get his works performed, mostly with the financial backings of others. Yet, he now possessed self-esteem and self-assurance.

But life's flighting and intensely lived moments of happiness were soon replaced again by long periods of frustration and expectation. At the end of May 1930, he left Paris for Brazil with stopovers and concerts in Brazil's Northeastern Recife in the state of Pernambuco. He arrived in Rio de Janeiro on June 15, 1930 on the SS "Araçatuba" in the firm belief to have returned for only a short while. His letter to Arnaldo Guinle (February 7, 1931)[38] is evidence that he yearned to return to France as soon as possible. Paris, he fancied, was

... porated as the second in his three-piece song series which he called "Três Poemas Indígenas" (Three Indigenous Poems) and which was expanded and enlarged in a similiar fashion as "Canide-Ioune Sabath", the first song of this cycle.

the only place where he could live and work. He did not return then or in the foreseeable future. His musical fecundity, that rich source of creation should be halted for the next fifteen years except for some sporadic works, including his famous "Bachianas Brasileiras" series. Instead the next fifteen-year-period foresaw for Villa-Lobos a completely different field of activity, as unexpected for him as for his friends and foes. The self-taught composer, lacking in formal pedagogical and administrative training, was to become an administrator, a pedagogue and inventor of an ingenious music-educational teaching device. He and those around him were to witness an additional talent of this versatile composer which neither he nor anybody else had suspected of this self-taught musician.

Villa-Lobos looked not for this change. It happened unexpectedly as before, and also, later in his life, the unexpected should again turn the course of his life into another direction he had neither sought for himself nor wanted. An outside event – the revolution in Brazil in 1930 – and the emergence of its protagonist Getúlio Dornelles Vargas (1883 - 1954)[39] was responsible. These political events not only influenced his musical career but also his private life. Heitor Villa-Lobos stayed put in Brazil for the next fifteen years from 1930 until 1945 except for short trips to Prague and Berlin (1936) and Buenos Aires (1940), because fate or providence had carved out, once more, a different path for him than what he had planned for himself. It proved again that chance and outside events, bare of human beings' influences often alter a person's lifepath unwillingly. Yet, if the person understands the winds of change, grasps the right opportunity, possesses the readiness and capabilities to adapt to new circumstances, irrespective of possible gloating and malicious joy of others, who relish that the path is intercepted, nature has a way of bringing out the person's unknown best resources and talents that otherwise may have remained buried and undeveloped.

Villa-Lobos faced sudden fateful changes not with resignation. His approach was intellectual: he possessed talent, intelligence, interests, curiosity, perseverance and tenacity, coupled with those irrational phenomena as inspiration, intuition and phantasy. He also had the gift to apply past experiences to new circumstances with an uncanny drive, energy and a penchant for the colossal coupled with a yearning for originality. This led to the astounding manifestation that

38 Lisa M. Peppercorn, *Heitor Villa-Lobos, Leben und Werk des brasilianischen Komponisten*, Zurich, 1972, p. 95.
39 Getúlio Dornelles Vargas (1883 - 1954) was chief of the Provisional Government (1930 - 1934), President of Brazil (1934 - 1937), Dictator (1937 - 1945) and again President of Brazil from 1951 - 1954 when he committed suicide on August 24.

serendipity applied to him all through his life.

The October Revolution of 1930 with the emergence of Getúlio D. Vargas, first as provisional and later as definite President of Brazil, brought nationalistic tendencies in all fields. Guided by his sponsor and friend, Arnaldo Guinle, who judged the political movement favorable also for Villa-Lobos's career and advised him accordingly[40], Villa-Lobos, first intuitively, and later with drive and verve, hoped that the new developments would give him the chance to be instrumental in paving the way to educate the public to understand *his* music, as he was, by that time, at the age of forty-four, by no means, an accepted composer in his own country nor abroad. So he submitted to the government, in a memorandum, his ideas about the musical education of the public. Next, he settled in the then Federal District of Rio de Janeiro to be close to the government, should his ideas be approved to bring the masses via folk music to appreciate art music. This was in 1932. The previous year and while awaiting a government decision, he gave practical proof of his ideas. He began to act on his own. This was a typical quality of his character: He undertook a musical pilgrimage, together with a small group of professional musicians, into São Paulo's hinterland to bring to small towns and villages, deprived of any cultural life, classical music. It was organized in conjunction with the respective towns' municipality. In São Paulo city, however, he demonstrated with a large chorus what could be accomplished if school children and adults were to sing folksongs, children's and civic and patriotic songs. The pragmatically thinking Villa-Lobos was carving out his future. He tried with practical manifestations to convince the authorities. Next he began to furnish the material for such choral singing by setting nursery rhyms and folksongs for one or four voices which eventually were assembled in the collections later to be known as "Guia Prático" (Practical Guide) and "Canto Orfeônico" (Orpheonic Song). The result was not long in coming: Villa-Lobos was nominated Director of Rio de Janeiro's Music Educational Department. The post, previously non-existent in Brazil, was specifically created for him. It involved him in pedagogical and administrative tasks. In both fields he was completely inexperienced. Yet, the results were remarkable, even overwhelming. A proof how his will-power and serendipity unearthed dormant talents. Villa-Lobos, at the age of forty-five, had now, for the first time, a steady job with a fixed salary. His worries to earn his living were over. With this financial background and his usual enthusiasm for the new and progressive — in all fields — he

40 Letter from Arnaldo Guinle to Heitor Villa-Lobos, dated January 7, 1931 (Cf. Lisa M. Peppercorn, *Heitor Villa-Lobos, Leben und Werk des brasilianischen Komponisten*, Zurich, 1972, p. 95).

embarked on the realization of his plans which he accomplished in an incredibly short time, first in Rio de Janeiro, and later, in charge of all of Brazil.

In short succession he first organized a chorus to give demonstrations. Next, he trained future teachers who were to instruct school children, first in Rio de Janeiro – and after he had enough teachers – also in other parts of Brazil. In 1933 he founded the Villa-Lobos-Orchestra, dismantled again the following year for lack of support. With it, and later with other orchestras he gave Brazilian first performances of such works as Bach's Mass in b-minor and Beethoven's "Missa Solemnis". Then he gave choral demonstrations with 10,000 to 35,000 school children each Independence Day (September 7), broadcast throughout Brazil until 1944 which he conducted, clad in flaming colors, from a high platform. Alone the mobilization and logistics of these masses of children, the novelty and uniqueness of such choral singing, not to speak of the tremendous traffic commotion and public health preparations captivated not only thousands of families whose children participated in this heroic effort but also attracted millions of youngsters to Villa-Lobos's pragmatic music educational system. This was exactly what he had planned. He wanted to interest the younger generation, and, if possible, his contemporaries, in music, good music and possibly modern music. The best way was, so Villa-Lobos thought, to lead them from singing folksongs to appreciate serious music. Not enough with these activities, Villa-Lobos, in those years, had invented a special Manisolfa System, based on the Tonic Solfa System to instruct his chorus. The system employs less syllables and more hand signs and can thus serve for any key and any chromatic notes.[41]

By the middle of the thirties, Villa-Lobos had turned into a personality with whom one had to reckon. His bust, made in 1935 by the Argentine sculptor Luís Perlotti, was unveiled at Rio de Janeiro's Municipal Theatre the following year, an honor which only Antônio Francisco Braga before him experienced during his life time. On Villa-Lobos's initiative was founded the *Conservatório Nacional de Cánto Orfeônico* (November 26, 1942)[42] and three years later (July 14, 1945) the *Academia Brasileira de Música*. His compositorial creations, except for choral arrangements, was in those years sparing-

---

41 "Musical Education in Brazil", by Lisa M. Peppercorn, in *Bulletin of the Pan American Union*, 74 (10): 689 - 693, Washington, D.C. 1940. In 1952, Villa-Lobos demonstrated in Tel Aviv, Israel, his Manisolfa System with an ad hoc chorus consisting of pupils and faculty members from the Teachers' Training College during a three-day-visit (June 17 - 19) on the invitation of his old friend Leo Kestenberg (1882 - 1962) whom he had met for the first time in Prague in 1936 during an Educational Congress.

ly, save his now famous "Bachianas Brasileiras". These were, so it seems, a leftover from his Parisian sojourn where the neo-classic, in those days, was en vogue.

Villa-Lobos's activities during this fifteen-year-period also influenced his private life. In 1936, during a trip to Prague, Berlin and Barcelona, he wrote his wife Lucília that he would not return to their Rio de Janeiro home and leave her.[43] Since then they lived separately until his death in 1959. Lucília survived him by six and a half years (May 25, 1966). Villa-Lobos's companion of his last twenty-three years until his death, Arminda Neves d'Almeida, emerged from the younger generation within his music educational environment. She became known under her juridically acquired name of Arminda Villa-Lobos[44]. After Villa-Lobos's death, she was nominated Director of the Museum Villa-Lobos founded in 1960.

Villa-Lobos would have continued his now established life had it not been for the Second World War, or rather the end of it. Fate and providence again swept him off his feet. His stationary, settled life in Rio de Janeiro, interrupted only by short concert appearances in Buenos Aires and Chile, was nearing its end. He had moved in Rio de Janeiro just within one block of streets during those past fifteen years. From his three-room apartment in the Rua Araújo Pôrto Alegre 56 in down-town, he walked around the corner to take his meals in the *Clube Ginástico Português* in the Avenida Graça Aranha. He had to turn just another corner, to the Avenida Almirante Barroso to come to his office and turning yet another corner, he came to the Avenida Rio Branco where, at the Municipal Theatre, he conducted his concerts. All he did, was walk around the block.

During the final fifteen years of his life (1944 - 1959) he was destined to give it all up. In contrast to his stationary life he traveled in his final years constantly from one place to the other, in Europe, the USA, Israel and Latin America. Big events cast their shadows and so did the last change in Villa-Lobos's life. The fall of France in 1940 and the role which the United States was to play during the war, had its repercussion on Brazil, including on the cultural and intellectual life. Turned and tuned towards Europe, particularly towards France, prior to World War II and now practically shut off from Europe during the war, also left its marks on Villa-Lobos. Franklin D. Roose-

42 On September 22, 1967 was founded the *Instituto Villa-Lobos* by the Federal Government to succeed the old *Conservatório Nacional de Canto Orfeônico* in order to train teachers in music education of medium level school children.
43 *Villa-Lobos, Visto da Platéia e na Intimidade 1912 - 1935*, by Luiz Guimarães and collaborators, Rio de Janeiro (n.d.), p. 352.
44 From a letter by Arminda Villa-Lobos to Lisa M. Peppercorn, Rio de Janeiro, September 2, 1970.

velt's Good Neighbor Policy and its cultural exchange programs that went with it brought scholars, artists, orchestras and lecturers to Brazil and Brazilians to the United States. The 1939 World's Fair in New York City drew attention to the arts and culture of countries south of the Rio Grande. English replaced French in Brazil as foreign language spoken by the educated and taught in schools. Villa-Lobos, Latin America's musical exponent of that time, was suddenly lionized by all those who visited Brazil. They spoke French to him or through an interpretor, since he spoke no English then or ever later in his life. He was puzzled at first, since the American mentality and outlook of life was unfamiliar and foreign to him. He was surprised about this sudden interest in his music educational work, more, however, that the visitors and those who approached him directly from the U.S. were interested in his compositions. They wished to play his works in the U.S., also asked him to come and conduct them himself. For a long time he mistrusted all this commotion. Nobody had ever been interested to play his music except when he had fought himself to get it performen.

World War II ended in 1945. Only a few months prior began Villa-Lobos's final fifteen years of his life when, on November 26, 1944, he conducted, for the first time, an American orchestra in Los Angeles. Thus ended the fifteen-year-period of Villa-Lobos's sedentary music educational period and began fifteen years of whirlwind guest appearances everywhere. A lifelong dream came to be fulfilled – at last. Europe in ashes and debris, physically and intellectually, and the United States having emerged from the hollocaust as the greatest economic and cultural post-war power, had caused it all. Villa-Lobos was, this time, not fate's victim, he was, instead, fate's chosen angel. He rode on the crest of the wave that quite unexpectedly swept him to international fame. Curiously enough, nothing of significance had been added by way of composition, except his "Bachianas Brasileiras", since his Parisian days which would have justified this sudden interest in Villa-Lobos's music. His destiny, instead, was shaped by two political events beyond an individual's influence: the 1930 revolution in Brazil and World War II. Had the Almighty thus intended to intercept Villa-Lobos's career as composer to be, for fifteen years (1930 - 1945), an educator and administrator? To let Brazil benefit from Villa-Lobos's unexpected talent in those fields? Or to make Villa-Lobos who never succumbed nor crushed under fate's weight blossom while facing a new challenge?

Now fate struck again and determined Villa-Lobos's life and his career as it had done throughout his life. The unpredicted and unforeseen just happened again without his own doing. Fate asked him once more to be adaptable and with serendipity accept chances and make good use of them. When Villa-Lobos set out on his first trip to the United States, he was completely unsure what would await him except that first concert in Los Angeles and the first honorary degree bestowed on him by the Occidental College in Los Angeles a few days piror to his concert debut. But these two events in California were merely the upbeat of fifteen consecutive years full of triumphs and honors. Whether it was at first due to the American-Brazilian cultural relations policy or right on his own merits, is now a futile speculation. The fact remains that Villa-Lobos had to prove himself as composer-conductor to maintain a gradually extending world-wide fame. And he succeeded. He was wooed and cooed. He conducted all the major orchestras in the U.S. and Europe, Israel and some Latin American countries. He was showered in the U.S. and elsewhere with honors during his final fifteen years of his life. São Paulo commissioned him to write a composition for the fourth centenary celebration of that city. The Vatican and private persons also commissioned him to write works for them. Paris was Villa-Lobos's center in Europe, New York City that in the United States. There, on his seventieth birthday, an editorial appeared in *The New York Times.* Brazil made that year (1957) a Villa-Lobos-Year. São Paulo proclaimed a Villa-Lobos-Week. A Villa-Lobos Museum in Rio de Janeiro was planned but postponed since Villa-Lobos objected to it during his lifetime[45]. He now lived the life he had always envisaged for himself: write and conduct his music. And he wrote in those last fifteen years an astonishingly large number of works for a person his age. Yet, for exceptions, the productivity reminded of mass production, 'more of the same' of previous years. It revealed no late style, no mature style. Success, fame and artistically an enormously rewarding and fulfilled period, those flighting moments of life's blissfullness which fate seemingly offered him during his final fifteen years, were mared by a somewhat melancolic undertone which, in later years, and only occassionally in unguarded moments was noticeable to his companion and some of his close friends. Villa-Lobos knew only too well that his time on earth and this hilarious life which he so much enjoyed was to be cut short perhaps sooner than he had wished for himself.

The year was 1948. Providence had struck again. This time with

45 In 1956 Villa-Lobos objected to project No. 1,588 which Amarylio de Albuquerque, then Director of the Secretariat of the Chamber of Deputies, had launched to establish a Villa-Lobos Museum in Rio de Janeiro. On June 22, 1960 then President Juscelino Kubitschek de Oliveira signed the decree that established the *Museu Villa-Lobos* and Clóvis Salgado, former Brazilian Minister of Education and Culture, signed the enactment on January 20, 1961 which arranged for the organization of the Museum.

uncanny reality from which there was no escape and no serendipity could help. Destiny asked Villa-Lobos to fight again as providence had always asked him to do exactly that, once every fifteen years, during the seventy-two years of his life. Fight some hitherto unknown and meet the new challenge. This time, however, it was a different fight, a moral fight, a battle full of courage against the inevitable end that would prematurely cut off his lifeline. Cancer of the bladder was the doctor's fateful verdict. An operation in New York's Memorial Hospital in July 1948 was successful. Rigorous medical treatment until the end of his life, increasing blood uraemia and overcharged kidneys were the consequences.

Life's short intensely lived happy moments were again accompanied by long durations of defeat and loss in a struggle, God, the Almighty, had granted him for another eleven years. This time Villa-Lobos could not conquer this last stroke of destiny. In the end, death is always the winner. Why just this length of time? Nobody can say. To complete his last fifteen years almost to the exact day? Or did Villa-Lobos realize that his life was made up of fifteen-year-periods, (except his first one which lasted just thirteen years) and the last one was nearing its end? Did he feel that another fifteen years was not carved out for him and his proverbial vitality and will-power would just carry his exhausted and sick body through to the termination of this period? Had Providence forecast that his strength would last until he had reached the end of his last fifteen years just nine days short to be exact, counting from his U.S. debut in 1944 in Los Angeles?

Outside events and circumstances often shape a person's life. Villa-Lobos's was no exception. His was, at any rate, a life where providence and external occurrances moulded him. If these unforeseen circumstances had never happened, his life would probably have taken a different course. Maybe, he would have remained a mediocre composer. It also seems to show that those who grasp the situation, understand the wind of changes, coupled with energy, good health and a God-given natural talent, together with perseverance and a lot of hard work — and some luck — overcome periodic outside changes whose cause is beyond an individual's influence.

RESUMO

A vida do compositor brasileiro, Heitor Villa-Lobos (1887 - 1959), divide-se em períodos de quinze aos cada um, excepto o primeiro, que tem apenas 13 anos. Acontecimentos externos causaram a mudança dum período a outro. O primeiro período (1887 - 1900) abrange a infância e a adolescência. Durante o segundo período

(1900 - 1915), após a morte do pai (em 1899), Villa-Lobos ficou sem recursos financeiros para uma educação formal. Ele se movimentou numa roda de compositores e intérpretes de música popular, e como membro da orquestra do Teatro Municipal no Rio de Janeiro, aprendeu a música erudíta. O terceiro período (1915 - 1930), iniciado pela primeira representação de obras dele, instigou o compositor a dedicar-se definitivamente à música erudíta. Este período marcou os anos mais importantes de sua vida, durante os quais ele criou composições de grande relevo, que, no futuro, contribuiram a faze-lo famoso dentro e fora do Brasil. O quarto período (1930 - 1945), inciado pela revolução no Brasil, está marcado pela nomeação do compositor para o cargo do Superintendente da Educação Musical e Artística do Departamento de Educação da Prefeitura do (então) Distrito Federal, onde exerceu grande influência sobre a vida educacional e musical do Rio de Janeiro. O quinto e ultimo período, que começou pouco antes do fim da Segunda Guerra Mundial, destacou-se da grande fama mundial do Villa-Lobos, alcançada nos EE.UU. e na Europa.

Ibero-Amerikanisches Archiv, **5**(2), 1979, 179–97

Corrigenda

p69 *second paragraph line 6:*
For Goías read Goiás
FN 2, line 3 from bottom:
for regeny read regency
FN 3, line 2:
add date after Dom Pedro I (1798–1834)
line 4:
For April 1, read April 7
p71 *FN8 line 6*:
For calles read called
p73 *FN 17*:
For 1866–1945 read 1863–1946
p74 *line 15*:
For Scheherezade read Sheherezada
p75 *second paragraph line 4*:
delete bracket after 1915
FN 23, line 3:
For 1924 read 1921

p76 *second paragraph line 11*:
For Andrade Almeida read Andrade e Almeida
FN 25 line 10:
For Lígua read Língua
line 11:
For esthetics read aesthetics
FN 27:
For born 1895 read 1895–1981
p77 *third paragraph line 5*:
For Edgar read Edgard
FN 30:
For Andrade Almeida read Andrade e Almeida
p78 *FN 34 line 4*:
For Goías read Goiás
FN 35 line 4:
For 1920 read 1820
FN 36 line 1:
For in 1557 when he accompanied, read in 1556 where he joined
line 2:
for 1570 read 1575
FN 37 line 5:
For Chôrus read Chôros
p84 *end of first paragraph*:
For performen read performed
p85 *FN 45 line 5*:
For Clóvis Salgado read Clóvis Salgado da Gama

Villa-Lobos's Last Years

Villa-Lobos was 57 when, in the autumn of 1944, his career reached the stage of concertizing in the United States; thereafter he went there every year until his death in 1959. On that first occasion he made his *début* not in the great cultural centres of the eastern seaboard but with the Janssen Symphony of Los Angeles in the sunny, more relaxed atmosphere of California. There was a good reason for this. Villa-Lobos and Janssen had got to know and like each other during the second World War, when the latter gave some guest performances in Rio de Janeiro, presenting a Sibelius symphony to the Brazilian public for the first time. It was natural, therefore, that Janssen should invite Villa-Lobos to Los Angeles to conduct his orchestra. Not that this first concert in North America was well attended:

> Heitor Villa-Lobos, Brazil's gift to the musical world, conducted the Janssen Symphony Orchestra in a program of his own works Sunday afternoon, November 26, 1944, in the Philharmonic Auditorium before an audience that only partly filled the room, much smaller than the important standing of the South American composer might have been expected to draw. The program included his *Symphony No. 2*, *Chôros No. 6* and *Rudepoema*.[1]

At the close the audience expressed its gratitude to the composer it was meeting for the first time. Stravinsky, then resident in Los Angeles, was among those who visited him in the artists' room; the two had known and esteemed each other in the Paris of the '20s and never met since, Villa-Lobos not having revisited Paris after his return to Rio de Janeiro in 1930, and the second World War having driven Stravinsky to the United States.

The hospitality Villa-Lobos enjoyed in Los Angeles, thanks to Janssen's invitation, included that of the Southern California Council of Inter-American Affairs. Receptions were held and honours bestowed. Thus, at the suggestion of Raymond G. McKelvey, Professor of Political Science at the Occidental College and Executive Director of the Southern California Council, on 21st November—a few days before his first concert—the Occidental College honoured him with the award of an honorary Doctorate in Law; the Professor of the Music Department, Walter E. Hartley, introduced him, and the President of the College, Dr. Remsen Bird, conferred the distinction; Erico Veríssimo, who was spending a few days in Los Angeles before returning to the University of California at Berkeley, where he was lecturing on Brazilian literature, acted as

---

[1] *Pacific Coast Musician*, Los Angeles, 2nd December, 1944.

interpreter (the composer did not speak English). Unlike the Philharmonic Auditorium on the occasion of his *début*, the College was

> filled to capacity . . . for the ceremony. Werner Janssen made an address on the life and works of the distinguished South American. As a compliment to Villa-Lobos the London String Quartet played his *Third String Quartet* and the Glee Club of Occidental College sang his *Canção da Saudade* . . . .[2]

In December, Villa-Lobos travelled to New York. Not being immediately involved in concert-giving, in the following January he composed there the Fantasy for cello and orchestra.[3] The work was suggested by Walter Burle Marx, the Brazilian composer and conductor, who, for some years, had been living in Philadelphia. (Burle Marx had once before—in 1932—initiated a composition of Villa-Lobos: the *Caixinha de Bôas Festas*, which Burle Marx had performed at one of the Youth Concerts given in Rio de Janeiro by the Philharmonic Orchestra founded by him.) In New York Villa-Lobos now met Olin Downes, at that time music critic of *The New York Times*, who thought highly of his music. Downes's interest had been aroused by several works—amongst them *Chôros* no. 10, which had been performed at concerts of Brazilian music given in New York, at the World's Fair, on 4th and 9th May, 1939.[4] This interest had been renewed by a festival of Brazilian music held in New York's Museum of Modern Art in the autumn of 1940. The President of the Museum at that time was Nelson Rockefeller (1909–1979), whom Franklin D. Roosevelt had appointed Co-ordinator of Inter-American Commercial and Cultural Affairs and who, in the interests of "good neighbour" policy, had promoted the festival with help from Armando Vidal, Brazilian General Commissioner at the World's Fair. Between 16th and 20th October, three concerts, each repeated at a matinée, were given in the Museum's auditorium, the first two containing and the final one consisting entirely of works by Villa-Lobos as the outstanding representative of contemporary Brazilian music. The festival of Brazilian music was held in conjunction with an exhibition of paintings by Cândido Portinari, opened on 9th October. Numerous prominent figures in Brazilian and, especially, North American circles had patronized and promoted these undertakings.

At that festival, the directors of which had been Burle Marx and Hugh Ross (the head of the Schola Cantorum of New York, an old friend of Villa-Lobos and an experienced interpreter), a number of the composer's works had had their first hearing in the United States: *Chôros* nos. 2, 4 and 7; the *Nonetto*; three pieces for violin: the second movement (*Serenidade*) of the *Fantasia de movimentos mixtos;* *O Canto do Cisne Negro;* and the third number (*A maripôsa na luz*) of *O martírio dos insetos*. *Rudepoema*,* dedicated to Artur Rubinstein and on this

---

[2] *Ibid.* (The *Canção da Saudade* is a four-part choral work to words by Sodré Viana. Composed in 1933, it was first performed in Rio de Janeiro on 10th October that year. It is published in the pedagogic song-collection *Canto Orfeônico*, Vol. II.)

[3] Villa-Lobos conducted the first performance, in Rio de Janeiro, on 8th October, 1946. The soloist was the Brazilian cellist Iberê Gomes Grosso, the orchestra that of the Teatro Municipal.

occasion played by him, along with other pieces, was receiving its first performance in New York, as was the *Bachianas brasileiras* no. 1, for eight violoncellos. Already given in New York, the *Bachianas brasileiras* no. 5 was again given here in its still incomplete form of a single piece, *Aria (Cantilena)*. Hugh Ross and members of the Schola Cantorum also performed some Brazilian folk-songs set by Villa-Lobos for unaccompanied choir.

At the end of 1944, Olin Downes had expressed the hope that not only Los Angeles but also New York and other American cities would have the chance of hearing Villa-Lobos's music:

> His works merit special attention. Although we have not yet had the opportunity
> to evaluate his enormous output in its entirety, there is no doubt that Heitor Villa-
> Lobos is one of the great figures of contemporary music.[5]

Now, as never before, New York was given that opportunity! On Sunday evening, 28th January, 1945, in the auditorium of the Museum of Modern Art, the League of Composers arranged a concert of his chamber music, skilfully designed to present a balanced view of Villa-Lobos's many-sided art; the composer attended. First, the *Chôros bis* for violin and cello; then a group of short piano pieces: *As três Marias*, two numbers from *Cirandas* and the *Dança do Indio Branco* from the *Ciclo brasileiro;* then a group of five songs performed by the Brazilian artist Olga Coelho: *Canção do Marinheiro* and *Lundú da Marquesa de Santos* from the first volume of *Modinhas e Canções* (neither of which New York had heard before) and three of the *Serestas* songs. The piano Trio no. 2 rounded off the concert. Afterwards, a reception for Villa-Lobos was held in the foyer.

Shortly after—on 8th and 9th February—Villa-Lobos made his first public appearances in New York, conducting his *Chôros* nos. 8 and 9 in two concerts at which the other works were conducted by Artur Rodzinski. On 21st, 22nd and 23rd of the same month he appeared as guest conductor of the Boston Symphony Orchestra at the invitation of Koussevitzky. His next date was 27th February in Chicago, where the Department of Music at the University was giving a winter season of so-called "Composers' Concerts" directed by Remi Gassmann. The third concert of the series, held in the Mandel Assembly Hall of the University, consisted entirely of works by Villa-Lobos: *Quatuor* of 1921, *Bachianas brasileiras* no. 1, the piano Trio no. 3 and *Chôros* no. 7. The composer himself conducted, with members of the Chicago Symphony Orchestra participating, together with women's voices from the University of Chicago Choir under the direction of Gerhard Schroth. Finally, on 14th March, Villa-Lobos's *Rudepoema*, which the composer had introduced to Boston, together

---

[4] *The New York Times*, 14th May, 1939.
[*] This is the same work as the orchestral *Rudepoema* referred to in the quotation from *Pacific Coast Musician* made on the first page of Mrs. Peppercorn's article. Originally a piano piece, it was orchestrated by the composer at a later date. (Ed.)
[5] *The New York Times*, 17th December, 1944.

with *Chôros* no. 12, during his visit to that city the previous month, was included in a concert given at New York's Carnegie Hall by the Boston Symphony Orchestra under the baton of Koussevitzky.   Thereafter, a big reception in Villa-Lobos's honour was held in the Waldorf Astoria Hotel and attended by distinguished musical figures and other prominent personalities.

The consequence of his first visit to the United States was that Villa-Lobos was suddenly catapulted into the position of celebrated composer of international stature.   Eighteen years ago in Paris, he himself had had to organize his concerts with the aid of Brazilian patrons; and in Brazil he himself had always had to move heaven and earth to create opportunities to conduct his work.   Now, he was being invited by the most famous American orchestras and universities; now, important periodicals were concerning themselves with his music; now, it was being established that he was a great composer whose works should be heard, published and made available on gramophone records.

Villa-Lobos returned to Brazil very much satisfied with his reception in the United States.   The direct, open-hearted character of the people and the high cultural *niveau* had surprised and touched him, and the widespread interest of people of all ages in music—and this included modern music—deeply moved him.   He realized how wide of the mark his preconceptions had been: he had been welcomed with a readiness and sympathy he had never dreamt of.

Very soon he began—intuitively or deliberately—to compose with the United States in mind.   In the past, the outside world had often influenced him —indeed, external elements had affected his style of composition and the course of his career so overwhelmingly that it was largely because of them that he acquired the personality that stamps him today.   In the Paris of the '20s a South American composer could make his name only by supplying characteristically South American music: therefore, instead of writing in a traditional style, he had composed his *Chôros*, *Serestas* and, later, the *Bachianas brasileiras* and pseudo-folkloristic music.   In the Brazil of the early '30s, the upsurge of national consciousness under the presidency of Getúlio Dornellas Vargas had inspired him to revolutionize the teaching of music in the Brazilian state schools.   He took over the post of Superintendent, invented a pedagogic system and made choral arrangements of Brazilian nursery and folk-songs. Both of these external elements—the Paris of the '20s and the Brazil of the '30s—had proved fruitful: he had composed music of a unique character and had created an unrivalled system of music education.   He was not likely, therefore, to have been unaffected by his first experience of the United States.

Villa-Lobos at that time was in his late 50s and had composed many works of different kinds from which to choose his programmes.   For his *début* in Los Angeles he had chosen works so diverse as the Symphony no. 2, *Rudepoema* and *Chôros* no. 6.   Perhaps he did so in order to discover which type was most likely to succeed.   Perhaps, later, he unconsciously made concessions to the public; perhaps he had in mind the conservatism of American orchestras and concert agents; perhaps he felt that it was time to distance himself from the nationalism of his previous period. Whatever the reason, the striking fact remains that after his first visit to the United States he tended more and more to return to traditional musical forms and ended by completely doing so.

Four years before that visit he had completed music for a ballet based on a legend of the Indians living by the river Solimões in the Amazon region: *Mandú-Çarará* for orchestra and choirs of men, women and children.[6]   In that same year, 1940, Leopold Stokowski, an old friend of his Paris days, had toured South America with the All-American Youth Orchestra; Stokowski was looking for performances of Brazilian popular and folk-music to be recorded for the world's leading libraries; Villa-Lobos, returning from a guest performance in Montevideo, had visited him in Rio de Janeiro and thrown himself enthusiastically into the task of helping him to select the music and the performing-groups.   In 1941 Villa-Lobos had orchestrated *Bachianas brasileiras* no. 4, which, on 15th July, the following year, was performed in Rio de Janeiro under his baton.   It was in 1942 that he also composed *Bachianas brasileiras* no. 7 for orchestra, the first performance of which took place two years later—on 13th March, 1944—again under his baton.   In 1942 he had also been much involved in preparations for performances of his latest *Chôros* in Rio de Janeiro —no. 6 (on 18th July) and nos. 9 and 11 (on 15th July).[7]   In 1944 he wrote another *Bachianas brasileiras*—no. 8, for orchestra, which the Accademia di St. Cecilia of Rome was to perform, three years later, on 6th August, 1947;[8] and while he was in New York in 1945 he completed yet another—no. 9, for string orchestra or unaccompanied choir, which was first performed under the Brazilian conductor, Eleazar de Carvalho, on 17th November, 1948.   It is as though, with this last of the *Bachianas brasileiras*, he wished to finish off as quickly as possible the whole series and a whole period.

From 1944 onwards, as his thoughts turned more and more to the United States, the tendency to return to traditional forms increased.   In 1944 he had written the string Quartet no. 8 (brought out by the Iacovino Quartet in Rio de Janeiro on 5th September, 1946); in 1945 he composed his Symphony no. 7, which he entitled *Odisséia da Paz (Odyssey of Peace)* to celebrate the ending of the second World War.[9]   That year also saw a new work for piano and orchestra that was neither a *Chôros* nor a *Bachianas brasileiras* but simply entitled Concerto no. 1 for piano and orchestra.   Presumably he had had his fill of composing *Chôros* and *Bachianas brasileiras*—he had written fourteen of the

---

[6] Villa-Lobos conducted the first performance in Rio de Janeiro on 10th November, 1946, with the orchestra and choir of the Teatro Municipal and the Orfeão Artístico do Colégio Pedro II. A version for two pianos, percussion, full choir and children's choir was given in New York at the Carnegie Hall on 23rd January, 1948.   The Schola Cantorum, under the direction of Hugh Ross, and the Girls' Ensemble of the High School of Music and Art took part.   The pianists were Pierre Luboshutz and Genia Nemènoff.

[7] Lisa M. Peppercorn, "New Villa-Lobos Works", *The New York Times*, 11th October, 1942.

[8] The Brazilian first performance was given on 30th December, 1948 at a concert consisting entirely of works by Villa-Lobos.   On this occasion, the composer was presented with an ivory baton.   (Andrade Muricy, "Villa-Lobos, Músico Brasileiro", *Presença de Villa-Lobos*, Vol. VII, Museu Villa-Lobos, Rio de Janeiro, 1972.)

one[9a] and nine of the other. Be that as it may, the Concerto had been commissioned by the Canadian pianist Ellen Ballon, who performed it on 10th November, the following year, with the orchestra of the Teatro Municipal of Rio de Janeiro under his baton.[9b] 1945 also saw the symphonic poem *Madona*, commissioned by the Koussevitzky Music Foundation, dedicated to Natalie Koussevitzky[10] and first performed in the Symphony Hall of Boston on 26th (and 27th) December, 1947. He had received commissions before, but this one was the first of a whole long series. Among other things he also wrote the string Quartet no. 9 in 1945. That year he was also involved in something quite different: he initiated the founding of a Brazilian Academy for Music, its members to consist of the country's outstanding composers and musicologists, for the promotion of Brazilian music. He became its first President.

The conclusion of the war meant that Europe was now open to Villa-Lobos; in 1947 he went to Rome; but at this period it was still to the United States that he felt drawn. Thus, early in 1947—on 19th February—he conducted in New York the first performance there of *Bachianas brasileiras* no. 3 (composed in 1938) by the orchestra of the Columbia Broadcasting System with the Brazilian pianist José Vieira Brandão. He was, furthermore, commissioned by E. Lester, President of the Los Angeles Civic Light Opera Association, to compose an operetta *Magdalena*, which was produced in Los Angeles on 26th July, the following year. The receipts from this rather banal piece helped to defray the expenses of an operation he had to undergo in New York, in which city the piece was brought out at the Ziegfield Theatre on 15th November. Thereby hangs a rather amusing tale. Before the actual New York performances various alterations had been made necessitating some drastic alterations to the score. Reporting these, his friend Hugh Ross remembered his saying angrily: "At the first performance I shall stand up in my box and say: 'People of New York, this is not my music!'". Ross continued: "He did not actually do so because most unfortunately he was in hospital at the time".[11]

The year 1948 began well, for it was then that his busy round of concert-giving, hitherto restricted to Brazil and North America, began to include Europe. In the spring he was in Paris and Rome and also in London, whither he had been invited by the British Council. Then, feeling ill, he returned to Brazil; a serious disorder was diagnosed; he was advised to go to New York as

---

[9] The first performance was given in London, on 26th March, 1949, by the B.B.C. Symphony Orchestra conducted by Villa-Lobos.

[9a] There are also *Chôros bis* for violin and cello and the *Introdução aos Chôros* for guitar and orchestra, both belonging to Villa-Lobos's Paris period of the '20s.

[9b] Arminda Villa-Lobos, Director of the Villa-Lobos Museum in Rio de Janeiro, confirmed this date to me in her letter of 6th December, 1972. The catalogue *Villa-Lobos—Sua Obra* (2nd edition, 1974), published by the Villa-Lobos Museum, gives the date 11th October, 1946.

[10] Natalie Koussevitzky (*née* Ouchkoff) was Koussevitzky's first wife. They were married on 8th September, 1905. After her death Koussevitzky married her niece, Olga, who, on her husband's death in 1951, succeeded him as President of the Koussevitzky Foundation in New York and remained in that office until her death, at the age of 76, on 5th January, 1978.

[11] Letter from Hugh Ross to Lisa M. Peppercorn, New York City, 16th October, 1973.

quickly as possible for the best medical treatment. On 9th July he was received at the Memorial Hospital to be operated on for cancer of the bladder. The surgeon was Dr. Victor Marshall and the operation, involving removal of the bladder, successful. For another eleven years—albeit under constant medical treatment—Villa-Lobos was able to lead an active creative life.

In the ensuing years he visited the United States even more frequently, conducting performances of his works by leading orchestras of capital cities or attending their performance by conductors of international repute. In Europe, too, where he was held in the same high esteem, he conducted his works in capital cities, and both there and in America either made or supervised the making of records with leading artists. As he was a man of tireless energy, the rest of his time he devoted to composition. The operation appears to have done nothing to diminish his busy career as a conductor—but it did have perceptible effects upon the compositions of his later years: most, though not all, bear witness to a decline of creative power.

That Villa Lobos in these last years conducted so much and was nevertheless still capable of producing numerous new works, some of them very demanding, was largely due to his temperament and attitude to life. He was a jovial character, blessed with vitality and *joie de vivre*, a lover of his fellow-men and especially fond of children. During his convalescence in the Memorial Hospital he showed what a sense of humour he had and how he could laugh at himself. On his sick-bed shortly after the operation he composed an *Ave Maria* for six voices, and as soon as his strength allowed he resumed his travels as conductor. And, when he was hospitalized in New York again in 1950, he composed on his sick-bed the string Quartet no. 12, which was performed in New York on 11th March, 1951.

In 1952 Villa-Lobos made Paris his headquarters in Europe. When he was there twenty-five years before he took rooms; now he stayed at the Hotel Bedford in the Rue de l'Arcade, where Pedro II, the last Emperor of Brazil, had stayed in the closing years of the nineteenth century. Since he travelled in Europe far more than he had done in the '20s, hotel life suited him: he kept his room on even when he was away, and into it was put the writing-desk Pedro II had used—for Villa-Lobos a reminder of Brazil, a link between Paris and his homeland. Until his death seven years later this hotel served as his European home—so much so that in 1971, on Villa-Lobos's birthday (5th March), on the initiative of the Brazilian Ambassador, General Aurélio Lyra Tavares, a memorial tablet was affixed to the building, upon which was engraved: "The Brazilian composer, Heitor Villa-Lobos, great interpreter of the spirit of his country, stayed at this hotel from 1952 to 1959". The same façade also contains a memorial tablet to Pedro II.

In 1952, apart from travels within Europe, not to mention trips to Brazil, guest performances in Buenos Aires and stays in North America, there was a visit to Israel. He stayed there three days, from 17th to 19th June. On 18th June he conducted the Israel Philharmonic in the following programme:

Corelli's *Concerto grosso* no. 8; his own orchestral version of Bach's organ Prelude and Fugue in C minor (no. 6); his Concerto no. 2 for piano and orchestra (with the pianist Maxim Shapiro); and, to finish with, his *Chôros* no. 6.   He met his friend Leo Kestenberg, whom he had first met in 1936 at the first International Congress for Musical Education at Prague and who was now the director of a music teachers' training college in Tel Aviv.   Kestenberg invited him to lecture to the staff and students on his "Manisolfa" system and Villa-Lobos assembled a chorus of some students in order to give a practical demonstration of his method.   The country and the people inspired a symphonic poem, *Odisséia de una Raça (Odyssey of a Race)*, which he composed in Rio de Janeiro in September, 1953.   He dedicated the work to the State of Israel and ceded his composer's rights to a fund to be designated by the Israeli Minister for Education and Culture.   A few months later—on 30th May, 1954—the Israel Philharmonic Orchestra under Michael Taube gave the work its first performance at the twenty-eighth festival of the International Society for Contemporary Music, held in Haifa.

The period after Villa-Lobos's discharge from the New York Memorial Hospital was one of enormous productivity.   The series of string quartets reached the number of seventeen and that of symphonies the number of twelve.[12] He also wrote a great deal else, including works for solo instrument and orchestra commissioned and performed by artists of the day.   It is difficult to decide whether all this productivity was the result of genuine creative impulse or of the need to make money to cover the costs of medical treatment: the very considerable expenses of his illness had eaten into his savings.   Many friends, the Brazilian authorities and, later, even the Vatican came to his help, moved by reverence for a great master and by admiration for his moral courage in continuing, despite severe physical suffering, to create fresh works and to lead the arduous peripatetic life of a conductor.

Commissions of many kinds poured in.   One was for the Concerto for guitar and orchestra, written in 1951 and first performed by his friend Andrés Segovia, with the Houston Symphony Orchestra, on 6th February, 1956 under his baton.   Another was for the Concerto no. 4 for piano and orchestra, composed partly in Paris, partly in New York, for the Brazilian pianist Bernardo Segall, who, under Villa-Lobos's baton, gave it its first performances, with the Pittsburgh Symphony Orchestra, on 9th and 11th January, 1953.   Commissioned also was the Symphony no. 10, entitled *Sumé Pater Patrium*, composed in 1952.   For this monumental work for solo, mixed choir and orchestra, written to celebrate the four-hundreth anniversary of the city of São Paulo, Villa-Lobos

---

[12] Symphony no. 9, composed in 1952, was first performed during a South American tour made by Eugene Ormandy with the Philadelphia Orchestra in 1966.   This took place at Caracas on 16th May.   Other performances followed in Brazil: in Rio de Janeiro (18th May), in São Paulo (20th May) and in Pôrto Alegre (23rd May).

[13] The first performance had already been given on 4th April, 1957 in Paris by the Orchestre National et Chœur de la Radiodiffusion Française, the composer conducting.

used verses from the *De Beate Virgine* of the Jesuit father José de Anchieta, who, in the sixteenth century, lived in Brazil and exercised a great influence there.   In the presence of the composer, João de Souza Lima conducted the first Brazilian performance[13] in São Paulo as part of the celebrations arranged by the city's cultural administration in honour of the composer's 70th birthday.

To continue the record of commissions: those of 1953 included, *inter alia*, the *Fantasia concertante* for piano, clarinet and bassoon, written for the American pianist Eugene List but not given its first performance until 19th November, 1968—nine years after Villa-Lobos's death—when it was played in Rio de Janeiro.   Another commissioned work was the Concerto for harp and orchestra, written for his friend Nicanor Zabaleta and first performed, with the Philadelphia Orchestra, on 14th, 15th and 17th January, 1955, the composer conducting.[14]   Again, it was in 1953 that the Louisville Orchestra inspired him to write the symphonic poem *Alvorado na Floresta Tropical* (*Dawn in a Tropical Forest*)—first performed by that orchestra, under Robert Whitney, on 23rd January, 1954—and in 1953 also that he composed his string Quartet no. 14 for the Stanley Quartet—first performed on 14th August, 1954—and the second cello Concerto[15] for Aldo Parisot, the Brazilian cellist.   In 1954 he composed—in six weeks—the Concerto no. 5[16] for the Polish-born Brazilian pianist Felicja Blumental and also the string Quartet no. 15, commissioned by Janet Collins and brought out by the Juilliard Quartet in Washington on 19th April, 1958. In 1955 the Symphony no. 11,[17] commissioned by the Boston Symphony Orchestra and the Koussevitzky Foundation, was first on the list of completed commissions.   Those of that year included the Concerto for harmonica and orchestra written for the harmonica virtuoso, John Sebastián.[18]

Not that commissioned works were the only ones Villa-Lobos composed in those years.   He composed many others and, despite the round of concert engagements and studio recordings, gave lectures.   In those years his attitude to composing changed—that at least is the impression one gets.   Perhaps he had the feeling that his days were numbered—that he would not live to experience

---

[14] At that concert, Symphony no. 8, composed in 1950, also received its first performance. The programme was repeated in New York (18th January), Washington, D.C. (25th January) and Baltimore (26th January).

[15] First performed, on 5th February, 1955, by Aldo Parisot with the New York Philharmonic-Symphony Orchestra under Walter Hendl.

[16] First performed, on 8th May, 1955, by Felicja Blumental and the London Philharmonic Orchestra under Jean Martinon at the Royal Festival Hall, London.

[17] Villa-Lobos conducted the first performances, given by the Boston Symphony Orchestra on 2nd and 3rd March, 1956.   The work was commissioned to celebrate the orchestra's 75th anniversary and is dedicated "To the memory of Serge and Natalie Koussevitzky".

[18] The Brazilian musicologist, Luiz Heitor Corrêa de Azevedo, who spent many years in Paris as an important member of the Conseil International de Musique of UNESCO, relates that in Paris he saw a drawing made by John Sebastián for the composer in order to demonstrate the possibilities of the instrument—a drawing revealing an unusually wide register and combinations (*Presença de Villa-Lobos*, Vol. II, Museu Villa-Lobos, Rio de Janeiro, 1966).

[19] Limón was born in Culiacan, Sinalco on 12th January, 1908 and died of cancer in Flemington, New Jersey on 2nd December, 1972.

the performance of many of his works. Perhaps because he had already composed such an enormous amount, he felt he could afford to take a philosophic view and be content to execute the many commissions he received simply because he needed the money. Perhaps his ability to write music of any kind at any given time in any circumstances, pleasant or unpleasant, made him feel that composing was an everyday thing like writing a letter. Hence, maybe, that famous, oft-quoted remark of his made in those years: "I regard my works as letters addressed to posterity requiring no answer".

In the years 1955 and 1956 Villa-Lobos returned to the United States and spent a longer time there. He met Basil Langton, the organizer of the Empire State Music Festival, which, in conjunction with John Brownlee and Frank Forest, he had just inaugurated; Langton commissioned music for a ballet, *The Emperor Jones*, Eugene O'Neill's play of that name, for the Mexican-born dancer and choreographer, José Arcadio Limón.[19] On 12th (and 14th) July, 1956, at Ellenville, N.Y., the ballet was performed by José Limón and his troupe, with Lucas Hoving; the orchestra, "The Symphony of the Air" (originally the orchestra of the N.B.C. under Toscanini), was conducted by Villa-Lobos.[20] Afterwards, Limón performed the ballet in many parts of the world with considerable success.[21]

After the *première* of *The Emperor Jones* Langton proposed that Villa-Lobos write for the Empire State Music Festival an opera on the theme of Macbeth enacted in a Brazilian setting. Villa-Lobos, however, had already accepted the offer of another opera; he had received the commission from Hugh Ross, one of his earliest American admirers (Ross had performed *Chôros* no. 10 on 15th January, 1930 in New York long before the composer was acclaimed in the United States), and John Blankenship, the director of the drama department of the Sarah Lawrence College in Bronxville, N.Y.;[21a] early in the '50s Blankenship had had the idea of Federico García Lorcas's play, *Yerma, the Unfruitful*, as a subject for an opera by Villa-Lobos and he accordingly requested his friend, Hugh Ross, to sound the composer out. It was planned to have the play translated by Ross and the English poet, Alastair Reid, but Villa-Lobos could not wait: he procured the Spanish original from the nearest bookshop in New York and forthwith plunged into the composition, which he finished in Paris the following year. It was not only that a libretto in the language of the original would be more in the spirit of the work: he had no knowledge of English. (The

---

[20] In the second half of the programme, Villa-Lobos conducted his *Alvorado na Floresta Tropical*, his piano Concerto no. 4 (soloist: Bernardo Segall) and other works of his own.

[21] The ballet music was given its first concert performance in Rio de Janeiro on 17th November, 1972. It was played at the annual Villa-Lobos Festival by the orchestra of the Teatro Municipal conducted by László Halász.

[21a] Leopold Stokowski, also a friend of Villa-Lobos since their Paris days in the '20s, performed the orchestrated *Danças características africanas* with the Philadelphia Orchestra on 23rd and 24th November, 1928 in Philadelphia and on 27th November at Carnegie Hall, New York City. These were the first occasions, presumably, on which United States audiences heard a work of the Brazilian composer.

only words he knew were "vanilla ice-cream" and "strong, strong coffee"—
words that he often used whilst in America.)

Hugh Ross describes how he visited Villa-Lobos one day at his New York
hotel and asked how the composition was going:

> . . . he answered 'there is the score', pointing to a big sheaf of manuscript paper on his
> table. I opened it and discovered to my amazement page after page with all the clefs
> and bar lines with time signature, but no notes! So he had it all in his head but he had
> not written it down yet.[22]

Blankenship planned to have a Negro cast and, to this end, directly after the
completion of the score Ross arranged to have excerpts performed and recorded
to enable Villa-Lobos to select singers for the principal parts; Ross presented
Betty Allen and Adele Addison and also, for the final scene, some members of
his own choir at Tanglewood.[23] Writing for the stage was not one of Villa-
Lobos's favourite occupations; nevertheless, when it was eventually performed,
fifteen years later, the opera had a remarkable success with the public. Basil
Langton was the man responsible. He had shown the score to Covent Garden
and Sadler's Wells, who had been interested but insisted on a translation into
English; other European cities wanted a translation into German. Langton
was determined to have it brought out in the original Spanish, and finally he
succeeded: on 12th (and 18th) August, 1971, with the Spanish singer, Mirna
Lacambra in the title-role, the opera was performed by the Santa Fe Opera in
Santa Fe's open-air theatre. Hugh Ross reports how a last-minute obstacle
was overcome:

> Due to the fact that I was the only possessor of a full score and vocal score of *Yerma*
> other than those in the possession of Villa-Lobos' legal executor, or copies in Brazil, it
> was only my copies that were available for presentation to prospective performing
> organizations. It was my friend Basil Langton who finally secured the interest of
> Gaddes, and with some aid from the Sullivan Foundation, which I direct, Santa Fe
> agreed to buy the rights from the organization *Music Now*, which at that time held the
> option on the first performance.[24]

Basil Langton was the producer, José Limón the choreographer and the 24-year-
old Californian, Christopher Keene, the conductor of that first performance of
Yerma. The house was sold out and the work well received despite—or
perhaps thanks to—certain reminiscences of Puccini. "It's a piece much like
Turandot—polytonal Puccini"[25] the conductor said; and this was a view
expressed by many of the critics.

In 1956 it began to be increasingly felt in Brazil that Villa-Lobos was not

[22] From a letter to Lisa M. Peppercorn, 16th October, 1973, New York City.
[23] From the unedited transcript of an interview: Arminda Villa-Lobos, Hugh Ross and Richard
Gaddes (Artistic Administrator of the Santa Fe Opera Company) on 31st March, 1971 in New
York City. The transcript was made available by the Santa Fe Opera Company, New Mexico.
[24] Letter to Lisa M. Peppercorn, 16th October, 1973, New York City.
[25] *Newsweek*, New York City, 23rd August, 1971.
[26] Clóvis Salgado da Gama, "O Museu Villa-Lobos, Sua História e Perspectiva", *Presença de
Villa-Lobos*, Vol. VI, Museu Villa-Lobos, Rio de Janeiro, 1971.

receiving there the recognition he deserved as the composer honoured abroad as the country's most important composer. The idea of founding a Villa-Lobos Museum was mooted by, among others, the director of the secretariat of the Chamber of Deputies, Amarylio de Albuquerque. As he put it in a speech delivered in Rio de Janeiro on 4th November, 1970, there was a bad conscience about "the lack of interest that surrounds Villa-Lobos in Brazil". So in 1956 "Project No. I. 588 concerning a Villa-Lobos Museum" was circulated in the Chamber. But when Villa-Lobos heard of it he rebelled against the idea:

> A museum is for the dead and I'm still alive. It's as though they want to make an archive out of me, as though they think I'm incapable of anything more. Well, they're wrong. I feel stronger than ever and have no lack of inspiration for more works. My *métier*, my life, my joy is to make music—not a museum.[26]

This opposition of Villa-Lobos, together with other obstacles, led to the postponement of the project. But not for long. On 13th June, 1960, a few months after Villa-Lobos's death, Clóvis Salgado da Gama, the Minister for Education and Culture, took the initiative and put to the President of the Republic the proposal of founding a Villa-Lobos Museum. On 22nd June, President Juscelino Kubitschek signed a decree and, on 20th January, the following year, Salgado da Gama an executive order for the organization of the Museum. Arminda Neves d'Almeida, with whom Villa-Lobos had lived for many years, was appointed Director. Much younger than he, she had been his pupil and was a member of the circle that had formed around him in the '30s when he was active as a teacher in Rio de Janeiro. He had separated from his wife, Lucília, on 28th May, 1936;[27] she died six and a half years after his death; Arminda Neves d'Almeida then changed her name by deed-poll to Villa-Lobos.[27a]

In 1957 Villa-Lobos completed his Symphony no. 12[28] and then turned once again to chamber music. He produced the *Duo* for oboe and bassoon, first performed, ten years later, on 19th November, 1967, and the *Quinteto instrumental* for the unusual combination of flute, harp, violin, viola and cello. In his old age he once again demonstrated his mastery of fresh combinations—indeed, his ability to create original effects of tone colour was one of the most significant aspects of his art. The *Quinteto instrumental* was first given, on 16th November, 1962, in Rio de Janeiro at the Villa-Lobos Festival.[29] Villa-Lobos also wrote his string Quartet no. 17, destined to be his last.[30] (A no. 18, he has told us,

---

[27] Letter of 28th May, 1936 from Villa-Lobos to Lucília, from Berlin, published in facsimile in Luiz Guimarães, *Villa-Lobos, Visto da Platéia e na Intimidade 1912/1935,* Rio de Janeiro, 1972.
[27a] Letter from Arminda Villa-Lobos to Lisa M. Peppercorn, Rio de Janeiro, 2nd September, 1970.
[28] First performed by the National Symphony Orchestra under Howard Mitchell, on 20th April, 1958, at the first Inter-American Music Festival.
[29] In 1961, the Villa-Lobos Museum instituted a yearly Villa-Lobos Festival in November, the month of the composer's death. Concerts, lectures and competitions were organized and records and books displayed.
[30] First performed by the Budapest String Quartet in Washington on 16th October, 1959.

was conceived, but it was never written down.)

Villa-Lobos had now reached the age of 70. *The New York Times* congratulated him in a leading article[31] and on that same day (4th March, 1957) he was honoured at the Town Hall: Abe Stark, the President of the City Council, handed him a scroll signed by Robert F. Wagner, Jr., the Mayor. The text ran:

> Senhor Villa-Lobos has rendered "distinguished and exceptional service" in promoting cultural relations between the people of the Americas.[32]

Three weeks later (on 26th March) he appeared on the N.B.C. television programme *Tonight! America after Dark*, answering questions about his compositions and his handling of Brazilian instruments. At that ceremony at the Town Hall Villa-Lobos had already demonstrated these instruments and talked about them. "Existing systems of notation" he had said (he spoke in Portuguese and French[33]) "are incapable of transcribing the range of subtle effects these percussion instruments can create". In his view, the difficulty could be overcome only by the composer himself showing players how to handle them. Two days after his appearance on television he conducted the Philharmonic-Symphony Orchestra in his *Bachianas brasileiras* no. 1 for eight cellos, in his *Chôros* no. 6 and in the first New York performance of *Mandú-Çarará* with the participation of the Schola Cantorum under Hugh Ross and the Girls' Chorus of the High School of Music and Art under Chester Coleman.

When he returned to Brazil, his 70th birthday was celebrated after the event. He was made an honorary citizen of São Paulo, and in that city, from 23rd to 28th September, a festival—a "Villa-Lobos Week"—took place consisting of lectures, concerts and other celebrations. Furthermore, the Ministry of Education and Culture declared 1957 the "Villa-Lobos Year".

In 1958 Villa-Lobos returned to Paris and became once more involved in the composition of large-scale works. He then completed an opera in three acts begun the previous year: *A Menina das Nuvens (The Maiden above the Clouds)*. On 29th November, 1960, after his death, it was performed in Rio de Janeiro. Another work he wrote in Paris was the *Fantasia concertante* for an orchestra of cellos, which the Violoncello Society of New York, to which it was dedicated, performed on 10th December, 1958. From Paris he moved to North America, where he was commissioned by Metro-Goldwyn-Mayer to write music for a film, *Green Mansions*, based on the novel by W. H. Hudson; portions of the music not used in the film he converted into a work for solo, male choir and orchestra entitled *Os Cantos da Floresta Tropical (Songs from the Tropical Forest)*—the work sometimes known as *Floresta do Amazonas (Forests of Amazon)*. It was first performed in Rio de Janeiro on 21st November, 1969, the tenth anniversary

[31] *The New York Times*, 4th March, 1957.
[32] *Ibid.*, 5th March, 1957.
[33] *Ibid.*, 5th March, 1957.

of Villa-Lobos's death. The piece contains songs to words written by the Brazilian poetess, Dora Alencar de Vasconcellos (1910–73), for many years the Brazilian Consul-General in New York City. In 1958 Villa-Lobos also composed music of a completely different kind. In Paris he had written six unaccompanied choral pieces to Biblical words; these he assembled under the title *Bendita Sabedoria*, and on 3rd December, 1958 they were performed in New York by the Washington Square College Chorus under Maurice Paress.[33a] Another work of this kind was the outcome of a commission from Pope Pius XII, transmitted by the Archbishop of Milan, subsequently Pope Paul VI: the *Magnificat Aleluia*, a setting of Biblical words for solo, mixed choir and orchestra, which was first performed, on 8th November, 1958, in Rio de Janeiro by the Orquestra Sinfônica Brasileira and the Associação de Canto Coral conducted by Edoardo di Guarnieri. Before Villa-Lobos left New York that year the University of New York on 3rd December conferred on him an honorary doctorate.

1959, the last year of Villa-Lobos's life, was no less crowded and busy than the preceding ones. He fulfilled a number of concert engagements in Europe; orchestrated early songs, such as the *Modinhas e Canções* (*Lays and Melodies*), originally for voice and piano; composed the two Suites for chamber orchestra. At the UNESCO restaurant in Paris he still dined with Brazilian friends, among others with the musicologist, Luiz Heitor Corrêa de Azevedo, and the author, Erico Veríssimo. Then he flew to New York. At the Empire State Music Festival in the Anthony Wayne Recreation Area in Bear Mountain, Harriman State Park, N.Y., he conducted a concert with "The Symphony of the Air" Orchestra; this concert, which took place on the evening of 12th July at 7 p.m., was the last he ever conducted. He was in poor health when he returned to his home-town of Rio de Janeiro on 13th July in order to attend the 50th jubilee of the Teatro Municipal the following day and receive yet another honour—the Carlos Gomes Medal, one of the many distinctions which in these last years had been showered upon him from all parts of the world.

A few days later he entered the Hospital dos Estrangeiros. There he received the news that, in New York on 24th October, United Nations Day, a concert was being planned at which portions of his *Descobrimento de Brasil* would be given under Eleazar de Carvalho, the Brazilian conductor, with the participation of his old friend Hugh Ross and the Schola Cantorum. He also received records of his *Green Mansions* film music; a record-player was provided and, weak though he was, he listened. Shortly after, he was visited by the

---

[33a] The world *première* was given in October, 1958 on the occasion of the opening of the new UNESCO building at Place de Fontenoy, Paris; René Alix conducted the chorus of Radiodiffusion Française. The composer was conspicuously absent. He was known to be distrustful of, and reticent regarding, the international Secretariat of UNESCO in Paris, although much had been done in the past—but without any practical results—to entice and honour him. In 1949 Villa-Lobos was one of twelve composers commissioned by UNESCO to write a work each for a gala concert commemorating the centenary of Chopin's death. He responded with *Hommage à Chopin*, a piano piece played upon that occasion by the Brazilian pianist Arnaldo Estrela. (Letter from Luiz Heitor Corrêa de Azevedo to Lisa M. Peppercorn, 23rd April, 1979, Paris.)

Argentinian composer, Alberto Ginastera, an old friend, who was journeying back to Buenos Aires from Europe; Ginastera had read in the Paris press of Villa-Lobos's serious illness; when his ship reached Rio de Janeiro he had hurried to the Teatro Municipal to procure the address of the hospital. "Although obviously suffering he was full of spirit" Ginastera reported later.

> He spoke of plans for concerts in the United States, of the projected first performance of his opera, *Yerma*, of the struggle he had had to get the full score of his *Green Mansions* considered by Hollywood. He spoke too of his visits to Buenos Aires—of how he loved the city, his Argentinian friends, the Teatro Colón, where he had given so many unforgettable concerts, received so many ovations. I left him with the feeling that I was seeing him for the last time.[34]

The doctors could do nothing more for Villa-Lobos. The operation of eleven years ago had led to a massive congestion of the kidneys, and a condition of uraemia had gradually developed. This condition was already so far advanced when he entered hospital in Rio de Janeiro that, according to his doctor (Dr. Moacyr Santos Silva), only his exceptional vitality and powers of resistance had kept him going.[35] He was discharged from the hospital so that he could spend his last days at home.

On 8th November, he was still able to attend the performance of his *Magnificat Aleluia* under Edoardo di Guarnieri given at the Teatro Municipal. From a box he listened to his own music. When it was all over Villa-Lobos received an unforgettable ovation; it was as though, in premonition of his early death, the public were paying a final act of homage to their nation's great composer. "Visibly moved, Villa-Lobos, as though delivering a last farewell, waved a feeble, friendly hand".[36] Shortly afterwards, on 17th November, at the age of 72, he died at his home in the Rua Araújo Pôrto Alegre 56, Rio de Janeiro.

The news of his death spread quickly to all parts of the world. Announcing it, the daily bulletin of *The New York Times* Radio Station WQXR cancelled its bulletin and broadcasted instead a memorial programme. Thus the United States—which, exactly fifteen years before, had accorded Villa-Lobos the recognition denied him elsewhere—honoured the Brazilian master whom it regarded as the most important composer of the Western hemisphere of the first half of the twentieth century. It honoured him, too, in other ways. Early the following year, from the beginning of February to 23rd April, a Villa-Lobos exhibition of scores, sketches, photographs and books was held at the New York Public Library.[37] In 1961, on the anniversary of his birthday, a concert under

---

[34] Alberto Ginastera, "Homenagem a Villa-Lobos", *Presença de Villa-Lobos*, Vol. III, Museu Villa-Lobos, Rio de Janeiro, 1969.
[35] Eurico Nogueira França, *Villa-Lobos, Síntese Crítica e Biográfica*, 2nd edition, Museu Villa-Lobos, Rio de Janeiro, 1973.
[36] Edoardo di Guarnieri, "Villa-Lobos", *Presença de Villa-Lobos*, Vol. V, Museu Villa-Lobos, Rio de Janeiro, 1970.
[37] *The New York Times*, 9th February, 1960.

the patronage of the Brazilian government was given at Carnegie Hall by the Universal Symphony Orchestra and Music Institute (UNISOMI). A speech was delivered by Adolf A. Berle, Jr., whom President Kennedy had recently appointed to co-ordinate the interests of the U.S.A. with those of Latin America. The orchestra, conducted by Eleazar de Carvalho, included ninety members of the New York Philharmonic. The soloists were Anne Ayer and Aldo Parisot. Robert F. Wagner, the Mayor of New York, headed the honorary committee, which included permanent representatives of twenty-six countries of the United Nations, together with numerous prominent New York personalities.[38]

Brazil also took steps to honour the memory of its great son. In the middle of 1960 the establishment of the above-mentioned Museu Villa-Lobos was decreed. Early in 1961 its doors were opened, and ever since it has served as a perpetual stimulus.

---

[38] *Ibid.*, 12th February, 1961.

(Translated from the German by Robert L. Jacobs)

The Music Review, **40**(4), November 1979, 285–99

Corrigenda/addenda

p90 *last line*:
For Artur read Arthur
p91, *third paragraph, line 8*:
For Olga Coelho read Olga Praguer Coelho
p91, *last paragraph, line 4*:
For 22 and 23, read 23 and 24
p93, *line 19*:
Should read: Nos. 6 and 11 on 18 July
               No. 9 on 15 July
line 20:
Should read: Accademia Nazionale di Santa Cecilia
line 5 from bottom:
Delete entire line until next line including "World War"
FN. 6 first line:
For 10th November read 11 October

p94 *line 3*:
For Teator read Teatro
Second Paragraph, line 11:
For 15 November read 20 September
F.N. 12
for : "was first performed during a South American tour"
read: had its world première on 24 April 1961 by the National Symphony Orchestra of Washington, conducted by Guillermo Espinosa. It was first performed in South America during a tour made by Eugene Ormandy with the Philadelphia Orchestra in 1966....
p.97 *line 1*:
For Beate read Beata
second paragraph line 9:
Alvorado na Floresta Tropical (Dawn in a Tropical Forest) should be described as an overture and not a symphonic poem. The first performance given at the date cited and by the artists named, did not take place at a public concert but was undertaken specifically for a recording made by First Edition Records.
line 15:
It was not the string Quartet no. 15 that was commissioned by Janet Collins but the symphonic poem *Genesis* (written in 1954) to be used for a ballet with her arrangement and choreography.
line 20:
For Sebastián read Sebastian
FN 18:
For Sebastián read Sebastian
p98 *FN 20*:
For Segall read Segáll
p101 *lines 5/4 from bottom*:
delete: not used in the film
Last line:
for: "It was first performed in Rio de Janeiro on 21 November 1969, the tenth anniversary
    of Villa-Lobos's death"
read: "The world première was held on 12 July 1959 at the Empire State Music Festival
    at Bear Mountain, N.Y."
p102, *line 7*:
For Paress read Peress
FN 33a:
For: In October 1958 read 3 November 1958
For twelve read eleven
p102, *third paragraph, line 3*:
For *de* read *do*
p103, *third paragraph, line 1*:
For 8 November read 7 September
p104, *line 7*:
For Robert F. Wagner read Robert F. Wagner, Jr.

HEITOR VILLA-LOBOS: IL BURLONE

Il compositore brasiliano Heitor Villa-Lobos (1887-1959) amava prendersi gioco degli altri rimanendo impassibile, ridendo dentro di sé dell'umana debolezza che faceva accettare per veritiere — o così gli sembrava — le storie fantastiche che raccontava. Egli era capace di ridere degli altri, con gli altri, ma comunque — soprattutto – era capace di ridere di se stesso. Il suo senso dell'umorismo era contagioso per tutti coloro che lo hanno conosciuto. Chiunque sia stato in sua compagnia anche solo per pochi minuti è stato rallegrato da questo personaggio cordiale e spiritosissimo che era di buon umore sia nei momenti di frustrazione che in quelli di successo. Tutto ciò può spiegare perché, per quanto sicuramente Villa-Lobos abbia avuto in campo artistico nemici, avversari e critici, come essere umano godette di una larga cerchia di amici di ogni provenienza sociale, anche se era — come testimoniano in molti — un eccentrico che si annoiava facilmente e che perdeva la pazienza se la conversazione non si accentrava sulla sua persona, le sue opere, imprese, attività, speranze e frustrazioni. Per lui, Villa-Lobos era il centro del suo mondo, e se non era così per un motivo o per un altro anche solamente per pochissimo tempo, non lasciava nulla di intentato per rimettere la sua persona al centro dell'attenzione generale. Villa-Lobos era praticamente sempre circondato da un considerevole gruppo di ammiratori ed amici, sia quando componeva (cosa che faceva spesso in compagnia di amici che gli chiacchieravano accanto), sia quando pranzava, quando svolgeva la sua attività di amministratore o si dedicava ad altri compiti. Tutti si divertivano quando erano con lui, perché egli irradiava gentilezza, cordialità, immensa gioia di vivere ed energia vitale. Il suo amore per la vita non era del genere che prevede feste o mondanità o tutto quello che oggi si associa al prestigio o alla condizione sociale che si è raggiunta. Egli amava la compagnia di persone gioviali, senza cerimonie, che si comportano come esseri umani sia nei momenti di gioia che in quelli di dolore.

Il burlone che viveva nell'animo di Villa-Lobos si servì assai per tutta la vita di questo talento gioviale, e lo usò per accrescere il suo prestigio o, se non questo, la sua fama di originalità; meglio ancora, fece di lui una leggenda, in modo che il pubblico parlasse di lui e non lo dimenticasse. Non appena Villa-Lobos si accorse che questo modo di essere portava buoni risultati, lo fece diventare parte del suo bagaglio, anche se le modalità cambiavano a seconda delle occasioni, delle circostanze, persone e momenti. Quando ebbe capito che questo talento da burlone aveva successo, pare che Villa-Lobos lo abbia sviluppato a suo vantaggio e per la costernazione degli altri che, nonostante tutto, si divertivano moltissimo con questo originale personaggio brasiliano. In un certo senso la vita di Villa-Lobos fu una grande avventura. Perciò era per lui indispensabile esprimere questa passione per la vita, divertirsi e fare molti scherzi e, col suo modo di giocare, agire in modo tale da propagandare il suo personaggio e la sua musica. Col passare degli anni è diventato difficile capire cosa fosse in realtà frutto di scherzo e di umorismo, e cosa sia poi diventato leggenda. La sua arguzia lo aiutava a reclamizzarsi e, in ogni caso, a creare un mito intorno alla sua figura quando era vivo. Eppure alcuni, che evidentemente non avevano molto senso dell'umorismo, considerarono le debolezze di Villa-Lobos non come piccoli difetti umani, che lo rendevano solo più amabile. Quindi il suo modo di fare propaganda alla propria personalità e alla propria musica divenne spesso oggetto di incomprensione e di attacchi.

Credo che Villa-Lobos abbia tentato i suoi primi scherzi a Parigi, durante il suo secondo viaggio verso la fine degli anni Venti. Quando si rese conto della sua nuova arma, se ne servì per quasi tutta la vita, e in modo particolare quando andò per la prima volta negli Stati Uniti verso la fine del 1944. A quell'epoca a Parigi Villa-Lobos si sentiva finanziariamente abbastanza sicuro, poiché il suo soggiorno — che durò dal gennaio 1927 fino alla metà del 1930 — era finanziato dagli industriali filantropi brasiliani Arnaldo Guinle (1884-1964) e Carlos Guinle (1883-1965). Perciò Villa-Lobos potè concentrarsi sulla propaganda della sua carriera. Ciò non era così facile in quegli anni. Perché Villa-Lobos non era il solo compositore straniero che abitava a Parigi. Ce ne erano molti altri, alcuni dei quali facevano, o avrebbero fatto, una carriera molto notevole. Villa-Lobos li osservava e li considerava, per capire come riuscivano ad avere successo, come facevano per ottenerlo, e come raggiungevano fama e fortuna. Forse riteneva che la sua migliore qualità fosse l'essere una persona di un paese molto lontano e, come scoprì ben presto, di un paese che appariva in quei tempi ai parigini lontano quanto appariva la luna alla maggior parte della gente, fin quando l'uomo non ci ha messo piede. Villa-Lobos fu stupito quando scoprì che a quell'epoca i francesi sapevano ben poco del Brasile. Ma d'altronde, come avrebbero potuto? A quei tempi non esisteva la televisione, che ha rimpiccolito il mondo portandolo nel salotto di tutti. La radio era ai suoi primi passi, e probabilmente non esistevano trasmissioni da paesi lontani come il Brasile. Infatti c'era ben poco da riferire su questo paese, che avrebbe potuto interessare i francesi in quegli anni. Né si compivano i viaggi aerei che avrebbero potuto accelerare lo scambio di notizie dal Brasile all'Europa. La sensazionale trasvolata di Charles Lindbergh era avvenuta poco dopo l'arrivo di Villa-Lobos a Parigi. A quei tempi in Brasile ci si andava per mare. Ci volevano circa due settimane. In breve, il Brasile era geograficamente e intellettualmente assai distante. Quanti sapevano che la capitale era — allora — Rio de Janeiro? E che Rio de Janeiro era in Brasile e non in Argentina, come credevano molti? Certo, avevano sentito parlare del caffè brasiliano, e avevano sentito dire che a volte, a causa dell'eccessiva produzione, veniva bruciato o buttato nell'oceano. Ma coloro che Villa-Lobos frequentava a Parigi ignoravano totalmente quali ripercussioni avessero tali fatti sull'economia brasiliana. Certo i francesi sapevano che il Rio delle Amazzoni è in Brasile, da qualche parte nel nord del paese, ma cosa fosse veramente una foresta vergine che circonda l'immenso fiume con i suoi numerosi giganteschi affluenti, naturalmente questo non lo sapevano né si preoccupavano di saperlo. E perché mai avrebbero dovuto, dopo tutto? Vivevano in Francia e probabilmente non avevano mai pensato di andare in Sud America dove, come credevano alcuni, le strade principali delle grandi città erano ancora infestate dai serpenti.

Il fatto che tutti i francesi che conosceva fossero così ignoranti circa il suo paese non offendeva Villa-Lobos. Egli si offendeva raramente dell'ignoranza degli altri in ogni caso, qualsiasi cosa dicessero o facessero o pensassero, anche se avessero creduto che il Brasile era un paese selvaggio, una gran giungla da qualche parte del Sud America, un'entità che non ritenevano degna di esser conosciuta meglio. Villa-Lobos in ogni caso pensava che questo atteggiamento e quest'indifferenza erano stupide, o tutt'al più buffe. Così decise di dare una lezione ai francesi, a modo suo. Naturalmente non insegnò loro le bellezze, la grandezza, l'economia o la cultura brasiliane. Semplicemente si adeguò alle immagini curiose che i francesi evidentemente avevano del suo paese. E se i francesi pensavano che fosse tutto selvaggio, giungla e indiani, a Villa-Lobos andava benissimo: nutrì i loro desideri e sogni esotici esattamente con le fantasie esotiche che i francesi sembravano aspettarsi da chi era nato nel paese più grande dell'America latina.

Così cominciò col raccontare la storia seguente: « Catturato dai selvaggi, per tre giorni assistette alle cerimonie funebri celebrate in suo onore, poiché i suoi ospiti si accingevano a mangiarlo...[1]. Più morto che vivo, rimase tutto questo tempo in uno stato di ricettività inconscia che gli permise di registrare le parole dei celebranti... Liberato dai bianchi, tornò da questa terribile avventura con moltissimi ritmi e modulazioni che ha da allora usato spesso nelle sue composizioni[2]».

«Nel corso di una delle mie spedizioni, avevo portato con me un grammofono e alcuni dischi. Avevo un'idea diabolica: volevo vedere che effetto avrebbe prodotto sugli Indiani la musica del patrimonio europeo. Giunto presso una tribù dove, ne sono certo, i benefici della civiltà non erano mai penetrati, ho installato i miei macchinari e ho messo un disco con una musica perfettamente tonale e melodica. I miei Indiani si misero a urlare e colpirono la divinità meccanica che dovetti proteggere con molta difficoltà dal loro furore. Ma no, vi sbagliate: non avevano paura del mio vaso di Pandora, ma della musica stessa. La prova? Quando tornò la calma misi un disco di musica indiana, registrata presso un'altra tribù con cui questa non aveva potuto avere alcun contatto. I buoni selvaggi passarono da un estremo all'altro e cominciarono a gridare, cantare, danzare e manifestare al grammofono tutti i segni di religioso rispetto. Quando furono sufficientemente entusiasti, feci un esperimento: misi di nuovo il primo disco. Ci fu prima un

---

[1] René Dumesnil, *La Musique Contemporaine en France*, Parigi, 1930.
[2] « Le Monde Musical » n. 12, Parigi, 21 dicembre 1927.

momento di stupore, poi, un attimo dopo, il povero grammofono non era altro che un mucchio di legname e ferro vecchio... Come i selvaggi delle favole, i miei non potevano sopportare l'idea che fosse la stessa bocca a produrre alternativamente il fuoco e il ghiaccio. ...Ho ripetuto spesso questo esperimento e le reazioni che ho osservato sono quasi sempre state così decise se non così violente. ...Ciò mi è costato diversi grammofoni e anche qualche chitarra (a volte ho usato una chitarra). Progressioni di accordi melodici e consonanti suonati sulla mia chitarra erano accolti assai male, mentre invece le mie improvvisazioni su ritmi indigeni eccitavano l'entusiasmo degli Indiani. Fu uno dei successi più belli della mia carriera di strumentista ».[3]

Il pezzo forte delle storie di Villa-Lobos è probabilmente il racconto di come incontrò sua moglie in mezzo agli Indiani. Il fatto che le sue storie fossero state pubblicate deve aver divertito immensamente Villa-Lobos, come il fatto di esser riuscito a prendere in giro gente che ha così stupidamente creduto tutto, senza essere in grado di controllare certi fatti né quello che oggi si chiama materiale che fa parte del *background* e che qualsiasi musicologo può facilmente verificare in una biblioteca famosa come la Bibliothèque Nationale di Parigi o anche altrove. Quel burlone di Villa-Lobos era anche riuscito a crearsi una formidabile sicurezza di sé, dal momento che giornalisti ed editori, che si consideravano così intelligenti, colti e raffinati, e probabilmente assai superiori a qualcuno che proveniva dalla giungla, erano tutti caduti nella sua trappola. O si trattava di persone molto stupide per credere a tali favole, o di persone avide di assicurarsi quello che oggi sarebbe definito un colpo giornalistico o una storia in esclusiva, e allora saranno stati fieri di avere ottenuto storie del genere ed essere stati in grado di rivelare la verità e solo la verità su quest'uomo venuto dal Brasile che, prima che queste rivelazioni fossero pubblicate, era a Parigi un grande Sconosciuto. Villa-Lobos comunque con tutti i suoi scherzi si rivelò una persona estremamente intelligente, astuta e furba, che aveva improvvisamente scoperto un modo eccellente per fare le sue pubbliche relazioni e per reclamizzarsi, modo che non abbandonò più per tutta la vita.

Conobbi Villa-Lobos a Rio de Janeiro negli anni Trenta, e poco dopo tentò di far credere anche a me le sue fole sul suo paese

---

[3] Guide du Concert, 6 giugno 1930, citato in « O Globo », Rio de Janeiro, 18 ottobre 1930.

natale. Egli credeva, a ragione, che a quei tempi io non avessi molta dimestichezza con tutti gli affluenti del Rio delle Amazzoni, e, non essendo stata nel nord e nella regione amazzonica, che non fossi a conoscenza della situazione geografica e climatica della giungla, quindi era abbastanza sicuro che le sue favole sulle sue avventure in quella regione mi avrebbero certamente impressionato, e questo era esattamente quello che voleva: colpirmi ed affascinarmi col suo animo avventuroso, col suo coraggio e la sua audacia. In breve, mi raccontò dei suoi viaggi in posti come Paranaguá, nello stato di Paraná, come Minas Gerais, Mato Grosso, San Paolo e altri stati brasiliani, compreso un viaggio fatto da giovane risalendo il Rio delle Amazzoni fino alla città di Manaos, tutti viaggi questi che aveva veramente fatto e che sono assolutamente possibili; poi si lanciò in una storia che doveva aver tirato fuori di peso da una favola brasiliana: mi raccontò di aver veleggiato con un paio di amici, in una barca che si era costruito da sé, su e giù per i maggiori affluenti del Rio delle Amazzoni, per un certo numero di viaggi nel corso di tre distinte spedizioni, come se ciò fosse facile quanto lo può essere andare lungo lo Hudson, la Senna o il Reno. Per quanto allora fossi rimasta colpita da questo racconto fatto da un compositore così intraprendente, ebbi subito dei dubbi a riguardo, poiché, dopo tutto, i viaggi attraverso la regione amazzonica, specialmente all'inizio del secolo, non erano — e non sono — proprio dei picnic. Così andai a parlare con la moglie di Villa-Lobos, Lucília (1886-1966), che aveva sposato il 12 novembre 1913 ma da cui si era separato il 28 maggio 1936, per sapere se lei era in grado di ricordare, confermare o smentire questi avvenimenti. Lei rise di cuore e rispose che si trattava di uno dei suoi soliti scherzi, giocati per fare effetto sugli altri decantando il proprio coraggio e il proprio spirito avventuroso e giocherellone.

Villa-Lobos, l'avventuriero, diede il meglio di sé ancora una volta diversi anni dopo, stavolta per lo più con i molti americani che lo andavano a trovare dagli Stati Uniti durante la seconda guerra mondiale. La politica di buon vicinato di Franklin D. Roosevelt aveva dato inizio a un programma speciale di rapporti tra gli Stati Uniti e il Brasile, particolarmente in campo culturale. In Brasile vennero quindi in visita dagli Stati Uniti musicologi, scrittori, pittori, artisti e compositori, a volte per conto loro, a volte finanziati dai dipartimenti per gli affari inter-americani di entrambi i paesi. In quegli anni l'interesse per il folklore era un argomento in voga, specialmente in Brasile dove fu creata perfino una cattedra di folklore brasiliano alla Scuola nazionale di musica presso l'Università del Brasile (oggi Scuola di Musica dell'Università Federale di Rio de Janeiro) e dove, nel 1943, fu fondato un Centro per la ricerca sul folklore.

Quindi il burlone Villa-Lobos ebbe un'altra idea ingegnosa per affascinare le persone che venivano a visitarlo dagli Stati Uniti: per fare effetto egli mise insieme tre punti che erano secondo lui in voga a quell'epoca: l'interesse per gli Stati Uniti, la ricerca sul folklore e un naufragio spettacolare. Villa-Lobos raccontò loro — come aveva raccontato già ad altri in anni precedenti — che all'inizio del secolo, quando egli era ancora molto giovane, era in viaggio per gli Stati Uniti. Ma la nave su cui viaggiava non giunse mai a destinazione perché per una disgrazia ci fu un naufragio al largo dell'Isola di Barbados nei Caraibi. Villa-Lobos, così raccontava, fu tanto fortunato da riuscire a mettersi in salvo sull'isola. Naturalmente non ebbe altro scopo e interesse, subito dopo essersi salvato sull'isola, lontano dal nativo Brasile, con pochi soldi e pochi vestiti, se non quello di profittare di questa disgrazia e raccogliere materiale folkloristico sull'Isola di Barbados. Credo che neanche uno studioso dei nostri tempi, un ricercatore professionista, con tutta l'assistenza tecnica che potrebbe avere oggi per essere salvato e riportato sano e salvo a casa o dovunque volesse andare, penserebbe che la cosa più urgente da fare in una situazione di questo genere sia rimanersene lì e profittare al meglio della propria sventura, e iniziare immediatamente una raccolta di materiale folkloristico come se si trattasse di raccogliere delle mele da un albero, e tutto ciò specialmente all'inizio del secolo!

Ma Villa-Lobos, naturalmente, la pensava diversamente! La sua idea della raccolta di materiale folkloristico avrebbe dovuto colpire i suoi visitatori americani perché la ricerca sul folklore musicale era di moda durante i primi anni della seconda guerra mondiale. E il fatto di viaggiare verso gli Stati Uniti o, almeno, il desiderio di farlo, prima o poi, era press'a poco altrettanto di moda a quei tempi. Perché prima di allora il Brasile era più rivolto all'Europa, e specialmente alla Francia, e sia le influenze culturali che l'interesse da e per gli Stati Uniti erano, al principio della guerra, solo agli inizi. Interrogata, Lucília mi confermò ancora che anche questa era una pura invenzione di Villa-Lobos, sia il naufragio al largo della Barbados che l'idea della raccolta folkloristica, e che egli non aveva mai tentato di andare negli Stati Uniti in quegli anni lontani.[4]

A parte questa conferma, credo che ci siano altri fattori che contrastano la plausibilità di questa storia. Al principio del secolo, come abbiamo detto, l'interesse del Brasile era rivolto all'Europa, e non certo agli Stati Uniti: in quei tempi, a parte un qualche interesse in questioni folkloristiche da parte di compositori brasiliani come Alberto Nepomuceno (1864-1920) e Alexandre Levy (1864-1892), nessun compositore in Brasile pensava seriamente di raccogliere canzoni popolari nel modo raccontato da Villa-Lobos, e sicuramente non il giovane Villa-Lobos, che aveva ben altri pensieri per la testa, e più precisamente quello di guadagnarsi la vita suonando il violoncello e tentare di scrivere i suoi primi piccoli pezzi di musica.

Credo che la storia della Barbados non fu mai presa sul serio dal suo narratore, per quanto abbia potuto divertirsi a raccontarla agli altri e a guardare le espressioni stupite dei loro visi. Non era dopo tutto proprio Villa-Lobos il più astuto dei due — il narratore e l'ascoltatore? Il suo senso dell'umorismo non era forse ammirevole, la sua abilità di irridere gli altri e di trovare il soggetto giusto non era adorabile, come il suo modo di raccontare una storia che non solo avrebbe divertito i suoi ascoltatori ma, nei suoi disegni, avrebbe accresciuto il suo prestigio? Non erano forse un po' troppo ingenui i suoi ascoltatori che cadevano nelle sue trappole? Forse erano più perplessi che mai. Ma, tra i due, sicuramente Villa-Lobos era quello che si divertiva di più e che conosceva e giudicava meglio l'umana debolezza. Per quanto potesse parlare all'infinito di sé, delle sue opere e delle sue imprese, qualsiasi cosa dicesse e comunque l'arricchisse era certamente fonte di divertimento per i suoi compagni, amici e ammiratori. È difficile dire chi fosse più contento, Villa-Lobos o coloro che lo credevano a metà, o erano solo catturati e incantati dalle sue narrazioni iperboliche. Prendere

---

[4] Gli industriali e mecenati brasiliani Arnaldo e Carlo Guinle, che finanziarono il secondo soggiorno di Villa-Lobos a Parigi (1927-1930) mi raccontarono di aver inviato una volta un gruppo di musicisti nell'interno del Brasile del nord per raccogliere materiale folkloristico. Consegnarono questo materiale a Villa-Lobos poco prima ch'egli partisse per la Francia, con la richiesta di sceglierlo e prepararlo per la pubblicazione col titolo di *Alma Brasileira* (Anima Brasiliana). Su questa raccolta esiste un carteggio inedito tra Villa-Lobos e i fratelli Guinle che è in possesso della famiglia Guinle, e che mi fu concesso di consultare negli anni Trenta a Rio de Janeiro. Secondo i fratelli Guinle Villa-Lobos non restituì mai il materiale, che non si sa dove sia andato a finire. Forse è proprio questo materiale folkloristico quello che Villa-Lobos raccontava sempre di aver raccolto di persona nel Brasile settentrionale e nella regione amazzonica (Lisa M. Peppercorn, *Heitor Villa-Lobos, Leben und Werk des brasilianischen Komponisten,* Zurigo, 1972, pagg. 65-66).

in giro gli altri era parte della natura e del carattere di Villa-Lobos. Eppure, il fatto che componesse musica mentre conversava con gli amici e, contemporaneamente, ascoltava un romanzo trasmesso per radio (cosa che adorava) non è una favola ma pura realtà.

In conformità con i programmi di scambi culturali tra il Brasile e gli Stati Uniti, o con altri programmi analoghi per diffondere la musica americana in Brasile e la musica brasiliana negli Stati Uniti, anche Villa-Lobos fu invitato ad andare negli Stati Uniti come una specie di ambasciatore musicale brasiliano. Ma Villa-Lobos declinò questi inviti. Disse che sarebbe andato se fosse stato invitato da orchestre a dirigere la sua musica, ma non oberato da missioni di vario genere. Voleva essere invitato e riconosciuto negli Stati Uniti per quello che era sempre stato ed aveva sempre ambito essere: Heitor Villa-Lobos, il compositore brasiliano e nient'altro.

Per chiarire la sua posizione a coloro che erano interessati a invogliarlo a visitare gli Stati Uniti, Villa-Lobos descrisse loro in Brasile le sue idee e i programmi che aveva in mente di realizzare non appena fosse arrivato nel paese dello Zio Sam. E questa volta nessuno riuscì a capire se Villa-Lobos prendeva in giro gli altri o se stesso, se si lasciava andare a fantasie irrealistiche ovvero se dava segni di vera e propria megalomania. Si descriveva a New York in un elegantissimo appartamento di Park Avenue, intento a ritrarre le fattezze dei visitatori musicalmente, secondo linee di un sistema di millimetrizzazione che aveva inventato da poco e su cui aveva basato la composizione del suo pezzo *The New York Skyline Melody* per pianoforte e orchestra (1939).[5]

Villa-Lobos disse che si sarebbe fatto pagare una cifra enorme per l'epoca ma che, secondo lui, era giustificata per la sua invenzione e creazione ingegnosa. Inoltre voleva dimostrare di essere un abile uomo d'affari dichiarando che avrebbe concesso uno sconto del cinquanta per cento se avesse avuto più di cinque visitatori al giorno. Inoltre, per fare in modo che tutta New York fosse al corrente del fatto che Villa-Lobos era in città, pronto per questa avventura a base di ritratti per i quali i visitatori avrebbero soltanto dovuto inviargli la loro fotografia o quella dei loro familiari, avreb-

---

[5] Entrambe le versioni sono pubblicate da Max Eschig, Parigi. La melodia fu scritta su una fotografia di Manhattan che si staglia contro il cielo, per soddisfare la curiosità di un giornalista di « Time Magazine » che interrogava il compositore sul sistema di millimetrizzazione che aveva usato nella sua *Mountain Melody (Villa-Lobos, Sua Obra*, Rio de Janeiro, Museu Villa-Lobos, seconda edizione, 1972, pag. 160).

be tenuto una conferenza stampa non appena arrivato a Manhattan per informare attraverso i mezzi di comunicazione di massa otto milioni di cittadini newyorchesi sul fatto che il grande maestro era disposto a ritrarli musicalmente. Non si trattava di un'intuizione momentanea, impulsiva, perché me lo ripeté diverse volte nell'arco di mesi e di anni.

Forse Villa-Lobos cercava facili guadagni, o pensava di trovare un tesoro per liberarsi del lavoro amministrativo che svolgeva in quegli anni a Rio de Janeiro nel dipartimento municipale per l'educazione musicale? Eppure negli anni precedenti non aveva mai mostrato nessuna inclinazione o desiderio per il lusso, sia nel suo stile di vita che nella sua casa o nei suoi abiti. Non sembrava desiderare per sé tutto quello che oggi tanti desiderano ottenere, e cioé un tenore di vita imperniato sui simboli di appartenenza sociale, tipico del consumismo. Viveva intensamente, umanamente, felicemente e forse con più piacere, allegria e gusto di vivere di molti che, materialmente, avevano da spendere più di quanto non avesse lui; perciò probabilmente non era la ricerca di fortuna il punto chiave della fantasia che ho riferito circa quello che avrebbe fatto dopo il suo arrivo sul suolo americano. Forse pensava che « quando sei a Roma, devi agire da romano », e quindi può essere che abbia immaginato che il proverbiale uomo d'affari americano avrebbe agito così — dal momento che non parlava né leggeva una parola di inglese, lingua che non imparò mai, tranne le parole « caffè molto, molto forte » e « gelato di crema ». Pensava che negli Stati Uniti colui che « si è fatto da sé » fosse un uomo che gode di vasta stima, rispetto e popolarità, e che il successo finanziario fosse talmente ricercato al nord che sarebbe stata questa la strada migliore per avere successo e attirare l'attenzione su di sé. Perché di solito aggiungeva che una volta diventato ricco avrebbe dato concerti gratuiti, senza richiedere di essere pagato, e avrebbe lasciato che il pubblico venisse ai suoi concerti senza pagare il biglietto. Un po' ingenuo, a dir la verità, ma assai tipico di Villa-Lobos, l'allegro burlone che amava raccontare favole e crogiolarsi in fantasie iperboliche.

Verso la fine della seconda guerra mondiale, nel novembre 1944, Villa-Lobos andò finalmente negli Stati Uniti, per la prima volta. Era stato invitato dalla Werner Janssen Symphony Orchestra di Los Angeles, dove debuttò il 26 novembre 1944 dirigendo la sua musica. Il concerto non ebbe un gran pubblico. « Heitor Villa-

Lobos, il dono che il Brasile ha fatto al mondo musicale, ha diretto la Janssen Symphony Orchestra in un programma di suoi lavori il pomeriggio di domenica 26 novembre 1944 all'Auditorio filarmonico, davanti ad un pubblico che riempiva solo parzialmente la sala, un pubblico assai più scarso di quanto ci si aspettasse, data la gran reputazione del compositore sudamericano. Il programma comprendeva la sua *Seconda Sinfonia, Chôros n. 6* e *Rudepoema*».[6]

Janssen e Villa-Lobos erano amici fin da quanto, pochi anni prima, Janssen era stato a Rio de Janeiro a dirigervi alcuni concerti, in uno dei quali era stata eseguita per la prima volta in Brasile, per merito suo, una Sinfonia di Sibelius. A quell'epoca Janssen aveva una sua orchestra a Los Angeles, ed è per questo che Villa-Lobos fu invitato all'inizio a dirigere in California, dove ha preso il via la sua carriera americana, e non sulla costa orientale, come ci si sarebbe potuto aspettare. La sua carriera, nonostante un inizio di poco conto, gli diede comunque la fama negli Stati Uniti, e gli Stati Uniti vi contribuirono molto riconoscendo il suo grande talento. In seguito la sua fama si diffuse in Europa e, purtroppo assai tardivamente nella sua vita, anche nella sua patria, il Brasile, dove fino alla sua partenza per Los Angeles Villa-Lobos aveva dovuto farsi propaganda per attirare l'attenzione.

Contemporaneamente al suo debutto a Los Angeles, vennero organizzate una serie di cerimonie ufficiali per onorare il più grande compositore brasiliano e sudamericano di quegli anni. Durante la prima cerimonia fu conferito a Villa-Lobos il titolo onorario di dottore in legge presso l'Occidental College. Villa-Lobos era sempre molto orgoglioso e soddisfatto di tutte le onorificenze, i titoli, l'appartenenza a circoli e altri riconoscimenti che ricevette durante la sua vita, ma detestava le cerimonie che li accompagnavano. Stavolta, a Los Angeles, fu il Southern California Council per gli Affari inter-americani — organismo che ha cessato di esistere dopo la seconda guerra mondiale — che si associò all'invito di Janssen a Villa-Lobos, e che organizzò le cerimonie ufficiali per la laurea ad honorem pochi giorni prima del debutto di Villa-Lobos, il 21 novembre 1944. La decisione di conferirgli questa laurea era stata presa per iniziativa di Raymond G. McKelvey, professore di scienze politiche presso l'Occidental College e, allo stesso tempo, direttore esecutivo del Southern California Council per gli Affari Inter-

---

[6] Pacific Coast Musician, Los Angeles, 2 dicembre 1944.

Americani. Nel corso delle cerimonie Villa-Lobos fu presentato da Walter E. Hartley, professore presso il Dipartimento di musica (ora deceduto), e dal dottor Remsen Bird (anch'egli scomparso), allora presidente dell'Occidental College. Al contrario di quanto successe pochi giorni dopo al debutto di Villa-Lobos come compositore-direttore della Janssen Symphony Orchestra, il Salone dell'Occidental College era « gremito, la sera di martedì 21 novembre 1944, in occasione della cerimonia. Werner Janssen ha presentato la vita e le opere dell'illustre sudamericano. In onore di Villa-Lobos, il London String Quartet ha suonato il suo *Terzo Quartetto per Archi,* e il Glee Club dell'Occidental College ha cantato la sua *Canção da Saudade* ».[7e8]

A far da interprete nel corso della cerimonia, il Southern California Council aveva invitato lo scrittore brasiliano Érico Veríssimo che si trovava allora a Los Angeles perché aveva appena concluso un ciclo di conferenze sulla letteratura brasiliana, tenuto a Berkeley presso l'Università di California nell'anno accademico 1943/4. Veríssimo, come racconta lui stesso, era un po' preoccupato di fare l'interprete, perché conosceva l'impulsività di Villa-Lobos, i suoi scherzi imprevedibili e le sue azioni improvvise vòlte ad attrarre l'attenzione su di sé o sulla propria originalità. Come racconta Veríssimo,[9] le cerimonie iniziarono e Villa-Lobos non era ancora arrivato, pare a causa di un ritardo del suo aereo. Quando finalmente Villa-Lobos arrivò, dopo una mezz'ora, fu presentato subito al suo interprete, che aveva già conosciuto in precedenza ma che non riconobbe; non ricordava neanche il suo nome e lo chiamò col nome sbagliato di « Luis ». Poi fu subito indirizzato verso la cerimonia, e la processione delle autorità finalmente entrò nel salone tra i grandi applausi del pubblico. « Sto morendo dalla voglia di fumare » bisbigliò Villa-Lobos al suo interprete mentre salivano sul palco delle autorità. Dopo il breve discorso di Janssen il Glee Club cantò *Canção da Saudade* (Canzone della Nostalgia) di Villa-Lobos. Col suo più bel sorriso Villa-Lobos mormorò in portoghese a Veríssimo: « Gesù, come cantano male », e il presidente del College chiese subito cosa aveva detto il maestro. Veríssimo rispo-

---

[7] Pacific Coast Musician, Los Angeles, 2 dicembre 1944.

[8] Un pezzo a cappella per voci femminili su parole di Sodré Viana, composto nel 1933 ed eseguito per la prima volta a Rio de Janeiro il 10 ottobre 1933 dalla Orfeão de Professores dell'allora Distretto Federale diretta da Villa-Lobos.

[9] *Meus encontros com Villa-Lobos,* di ÉRICO VERÍSSIMO, in *Presença de Villa-Lobos,* vol. 3, prima edizione, 1969, Rio de Janeiro, Museu Villa-Lobos, pagg. 55 e seguenti.

se mentendo: « Ha detto che il coro è eccellente ». « Bene » rispose il presidente. Quando gli fu conferita la laurea, Villa-Lobos chiese — attraverso il suo interprete — se doveva fare un discorso. Gli fu risposto: « Se vuole parlare, tanto meglio ». Così Villa-Lobos avanzò verso il microfono, con le mani dietro la schiena, e cominciò a parlare prima del suo viaggio aereo verso gli Stati Uniti (cosa assai nuova a quei tempi per un passeggero non militare) e quindi disse « che era un figlio della natura e che aveva imparato la lingua della libertà ascoltando gli uccelli della giungla brasiliana ». Cosa il pubblico abbia capito di questo racconto enigmatico, nessuno lo sa.

Il giorno dopo il Council offrì una cena ai suoi ospiti illustri presso un grande albergo alla moda. C'erano tutte le persone importanti dell'industria cinematografica di Hollywood, scrittori, artisti, musicisti, registi. Seduto a tavola con il sindaco e i dignitari, a Villa-Lobos furono presentate tutte le celebrità una per una. Gli fu anche presentato un rappresentante degli studi di Walt Disney, che avevano appena terminato il film *Adiós, Amigos*. Villa-Lobos, quando gli fu presentata questa persona, ebbe l'audacia e la presunzione di esclamare davanti a tutti che il film era « una vera fesseria », e fumando il suo sigaro rise alla faccia sconcertata del suo interprete, che però non poté fare a meno di pensare che nessuno alla cena si divertiva di più del grande ospite d'onore.

Il pomeriggio seguente uno dei grandi magnati dell'industria cinematografica offrì a Villa-Lobos, nella sua imponente villa di Bel Air, un sontuoso ricevimento con i soci del circolo femminile. Dopo aver chiacchierato un po', racconta Veríssimo, Villa-Lobos si accomodò in una grande poltrona con un'espressione sul viso che lasciava prevedere delle sorprese. Fu presto circondato da signore del circolo, che erano molto onorate di avere Villa-Lobos con loro. Una di esse chiese a Veríssimo di dire a Villa-Lobos che il circolo aveva ricevuto molti grandi artisti, come Toscanini, Stokowsky, Rachmaninoff e altri; al che Villa-Lobos reagì, quando gli fu tradotto, dicendo con espressione terribilmente annoiata: « Non mi interessa, non mi interessa affatto ». Sorridendo, la signora americana chiese la traduzione delle parole del maestro, e Veríssimo, per salvare la situazione, mentì nuovamente e disse che « Villa-Lobos ne era molto contento ». Poi disse a Villa-Lobos che le signore lo ammiravano molto e che non aveva importanza che lui non parlasse inglese; la risposta di Villa-Lobos fu: « Dica a queste signore che non sono un pappagallo e neanche un pagliaccio da circo ». Veríssimo si vergognò e tacque per un momento. Poi — ed è lui stesso a raccontarcelo — tradì nuovamente il suo connazionale e rispose: « il signor Villa-Lobos ha detto che è molto felice di essere qui ». La commedia andò avanti così fino a quando, improvvisamente, Villa-Lobos si alzò e disse: « Basta con questa conversazione. Se vogliono, posso suonare un po' di musica mia e poi me ne vado ». La proposta fu accolta con un applauso. Quindi suonò due o tre delle sue *Cirandas*, ma tra il primo e il secondo pezzo si lamentò: « Questo piano è scordato. Sembra l'organetto a manovella di un cieco ».

Nonostante questo strano comportamento e la noia che manifestava chiaramente nei confronti dei soggetti e delle persone con cui non poteva avere un rapporto diretto per la mancanza di un mezzo di comunicazione linguistico comune, e che non condividevano i suoi punti di vista, il suo stile di vita e la sua posizione nei confronti della vita, Villa-Lobos si avvicinava all'apice della sua carriera, per quanto riguardava la sua fama nel mondo. Il suo debutto a Los Angeles fu seguito da una serie ininterrotta di impegni quale direttore d'orchestra ospite, invitato a presentare e interpretare la sua musica, prima con le orchestre più importanti degli Stati Uniti, poi con quelle delle capitali europee, con viaggi intermedi in Brasile e in altri paesi dell'America Latina, ed un viaggio in Israele. Ci si chiede se Villa-Lobos avrebbe mai raggiunto la fama mondiale se non fosse stato per la politica americana/di buon vicinato, che gli diede la possibilità di essere ascoltato in tutta la nazione, di essere invitato a fare conferenze nelle università, che gli conferì un'altra laurea ad honorem all'Università di New York (il 3 dicembre 1958) e che fece eseguire per la prima volta molte delle sue opere, alcune delle quali erano state commissionate da fondazioni americane e da artisti americani o che abitavano negli Stati Uniti. Nonostante il suo declino fisico, aveva subíto nel 1948 presso il Memorial Hospital di New York un'operazione per l'asportazione di un cancro alla vescica, che gli lasciò ancora undici anni di vita, il successo raggiunto parve dargli la forza e l'energia che qualcun altro con la sua età ormai avanzata e dopo un simile intervento non avrebbe forse avuto.

In quegli anni Villa-Lobos non solo diresse la sua musica e compose, ma viaggiò molto per i suoi impegni, che comprendevano anche conferenze presso università. Così nel 1953 l'Università

di California a Los Angeles (UCLA) lo invitò a fare delle conferenze. Lì, per caso, Villa Lobos incontrò di nuovo Érico Veríssimo, che si trovava a Los Angeles in un intervallo dei suoi impegni
come conferenziere presso le Università della Costa Orientale degli
Stati Uniti. Entrando nel campus dell'UCLA, Veríssimo vide con
stupore l'annuncio di una conferenza di Villa-Lobos, e non resi-
stette alla tentazione di andare ad ascoltarlo. E ne valeva veramente
la pena, come ebbe poi a raccontare:[10] « C'erano circa trenta persone. Villa-Lobos era sulla pedana, affiancato da Lukas Foss, il
compositore, pianista e musicologo, che fungeva da interprete. Villa-Lobos, un gran sigaro tra le dita, iniziò a parlare ». Secondo
Veríssimo, fu questa la prima volta che vide un oratore fumare
durante una conferenza, specialmente poi in un'università. Villa-
Lobos non aveva un argomento prestabilito per il suo discorso,
cosa assai tipica in lui, ma raccontava — in francese, poi tradotto
in inglese — un aneddoto dietro l'altro sulla musica e sui musicisti,
e a quanto pare non dava nessuna importanza al fatto che gli
aneddoti non avevano nessun rapporto gli uni con gli altri. Si
comportava, racconta Veríssimo, come se fosse stato seduto in un
caffè di Montparnasse a Parigi, a chiacchierare con gli amici davanti a un bicchiere di vino. Il suo pubblico dell'UCLA rideva alle sue
spiritosaggini, e Villa-Lobos rideva con loro e sembrava divertirsi
molto. A un certo punto, improvvisamente, non seppe cos'altro
dire. Cominciò a guardarsi intorno da destra a sinistra, come per
cercare qualcosa di cui aveva bisogno. Poi dichiarò: « Voglio un
pianoforte, dov'è un pianoforte, portatemi un pianoforte ». Lukas
Foss si occupò immediatamente di soddisfare questa richiesta, e un
pianoforte a coda fu portato sul palcoscenico. Col suo sigaro sempre tra i denti, Villa-Lobos annunciò in francese: « Suonerò
Brahms ». Dopo qualche battuta di una Sonata di Brahms disse:
« Et le piano ne bouge pas ».[11] Poi suonò dei brani di una Sonata
di Beethoven, si girò al suo pubblico e disse: « Suono Beethoven,
ma il piano "ne bouge pas" ». Poi suonò Schumann, Schubert,
Chopin, e secondo Villa-Lobos il piano continuò a non
« bouger ». Alla fine Villa-Lobos dichiarò: « E ora suonerò Villa-
Lobos » e iniziò a suonare un brano dal suo *Rudepoema*. Pochi
minuti dopo si rivolse sorridendo al suo pubblico e disse: « Il
bouge, il bouge ». Evidentemente desiderava fare il pagliaccio per

---

[10] Érico Veríssimo: *ibidem.*
[11] « E il piano non si muove ». (n.d.t.).

fare effetto sui suoi ascoltatori. Eppure, alcuni di questi scherzi abbastanza stupidi erano al limite del buon gusto, e indegni del sessantaseienne compositore che tentava di esser preso sul serio. Così come i suoi modi assai scortesi nel corso delle cerimonie ufficiali e i mezzi espliciti con cui voleva fare amicizie o influenzare la gente non erano esattamente graditi a tutti. Ci si chiede se questo comportamento avrebbe portato a Villa-Lobos il risultato desiderato, se non fosse stato per la diplomazia di Érico Veríssimo, che con il suo tatto salvò più volte la situazione in un momento, subito dopo la guerra, in cui Villa-Lobos non era ancora un compositore famoso né ricercato, come divenne più tardi.

Due anni dopo la sua prima apparizione all'Università di California a Los Angeles (UCLA), Veríssimo e Villa-Lobos si incontrarono di nuovo nel 1955 dopo un concerto che il compositore aveva diretto con la National Symphony Orchestra a Washington, D.C. Villa-Lobos aveva l'aria stanca e appariva sfinito, ricorda Veríssimo. Al ricevimento che l'ambasciatore brasiliano João Carlos Muniz dette in onore del compositore presso la sua residenza dopo il concerto, Veríssimo cercò invano Villa-Lobos tra gli ospiti. Fin quando, improvvisamente, si sentì chiamare, e riconobbe la voce di Villa-Lobos. Il compositore sedeva in cucina, senza cappotto, circondato dalla servitù dell'ambasciatore, e mangiava un pezzetto di carne con riso conditi con una salsa fatta di fagioli neri brasiliani. « Si sieda qui, Veríssimo », disse Villa-Lobos allo scrittore. E si accese un sigaro, lentamente.

Dopo quel giorno Villa-Lobos aveva ancora quattro anni di vita. In quegli ultimi anni diventò più calmo, sentendo — come ebbe a dire a qualcuno — che il suo fisico minato non gli avrebbe consentito di vivere a lungo. E quando morì, il 17 novembre 1959, lasciò non solo un gran numero di opere musicali di tutti i tipi, ma il ricordo di essere stato una persona franca che non aveva paura di dire quello che pensava, di affrontare il futuro con ottimismo, di scherzare su tutto e su tutti quelli che prendevano se stessi e il mondo troppo sul serio — eccetto, naturalmente, lui, il compositore Villa-Lobos.

(Traduzione dall'inglese di Caterina D'Amico de Carvalho)

Nuova Rivista Musicale Italiana, **XIV**(3), July/September 1980, 378–92

Corrigenda

p107 *line 3 from bottom*:
For 1965 read 1969

p114 *line 10 from bottom*:
For 'e' read 'o'

CORRESPONDENCE BETWEEN HEITOR VILLA-LOBOS AND HIS WIFE LUCÍLIA

NINE LETTERS survive exchanged between Heitor Villa-Lobos (1887–1959) and his wife Lucília (1886–1966), a music teacher, pianist, composer and interpreter of her husband's music, during a crucial six years of the composer's professional and personal life.[1] At the time of the first letter, in 1930, Villa-Lobos, the devoted husband, was beginning his struggle for recognition in his native Brazil; by the time of the last, in 1936, he was professionally established and had decided to separate from his estranged wife.

On 15 June 1930, only about two weeks before the first of these letters, Villa-Lobos and Lucília had returned to Rio de Janeiro after a three-and-a-half-year stay in Paris sponsored by two Brazilian industrialists and philanthropists. On their way home they had taken part in concerts on 6 and 10 June at the Teatro Santa Isabel in the north-eastern city of Recife in the Brazilian state of Pernambuco, performing some of his early works. Villa-Lobos did not expect to remain permanently in Brazil: he planned to return in due course to Paris, which he regarded as better suited to his artistic development and professional life. This dream did not come true.

Already at the time of his arrival there were premonitions of the revolution in Brazil that was to break out in October 1930. Without regard for the threatening political situation, Villa-Lobos embarked on the concert engagements that had been arranged in advance from Paris, and immediately set out for São Paulo to begin rehearsals. In his excitement at the vivid musical life of Paris in the twenties, he had planned, with his customary enterprise, to enliven Brazil's musical life with first performances in his native country of works by his non-Brazilian contemporaries, and he had brought the orchestral material with him from Paris. The programmes included such novelties for Brazil as Darius Milhaud's *Saudades do Brasil*, written to commemorate Milhaud's stay in Brazil as secretary to Paul Claudel, at that time (1918) Minister at the

[1] The letters, in the possession of Lucília Villa-Lobos's family, were published in facsimile in a privately printed publication issued by Villa-Lobos's brother-in-law Luiz Guimarães in collaboration with his brothers Oldemar and Alvaro de Oliveira and his sister Dinorah Guimarães Campos, *Villa-Lobos, Visto da Platéia e na Intimidade (1912–1935)*. Rio de Janeiro, 1972. pp. 340–55. Particular thanks are due to Dr. R. W. Truman of Christ Church, Oxford, for his help with the translation from the Portuguese. Only Villa-Lobos's original layout (often with a new paragraph for each sentence, however short) has occasionally been altered here for the sake of greater continuity.

French Legation in Rio de Janeiro. Other works conducted by Villa-Lobos under the patronage of the Sociedade Sinfônica de São Paulo were Honegger's *Pacific 231* and music by his friend and Paris publisher Eugène Cools (1877–1936), director of Editions Max Eschig from 1927 to his death. There was also music by Coppola, Albeniz and the talented but then relatively unknown Brazilian composer Mozart Camargo Guarnieri (b. 1907).

Shortly after his arrival in São Paulo,[2] Villa-Lobos wrote to his wife:[3]

> Go to the Licêo de Artes e Officios in the street that runs in front of the Teatro Lyrico and look for that 'mulatto' gentleman whose name I don't remember but who organized that concert of Brazilian music I conducted two or three years ago—remember?
>
> Well, find that gentleman, or someone in his place, and ask him about an instrumentation I did, for that concert, of a song by Felix Othero called 'A Flor e a Fonte'. Would he look for it and do me the great favour of lending it to me, since I intend to perform it here in São Paulo with Bidú Sayão in honour of the author, who very much wants to get to know the instrumentation.[4] See if you can manage to bring this instrumentation along with you when you come, with the promise that it will be returned.
>
> As far as Pery is concerned,[5] I am seeing if I can arrange a fee of one *conto-de-reis* for him.[6] It will be difficult, though, since the finances of the Villa-Lobos season are not very good, it seems.
>
> I have had no news of my pianos from Arnaldo.[7] I have just written to him to this effect.
>
> What is being said about Luiz[8] is so much posturing and pretence, because I know that I am fully entitled to a refund of those 'crooked' duties I paid to the Customs.
>
> It's very cold here, so when you come, put on warm clothes.
>
> Nothing else, kisses and greetings.
>
> PS: On presentation of this chit you will receive at the Rio branch of this bank the sum of 500 *milreis*. You can expect a communication [from the bank].

Three days after his first concert (12 July) Villa-Lobos wrote again:

[2] The letter is undated, but according to Villa-Lobos's brother-in-law it dates from 1930 (communication to the author from Oldemar Guimarães, 1 December 1972).

[3] The 1930 letters are addressed 'Lucas' or 'Luquinha'; thereafter Villa-Lobos uses the full form 'Lucília'. Except for his valedictory letter, signed 'Villa-Lobos', he signs himself not 'Heitor' but 'Villa', the name by which he was universally known. Lucília addresses him the same way. Her first letter is signed 'Lucília', her second is without signature.

[4] The orchestration (unpublished) of the song by the Brazilian composer Araújo Viana (1870–1916) was performed on 24 September 1930 at the Teatro Municipal, São Paulo. Villa-Lobos conducted. The soloist was not Bidú Sayão, Brazil's leading concert and opera singer, but Sira Monossi.

[5] Pery Machado, violinist, friend of Villa-Lobos and interpreter of his music.

I sent you 500 *milreis* to cover your present needs and to pay for your journey to S. Paulo when the time comes. Simply let me know the day when you will be arriving, and I'll meet you at the station. If by chance this is not enough, let me know right away, and I will send more, at whatever sacrifice.

The concert on the 12th went well, though it could have been better if I had had more rehearsal. The second [concert] has been fixed for the 26th of this month and the third for the 30th or 31st.

I think you will find me very slim, for I eat almost nothing and work like a madman. I don't know when I can manage to get some rest.

I think it would be as well for you to get here only at the end of this month, because by then I shall have more money and be able to cope with our expenses at the hotel here, which will be 50 *milreis* a day.

When you come to the concerts I am conducting, the best programmes will be those in August and September. Regarding our chamber music concerts, I am awaiting final arrangements from various impresarios here. When you come, bring the two orchestral batons I left behind.

Nothing else, kisses and greetings to Mama and lots more for you.[9]

Villa-Lobos was clearly anxious to have Lucília with him, as she had been in Paris, though on second thoughts he suggests delaying her arrival in São Paulo until his precarious financial situation had improved. At the time he had no steady income. The second concert, scheduled for 26 July, took place two days later than planned, and the third did not materialize on the appointed day. Only the next month were there more concerts, on 11, 25 and 31 August, one of which was dedicated exclusively to Florent Schmitt, Villa-Lobos's Parisian friend and patron, and another to works by Debussy and Casella. The concerts a month later that Villa-Lobos refers to without giving dates took place on 24 and 30 September, but he does not mention the concert in his honour arranged for 20 October or the series (25 and 28 November, 12 December) in which he was to present works of his own from his early years, songs from his Paris stay and new ones written especially for the São Paulo concerts.

Only two days after his previous letter, Villa-Lobos speaks of his struggle for recognition at home and of his dissatisfaction with the musical and artistic life of his native city:

[6] The Brazilian currency was at that time based on the *real* (plural *reis*), the effective unit being the *milreis*. One million *reis* totalled one *conto-de-reis*.

[7] Arnaldo Guinle, one of Villa-Lobos's Brazilian sponsors, who with his brother Carlos financed his stay in Paris.

[8] Unidentified but apparently connected with the Guinle brothers, according to the Guimarães family.

[9] Villa-Lobos, who had lost his father at the age of twelve, was always especially close to his mother.

S. Paulo, 17 July 1930

The day before yesterday I sent you 500 *milreis* through the Banco Nordeste de S. Paulo and went to the Post Office myself to mail you a long letter. I now write in answer to your letter which I have just received, in which you tell me about a radio festival with Newton.[10]

I really don't want you to take part in any concert without earning at least 200 *milreis* or so. If they want to put on some festival, they should do it on their own, for I *will not countenance the use of my works there in Rio* except on payment of a fee. I am tired of 'mockery' and injustices, and for me Rio is artistically dead already.

Nothing . . . Nothing and Nothing! . . .

I want you to pack your bags and come to me, where you belong.

Newton, whom as you know very well I value as an excellent friend and committed artist, will forgive me this protest; for, even with due regard to him, I want to hear no more of concerts in Rio unless they pay us as if we were good foreigners. So don't write to me any more in these terms. And if you do take part, then only for a minimum of 200 *milreis*.

As for your complaint about my not having written more often, that is unfair, for I have already written to you five times, and you know very well that I hate writing letters.

I have had a letter from Pery, which I will answer as soon as I can. Another from our concierge in Paris telling us that all is well.

Here everyone is waiting for you so that they can fête us jointly. Souza Lima,[11] Fonseca,[12] D. Olivia,[13] Baby de Guilherme,[14] who ask after you all the time—and others.

You need only let me know for certain which Cruzeiro[15] train you will be taking—for, unless I am mistaken, you will be visiting Bilita first[16]—and I can meet you at the station.

I have been ill, I don't know what with. I have lost weight to the extent that everyone notices, and I feel exhausted and despondent, although I am always surrounded by admirers and made much of. I can't acccount for my present state of physical decline. Perhaps I am worn out by my constant protests against the endless injustices that I have suffered lately. Oh! How I wish I could overcome everything and flee to 'inferno'! In short, my problem is how to achieve calmness and perseverance.

The first symphony concert (12 July) was so-so, and I am rehearsing every day for the second concert, which will be perhaps on the 26th of this month. I hope you will be here by then.

Nothing else, a thousand kisses to our beloved Grandma, and more to you and greetings.

[10] Newton Pádua, Brazilian cellist, friend of Villa-Lobos and interpreter of his music.
[11] João de Souza Lima, Brazilian pianist, composer and conductor.
[12] Unidentified, presumably another of Villa-Lobos's friends.
[13] Dona Olivia Guedes Penteado, Brazilian socialite and patroness of the arts, resident in São Paulo.
[14] Wife of Guilherme de Andrade e Almeida (1890–1969), Brazilian poet, essayist and journalist.
[15] A Brazilian railway company.
[16] The familiar name of Villa-Lobos's sister Carmen, married to the late Danton Condorcet da Silva Jardim.
[17] *Villa-Lobos, Visto da Platéia e na Intimidade*, p. 228.

At a time when he was anxious and physically unwell, Villa-Lobos particularly missed the support of his wife. This and occasionally other letters reveal a preoccupation with his health—though he had consulted a doctor for the first time only at the age of 39[17] and enjoyed robust good health until he was 61, when cancer of the bladder necessitated a successful operation in New York in 1948. His concern here was probably less an anxiety about his present indisposition than a fear that he might lack the stamina effectively to carry on his work in the face of difficulties. He is not self-indulgent: he diagnoses his ill-health as being of a psychosomatic nature and prescribes his own medicine—'calmness and perseverance'.

Between this letter to Lucília and the next there is a gap of two years, during which Villa-Lobos's life had taken a new—and unexpected—turn. The composer had become an organizer and administrator, teacher, deviser of a teaching method for choral singing and arranger of songs for chorus. He did not return to Paris, as he had wished, but remained in Brazil until the end of World War II apart from a few concert engagements in Buenos Aires and a short visit to Europe. This change of direction was a result of the nationalist developments that took place in Brazil under the presidency of Getúlio Dornelles Vargas (1883–1954). In February 1932 Villa-Lobos was appointed head of SEMA (Superintendencia da Educação Musical e Artística do Departmento de Educação da Prefeitura do Distrito Federal), the Department of Musical Education, a post that was created specifically for him. This alone represented a striking change in his life: at the age of 45 he had for the first time a salaried position.

Before his appointment, Villa-Lobos had demonstrated his theories about the use of massed choruses to involve the general public in good music. In the previous two years, with Lucília and a selected group of musicians, he had made pilgrimages to small towns in the hinterland of São Paulo, bringing music to places that were otherwise without culture. The whole of his career shows his chameleon-like adaptability to new circumstances and opportunities. His musical style as well as his professional life was a response to changing demands. He had abandoned 'internationalism' when his first visit to Paris (1923–4) showed him that folk-like elements were what Europe wanted at that time. Now, in the Brazil of the early 1930s, he saw the opportunities offered by musical education—and the promise of financial stability. Later, after the end of the war, he was ready to take the chance of joining the international circuit as a guest conductor, presenting his works on both sides of the Atlantic. He was an opportunist, it is true. Yet it was this pragmatism, coupled with his extraordinary musical ingenuity, intelligence, organizing ability and hitherto unsuspected pedagogical gifts, that made Villa-Lobos Brazil's most outstanding composer of his age.

The next letter to his wife, written only three months after his SEMA appointment, shows a new self-assurance. It also demonstrates the degree of influence he already enjoyed and was willing to exercise in obtaining the right teaching posts for Lucília.

Rio 5 May 1932

Today Dr. Pedro Ernesto[18] signed your appointment as a teacher in one of the Technical Secondary Schools, which establishes the right of assigning you to the Orsina da Fonseca School, as you and the headmistress there both want. Also the Minister of Education is appointing you under contract at the Ginásio [secondary school] Pedro II, according to a telegram which I am sending you along with another sent to me by the Minister himself. I have thanked all concerned by telegram.

You can be confident that they can wait a month for you with these appointments, which will bring you a further 1,750 *milreis*. So it is best for you to stay on [there] as long as you can so as to be really strong when you come, because you will have a lot of work to do. (My mother has today sent you 200 *milreis* by post.) I shall be sending you in the coming ten to fifteen days a further 200 *milreis* for your fare, and if you need any more, let me know in time.

You can arrive here at the end of this month or the start of next, because I am tying up the whole business of your appointment, and only your signature is necessary to bring it to a conclusion, which could be a month from today.

I think it is best for you to write two letters, one to Mme Anísio Teixeira[19] and another to Dr. Roxo.[20]

No more for now. All is well.

Another two years elapsed before the next letter, the briefest of notes from Bahia, in north-eastern Brazil, dated 4 July 1934, reporting that he is there to catch a flight to Recife and adding an affectionate postscript to his mother. The next day, on 5 July, at the invitation of the Pernambuco state government, Villa-Lobos took part in performances at the Santa Isabel Theatre including demonstrations of choral singing of the sort that he had been mounting in Rio de Janeiro. He also gave two lectures and a press conference on the subject. He was to return to Rio only in time for two 'Historical Concerts of Brazilian Music' on 18 and 20 July sponsored by the Fourth South American Theosophical Congress. Meanwhile he reported to Lucília from Recife.

Recife, 9 July 1934

Here everything has gone well apart from my stomach. I have done everything possible to improve my digestion, but palpitation on my left side is thoroughly unwelcome. I was afraid of travelling by air because of this, but I decided that a journey by air is much less upsetting than one by sea or land. So I am returning by plane and think I shall be leaving here on the 16th or 17th, on a Panair or Condor sea-plane, and will be two days travelling. I cannot say which day for certain, because my work here is not yet finished and I am very busy with speeches, interviews etc. I think we shall be going in an official and thoroughly artistic and educational party to visit the states of Paraiba and Rio Grande do Norte. We shall travel in a number of official cars. I shall of course find it extremely hard going; still, no matter: there will surely come an end to my involvement in this peregrination.

Please don't say anything to my people about my health.

Are you in office at [the Ginásio] Pedro II now? Have you received your salary from the city hall? Have they sent you 800 *milreis* from SEMA?

You can reply to me by airmail when you receive this, writing to the following address, and I shall still receive it in time:

Pensão Palácio
Rua de Concordia 148
Recife, Pernambuco

Give my remembrance and greetings to my mother and Candonguinha;[21] also to you.

PS: A letter is in the post with cuttings and reports from the newspapers here.

During the ensuing years Villa-Lobos was immersed in his SEMA activities: teaching (with much less time to compose new works), organizing and conducting choruses and concerts. He was esteemed in his own country. He led a settled life and could look forward to a future without worries—or so it seemed on the surface. For his personal life was apparently less smooth than it had been at the time of his last letter, in 1934. Only two years later, in May 1936, he separated from his wife. It is impossible to say what the cause was. Villa-Lobos's letter announcing his intention and explaining his reasons scarcely tells the full story, and gives little

[18] Pedro Ernesto do Rego Batista (1886–1942), Federal Interventor of the (then) Federal District, later mayor of Rio de Janeiro.
[19] Anísio Spinola Teixeira (1900–1971), in 1932 director of the Department of Education.
[20] Unidentified.
[21] Familiar name (diminutive of *candonga*—'darling') of Villa-Lobos's niece and godchild Laiseni, daughter of Luiz Guimarães (communication from Oldemar Guimarães, 27 November 1978).
[22] Villa-Lobos and the Brazilian Antônio Sá Pereira were the only Latin American delegates at the International Congress for Musical Education held in Prague between 4 and 9 April 1936. On his return journey to Brazil Villa-Lobos passed through Berlin and also gave a concert including his music in Barcelona.

clue to the difficulties that must have preceded his decision. Nor are Lucília's two letters in reply any more revealing. There is no more to be said, and the three letters are given here without further comment.

Berlin, 28 May 1936

This three-month trip of mine to Europe was undertaken especially to decide my personal life, once and for all, and not really to fulfil my obligations as a delegate to the International Congress for Musical Education.[22]

I am sure that the decisive news that follows below will come as no surprise to you. For a long time I have been reflecting on this resolution. The reasons are few but just. I cannot live in the company of someone from whom I feel entirely estranged, isolated, [and by whom I feel] constricted, in short without any affection save for a certain gratitude at your faithfulness for many years in my company.

I proclaim our absolute liberty [from one another]. I do so, however, with a quiet conscience, in the knowledge that I have done everything to ensure that you lack for nothing. It was entirely through my own efforts that I secured for you the excellent positions you now hold, as a result of which you earn more than I do and have better prospects.

I should wish you never to feel resentment towards me or anyone else, but to accept that our situation could not end in any other way than this. Hence, when I return I shall not come back to our home at 10 Rua Didimo, which I regard as being henceforth entirely your responsibility.

Naturally I must accept responsibility for all the expenses that result from this change in our lives. I will send a reliable person to fetch my personal belongings, and I will live alone with my mother.

Wishing you much happiness in your new life.

Lucília's answer dates from 14 June 1936, written in Rio de Janeiro:

I received your letter of 28 May but did not reply at once because I did not know where to write, seeing that you were on your way back here. I am replying now.

It is unnecessary for me to comment on the fact of your outrageous and absurd decision, but I am bound to point out that I am your wedded wife, that you undertook responsibilities towards me, and that you owe me personal satisfaction. I do not speak of your duties towards society, above all as regards the position you occupy in it as one concerned with education, because this I leave to your conscience to direct you.

However much I read your letter and try to draw deductions to lead me to a conclusion concerning the motives that have led you to this decision, I find no point of departure to set me in the right direction, unless it is that the last trace of feeling for me on your part has disappeared. You say that, when you agreed to go to Europe, it was with the aim of taking the opportunity of following a new course relative to our life [together]. This does not seem very probable to me, because, in that case, the cards you wrote to me earlier would make no sense. You also said that all you recognized as a common bond in my life with you was my virtue [as a wife], and as regards that I take pride in telling you that I owe you no debt on that score.

If latterly I have not shared your joys and sorrows, it is simply due to the fact that you have given me no opportunity to do so, since I do not even know what I have meant to you. This letter does not contain an appeal to you to return, because I cannot tell how far your animosity towards me has gone.

Meanwhile, it is my pleasure and duty to tell you that, so long as you do not give me the satisfaction to which I am entitled, I continue as before in my place [as your wife], waiting for you. But you should know that I have not even the slightest idea of putting pressure on you to return home, but simply desire that you should, as I do not see any reasons why you should do otherwise.

As regards your remarks to the effect that what I am I owe to you, I accept that as true, and if my gratitude is what you want, this [letter] brings it to you, though I take the opportunity of reminding you that this could not have been otherwise since, in a situation involving husband and wife, my cooperation could not but play its part.

And so, Villa, I am ready to submit myself to God's will, but for the satisfaction at least of my own conscience I shall continue to wait to hear your reasons or to await your final word.

Lucília's last letter is clearly in reply to Villa-Lobos's answer, now lost,[23] to her letter of 14 June:

19 June 1936

Your last letter has caused me surprise and very great offence.

I never imagined that, open and impulsive as you admit you are, and enjoying *absolute liberty*, you would endeavour to hide the real reason for your conduct, casting around for excuses which are in any case quite unjust and without foundation for a decision as serious as our final separation.

I cannot in the least accept your allegations. Nor can I stay silent in the face of such a serious and utterly untrue charge of which I am accused. It is unbelievable that you should have lived with me for twenty-two and a half years, knowing my shy temperament and trustworthy character, and now be capable of listening to such base and outrageous insinuations. I am astonished above all that you should never have said a word to me about the matter and did not make the slightest reference to it in your letter from Berlin, despite the fact that now you have judged it 'extremely serious' and *latterly* a matter of observation.

My attitude has always been one and the same and known to all: to be your sincere companion and collaborator.

If the many enemies you have have been busy spreading this *infamous nonsense*, quite certainly your work, your response, your compositions have by themselves crushed any such outrageous

[23] Communication from Oldemar Guimarães, 27 November 1978.

allegation. The proofs I have given to the contrary are countless and you would see them well enough if your present pride and obsession did not prevent you. And despite the humiliations I have suffered, I continue encouraging interest in your work and making it known in every post I hold, even though you are not there to see it.

My devotion and sincerity have not grown less. I regard Villa[-Lobos] the man and Villa[-Lobos) the artist as quite distinct. I think, in any case, despite your insisting in your decision not to return home, that it would be better for us to have, as I already asked, a personal understanding between us. Meanwhile, our situation, should you not respond to this request, will be what you have made it, since all that interests me is that you return of your own free will, if there is any affection still on your part.

My attitude will not be one of hostility but of all possible loyalty and discretion, as I am already proving by entrusting my own brother, as a person in one's confidence, with the delivery of this letter.

However, you should quite clearly understand that I will not relinquish any of my rights as your wedded wife and shall continue to sign myself Lucília Guimarães Villa-Lobos. This I must emphasize, as I cannot but mention the offence your present attitude caused me, addressing the reply your chauffeur brought me to 'Lucilia Guimarães V.L.'—a form of address I compared with those on the cards you sent me from Europe ('Lucília Villa-Lobos') when you had not yet got to the point of charging me with this 'infamous nonsense'.

Villa-Lobos did not return to his wife. They each went their separate ways until the composer's death in 1959. Lucília survived him by six and a half years.

Music and Letters, **61**(3/4), July/October 1980, 284–92

Corrigenda

p127 *second paragraph, fourth line from bottom*:
For Educacáo read Euducação
p129 *FN 22*:
For 4 and 9 April read on 25 April
p132 *line seven from bottom*:
For Lucilia read Lucília

HEITOR VILLA-LOBOS EN ZIJN FAMILIE*

„Op Allerheiligen (1 november) van het jaar 1912 was Heitor Villa-Lobos bij ons te gast. Arthur Alves, een vriend van mijn ouders, had hem meegenomen zodat we zijn uitstekende gitaarspel konden horen. Indertijd woonden wij – mijn moeder, mijn zes broers en zusters en ik – in de Rua Haddock Lobo in de wijk Vila Itala, tegenwoordig Rua Domicio da Gama geheten. Ik had mijn pianostudie aan het Instituto Nacional de Música (de huidige Escola de Música da Universidade Federal do Rio de Janeiro) afgesloten en was als pianolerares verbonden aan het Colégio Sacré Coeur; verder gaf ik aan enkele privé-leerlingen piano- en solfègeles. De muziekavond met Villa-Lobos verliep aangenaam. Nadat hij gitaar had gespeeld, wilde hij mijn pianospel horen. Ik koos Chopin. Toen ik mijn spel had beëindigd, was Villa-Lobos somber en terneergeslagen. De gitaar was toentertijd nog geen instrument voor ernstige muziek; men gebruikte hem voor serenades.

Plotseling vertelde Villa-Lobos dat hij eigenlijk cello speelde en met dat instrument een andere keer terug wilde komen. We maakten een afspraak voor de zaterdag daarop en hij beloofde me de muziek op te sturen zodat ik die kon instuderen en hem op de piano kon begeleiden. Na die zaterdag volgden nog meer bijeenkomsten. Bij de gemeenschappelijke artistieke interesse voegde zich al gauw wederzijdse persoonlijke genegenheid. We verloofden ons en op 12 november 1913 trouwden we. Ik bleef de twee geven en Vila[1]) speelde overdag cello in het Confeitaria Colombo[2]) en 's avonds in Assirio[3]). We woonden in bij mijn familie die ondertussen verhuisd was naar de Rua Fonseca no. 7 in de wijk São Cristovao. Ondanks de talrijke problemen die het dagelijks leven met zich mee bracht, begon Villa nu serieus te componeren. Omdat hij toen nog geen piano kon spelen, speelde ik hem gedeelten van zijn composities voor."[4])

Zo startte, beginnend bij de vriendschap en het huwelijk met Lucília Guimarães (1886-1966) die hem bij tijd en wijle muziektechnische hulp bood, de compositorische loopbaan van Heitor Villa-Lobos (1887-1959), de beroemdste Braziliaanse en belangrijkste Latijns-Amerikaanse componist van zijn tijd, wiens werken vooral sinds het einde van de Tweede Wereldoorlog in vele landen worden

uitgevoerd. Lucília's invloed op de composities uit deze vroege periode waarin Villa-Lobos zijn weg als componist nog bijna geheel autodidactisch zocht, moet niet worden onderschat. Zo vertelde ze ons in Rio de Janeiro dat Villa-Lobos eens met veel moeite trachtte de tonen van een thema dat hij voor een Ave Maria wilde gebruiken, op de piano te vinden. Lucília speelde hem het thema driemaal zo snel voor en merkte op dat ze het meer geschikt achtte voor een tarantella. Villa-Lobos was het daarmee eens en zo ontstond de Tarantella opus 30 voor twee piano's; het stuk werd in april 1911 op papier gezet. En aan de wereldpremière (op 17 november 1917 in Rio de Janeiro) werkte Lucília mee.[5]) Het was het eerste stuk dat niet meer tot Villa-Lobos' jeugdwerk kan worden gerekend, maar al tot de reeks serieuzere composities die eveneens nog in 1911 ontstonden.

Lucília was een begrijpende partner voor haar echtgenoot, die met zijn hoge ambities niet gemakkelijk in de omgang was. De lange, moeizame weg naar het succes betekende een hele opgave voor de jonge, pasgetrouwde vrouw die zelf een gevoelig kunstenares was. Lucília vertolkte vele van zijn composities met piano, zowel muziek voor piano-solo, als begeleidingen en partijen in zijn kamermuziek. Ze was een goede huisvrouw en een attente gastvrouw voor de vele vrienden, kameraden en collega's die Villa-Lobos geheel onaangekondigd mee naar huis nam voor het eten, zowel in Rio de Janeiro als later in Parijs (1927-1930). Lucília stond hem terzijde in al de zware, zorgelijke en moeilijke jaren van strijd om het hoofd boven water te houden en artistieke erkenning te vinden. Dit duurde voort tot Villa-Lobos in 6932 op vijfenveertigjarige leeftijd voor het eerst een vaste betrekking als ambtenaar had gekregen. Hij moest het muziekonderwijs in Rio de Janeiro organiseren en leiden en begon net als componist in binnen- en buitenland naam te maken. Toen kwam de breuk. Villa-Lobos ging in het late voorjaar van 1936 bij zijn vrouw weg om nooit meer terug te komen. In aansluiting op een muziekpedagogisch con-

---

*Dit oorspronkelijk in het Duits geschreven artikel is vertaald door Sabine Lichtenstein.

gres in Praag waaraan hij op uitnodiging van Leo Kestenberg (1882 – 1962) had deelgenomen, schreef hij vanuit Berlijn aan zijn vrouw:

„Lucília,

Mijn reis van drie maanden door Europa werd voornamelijk ondernomen om eens en voorgoed een einde te maken aan mijn innerlijke onzekerheid en pas in tweede instantie om mijn taak als gedelegeerde bij het Internationale Congres voor Muziekpedagogie te vervullen. Ik ben ervan overtuigd dat het zeer beslissende bericht dat hieronder volgt, geen verrassing zal zijn. Ik ben lang bij mezelf te rade gegaan om tot een besluit te komen. De redenen zijn gering in aantal, maar gerechtvaardigd. Ik kan niet leven in gezelschap van een persoon door wie ik mij geïsoleerd, vervreemd, gedeprimeerd voel – kortom zonder enige genegenheid, of het zou een zekere dankbaarheid moeten zijn voor de jarenlange trouw jegens mij. *Ik proclameer onze absolute vrijheid.* Ik doe dat met een gerust geweten: ik heb al het mogelijke gedaan om het je aan niets te laten ontbreken. Het is uitsluitend aan mij te danken dat je nu uitstekend werk hebt waarmee je meer verdient en meer zekerheid voor de toekomst hebt dan ik. Ik hoop dat je nooit wrok jegens mij en anderen zult koesteren, maar dat je kalm en berustend vast zult stellen dat er aan onze situatie op geen andere wijze een eind kan worden gemaakt dan nu is gebeurd. Ik zal dus na mijn aankomst niet meer terugkeren in de woning Rua Didimo 10; daarvoor acht ik vanaf die datum uitsluitend en alleen jou verantwoordelijk. Uiteraard moet ik opkomen voor alle kosten die deze verandering in onze levens met zich meebrengt. Ik zal een vertrouwensman sturen om mijn persoonlijke bezittingen op te halen en zal bij mijn moeder intrekken. Je veel geluk toewensend in je nieuwe leven,

Villa-Lobos"[6]).

Daarmee kwam ook een eind aan Villa-Lobos' contact met Lucília's broers en zusters, die hem in zijn moeilijke beginperiode eveneens een niet onbelangrijke morele steun hadden verleend en hem ook in artistiek opzicht nader stonden dan zijn eigen moeder, broers en zusters.

Villa-Lobos' moeder, Noêmia Umbelina Santos Monteiro (1859-1946), kwam uit een eenvoudig milieu. Hoewel haar vader, Antônio Santos Monteiro, die van Portugese afkomst moet zijn geweest, als pianist was opgetreden bij feesten en ook quadrilles en andere toentertijd populaire dansen schijnt te hebben gecomponeerd, was Noêmia volstrekt niet geïnteresseerd in muziek; dit in tegenstelling tot haar cellospelende echtgenoot Raúl (1862-1899), een uit Spaanse ouders geboren assistent-bibliothecaris, die al op zevenendertigjarige leeftijd in Rio de Janeiro aan malaria stierf. Villa-Lobos' broers en zusters erfden de amuzikaliteit van hun moeder: zijn jongste broer Othon (1897-1918) was elektricien en woonde, toen de componist nog vrijgezel was, met hem samen. Nadat Othon getrouwd was, distantieerde hij zich echter van Heitor die het reeds op negentienjarige leeftijd gesloten huwelijk van zijn broer met Octavia namelijk niet kon billijken, aangezien zij, aldus de broers en zusters[7], uit een ander milieu stamde. Othon interesseerde zich bovendien meer voor sport, vooral voetbal – zaken waar de componist een afschuw van had – en toonde volstrekt geen artistieke of intellectuele neigingen. Villa-Lobos' twee zusters waren evenmin geïnteresseerd in muziek en hadden dan ook weinig begrip voor het leven en het streven van hun broer. Zijn zuster Bertha (1885-1976), ook wel Lulucha genoemd, trouwde met Romeu Augusto Borman de Borges. Haar aandacht was voornamelijk gericht op haar man en hun drie kinderen: Clélia, Haygara en Paulo Emygidio. Haar drie jaar jongere, ietwat hardhorende zuster Carmen (1888-1970), in de huiselijke kring Bilita genoemd, was lerares. Uit haar huwelijk met Danton Condorcet da Silva Jardim werd een dochter, Yacyra, geboren.

In het gezin van Lucília trof Villa-Lobos meer begrip voor zijn werk en zijn compositorisch streven. Haar broers en zusters waren, net als zij, muzikaal en muziekminnend zodat ze alleen daardoor al veel meer aan Villa-Lobos' leven en werk konden deelnemen. Lucília's oudste broer Juca had zelfs een absoluut gehoor. Haar broer Alvaro de Oliveira verhuisde na beëindiging van zijn medicijnenstudie naar een andere stad. Haar broer Luiz had het langdurigste en intiemste contact met Villa-Lobos. Hij paste ook tijdens het verblijf van het echtpaar Villa-Lobos in · Parijs (1927-1930) op de woning in de Rua Didimo 10 die de componist en zijn vrouw in 1919 hadden betrokken. Ook redigeerde en verkocht hij twee artikelen die Villa-Lobos hem vanuit Parijs had opgestuurd aan de Braziliaanse pers. Bovendien stonden Lucília's broers Villa-Lobos ook met raad en daad ter zijde tijdens de Week van de Moderne Kunst in São Paulo (11-18 februari 1922). Het deerde hen volgens eigen zeggen niet om voor hun zwager, wiens carrière zich nog in een beginfase bevond, min of meer als loopjongen te fungeren. Ze bewezen hem allerlei diensten en traden als koerier op zodat zijn aandacht niet werd afgeleid door bijzaken; ze zorgden ervoor dat hij bij deze manifestatie probleemloos en succesvol kon functioneren. Lucília en haar broers en zusters omringden Villa-Lobos met warmte en sympathie en pasten zich aan bij zijn steeds krachtiger naar buiten tredende, onbuigzame en heftige temperament. Ze boden hem samen de morele steun die hij in die jaren en zelfs later nog zo veelvuldig behoefde en moedigden hem aan vol te houden in perioden waarin de Braziliaanse pers wel over Villa-Lobos discuteerde, maar het grote talent in hem nog lang niet wilde erkennen, laat staan bereid was te constateren hoe belangrijk hij voor de muziek van zijn land al was en nog zou worden.

Toen Villa-Lobos en Lucília twintig jaar waren getrouwd, namen ze een eigen woning. Ze huurden de parterre in de Rua Didimo 10 in de wijk Vila Rui Barbosa. Deze weinig bekende straat loopt van de Rua do Senado tot aan de Avenida Henrique Valadares. Ze ligt in het centrum van de stad, dicht bij het Hoofdbureau van politie en het Braziliaanse Rode Kruis. Het huis valt nog steeds niet onder de monumentenzorg noch bevindt er zich een gedenksteen[6]) om er aan te herinneren dat Villa-Lobos er ruim zestien jaar woonde (tot begin 1936) en er gedurende die tijd de werken schreef die zijn roem in binnen- en buitenland definitief vestigden. In deze periode ontwikkelde hij de compositiestijl die karakteristiek voor hem werd en die nadien ook nauwelijks zou veranderen.

Ook al waren de materiële middelen bescheiden, toch heerste er in deze woning een actief, cultureel en sociaal klimaat. Villa-Lobos' tekstdichter en andere toenmalige schrijvers, componisten, schilders en uitvoerende kunstenaars kwamen er regelmatig over de vloer. Later, in de jaren dertig, toen hij een post als ambtenaar bekleedde, had hij ook vaak mensen om zich heen die hoopten dat hij zijn invloed voor hen zou aanwenden. In deze woning bracht Villa-Lobos de meest beslissende jaren in zijn artistieke ontwikkeling door. Hij streed er niet alleen de dagelijkse strijd om het bestaan, maar beleefde er ook vele gelukkige uren en vierde er menig vrolijk feest. Zelfs gaf Villa-Lobos hier, zij het slechts gedurende korte tijd, les aan de enige celloleerling die hij ooit heeft gehad. Hij bezat in die jaren weinig geduld voor amateurs; zijn buitengewoon grote pedagogische talent, waarvan hij zich toen in het geheel nog niet bewust was, ontplooide zich pas in de dertiger jaren toen de tijden veranderden en er zich volledig onverwacht allerlei mogelijkheden voordeden. Toen zou hij op dat gebied het onmogelijke waarmaken en voor Brazilië

een eenmalige prestatie verrichten.[9])
Tot aan het begin van de dertiger jaren interesseerde hij zich echter uitsluitend voor het componeren. Zijn ongewoon robuuste gestel gecombineerd met een eenvoudige leefwijze en bescheiden eetgewoonten maakten het hem mogelijk vaak tot in de vroege ochtend te componeren. Lucília's familie vertelde dat hij bij wijze van ontbijt slechts één of twee koppen zeer sterke Braziliaanse koffie dronk. Zijn warme maaltijd bestond uit rijst of pommes frites, een biefstuk en waterkers of kool. Tussendoor at hij niets. Wel weer dronk hij veel kopjes koffie die buitengewoon sterk moesten zijn – ,,jodiumtinctuur'' zoals Lucília en haar familie het noemden. Afgezien van een enkel glas donker bier dronk hij geen alcohol. Zijn koffie-traditie hield Villa-Lobos zijn hele leven vol, ook in de Verenigde Staten waar hij na de oorlog een deel van het jaar doorbracht. Behalve ,,Vanille Ice Cream'' zijn ,,strong, strong coffee'' dan ook de enige Engelse woorden die hij ooit heeft geleerd.[10]) Een uitzondering op zijn spartaanse leefwijze vormde zijn verslaving aan sigaren. Maar noch de koffie noch de tabak schenen zijn gezondheid tot aan zijn eenenzestigste levensjaar schade te berokkenen. Zijn zwagers vertelden dat Villa-Lobos nooit klaagde over hoofdpijn en nooit griep had. Zelfs de Spaanse griep, waaraan zijn vrouw en haar broers en zusters in 1918 moesten geloven, ging aan hem voorbij. Slechts eenmaal was hij niet geheel in orde; hij leed toen aan een door parasieten veroorzaakte afwijking aan zijn voet. Dat speelde zich precies af in de Week voor Moderne Kunst (1922) in São Paulo, zodat men hem uitlachte toen hij met één voet in een pantoffel gestoken in het openbaar verscheen. Op negenendertigjarige leeftijd (in april 1926) moest Villa-Lobos in het Pedro Ernesto-ziekenhuis een kleine chirurgische ingreep ondergaan. Het was, volgens zeggen van zijn familie, de eerste keer in zijn leven dat hij een arts consulteerde. In de dertiger jaren leed hij tenslotte bij tijd en wijle aan een ,,typische overproduktie van maagzuur'' zoals hij het noemde. Dat blijkt uit een brief van 9 juli 1934[11]) aan Lucília die hij schreef vanuit Recife in het Braziliaanse departement Pernambuco. Een en ander had tot gevolg dat hij zijn reis per vliegtuig in plaats van per trein of schip voortzette.
Zijn ijzersterke gestel had na zijn zestigste levensjaar een grote schok te verduren. Op advies van zijn Braziliaanse artsen vloog hij in 1948 naar New York City waar hij op 9 juli in het Memorial Hospital werd opgenomen voor een operatie in verband met blaaskanker. Ondanks het feit dat hij tot aan zijn dood een rigoureuze behandeling moest blijven on-

dergaan, was het hem met zijn sterke gestel en wilskrachtige karakter vergund zich nog elf jaar lang aan zijn vermoeiende dirigententaken in de VS, Europa, Zuid-Amerika en Israël te wijden. Daarnaast ontvouwde hij een onwaarschijnlijk grote compositorische produktiviteit, totdat overbelaste nieren en een uremie op 17 november 1959 een eind aan zijn leven maakten.

Villa-Lobos' huwelijk met Lucília bleef kinderloos. Misschien moet men zijn grote liefde voor kinderen en zijn talrijke voor kinderen gecomponeerde pianostukken hiermee in verband brengen. Misschien ook is het de oorzaak van zijn bepaald kinderlijk plezier in het oplaten van zelfgemaakte vliegers. Een plezier dat hij zich zelfs nog als veertigjarige in zijn tweede Parijse periode gunde, tijdens een tochtje in gezelschap van zijn vriend de pianist Tomás Terán (1896-1964) en diens vrouw. Deze gebeurtenis is ook fotografisch vastgelegd.[12]) Villa-Lobos bleef het biljartspel, dat hij in zijn eerste huwelijksjaren met zijn twee zwagers Juca en Oldemar had beoefend, ook later, na zijn scheiding van Lucília, trouw. Toen frequenteerde hij de biljartkamer van de Associação Brasileira de Imprensa (ABI), de Braziliaanse persvereniging; deze bevindt zich in een pand, gebouwd in de stijl van Le Corbusier tegenover zijn in het centrum gelegen driekamerwoning in de Rua Araújo Pôrto Alegre 56 die hij kort na zijn scheiding had betrokken. Villa-Lobos was zijn leven lang dol op de bioscoop waar hij heen ging om wildwestfilms te zien; en op vervolghoorspelen waar hij thuis aan de radio naar luisterde. Het laatste belette hem niet gelijktijdig te componeren.

In het jaar 1936 vond de grote breuk in zijn privé-leven plaats. Bijna vijftig jaar oud wendde hij zich af van de één jaar oudere Lucília en daarmee tevens van haar familieleden. Villa-Lobos had een andere partner – Arminda Neves d'Alemida – gekozen. Ze behoorde tot de jongere generatie, was zijn leerlinge geweest en kwam uit de kring die zich om hem heen had gevormd toen hij zich als ambtenaar aan zijn pedagogische activiteiten wijdde. Tot aan zijn dood, drieëntwintig jaar later, deelde ze lief en leed met hem; ze bezochten na de oorlog samen talrijke plaatsen waar Villa-Lobos als gevierd componist met alle grote orkesten zijn werken dirigeerde. Na zijn dood gaf men haar de leiding van het Villa-Lobos Museum in Rio de Janeiro dat in het begin van de zestiger jaren was opgericht met als doel behartiging en verspreiding van Villa-Lobos' muziek. Villa-Lobos' levensgezellin uit zijn latere jaren is bekend geworden onder de naam Arminda A. Villa-Lobos die ze op grond van een gerechtelijke beslissing had aangenomen.[13])

Noten

1. Villa-Lobos werd in het ouderlijk huis „Tuhu" genoemd, wat zoveel betekent als vonk. Lucília, haar familie en alle binnen- en buitenlandse vrienden en kennissen van de componist spraken hem nooit aan bij zijn voornaam „Heitor", maar noemden hem altijd „Villa".
2. Het in 1894 opgerichte Confeitaria Colombo in de Rua Gonçalves Dias 32-36, een straat genoemd naar de Braziliaanse dichter Antônio Gonçalves Dia (1823-1864); Rio de Janeiro's beroemdste tearoom.
3. Het restaurant Assirio bevond zich in het souterrain van het Teatro Municipal in de Avenida Rio Branco, de hoofdstraat van Rio de Janeiro. Sinds 1949 bevindt zich op die plaats het Museum dos Teatros do Rio de Janeiro.
4. Uit de ongepubliceerde *Memoires* van Lucília Guimarães Villa-Lobos overgenomen in *Villa-Lobos, Visto da Flatéia e na Intimidade* (1912-1935), samengesteld en uitgegeven door Villa-Lobos' zwager Luiz Guimarães, met medewerking van zijn familieleden Oldemar Guimarães, Dinorah Guimarães Campos en Alvara de Oliveira Guimarães, en gepubliceerd in een niet in de handel zijnde uitgave in Rio de Janeiro, p. 223-224.
Intussen is aan het licht gekomen dat de memoires van Lucília Guimarães onvindbaar zijn en hoogst waarschijnlijk verloren zijn gegaan. Het hier gepubliceerde korte fragment eruit is het enige waarover we nog beschikken. (Uit een brief van Villa-Lobos' zwager, Oldemar Guimarães, aan Lisa M. Peppercorn, Rio de Janeiro, 12 december 1979.)
5. *Heitor Villa-Lobos, Leben und Werk des brasilianischen Komponisten* door Lisa M. Peppercorn. Atlantis, Zürich 1972, p. 30, 111/112, 178, 179. Uit dit verhaal van Lucília moet men concluderen dat haar eerste ontmoeting met de componist niet heeft kunnen plaatsvinden op 1 november 1912, maar reeds in 1911. Op de ontstaansdatum van de compositie die we indertijd in Rio de Janeiro overnamen van het manuscript zou onjuist zijn. Ook andere factoren spreken er voor dat de eerste ontmoeting eerder zou hebben plaatsgevonden dan in Lucília's *Memoires* staat aangegeven. Mogelijk is nog dat in het onder 4.) vermelde boek een drukfout is geslopen bij de vermelding van de ontmoetingsdatum.
6. Deze brief, geschreven in het Portugees, is voor het eerst gepubliceerd in facsimile in het in 4.) vermelde boek *Villa-Lobos, Visto da Flatéia e na intimidade*, p. 352/353.
7. *Villa-Lobos, Visto da Flatéia e na Intimidade*, p. 224.
8. In Parijs daarentegen onthulde men naar aanleiding van Villa-Lobos' vierentachtigste verjaardag (die hij niet mocht beleven) in 1971 een gedenkplaat aan de buitenmuur van het hotel Bedford, Rue de l'Arcade 17, Paris 8ième. Villa-Lobos woonde vanaf 1952 tot aan zijn dood in 1959 in dit hotel dat voor hem dienst deed als Europees hoofdkwartier. In hetzelfde hotel bracht de laatste keizer van Brazilië, Don Pedro II. na zijn aftreden en het uittreden der republiek (15 november 1889) tot aan zijn dood (5 december 1891) er zijn jaren van ballingschap door. Boven de gedenkplaat voor Villa-Lobos hangt nog een plaquette ter nagedachtenis aan de keizer. Pedro II (1825-1891) was de zoon van Don-Pedro I (1798-1834) en aartshertogin Leopoldina van Oostenrijk (1797-1826).
9. *Musical Education in Brazil* door Lisa M. Peppercorn, Bulletin of the Pan American Union, Washington DC, Vol. 74 no. 10, okt. 1940.
10. Uit een transcript van een interview dat op 31 maart 1971 in New York City plaatsvond tussen Arminda A. Villa-Lobos, Hugh Ross, leider van de Scola Cantorum te New York en Richard Gaddes, de artistiek leider van de Santa Fee Opera Company. Dit manuscript werd ons als gebruiksmateriaal ter beschikking gesteld door de Santa Fee Opera Company in Santa Fee, New Mexico.
11. Deze brief, geschreven in het Portugees, is voor het eerst in facsimile afgedrukt in het 4.) vermelde boek *Villa-Lobos, visto da Flatéia e na Intimidade*, p. 348.
12. Tomás Terán, Braziliaans pianist en muziekpedagoog van Spaanse origine, leefde vanaf 1929 in Brazilië waar hij van grote invloed was op een groep jonge Braziliaanse pianisten.
13. Uit een brief van Arminda A. Villa-Lobos aan Lisa M. Peppercorn.

Mens & Melodie, September 1980, 457–60

Corrigenda/addenda

p133 *second column line 14 from bottom*:
For 6932 read 1932
p136 *FN 4 line 2*:
For Flatéia read Platéia
FN 6 line 3:
For Flatéia read Platéia
FN 7 line 1:
For Flatéia read Platéia
FN 11 line 3:
For visto da Flatéia read Visto da Platéia
FN 13:
add at the end: dated Rio de Janeiro 2 September 1970

A Villa-Lobos Autograph
Letter at the Bibliothèque
Nationale (Paris)

The Bibliothèque Nationale in Paris possesses an autograph letter of the Brazilian composer Heitor Villa-Lobos (1887–1959), written from his Rio de Janeiro downtown apartment (at Rua Araújo Pôrto Alegre 56) on September 25, 1951, to his long-time friend, the French composer and music critic Florent Schmitt (1870–1958). François Lesure, curator of the Bibliothèque Nationale's Music Department, mentioned the autograph to me when I visited him in March 1979 and offered, at my request, a photocopy with his permission for publication. Arminda Villa-Lobos, the composer's companion during his last twenty-three years and, since 1961, director of the Villa-Lobos Museum, also consented to the publication of this letter, which she had cosigned.

To my knowledge, the letter is the only one that Villa-Lobos wrote to Florent Schmitt (or, at least, the only one presently available), although their acquaintance, and later their friendship and mutual artistic admiration, dates back to the period 1927–1930. At this time Villa-Lobos, with his wife Lucília, took up residence in Paris at Place St. Michel 11, where the composer's Brazilian sponsors, the brothers Arnaldo Guinle (1884–1964) and Carlos Guinle (1883–1969), two philanthropists and industrialists, had set him up in a well-furnished apartment and financed not only his sojourn but also some of his Paris concerts and early publications with Editions Max Eschig to help him get a footing in the European musical world.

Nearly twenty-five years separate the date of this letter (1951, when both he and Schmitt were already close to the end of their lives) and their first artistic encounter in the fall of 1927. The then fifty-seven-year-old Florent Schmitt, with extensive foreign

Latin American Music Review, Vol. 1, No. 2, October 1980
© 1980 by the University of Texas Press   0163–0350/80/020253–12$01.10

travels and a post as director at the Lyon Conservatoire (1921–1924) behind him, was again in Paris at the time Villa-Lobos presented to the Parisian public his latest compositions in two concerts, on October 24 and December 5, 1927. These works (see below) were, as time has shown, among his most characteristic ones. They indisputably manifested an unusual style and an outspoken personality. At that time, Villa-Lobos was forty years old, an unknown composer in Europe except for some smaller pieces that Artur Rubinstein and Aline van Barentzen had played occasionally and that were reviewed in the musical press. Even then, Florent Schmitt wrote quite enthusiastically about Villa-Lobos's *A Prole do Bebê No. 2* for piano, devoting a full page in his column "Les Arts et la Vie: La Musique" in *La Revue de France*, on October 1, 1927 (pages 522–523), to the first performance of this work, dedicated to its interpreter Aline van Barentzen. He was undoubtedly impressed by Villa-Lobos's music and concluded his review by saying: "En vérité, il faut retenir entre nous le nom de Villa-Lobos. Ou plutôt point n'est besoin de le retenir: ses oeuvres se chargeront de nous le rappeler."

The two concerts of 1927 at the Salle Gaveau were a much more formidable event, inspiring Florent Schmitt to write an almost four-page review and analysis in his *La Revue de France* chronicle.[1] He wrote:

> Mais l'évènement, jusqu'alors, fut la révélation, en deux séances salle Gaveau, des oeuvres de chambre et d'orchestre de Heitor Villa-Lobos, l'extraordinaire musicien dont nous comble momentanément le Brésil. Que nous voilà loin, en présence de ce jeune trois-quarts de dieu aux dents de crocodile à travers lesquels, jusqu'alors, nous étions réduits à juger comme nous pouvions de la richesse et de la variété d'un folklore somptueux entre nous. Car, si personnel pourtant, l'art de Villa-Lobos s'inspire en droite ligne des simples scies et rengaines natales que son génie s'est merveilleusement assimilé.
>
> A la première séance voici d'abord trois *chôros,*—prononcez à la Shakespeare: sérénades, 'façons de synthèses, nous explique l'auteur, des différentes modalités brésiliennes et indiennes', avec pour principaux éléments, outre le rythme, qui, roi chez Chabrier, est ici dictateur, quelque mélodie typique qui apparaitra incidentellement et sous des aspects toujours renouvelés. De ces trois chôros de chambre écrits, le premier pour trois cors et trombone et dans une gravité de sentiment adéquate, le second en forme de divagation ingénue et touchante entre la flûte et la clarinette, c'est le troisième, septuor pour instruments à vent dont saxophone, pour violon, violoncelle avec, par surcroit, d'après troisièmes temps sur quatre de tam-tam extra, c'est le troisième qui est le plus original, le plus émouvant aussi, d'une invention mélodique et

rythmique qui nous décamoufle des routes vierges et des atmosphères irrespirées.

Puis le *Rude Poème*, long et passionné monologue où, même après l'étonnante richesse de timbres du morceau qui précède, réduit à ses propres moyens, le piano trouve *celui* de ne nous point décevoir. Car si Villa-Lobos traite l'instrument avec une vieille maîtrise, c'est aussi avec une virtuosité très nouvelle et de vastes ressources.

Et parce qu'il faut que l'intérêt aille toujours en croissant, nous arrivons au gigantesque *Chôros VIII*, le point culminant de cette soirée mémorable du 24 octobre. Là, parallèlement à l'orchestre redevenu normal, ses quatre-vingts rouages enfin assemblés et prêts à entrer en lutte, nous voyons se déchaîner sans plus aucune hypocrisie les pires instincts de ce rescapé de l'âge de pierre. La fantaisie y coudoie le sadisme, mais un sadisme stylisé d'homme bon et d'âme haute, qui n'est pas à la portée du premier fêtard venu, ou du premier chemineau, et se tient jalousement dans le cercle de la beauté. L'orchestre hurle et délire, en proie au *jazzium tremens*, et, alors que vous croyez atteintes les limites d'un dynamisme presque surhumain, voici que, d'un coup, quatre bras de titans s'abattent, ceux d'Aline van Barentzen et de Tomas Teran, vingt doigts d'acier qui en l'espèce en valent cent, brandissant deux formidables tanks-Gaveau de quinze octaves qui, sur ce fond tumultueux, explosent avec un fracas de séisme aux enfers. C'est le coup de grâce. Cela devient démoniaque, ou divin, selon votre entendement. Car vous adorerez ou abhorrerez: vous ne resterez pas indifférents. Irrésistiblement vous sentirez que le vrai grand souffle a passé.

Entre temps, Miss Elsie Houston[2], d'une voix magnifiquement timbrée, dialogua avec l'orchestre dans une suite de cinq *Serestas* dont la première, *Abril*, la quatrième, *Cantiga de Viuvo*, d'une mélancolie prenante et étrange, sont parmi les choses les plus suggestives que je sache.

La seconde séance ne fut pas moins passionnante. Comme frontispice, un fier triptyque de choeurs avec orchestre: *Cantiga de Róda*—chanson de ronde—inspirée d'un thème populaire enfantin dont la poésie, précieuse et naïve, vaut d'être citée: 'Allons, soeurette, nous promener sur la grève. Allons voir la barque neuve tombée du ciel sur la mer. Elle porte Notre-Dame et les anges vont ramant. Ramez, rameurs, car ces flots sont des fleurs'. Puis *Na Bahia tem*, d'après des thèmes et des argots séculaires de l'État de Bahia plus connu par ses obligations 1910 que par son folklore. Le troisième, *Pica-paó*, composé sur une légende des Indiens Parécis, est sans doute le plus original, avec ses bizarres onomatopées qui tiennent lieu de tout texte et ses vocalises qui datent des premiers âges du monde. Ces choeurs, dont le premier pour voix de femmes, les deux autres pour voix d'hommes, furent chantés par l'*Art choral* avec infiniment de souplesse, sous la direction de M. Robert Siohan, à qui il faut rendre grâce pour les efforts persévérants et intelligents dont nous commençons sérieusement à recueillir les fruits, car sa jeune société est en progrès flagrant, et entrevoir enfin dans un avenir proche une ère—pour parler comme Zola—de vérité et de justesse.

En suite Mme. Aline van Barentzen s'en vint défiler la série des *Os Bichinhos*—Les petites bêtes—avec sa sollicitude un peu égoiste d'heureuse dédicacée. Je vous ai parlé, il y a trois mois, de cette pittoresque et divertissante suite composée à l'usage des enfants prodiges. Qu'il me suffise aujourd'hui de célébrer la rare musicalité, la virtuosité et le mécanisme invraisemblable, la puissance et aussi l'intelligence et la compréhension, et encore la docilité, la simplicité, la modestie d'une interprète qui ne nous surprend que malgré elle et parce qu'elle ne peut faire autrement. Elle est certainement de la pléiade sacrée, des quatre ou cinq élus que j'évoquais tout à l'heure à propos de la *Valse de l'Adieu,* et cela résume tous les éloges.

Mais le fauve apparaît au pupitre, salué d'une longue ovation, pour diriger avec une incontinence d'échappé de la jungle son *Nonetto* pour choeur mixte, cinq instruments à vent dont saxophone. puis célesta, harpe, piano et batterie. Ce nonetto, qui veut exprimer toute l'ambiance sonore du pays natal et toute l'originalité du rythme, est, parmi tant de belles pages, une des plus saisissantes. Transportés loin de notre Europe étriquée et calculatrice, nous vivons un instant de la vie instinctive de ces sauvages, la vraie, la seule peut-être, avec leurs joies, leurs terreurs et leurs superstitions. C'est le déchaînement des forces brutes, bonnes ou mauvaises, où la quiétude d'un fond vocal parfois apaisé vient atténuer l'angoisse et la torture du rythme.

Suivant trois poèmes indiens pour chant et orchestre. Le premier *Canide-Ioune-Sabalet* est une chanson élégiaque de la légende de l'*Oiseau jaune*; le second célèbre la mort du cacique, prince de U. . .— suit un nom que nul Français n'entreprendrait de lire; le troisième, *Iâra*, d'après une poésie de Mario de Andrade, décrit en style populaire et dans l'idiome dérivé, sous l'influence des races et du climat, de la langue portugaise, un être légendaire de l'île de Marajo, à l'embouchure de l'Amazone, un être tour à tour serpent, sirène . . . et femme, ce qui devait arriver. Ces trois poèmes, d'une barbare désespérance, furent chantés par Mme. Vera Janacopulos[3]. sud-Américaine d'éducation, sinon de naissance, avec un sens et une âme d'indigène authentique.

Et voici le counronnement: le puissant *Chôros X* d'après la poésie populaire, nous dit le musicien, d'un grand poète typique, Catulle Cearence. A ce magnifique *Chôros X, Rasga o coração,* je comparerai, pour éviter de me répéter, le *Chôros VIII* de la première séance. Même mélange de grandiose et d'intimité, de tumulte et de tendresse, de sauvagerie et de préciosité, même débordement d'invention. Si le piano y a un rôle moins dominateur, en revanche la percussion est à l'infini, mobilisant tous les instruments du terroir, depuis le réco-réco, sorte de râpe qui rapelle à la centième puissance les rauquements de nos crécelles du vendredi saint, jusqu'aux Ucalho, massue bourrée et

mitraille et de tonnerre, bref un ensemble chirurgical qui, déchirant
l'air et parfois le tympan, scande le choeur d'une péremptoire impulsion.
Sous la direction de l'auteur, l'oeuvre subjugue l'auditoire et balaye
les dernières résistances.

The review of these concerts caused a considerable repercussion.
Quotations were published in Paris and in Brazil,[4] probably because
". . . dans la médiocrité des concerts quotidiens [les deux concerts]
produisirent une impression profonde sur les auditeurs: révélation
d'un nouveau monde sonore."[5] More important, however, was that
Villa-Lobos had found in Florent Schmitt, his elder by seventeen
years, an admirer of his music and a sincere friend. The esteem and
high regard they held for each other and the genuine friendship that
developed between them after those two memorable concerts en-
dured the rest of their lives.

During Villa-Lobos's Parisian sojourn before World War II,
he was dependent on Florent Schmitt, who encouraged him and
gave him moral support by his understanding and considerate reviews
and his personal interest in his music. The warm friendship he
offered his younger colleague presumably helped also to introduce
him to other composers and artists, both French and foreign, who
lived in Paris, the center of the cultural world of the 1920s. Florent
Schmitt's column in *La Revue de France*[6] also reviews the first Paris
performance of Villa-Lobos's *Danses Africaines*, included, on April
4, 1928, in one of the Walter Straram concerts. Schmitt, however,
cared less for this type of music. He wrote: "Sans doute leur pré-
férerai-je les magnifiques *Chôros VIII* et *X* de l'automne." But
Schmitt remained conspicuously silent all through the following year
(1929), although Villa-Lobos's music was performed in several concerts. One of them, on February 2–3, 1929, produced quite a
scandal and "une atmosphère de fièvre et de bataille"[7] with the
repeat performance of Villa-Lobos's *Chôros VIII* given during one
of the Concerts Lamoureux conducted by Albert Wolff. The 1927
Paris presentation of *Chôros VIII* was reviewed factually, thoroughly,
and with *sagesse* not only by Florent Schmitt but also by Henry
Prunières. But now the press were vying with one another in recording the audience's outraged reactions to the music.

Florent Schmitt's silence stemmed from the fact that at the beginning of 1929 the music column in *La Revue de France* ceased to
appear under his name. It was henceforth written by Louis Schneider.
Le Temps's music chronicle, published on Wednesdays, was signed
by Henry Malherbe (1870–1963). Only in the fall of 1929 did
Florent Schmitt's music column appear for the first time in *Le*

Temps (October 19, 1929). He was to write this column for the next ten years. This may explain why Villa-Lobos's performance of his *Amazonas* in the Salle Gaveau during one of the Gaston Poulet concerts on May 30, 1929, received no written attention from Schmitt although it was reviewed in *Le Monde Musical*. On December 28, 1929, a little more than two months after he had joined *Le Temps*, Florent Schmitt voiced his opinion on the Paris performance of Villa-Lobos's *First Symphony*, op. 112, composed at age twenty-nine and based on his own philosophical text written as a youthful twenty-year old, and premiered on August 30, 1920, in Rio de Janeiro. In Paris, the symphony was played in one of the Concerts Gaston Poulet on December 15, 1929. Florent Schmitt wrote: -

> . . . Nature généreuse, violente, d'une mobilité paradoxale, il crée des oeuvres à son image. Non qu'il ne sache à l'heure dite, fût-ce pour narguer toute classification, déposer sa cuirasse d'airain et tout comme un autre faire chanter son coeur de velours. Mais, même dans les plus pathétiques attendrissements et les plus intimes confidences, on sent sourdre impérieusement la folie latente du mouvement et du rythme, et gronder l'impatience de l'ordre établi.
>
> Sans atteindre encore à l'incomparable maîtrise, à l'inouie virtuosité orchestrale du *Chôros VIII*, par exemple, du *Chôros X* ou des *Amazones*, sa première symphonie, écrite en 1916, les fait pressentir. L'auteur n'y désavoue ni les formes classiques ni les quatre divisions traditionnelles; allegro, adagio, scherzo, allegro. Il ne rougit pas de recourir aux artifices du contrepoint, de l'imitation, de l'exposition fuguée, comme dans le scherzo, voire de sacrifier sur l'autel du cyclisme dont Franck et d'Indy furent les grands prêtres. Ainsi le thème des contrebasses par lequel débute l'allegro initial, imité à la sixte par les bois, constituera l'axe de l'oeuvre, engendrant des motifs qui à leur tour deviendront, dans les morceaux ultérieurs, des éléments de développement. Mais tout cela n'est que de négligeable surface; le fond reste immuablement à Villa-Lobos dont l'indiscutable originalité éclate à chaque pas. Et tout, depuis ces rauques mélopées de contrebasses qui inaugurent l'oeuvre, depuis les grâces un peu ironiques du scherzo, la meilleure partie à mon avis, jusqu'aux ultimes pages où explosent, en une mêlée presque tragique, les innombrables thèmes, jusqu'à cette obsédante pédale au rythme dévastateur qui aboutit sur un immense unisson triomphant comme un défi, tout en est la preuve péremptoire. Forcené, intraitable, insociable, véritable possédé de Belzébuth, il mourra dans l'impénitence finale et dans toute la vierge splendeur de son péché originel.

Two months after this encouraging review another Villa-Lobos work was played in Paris. The Orchestre Symphonique de Paris had

scheduled for Sunday, February 23, 1930, at the Salle Pleyel, the
world premiere of a piece for piano and orchestra entitled
Momoprecoce, which the composer had written at the request of the
Brazilian pianist, Magda Tagliaferro, who lived in Paris and to
whom the work is dedicated. Lacking time to write a new composition, Villa-Lobos resorted—as he was to do on similar occasions
throughout his life—to orchestrating a previously written work for
piano[8] during his vacation in Brazil in the summer of 1929. Florent
Schmitt reviewed the work in *Le Temps* on March 8, 1930:

> "Puis voici un Villa-Lobos tout neuf, *Momoprecoce*, façon de mannequin
> d'osier qui serait au Brésil ce qu'est, nous dit André Obey, Gayard
> à Douai. Il semble que dans ce poème pour piano et orchestre, dédié
> à Mlle. Tagliaferro qui le joue délicieusement, notre Heitor
> équatorial s'est, si j'ose dire, un peu apprivoisé. Non pas affadi, grands
> dieux. Simplement, de fauve de la jungle, il est devenu la faune des
> bois. De fait, sa musique nous apparaît d'humeur étrangement
> sociable. Mais il ne faut pas s'y fier. Dans le *Lento*, par exemple, de
> substance si délicate et si souple, l'attendrissement est celui du
> crocodile qu'il faudrait ne contrarier que très peu pour que l'animal,
> séchant ses larmes, rebondisse avec toute sa férocité native. A parler
> franc, ce poème ne me rendra pas ingrat, envers les magnifiques
> *Chôros* de l'an passé. Soyons toutefois reconnaissant à Villa-Lobos de
> cet avatar inattendu. Il a compris qu'il devait se renouveler. Soit. Mais
> qu'il ne renie pas son origine. Il serait désastreux que sa puissante
> personnalité fût poluée aux attouchements de notre triste civilisation
> européene."

This was, to our knowledge, the last time that Florent Schmitt
published his opinion on the music of his Brazilian friend.
Thereafter, he recorded no further performances of Villa-Lobos's
music in *Le Temps* prior to Villa-Lobos's departure from Paris at the
end of May 1930, although three more concerts of his music were
given, one each during his last months in Paris. These concerts
were scheduled for March 14,[9] April 3, [10], and May 7.[11] The first of
these concerts took place at the Salle Chopin and was labelled
"Festival de Musique Moderne," and the two others were performed
in the Salle Gaveau. Malherbe's Wednesday music column in *Le
Temps*, which he wrote in Florent Schmitt's absence, mentioned
none of these works. If Florent Schmitt was in Paris at the time,
he may possibly have felt that some of Villa-Lobos's compositions
presented in the spring of 1930 had already been heard, with the exception of those he may have considered too uncharacteristic to
warrant a review.

Schmitt may also have felt what ensuing years have proven true: that Villa-Lobos's works presented in Paris up to this point had established and demonstrated his style once and for all, and little, if anything (with the exception of the *Bachianas Brasileiras* written later), in the way of maturing was added. In any case, Villa-Lobos's music reflects the continuity of an already established style rather than steps of development or change. Schmitt expressed this idea somewhat when he mentioned in his *Le Temps* reviews, on two occasions, that he was most impressed by the *Chôros*. So why write any more about something that in essence, Schmitt must have felt, had been amply expressed in his previous chronicles?[12]

Stimulated by the lively Paris concert life, Villa-Lobos organized, right after his return to Brazil in the summer of 1930, a number of symphony concerts in Rio de Janeiro and São Paulo that he devoted to contemporary works of non-Brazilian composers, for which purpose he had brought along his orchestral material from Paris. One of these concerts was entirely dedicated to works of his friend and Parisian sponsor, Florent Schmitt, as a tribute and expression of gratitude. They did not meet again until after the Second World War. Villa-Lobos stayed in Brazil and devoted himself to the musical education of schoolchildren in a position created for him by the Rio de Janeiro municipality. Florent Schmitt, on the other hand, was tied to his post as music critic of *Le Temps* until July 1939, when his last chronicle appeared.

After the war, the two friends met once again in Paris. A few months prior to Villa-Lobos's operation for cancer of the bladder at New York's Memorial Hospital in July 1948, Florent Schmitt was honored by the Brazilian composer in Paris by being the only Parisian guest at an otherwise all-Brazilian birthday luncheon party given for Villa-Lobos on March 5, 1948, in La Maison de l'Amérique Latine. Also present were Arminda Villa-Lobos, Luísa Bailley from the Brazilian Embassy in Paris, the singer Cristina Maristany,[13] the cellist Iberê Gomes Grosso,[14] the pianist Arnaldo Estrella[15] and his wife, the violinist Mariuccia Iacovino,[16] and the eminent musicologist who, at that time, held an important post with UNESCO, Luiz Heitor Corrêa de Azevedo[17] and his wife Violeta.

It must be assumed that Villa-Lobos may have suggested to Schmitt then, or at a later date, that he include Brazil in his many foreign travels, assuring him of a hearty welcome and the performance of his works in Brazil. Villa-Lobos felt compelled to use his influence in favor of Schmitt's music since, after all, Villa-Lobos had by that time attained recognition and a fine reputation in his own country. Schmitt decided to go to Brazil. In September of the following year - (1949), he crossed the Atlantic on the S. S. Kergueleu and was greeted in Rio de Janeiro's port with flowers and music by Villa-Lobos. On Monday evening, October 31, 1949, Florent Schmitt conducted his *La Tragédie de Salomé* at Rio de Janeiro's Municipal Theater in the presence of several high Brazilian dignitaries. Villa-Lobos conducted three of Schmitt's six *Choeurs* for women's voices and orchestra, *Ronde Burlesque*, and *In Memoriam* (à Gabriel Fauré). The concert ended with Schmitt conducting his *Psaume* with Christina Maristany as soloist.

The almost eighty-year-old Schmitt was honored the following afternoon, November 1, 1949, by the Academia Brasileira de Música, founded by Heitor Villa-Lobos four years before. The reception took place in the Brazilian Press Association Building, where a concert of Brazilian music and Schmitt's *Trois Rhapsodies* for two pianos were played. In the evening of November 4, 1949, a Florent Schmitt Chamber Music Festival was held in the auditorium of the Ministry of Education and Culture; the music played included his *Quatuor de flûtes*, *Quatre poèmes* of Ronsard for voice and piano, the *Andante* from the Piano Quintet with the composer at the piano, *Trois Danses* for piano solo, and *Trois Rhapsodies* for two pianos. During the next days, Villa-Lobos showed his guest the sights of Rio de Janeiro and its surroundings. He took him to Petrópolis, the mountain resort near Rio de Janeiro, where Schmitt savored all the beauty and lush nature of Brazil. He also visited São Paulo, which he found attractive in other ways, and finally returned home, also by boat.

The last observable evidence of their great friendship is Villa-Lobos's letter, written two years later, on September 25, 1951, and whose autograph is today in the Bibliothèque Nationale in Paris. This letter is reproduced here for the first time.

Chers Amis:

C'était pour nous une grande joie recevoir votre lettre, toujours bienvenue.

Nous étions déjà inquiets sans rien de nouvelle de vous deux. Nous ne savons pas pourquoi les lettres n'arrivent pas.

Nous sommes très content de savoir de les exécutions des oeuvres de nôtre cher Florent, et qu'elles ont beaucoup de succèss comme meritent.

Merci beaucoup pour la lettre si gentil de notre cher Florent. Nous esperons être ensemble en février, et c'est domage que nous ne pouvons pas monter le *Pão de Assucar* avec vous deux.

Tous les amis d'ici ont rappelent toujours de vous, et ils vous envoyent les affectueux souvenirs.

Il y a longtemps que je ne vois pas Jean Français. Nous avons été beaucoup de fois avec Mme. Mineur,[18] charmante, si gentil avec nous, et qui a parlé beaucoup de vous.

Dans l'espoir de vous revoir bientôt, nous vous embrassons cordiellement.

Arminda e Villa-Lobos

The letter was sent to Florent Schmitt's address at "44 Quai du Passy," in Paris.

The contents reveal that Villa-Lobos and Florent Schmitt, despite the former's heavy conducting schedule on both sides of the Atlantic and Schmitt's advanced age (he was now over eighty), were still in touch. The warmth that Schmitt once imparted to his younger colleague in the early days in Paris also radiated in Villa-Lobos's letter toward the friend he admired. It even seemed that Schmitt had planned a second trip to Rio de Janeiro, as the letter hints at an excursion planned with the composer and Arminda Villa-Lobos to the Sugar Loaf by cable car. But, at his age, Florent Schmitt may have eventually decided against another strenuous trip. With great affection Villa-Lobos recalls Schmitt's 1949 sojourn in Brazil, and in a somewhat nostalgic mood he reminds him of how much he had endeared himself to his many new friends and admirers in Brazil. Keeping him informed on topics of mutual interest, Villa-Lobos tells him that he is still in contact with the French composer Jean Français, though as of late he has had no news from him, indicating how much he cherished his ties with France. This is also clear from his remark about the charming Mme. (Gabrielle) Mineur, and it must have delighted the aging Schmitt that she, too, remembered him affectionately.

Seven years later, on September 29, 1958, Florent Schmitt died, and fourteen months thereafter, on November 17, 1959, Villa-Lobos passed away. It is difficult to say if Villa-Lobos would have ever gained as much success as he did in his early days in Paris without Schmitt's analysis and reviews of the composer's works in reputable publications, or without the attachment and affinity the artists felt and expressed for one another. This relationship is recorded here for the first time, based on all available primary sources, including Villa-Lobos's letter to Florent Schmitt.

Notes

1. January 1, 1928, pp. 138–141.
2. Elsie Houston (Rio de Janeiro, 1902—New York City, 1943), Brazilian singer. She studied in Rio de Janeiro and made her debut in Paris. Principally known as an interpreter of Brazilian folk music, she toured Europe and the United States.
3. Vera Janacópulos (Petrópolis, 1892—Rio de Janeiro, 1955), Brazilian singer and teacher. She studied violin and singing, living in France from 1896–1916. She retired from concert life at the prime of her career and dedicated herself to teaching in Brazil.
4. Henry Prunières published quotes in his review of the two concerts in *La Revue Musicale* (9, no. 3 [January 1928]: 258–259). Quotes are also found in *150 Anos de Música no Brasil* (Rio de Janeiro: 1956), p. 262, note 4, by Luiz Heitor Corrêa de Azevedo. Vasco Mariz, in his book *Villa-Lobos* (Rio de Janeiro, 1977), p. 103, note 52, publishes quotes in Portuguese. The *Revista Musical* (Rio de Janeiro), January 1928, p. 4, gives the review in French of only the first concert on October 24, 1927. All three Brazilian publications quite mistakenly attribute Florent Schmitt's review to the *Paris Matinal*. However, the *Paris Matinal* has no reviews by Florent Schmitt whatsoever. They are all signed Jean Lasserre.
5. Henry Prunières in *La Revue Musicale*, January 1928, p. 258–259, Paris.
6. July 1, 1928, pp. 134–135.
7. *Comoedia*, February 4, 1929.
8. *Momoprecoce* is the orchestration of the piano work *Carnaval das Crianças Brasileiras* (composed 1919–1920 and first performed September 22, 1925, in Rio de Janeiro).
9. The works included: *Quinteto em forma de Chôros, Saudades das Selvas Brasileiras* for piano, *Deux Chôros Bis* for violin and cello, *Poème de l'enfant et de sa mère* for voice. flute, clarinet, and cello, some *Cirandas* for piano, and four of the *Chansons Typiques Brésiliennes*.
10. The works included: *Danses Africaines, Quinteto em forma de Chôros, Quatuor, Suite Suggestive* (which was previously performed in a private hearing at the home of Mme. Frédéric Moreau on June 29, 1929), and a repeat performance of *Momoprecoce*.
11. The works included: Suite for Strings, Cello Concerto, *A Mariposa na Luz* for violin and orchestra. two movements from *Fantasia de Movimentos Mixtos, Chôros VIII*, and *Missa-Oratório* (the published edition of this work is called *Vidapura*).
12. *Liberté, Le Ménestrel*, and *La Semaine à Paris* recorded the above-mentioned concerts.
13. Christina Maristany (Porto, Portugal, 1918), Brazilian singer who specialized in chamber music. She studied in Paris and gave concerts in Europe, the United States, and Latin America. A member of the Brazilian Academy of Music, she is also the holder of the Carlos Gomes Gold Medal (1965).
14. Iberê Gomes Grosso (São Paulo 1905), Brazilian cellist. He studied with his uncle Alfredo Gomes, later obtaining prizes at the Instituto Nacional de Música in Rio de Janeiro (today Escola de Música da Universidade Federal do Rio de Janeiro). He continued his studies in Paris with Pablo Casals. He teaches at the Escola de Música da Universidade Federal do Rio de Janeiro and at the Conservatório de Canto Orfeónico. In 1964 he toured Europe and Israel playing only Brazilian music.
15. Arnaldo Estrella (Rio de Janeiro, 1908–1979), Brazilian pianist. He won first

prize of Columbia Concerts and undertook concert tours in the United States, Cuba, Europe, China, and Africa as soloist with leading international conductors and as recitalist. He participated in various festivals. He taught at the Escola de Música da Universidade Federal do Rio de Janeiro.

16. Mariuccia Iacovino (Rio de Janeiro, 1912), Brazilian violinist, the wife of pianist Arnaldo Estrella. She studied with Paulina d'Ambrosio, well-known Brazilian violinist, obtained various prizes, and founded several quartets. She toured Brazil and Europe as soloist and chamber-music player.

17. Luiz Heitor Corrêa de Azevedo (Rio de Janeiro, 1905), Brazilian musicologist. He studied in Brazil. He became librarian (1932) of the Instituto Nacional de Música, where he edited the *Revista Brasileira de Música* until 1942. At the same institution he founded the chair of Musical Folklore in 1939. In 1941, he acted as consultant of the Music Division of the Pan American Union, Washington, D.C. From 1947 until his retirement he held an important position at UNESCO in Paris. He is the author of many books and contributor to music journals and dictionaries.

18. During many years Gabrielle Mineur was cultural attaché at the French Embassy in Rio de Janeiro. A scientist who married into the Brazilian Lage family, she now lives just outside Paris (from a letter of Luiz Heitor Corrêa de Azevedo to Lisa M. Peppercorn, Paris, April 23, 1979).

Latin American Music Review, **1**, (2), October 1980, 253–264

Corrigenda/addenda

p139, *line 9 from top*:
For Artur read Arthur

Insert, line 1:
For évènement read événement

p143, *line 2*:
For the sentence beginning with "This may explain...." read
'Only very belatedly, in January 1930, received the performance of Villa-Lobos's *Amazonas* in the Salle Gaveau during one of the Gaston Poulet's concert on 30 May 1929, a written attention once more in *La Revue de France* by Florent Schmitt; it was also reviewed in *Le Monde Musical*'.

p144, *insert, last line*:
For européene read européenne

p146, *line 3:*
For Kergueleu read Kerguelen

A LETTER OF VILLA-LOBOS TO ARNALDO GUINLE

There were at least fifteen letters exchanged between the Brazilian composer Heitor Villa-Lobos and the brothers Arnaldo Guinle (1884-1964) and Carlos Guinle (1883-1969), two well-known Brazilian industrialists and philanthropists who sponsored the composer's three-and-a-half year sojourn in Paris, from January 1927 until May 1930, and financed the first publication of his compositions there with Éditions Max Eschig. All these letters but one were in the possession of the Guinle brothers and were made available to this writer for use and publication until Carlos Guinle's death. Quotations from this correspondence were included in this writer's biography of Villa-Lobos.[1] Since then the letters have disappeared. They could not be traced in spite of this writer's inquiries with the Guinle heirs and diligent search with other sources. Presumably, they have gone astray and should be considered lost.

However, one of Villa-Lobos' letters, which he wrote to Arnaldo Guinle on 24 February 1930, is not in this collection of correspondence. It was left in the estate of the composer's wife, Lucília Guimarães Villa-Lobos (1886-1966), and is presently in the possession of her brothers and sister, Oldemar Guimarães, Luiz Guimarães, Alvaro de Oliveira Guimarães and Dinorah Guimarães Campos, who reside in Rio de Janeiro. A facsimile of this letter, in its original Portuguese language, was published for the first time in a volume containing reprints of concert programs, reviews of concerts and photographs, which Villa-Lobos' in-laws had privately printed at their own expenses in Rio de Janeiro.[2]

Villa-Lobos writes to Arnaldo Guinle (in this writer's translation):

Dear Arnaldo,

I waited until the 23rd inst. to write to you not only about the Gaveau pianos, but also to send you the latest news and the first reviews concerning the performance of my Fantasia for piano and orchestra – given for the first time yesterday by the Symphony Orchestra of Paris conducted by Arbos; it was very well received by the audience – as well as other previous reviews.

A few days ago I received a sort of call from the administration of the Maison Gaveau, though in very delicate terms, to settle my commitment in

---

[1] L. M. PEPPERCORN, *Heitor Villa-Lobos, Leben und Werk des brasilianischen Komponisten*, Zürich 1972.

[2] *Villa-Lobos, Visto da Platéia a na Intimidade 1912-1935*, Rio de Janeiro, n.d., pp. 337-339.

the amount of 80 ... for the four pianos which I took to Brazil. They tell me that the administration of the M[aison] G[aveau] is going to close their books for this year; they absolutely counted on the good result of the sales in Brazil of the four pianos, which they entrusted to me, completely relying on my word. They expect me to go personally to one of their Directors or assume this obligation in writing.

It made me dizzy, as you may well imagine.

They waited precisely for the moment when the dates of my festivals are approaching to hold a knife to my throat. As you may remember, the Maison Gaveau offers me the large hall gratuitously and does good publicity for my concerts; without this important support and prestige I couldn't realize any concert at present, since I have no material protection at this moment.

Now, it is absolutely impossible to give up the realization of these concerts in Paris at this time, because they mean the continuation of my artistic image in all of Europe. Otherwise, I shall be forgotten and all the efforts we have made, you, Dr Carlos and myself, to have me attain the excellent moral and artistic situation in which I find myself today, will go to the drain.

I figure that the only solution of this case is the following: to find some one in Rio or São Paulo who is willing to lend me, against pledge of the pianos which have not yet been sold, the amount of 80 ..., and to deliver it to the Maison Gaveau as soon as possible, to avoid prejudicing the organization of my festival next month.

According to the calculations which I left with Mário,[3] the four Gaveau pianos represent the following, in Brazilian currency, in my favor:

1 Grand Piano for Dr Carlos	14,867
2 Baby-grand pianos	28,000
1 Grand Piano, the last three to be sent to D. Olívia Penteado[4]	12,000
	54,867
Deducting 16,000 francs which Dr Carlos advanced me in Paris	5,396
Deducting 4 Contos[5] which you paid on my behalf for the hotel expenses of Terán[6] and Raskin[7]	4,000
Deducting 2 Contos which D. Olívia was to give to Raskin for his return to Europe	2,000
Deducting (what amounts to approximately 1,000 for expenses you may have for the pianos)	1,000
	12,396

---

[3] Mário Polo was Arnaldo Guinle's secretary.

[4] Dona Olívia Guedes Penteado is a São Paulo socialite and patroness of the arts.

[5] One Conto (plural Contos) has one thousand cruzeiros. At the time of Villa-Lobos' letter to Arnaldo Guinle the Brazilian currency was called milreis, not yet cruzeiro.

[6] Tomás Terán (Valencia 1896 - Rio de Janeiro 1964), a Brazilian pianist of Spanish origin, lived in Brazil since 1929 and had great influence on many young Brazilian pianists.

[7] Maurice Raskin (Luttich, Belgium, 1906) is a Belgian violinist.

There remain 42,471 in my favor, which, converted into French francs, represent approximately 128,000 francs.

I then have a substantial amount at your disposal to make you find somebody there who at least lends me the sum that the Maison Gaveau asks from me for 30 March, which is simply 80 ...

I beg you, as a good friend of all times, to get me out of this trouble with the Maison Gaveau, which is a terrible precipice for me.

Or else you may wire directly to Gaveau to postpone this transaction until the end of next June, at wich time I shall be in Brazil and therefore have better chances to settle those ' annoying ' pianos.

Personally I can ask nothing from the Maison Gaveau, because, as I said above, I would loose all my artistic prestige in Paris. This means that I am on the brink of an unforeseen precipice.

I beg you to wire me upon receipt of this letter to tranquillize me because I am more than very much worried.

On the same day on which I received your last telegram I wired to Dona Olívia and wrote an airmail letter to you, but I have had no answer as of today.

[no signature]

The Fantasia for Piano and Orchestra which Villa-Lobos mentions in the opening of his letter is the *Momoprecoce*, Fantaisie pour Piano et Orchestre sur « Le Carnaval des enfants brésiliens ». The work is dedicated to the Brazilian pianist Magda Tagliaferro (born 1893 or 1895 in Petrópolis, near Rio de Janeiro) who lived in Paris. She had asked Villa-Lobos the year before (1929) to write a Concerto for piano and orchestra for her, wich she intended to give its first performance in Paris in 1930. The piece was first performed on Sunday afternoon, 23 February 1930, in the Salle Pleyel by the Orchestre Symphonique de Paris conducted by Enrique Fernández Arbos (1863-1939). The work was generally well received by the press. The only exception was Florent Schmitt, the music critic and composer, and a great admirer of Villa-Lobos, who commented in *Le Temps*, on 8 March 1930, that: « à franc parler, ce poème ne me rendra pas ingrat envers les magnifiques *Chôros* de l'an passé ».

Momoprecoce is a pièce d'occasion: it is an orchestration of a series of eight little piano pieces, written in 1919-1920, called *Carnaval das Crianças Brasileiras* (Carnival of Brazilian Children), the last of which, entitled *A Folia de um Bloco Infantil* (The Folly of a Group of Children) had originally been set for four hands, and orchestrated a little later in the same year.[8] Then years later, in 1929, orchestration of this Finale

---

[8] The first performance of the *Carnaval das Crianças Brasileiras*, the first seven numbers for piano solo and the eigth and final number with orchestral accompaniment, took place on 22 September 1925 in Rio de Janeiro, in the Concert Hall of the Instituto

was, with a few changes, incorporated into the complete orchestration of the entire set during Villa-Lobos' vacation in his home town, Rio de Janeiro. He called this new work *Momoprecoce*.

When Villa-Lobos was pressed for time or did not feel inclined to write a new piece for those who commissioned him one, he resorted at times to orchestrating an old composition or finishing an incomplete work. This applies not only to *Momoprecoce* but also to *Chôros No. 11* for piano and orchestra; based on sketches made in 1928, it was eventually written in 1941, when Arthur Rubistein, during one of his South American concert tours, asked the composer to write a Piano Concerto for him.[9] Similar circumstances apply to the *Fantasia de Movimentos Mixtos* for violin and orchestra. Begun in 1920 and originally conceived for violin and piano, it was never completed nor fully orchestrated until 1940, when Villa-Lobos met again his old Parisian friend Albert Wolff in Buenos Aires. The two discussed the possibility of having a work by Villa-Lobos performed by Wolff in Rio de Janeiro during the next season. Villa-Lobos completed the work for the event, which took place on 23 April, 1941, at the Municipal Theatre, with the Brazilian violinist Oscar Borgerth (born Rio de Janeiro, 1906) as soloist.

Momoprecoce, whose first performance Villa-Lobos so anxiously awaited before writing to Arnaldo Guinle, is not the only piece for a solo instrument and orchestra lacking the customary classical name Concerto. Apart from the aforementioned compositions *Chôros No. 11* for piano and orchestra and the *Fantasia de Movimentos Mixtos*, Villa-Lobos had written, as early as 1913, a work for piano and orchestra which he called *Suite*, and, many years later, in 1945, he wrote a composition for violoncello and orchestra which he entitled *Fantasia*. The majority of his other works for a solo instrument with orchestral accompaniment, mostly written after the Second World War, when Villa-Lobos had become a well-known composer conducting his music on both sides of the Atlantic, have the classical title Concerto. Many of these works had been commissioned to him.

At the time when Villa-Lobos wrote to Arnaldo Guinle, at the beginning of the 'thirties, he was, by no means, much acknowledged either in Brazil or in Paris; he had lived in Paris intermittently with his wife

---

Nacional de Música. Lucília Guimarães Villa-Lobos, the composer's wife, was the soloist, substituting for the pianist Antonieta Rudge (São Paulo, 1886), with the composer conducting a small orchestral ensemble.

[9] The work was first performed on 18 July 1942 in Rio de Janeiro, though not with Arthur Rubinstein as soloist but with the Brazilian pianist José Vieira Brandão (Cambuquira, state of Minas Geraes, 1911) and the orchestra of the Municipal Theatre conducted by Villa-Lobos.

Lucília since the beginning of 1927, following a previous one-year sojourn in Paris from the sumer of 1923 until the summer of 1924, on a grant of the Brazilian government, this time without his wife. Early in 1930, after three years of residence in Paris, Villa-Lobos, aged 43, was still a financially insecure artist who struggled hard to get his music performed, to attract the attention of the press, and to interest Éditions Max Eschig in the publishing of his latest compositions. Villa-Lobos' apprehension and anxiety are apparent in his letter to Arnaldo Guinle, whom he implores to get him out of trouble in regard to the financial transactions for some pianos which he had brought into Brazil during a previous vacation at home. The composer's trepidation and concern lest the apparently still unsettled bills of some Gaveau piano purchases could jeopardize the performance so carefully planned of his works at a forthcoming Villa-Lobos Festival, is easily understood. Yet, it also reveals how fragile he considered his artistic position in Paris at the time, and how much he lacked self-confidence and self-assurance at his already advanced age. The style and contents of his letter tell of his evident submissiveness to and dependence on his financial sponsors, playing up to their generosity and goodwill, albeit hinting at the same time that he may become some day independent of their largess towards him. The tenor of the letter gives the picture of a composer who fails to have faith in his success and in his future as an artist, quite in contrast to the talks and interviews which he gave in his own country, Brazil. There, at home, just a few months earlier, he had boasted about his Parisian success and his being a much sought-after artist and composer.

The festival to which Villa-Lobos refers in his letter to Arnaldo Guinle consisted of two concerts which were to take place on 3 April and 7 May of that year. The first concert in the Salle des Concerts Gaveau included the *Quinteto em Forma de Chôros* for flute, oboe, clarinet, English horn and bassoon (1928). It had been given once before in Paris in the Salle Chopin on 14 March 1930, and unfavorably received by the press. At the concert in the Salle Gaveau the *Quatuor* for harp, flute, celesta, saxophone and women's voices (1921), the *Danses Africaines (Danses des Indiens Métis du Brésil)* (1916) and the *Suite Suggestive* (1929) were also performed. Neither did this concert meet with much approval, but at least it called attention to the composer: « C'est [...] un compositeur étrange autour duquel on fait quelque bruit, et qui en fait lui-même [...] Il est quelquefois diffus et difficile, presque agressif [...] ».[10]

---

[10] « La Semaine à Paris », April 18, 1930.

The second concert, on 7 May 1930, was, according to contemporary opinion, the more important and more interesting of the two. The heavy program made great demands on the audience. Except for *Chôros No. 8* (1925), all the other works presented were having their first performance in Paris. They included the *Suite Característica* for strings (1913), the *Concerto No. 1* op. 50 for violoncello and orchestra, the *Fantasia de Movimentos Mixtos* (1920-1940; two movements only), *A Mariposa na Luz* and the *Mass-Oratório* (1919-1920).[11]

This was the last concert that Villa-Lobos gave in Paris or anywhere else while still under the patronage of his Brazilian sponsors and friends, the Guinle brothers. Unselfishly, they had helped a struggling composer, then aged 40, to get a footing in Europe, especially in Paris, Europe's cultural center in the 'twenties. They had enabled him to live a good life at a well-furnished apartment at Place St. Michel, 11, and to entertain friends and colleagues. The Guinles also supported financially the realization of his first concerts and the publication of his music. It was Arthur Rubinstein who had made the suggestion and encouraged the Guinle brothers, particularly Carlos, to send this gifted composer to Europe to broaden his mind and get a chance to be heard and seen. This was a few years after Rubinstein had met Villa-Lobos in 1918, realizing a suggestion of Ernest Ansermet. The Swiss conductor had first heard of Villa-Lobos when the Brazilian composer and violoncellist was still a member of the orchestra of the Municipal Theatre in Rio de Janeiro; at that time in the 'teens Ansermet was visiting Brazil on a South American tournée as the conductor of Serge Diaghilew's Ballets Russes. There is no doubt that, had it not been for the Guinle brothers' generous financial and moral support, Villa-Lobos might never have made headway in Europe in those years as a composer-conductor or have found an European publisher for his works. The Guinles offered him an unique chance and Villa-Lobos knew how to use it: he worked diligently, wrote new compositions, arranged concerts, obtained publicity and reviews and found a favorably inclined publishing house.

Although Villa-Lobos still corresponded with the Guinle brothers within Brazil during the following year (1931), the letter of 24 February 1930 to Arnaldo Guinle is the last he ever wrote to either brother from Paris. The concert of 7 May 1930 was also the last he gave before returning to Brazil at the end of May and arriving at Recife, state

---

[11] This work was called *Segunda Missa* when it was performed for the first time on 11 November 1922 in Rio de Janeiro. At the Paris first performance on 7 May 1930 it was entitled *Missa-Oratório*. The title of the printed edition is *Vidapura (Missa-Oratório)*.

of Pernambuco, on 1st June 1930. Villa-Lobos considered his absence from Paris to be only a short vacation, and hoped to return to Place St. Michel in a little while. The October 1930 revolution in Brazil and the ensuing events prevented him from realizing his dream to go back and live in Paris, which he only visited again many years later, after World War II, when he made his re-entry as an internationally acclaimed and successful composer, long since independent of the Guinles' protection. This time he made his European headquarters in Paris at the Bedford Hotel, Rue de l'Arcade, 17, where eventually, twelve years after his death, and on the occasion of the 84th anniversary of his birth, a plate to his memory was unveiled on the Hotel's façade, on 5 March 1971.

THE ORIGINAL PORTUGUESE TEXT
OF VILLA-LOBOS' LETTER

Querido Arnaldo

Esperava o dia 23 do corrente para não só escrever sobre os pianos de Gaveau como para enviar-te notícias e criticas frescas de execução da minha Fantasia para piano e orchestra levada ontem em 1ª audição pela Orch. S. de Paris, com excellente acolhimento do publico e regida pelo Arbos – e outras criticas anteriores.

Recebi há alguns dias da administração da Maison Gaveau, uma especie de convite, embora em termos muito delicados, para liquidar a minha responsabilidade de quantia de 80 ... dos 4 pianos que levei para o Brasil, dizendo-me que como a administração da C. G. ia fechar o balanço deste anno, e que elles contavam absolutamente com o bom resultado das vendas para o Brasil dos 4 pianos que me confiaram em absoluta confiança da minha palavra, esperavam que eu fosse perante a um dos Directores, pessoalmente ou por carta, assumir este compromisso.

Fiquei tonto, come deves bem imaginar.

Estes homes esperaram justamente o momento em que se aproxima as datas dos meus festivaes, para me botarem a faca no peito. Come deves te lembrares, a Casa Gaveau, me sede gratuitamente a grande sala e me faz um bom reclame dos meus concertos, que sem esse importante auxilio e prestigio eu não poderia realizar nenhum concerto actualmente, pois não tenho nenhuma proteção material neste momento.

Ora, é completamente impossivel deixar de realizar estes festivaes em Paris neste momento, porque elles representam a minha permanencia de destaque artístico em toda Europa. Do contrário, ficarei esquicido e lá se vae todo o esforço que nós tivemos, Você, o Dr Carlos e eu para que eu chegasse a excellente situação moral e artistica que me eoncontro hoje.

Vejo que a unica solução deste caso é a seguinte: encontrar no Rio ou em S. Paulo quem queira emprestar-me sobre a penhora dos pianos que ainda não foram vendidos ahi, a quantia de 80 ... e entregar a casa Gaveau no mais breve possivel para que não seja prejudicada a organisação dos mes festivaes no mez proximo.

Pelas contas que deixei em mãos de Mario, os 4 pianos Gaveau representam em dinheiro brasileiro em meu favor o seguinte:

1 Piano de grande cauda para o Dr Carlos	14.867
2 Pianos de 1/4 cauda	28.000
1 Piano Cropô que todos os 3 ultimos deveriam ter sido enviados para Da. Olivia Penteado	12.000
	54.867

Deduzindo (16.000 francos) que o Dr Carlos me adiantou
em Paris 5.396
Deduzindo 4 contos que Vocé pagou por mim das despesas de
Hotel de Terán e Raskin 4.000
Deduzindo 2 Contos que Da. Olivia deveria ter entregue ao
Raskin para sua volta a Europa 2.000
Deduzindo (mais ou menos augmentou de 1.000 de despezas
provaveis pelos pianos) 1.000

                                                    12.396

Resta a meu favor 42.471 que passados a francos representam aproximada-
mente uns 128.000 francos.

Por conseguinte tenho authentica quantia as tuas ordens para poderes me
arranjar ahi quem me empreste ao menos a somma que a Casa Gaveau me exige
até o dia 30 de Março proximo que é simplemente de 80 ...

Peço-te, como o bom amigo de todos os momentos que me tire destes
apuros com a Casa Gaveau que é un precipicio terrivel para mim.

Ou então tu telegraphes directamente a Gaveau para elle protelar este compromisso até o fim de Junho proximo, epocha que estarei no Brasil, por conseguinte com as maiores probabilidades de liquidar estes ' cacetes ' pianos.

Eu, pessoalmente nada posso pedir a C. Gaveau, pois, como já te disse
acima, perderei todo o prestigio artístico em Paris. Quer dizer que estou na
beira de um precipicio imprevisto.

Peço-te para me telegraphar llo receberes esta tranquillisando-me porque
estou, mais do que nunca, preoccupadissimo.

No mesmo dia que recebi o teu ultimo telegrama, telegraphei para Da.
Olivia, assim como lhe escrevi uma carta, por avion, até hoje nada de resposta.

                                        Studi Musicali, **X**(1), 1981, 171–9

Corrigenda/addenda

p150 *first line*:
For fifteen read thirteen
FN 2:
For 'a' read 'e'
p151 *FN 5 add*:
And renamed in February 1986 *Cruzado*, to *Cruzado novo* in 1989 and again to *Cruzeiro*
in March 1990
p153 *second paragraph line 6*:
For Rubistein read Rubinstein

p157 *line 1*:
For escrever sobre read escrever-te sobre
fifth paragraph line 3:
For todo Europa read toda a Europa
For contrário read contrario
For lá read la
line 4:
For nós read nos
last paragraph line 1:
For de Mario read do Mario
p158 *line 3*:
For quantia read garantia
line 4 from bottom:
for llo read ao

The Paris Bibliothèque Nationale's autograph letter of Villa-Lobos to his sponsor

The world knows Heitor Villa-Lobos (1887–1959) as the most distinguished Brazilian composer of the first half of the twentieth century, and as a tremendously prolific writer who allegedly produced more than a thousand works. Few outside his native country know of — or give credit to — his singular aptitude as pedagogue and his eminent organizational talent as promoter of choral and symphony concerts. For neither of these activities — education and administrative organization — did Villa-Lobos have any earlier training nor had he any experience in them until unforeseen events in Brazil suddenly afforded him the opportunity to prove his talents. Nobody in Brazil, including the composer himself, either sensed or presumed the existence of such extraordinary ability and ingenuity which, all along, lay dormant. Because of his innate pragmatism, Villa-Lobos produced results unprecedented in Brazil until that time.

It so happened that in the early thirties Villa-Lobos was very unexpectedly appointed to an important public service position in Rio de Janeiro's Municipality. This gave him the opportunity to influence Rio de Janeiro's musical life both in the field of education and in the organization of symphony concerts. With native sensitibility Villa-Lobos perceived his chance to influence the neglected concert situation in Rio de Janeiro that existed in the middle of the thirties, contrasting with a previously active and stimulating period of symphony concerts by various orchestras and organizations. So he decided to give the concert-going public what he felt was their due — good music with interesting

J. of Musicological Research, 1981 © Gordon and Breach Science Publishers, Inc., 1981
Vol. 3, Nos. 3/4. pp. 423-433 Printed in Great Britain
0141-1896/81/0303-0423 $06.50/0

programs, including works never before performed there. His public service position enabled him to do this.

A decisive turn in an individual's life and with it the outburst of unexpected and unknown capabilities often arises from unforeseen and sudden external events and the individual's ability to adjust and adapt to such new circumstances and grasp their opportunities. Exactly this applied to Villa-Lobos. On June 15, 1930 the composer, together with his wife Lucília (1886–1966) had returned to Rio de Janeiro on the S.S. Araçatuba after a three-years' sojourn in Paris which was financed by two Brazilian industrialists and philanthropists, the brothers Arnaldo Guinle (1884–1964) and Carlos Guinle (1883–1969). Villa-Lobos considered his stay in Brazil only a temporary one. He longed to return to Paris where — so he felt — the artistic atmosphere was more congenial to his taste, talent and career. Although concerts with his own works, which he gave upon his return to Brazil, were well received by the press and the public, he was, nevertheless, dissatisfied with his life in Brazil, expressing his discontent and his precarious financial situation in a letter to Arnaldo Guinle a few days after Christmas 1930.[1]

However, his long-time friend and patron, Arnaldo Guinle, was more far-sighted and more realistic than Villa-Lobos. Guinle foresaw for the composer the possibilities and opportunities that might open up right then in Brazil after the October 1930 Revolution. The revolution had given rise to many changes with nationalistic tendencies, first during the temporary, and later during the permanent, Presidency of Getúlio Dornelles Vargas (1883–1954). This consideration would and should decidedly have influenced Villa-Lobos's future career, Arnaldo Guinle felt. "You must face the situation," Arnaldo Guinle wrote to Villa-Lobos, "and fight, as you fight presently, because history's unforeseen events are also fruitful and perhaps you may find yourself on the eve of some compensations for your efforts."[2]

Villa-Lobos was of a different opinion. Only one month later, on February 7, 1931, he wrote to Arnaldo Guinle: "I shall do all I can to be able to leave for Europe as soon as possible because, as you know very well, I have to live in a different kind of atmos-

phere where I can work quietly.''[3] Villa-Lobos felt that in Brazil
the public's taste was not yet ripe and people were not yet prepared to accept him and his works. However, Guinle's suggestion
— that Villa-Lobos could influence and modify the musical taste
of Rio de Janeiro's concert-going audience so that it would accept
him and his works — finally prevailed, principally, perhaps, because
his friend and former sponsor had made it quite clear that he was
not willing to finance any further sojourns in Paris or elsewhere
in Europe. Hence, Villa-Lobos felt compelled to keep his eyes
open for chances at home, put out his own feelers, be aware of the
new political situation in Brazil. The opportunities came sooner
than expected, and were overwhelmingly advantageous for a
jobless, financially insecure, artist.

Various external events and happenings, Villa-Lobos's own
contacts with public servants in high ranks and his own strenuous
efforts coupled with ingenious ideas and their practical applica-
tions demonstrated before responsible authorities, eventually
prepared the way for him to become the holder of a position as a
public servant. In February 1932, at the age of 45, he was appointed head of the School Music Department in Rio's municipality.
This was a decisive change in Villa-Lobos's life, perhaps *the* biggest
change that ever occurred in his lifetime: For the first time in his
life he had a steady job which guaranteed him a fixed monthly
salary. His financial worries were over. At the same time, this
position offered him never before dreamed-of opportunities and a
vast field of activities. He had an almost free hand to prove and
realize his talents. Henceforth, in short succession, he introduced
and developed music education for adults, for young people,
trained music teachers to instruct school children in choral singing, gave demonstrations with mass choruses ranging from 10,000
to 35,000, in later years.[4] Music education of the masses was a
novelty in Brazil. It was even a greater novelty that this was conducted by an artist whose talents as a composer were accepted,
though his qualities as educator and organizer were doubted,
belittled and treated with condescension, since he had neither an
academic education nor administrative training. Villa-Lobos was
a complete amateur in both fields, yet possessed a forceful natural

talent for both. Eventually, his overwhelming success over the years silenced even his greatest critics.

It did not take long before Villa-Lobos also turned to organizing symphony concerts. For this purpose he first founded an orchestra that took his name but it folded again after a while for lack of funds and official support. But, holding an important position in the municipality's administration Villa-Lobos could, henceforth, organize symphony concerts with the orchestra of the Municipal Theatre. So, in 1935, he planned three memorable concert series: Firstly there were the educational concerts which took place either in the Teatro João Caetano or the Instituto da Educação in Rio de Janeiro and were also relayed over the radio station of the municipality; in addition, he organized the so-called Cultural Symphony Concerts, which included the Brazilian premi-ère (in concert form) of his early work *Uirapuru* (composed 1917, performed November 9, 1935)[5] and also such ambitious works as Beethoven's *Missa Solemnis* and Bach's *B-Minor Mass*; and finally he organized Extraordinary Cultural Concerts.

In 1937 Villa-Lobos again planned the Cultural Symphony Concerts at popular prices at the Municipal Theatre in Rio de Janeiro. To ensure a sufficiently large attendance and at the same time interest an audience from all social levels, he turned to an old friend and sponsor of his, Madame Laurinda Santos Lobo, a Rio de Janeiro socialite and patron of the arts. Sometime in 1937 he wrote to her:

Departamento de Educação
Laurinda Santos Lobo   1937

Inesquecí vel Amiga:
Na feliz luta pela educação civica-artistica do nosso Brasil os nomes de D. Laurinda Santos Lobo e D. Olivia Guedes Penteado não poderão deixar de serem sempre lembrados, como legítimas bandeiras de Arte Nacional.

No momento a minha prezada amiga está eleita a generalissima do ilustre exército social da nossa melhor elite carioca afim de arregimentar assinantes para os Concertos Sinfônicos Culturais a precos populares a se realizarem no Teatro M [unicipal], no proximo mez de outubro.

Envio juntamenta alguns prospectus para facilitar a propaganda e os meus infinitos respeitos e eterna admiração pela prezada amiga e todos os que lhe são caros.   Villa-Lobos

(English translation)

Department of Education
Laurinda Santos Lobo   1937

Unforgettable Friend:
In the happy fight for civic-artistic education in our Brazil, the names of
D. Laurinda Santos Lobo and D. Olivia Guedes Penteado could not but be
always remembered as legitimate supporters of National Art.

At this moment, my esteemed friend is elected as commander-in-chief of
the illustrious social army of our best Rio de Janeiro élite, in order to enlist
subscribers for the Cultural Symphony Concerts at popular prices, to take
place at the M [unicipal] Theatre next October.

I enclose some programs to facilitate the propaganda and send my infinite
respects and eternal admiration for my esteemed friend and all those who
are dear to her.

Villa-Lobos

The autograph of this letter is in the Bibliothèque Nationale,
Paris, as François Lesure, Curator of its Music Department, told
this writer, when she visited him in early March 1979 and upon
her request was offered a photocopy of the letter for use and
publication.

The letter reflects Villa-Lobos's character *and* temperament; it
also shows how he inspired the confidence of others and knew
how to win support for his own ideas and plans. Most of the time
he succeeded, now in 1937, just as he had done in former years,
when he was still a struggling artist. More often than not, he used
hyperbolical expressions and eulogy; he cajoled, coaxed and
wooed. He was psychologically adept in winning the other
person's support. He certainly knew very well how to persuade
and animate Laurinda Santos Lobo and therefore pulled out all
the stops to make her feel important, indispensable and noble.
With real or feigned devotion and gratitude, he purposely placed
himself in a polite and even subservient level. In the end Villa-
Lobos, forced into this position and employing his typical literary exaggeration, was the winner in life's intricate play of
human relationships. With Laurinda Santos Lobo — as often
before and after with others — Villa-Lobos played his hand well,
turning on his charm, showing himself to be a great connoisseur
of human foibles, and knowledgeable as to which tune to play

DEPARTAMENTO DE EDUCAÇÃO

ORIGEM: N.

Distrito Federal, de de 193

1

Ilustrissimo amigo

Na feliz luta pela educação
cívica-artística de nosso
Brasil os nomes de D. Laurinda
Santos Lobo e D. Olivia Guedes
Penteado não poderão deixar
de serem sempre lembrados, como
legitimas bandeiras da
Arte Nacional.

No momento, a minha
presada amiga está eleita
a generalissima do ilustre
exercito social da nossa melhor
elite carioca afim de aregimentar

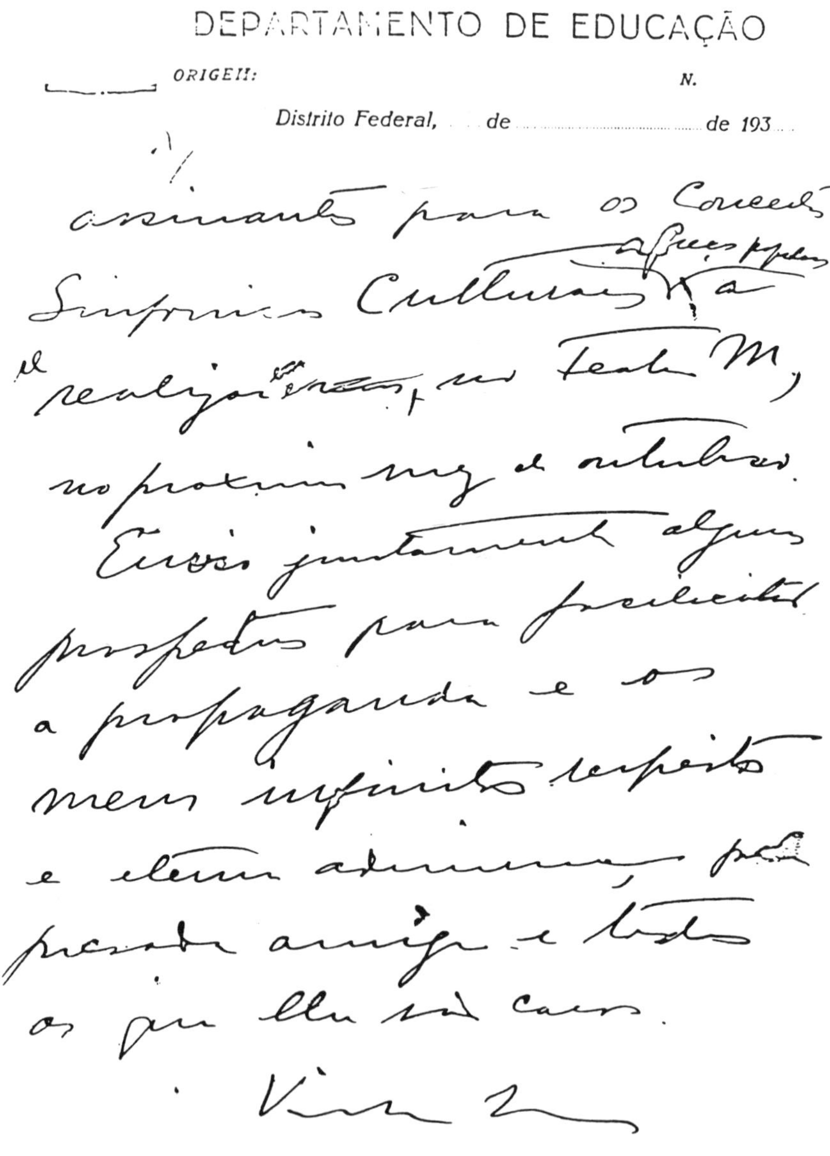
DEPARTAMENTO DE EDUCAÇÃO

ORIGEM: N.

Distrito Federal, de de 193

assinantes para os Concertos Sinfonicos Culturais que a se realizarão no Teatro M. no proximo mez de outubro. Envio juntamente alguns prospetos para facilitar a propaganda e os meus infinitos respeitos e eterna admiração, prezada amiga e todos os que lhe são caros.

Villa Lobos

Figure 1. Copy of Villa-Lobos' letter to Laurinda Santos Lobo.

to achieve his end. He did it with tolerance, delight, worldly and humane wisdom. He applied this art of human relations to the socialite Laurinda Santos Lobo, but he also applied it to the subordinates at his office, his pupils, the school-children's chorus, his superiors in the public service and his colleagues. Even his critics in all fields were eventually disarmed by Villa-Lobos's hilarious sense of humor and his infectious enthusiasm.

The year 1937 was not the first time that Villa-Lobos had approached Laurinda Santos Lobo for help. Their aquaintance dated from the time in the twenties when Villa-Lobos hoped to enlist the support of wealthy patrons such as herself to get his music performed in Brazil and to have a sojourn financed in Europe, for himself and his wife Lucília. In those early years, at the beginning of his career, Villa-Lobos chose to dedicate his compositions to those patrons and those who were instrumental in furthering his career, to show his appreciation for their help, or to make them more inclined and willing to back him. These works include the *Quatuor* for Harp, Celesta, Flute and Saxophone and women's voices, written in 1921, which he dedicated to Laurinda Santos Lobo. The work was premiered the same year (October 21, 1921) in a concert which Villa-Lobos specifically dedicated to his patron. At its first performance, the composition appeared in the program with the title *Quarteto Simbólico*. The composer probably selected this name in appreciation of Debussy, by whom he was still very influenced at that time. When this work was published nine years later (1930) Villa-Lobos's musical taste and interests had changed, as had the trend of the times and he replaced the original title with the simpler title of *Quatuor*. At the same time he also dispensed with a rather odd introductory text in which he expressed, rather wordily, his distaste and aversion for the conventional life at those times.

In the early twenties Madame Laúrinda Santos Lobo had Villa-Lobos's music played at her home and gave him whatever support she could. But she also came to his rescue later when Villa-Lobos, together with his wife Lucília, spent a three-year sojourn (1927/1930) in Paris. This Paris stay was principally financed by the Guinle brothers. They also footed the bill for the publication of the composer's first works by Editions Max Eschig in Paris and helped Villa-Lobos to launch two concerts (Oct. 24 and Dec. 5, 1927) with his own works. Yet before the second concert had even taken place, Villa-Lobos was already eager to have similar concerts organized in other European cities. To win the Guinle brothers' help in realizing his yearnings, Villa-Lobos described the success of his first concert in the most vivid color. Since he was not at all sure whether the Guinle brothers would grant him his wish, he added that it was principally Eschig's idea that such concerts in other European cities would help with the sale of his recently published works. He also addressed himself to other patrons in Rio de Janeiro and São Paulo who in previous years had come to his rescue when he wanted to perform his music in Brazil. However, most of these addressees failed to respond or were not interested. So Villa-Lobos had to depend, in the end, almost entirely on the Guinle brothers. "Only Dona Laurinda Santos Lobo and our Arnaldo [Guinle] have responded right away," he writes to Carlos Guinle, ". . . the others keep absolute silence. I don't know why . . ."[6]

In the following ten years (1927–1937) Villa-Lobos's career had taken a turn for the better. Thus, by 1937, his attitude towards Laurinda Santos Lobo was no longer that of the petitioner hoping for a request to be granted. (This is shown clearly in Villa-Lobos's 1937 letter to her.) The composer's approach to Laurinda Santos Lobo was that of the head of a municipal department, commanding authority and being able, and in a position, to enlist the best elements of the citizenship to support his plans in the interest of "National Art." The tenor of his letter gives ample proof of his changed attitude.

Olivia Guedes Penteado whom Villa-Lobos mentions in the 1937 letter in one breath with that of Laurinda Santos Lobo, was also one of the composer's sponsors. A São Paulo socialite, Madame Penteado, like others in that city, (much as Laurinda Santos Lobo in Rio de Janeiro) sponsored Villa-Lobos and his music at the beginning of the composer's career. Villa-Lobos had frequented her home though he was not altogether enthusiastic about high society's musical taste and their way of life. He knew, nevertheless, how to appreciate such hospitality and help if it meant advancement for himself and public performances of his recently completed compositions. Madame Penteado also belonged to the group of persons to whom Villa-Lobos dedicated compositions, at the time, out of sheer thankfulness for what she — as others — had done to help him launch his career in composition.

Thus, on January 3, 1925, Villa-Lobos composed (to words of Goffredo da Silva Telles) a piece for voice and accompaniment, entitled *Tempos Atrás* which he dedicated to Olivia Guedes Penteado and a second piece, entitled *Tristeza*, dedicated to her daughter Carolina da Silva Telles. Both compositions, originally set for voice and piano accompaniment, were soon orchestrated because of the possibility of having them performed fairly soon at a São Paulo concert. Villa-Lobos chose the following instrumentation for *Tempos Atrás*: flute, oboe, clarinet, saxophone, bassoon, battery, string quartet and piano; and for *Tristeza* flute, oboe, clarinet, saxophone and bassoon. Both works were premiered on February 18, 1925 during an all Villa-Lobos program, given at the Teatro Sant'Ana in São Paulo. The concert was dedicated to Dona Olivia Guedes Penteado. Eventually Villa-Lobos joined *Tempos Atrás* and *Tristeza* under the collective title: *Coleção Brasileira*. Four years later, on September 14, 1929, Villa-Lobos again dedicated a further concert to Olivia Guedes Penteado.

This autograph letter represents a fascinating moment in the establishing of the musical career of a great international composer and a witty and chivalrous student of the human race, particularly that better endowed part of it able to promote — despite itself — music for the people.

Notes and References

1. Letter from Villa-Lobos to Arnaldo Guinle, December 27, 1930, as quoted in *Villa-Lobos, Leben und Werk des brasilianischen Komponisten*, by Lisa M. Peppercorn, Zurich, 1972, p. 94.
2. Letter from Arnaldo Guinle to Villa-Lobos, January 7, 1931, *ibid.*, p. 95, footnote 3.

3. Letter from Villa-Lobos to Arnaldo Guinle, February 7, 1931, *ibid.*, p. 95.
4. Villa-Lobos's educational career and his activity in this field are described in detail in "Musical Education in Brazil" by Lisa M. Peppercorn, *Bulletin of the Pan American Union*, Vol. 74, No. 10, October 1940.
5. The world première, as ballet, was on May 26, 1935 at the Teatro Colón, Buenos Aires, Argentina. Villa-Lobos was the conductor.
6. Letter from Villa-Lobos to Carlos Guinle, December 9, 1927, as quoted in Lisa M. Peppercorn, above, p. 78.

Corrigenda

p163, *beginning of insert of letter*: For Inesqueci vel read Inesquecivel
p170, *FN5* for May 26, read May 25

VILLA-LOBOS'S STAGE WORKS

The Brazilian composer Heitor Villa-Lobos (1887-1959) wrote four stage works: *Izaht* (1914-1940), *Magdalena* (1947), *Yerma* (1955/56) and *A Menina das Nuvens* (A Girl on Clouds) (1957/58). The first and last ones — *Izaht* and *A Menina das Nuvens* — were first performed in Rio de Janeiro, the composer's native city; the two others — *Magdalena* and *Yerma* — both commissioned works, were premiered in the United States. Villa-Lobos also projected other dramatic compositions which, however, he never realized. From a planned operetta 'with thirty-six numbers and ten dansantes' exists only an Intermezzo from the fourth act. According to the manuscript, the operetta's title was to be *Dulcinda*. There is another manuscript from this early period (1904-1911): a piano reduction of an unfinished *Comédia Lírica* based on a libretto by Octávio F. Machado which was to have three acts. Preserved are the prelude to the first act and its numbers one, two and four; a prelude to the second act and its numbers 1-9 and an incomplete waltz. Numbers four and six are called 'Côro dos Convidados' (Chorus of the Invited), number seven is entitled 'Fábula Canção' (Fable Song) and number nine is called 'Quarteto dos Amantes' (Quartet of the Lovers).

In the late nineteen-twenties, during a three-year sojourn in Paris, Villa-Lobos stated that four more stage works of his were performed in Rio de Janeiro: *Femina, Jesus, Zoé* and *Malazarte*. These works were, to our knowledge, neither composed nor performed. But the enterprising and ambitious Villa-Lobos who, all his life, was his own best publicity and promotion manager, seized at an opportunity in Paris to boast about his operatic successes in — at that time — far-off Brazil, tales which neither the music press nor the director of the Paris Opera could — or would check or verify but, in good faith, accepted at face value.

It so happened that Villa-Lobos, at the beginning of 1928, had met the director of the Paris Opera who, apparently, showed interest to perform a Villa-Lobos opera 'towards the end of the following year', as Villa-Lobos mentions in a letter to his friend and sponsor Arnaldo Guinle (1884-1964) [1], a Brazilian industrialist and philanthropist who, together with his brother, Carlos Guinle (1883-1969) financed and underwrote Villa-Lobos's second Parisian sojourn (1927-1930). Nothing, in fact, happened thereafter. It seems that even the composer was not particularly keen on his opera performance in Paris.

---

[1] Letter from Villa-Lobos to Arnaldo Guinle, March 12, 1928 quoted in *Heitor Villa-Lobos, Leben und Werk des brasilianischen Komponisten* by Lisa M. Peppercorn, Zurich, 1972, page 79.

'Because', as he writes to Arnaldo Guinle, 'in my opinion the genre opera is a grave for a composer who is far-sighted, and I prefer to be known, one day, with my *Chôros* instead of becoming a very popular opera writer which has nothing solid from an artistic point of view' (¹).

Since dramatic works were never Villa-Lobos's favorite compositions, he believed that they represent 'nothing solid'. On the other hand, his only — at that time unfinished — opera was *Izaht* but seemingly he was not inclined to complete it then. This, of course, he did not want to admit, but instead resorted to typical Villa-Lobos hyperbole and phantasies to cover up the real facts and impress the French. To begin with he said that *Izaht* 'eut quatre représentations et la série en fut arrêtée par Villa-Lobos lui-même qui ne voulut plus donner au théâtre que des œuvres d'une construction entièrement originale' (²). And to prove his being different from others, Villa-Lobos declared that he wrote 'en quatre mois un opéra à grand orchestre, avec chœurs, nombreux personnages, etc...., le pari est gagné et c'est *Izaht*... qui marque le moment où l'auteur devint célèbre dans son pays' (²). This, however, is incorrect. *Izaht* made Villa-Lobos neither famous in his own country nor was the opera written in four months. It can well be assumed that in 1928 Villa-Lobos was not at all interested in what others thought about his opera. But he was interested in seizing the opportunity that others apparently wanted his opinion on opera writing in general.

And here is what happened with *Izaht:* the overture, conceived in September 1915, was first performed on May 15, 1917 on the occasion of a benefit concert for the Patronato de Menores, in Rio de Janeiro. Villa-Lobos conducted. Thereafter, the *Izaht* overture was repeatedly played over the following years. The fourth act of the opera, completed in 1918, was first performed on August 15, 1918 at the Teatro Municipal in Rio de Janeiro during a symphony concert which also included other orchestral works by Villa-Lobos. While the overture pleased the press, the fourth act disappointed: 'Nobody understood what happened on the stage and moreover the composer occupied himself only with the orchestra without taking care of the voices' (³). The third act, according to the manuscript, was conceived in 1914. It was first performed on June 13, 1921 (⁴) together with a repeat performance of the fourth act during a symphony concert at the Teatro São Pedro in Rio de Janeiro. The completed opera *Izaht* was premiered as late as April 6, 1940 when Villa-Lobos had just turned fifty-three

---

(²) *La Revue Musicale,* Paris, November 1929.
(³) *Jornal de Comércio,* Rio de Janeiro, August 16, 1918.
(⁴) *Villa-Lobos, Sua Obra,* MEC/DAC/MVL, Second Edition, Rio de Janeiro, 1972 gives the date of November 16, 1921 (page 148). This date seems unlikely because the third and fourth acts were given together already on June 13, 1921. In *Villa-Lobos, Leben und Werk des brasilianischen Komponisten* by Lisa M. Peppercorn, Zurich 1972 appear two printing errors regarding this date: it should read June 13 (not 11), 1921 (page 45) Footnote 7 and June 13, 1921 (and not 1922) on page 50.

years, however, not on the stage, but as a concert performance, conducted by the composer at the Teatro Municipal in Rio de Janeiro. It, therefore, may be assumed that the first and second acts were not written until shortly before the 1940 performance. At any rate, these two acts were unavailable, upon request, prior to this date. Very much later, on December 13, 1958, was *Izaht* finally performed on stage in Rio de Janeiro at the Teatro Municipal. Edoardo di Guarnieri (1899-1968) conducted. This was eleven months prior to Villa-Lobos's death.

The libretto is written by Fernando Azevedo Junior and Epaminondas Villalba Filho. The latter is Villa-Lobos's pseudonym which he occasionally used; it was borrowed from his father Raúl Villa-Lobos (1862-1899), a librarian and prolific writer. Villa-Lobos simply added the word *Filho* (Son).

Izaht's story and music reflect exactly what Villa-Lobos thought then — and all through his life — about dramatic compositions. 'For him it is the lowest class of serious music, a music essentially meant for the great public and the masses which want to be entertained. In his opinion one has, therefore, to meet the public's taste and sacrifies one's own ideals to such an extent that tuneful and almost vulgar melodies should take the place of proper ones. This makes the extraordinary plot understandable' ([5]).

The plot indeed is extraordinary. '*Izaht,* a depraved gypsy girl, belongs to a gangster band in the suburbs of Paris and has to entice rich people. For the first time in her life she falls in love with a viscount who rescues her from the slaps of her father. In the meantime, the gangsters plan to rob the house of the viscount's fiancée, and later on that of the viscount. Izaht rescues him from the gangsters. Izaht dies when the gangsters are about to kidnap the count's fiancée. Finally, the leader of the band, a decayed nobleman, recognizes in the viscount's fiancée his own natural daughter' ([5]).

The Puccini elements in *Izaht* are quite intentional. They were intentional not only in those early years but also as late as 1955/56 when Villa-Lobos wrote his opera *Yerma;* he was then in his late sixties. 'He loved Puccini' even at that time, as Arminda Villa-Lobos, Director of the Museum Villa-Lobos in Rio de Janeiro, recorded ([6]).

Villa-Lobos expressed his rather odd opinion on opera composers at the beginning of his career in quite an interesting document whose exact year could not be ascertained. Because there exist, signed with Villa-Lobos's pseudonym — Epaminondas Villalba Filho —, some opera reviews though neither the name nor the date of those publications were mentioned on the clippings. Amongst the reviews is one on Puccini's *Madame Butterfly* and one on Verdi's *Traviata.*

([5]) «A Villa-Lobos Opera» by Lisa M. Peppercorn, *The New York Times,* New York, April 28, 1940.

([6]) Quoted in an unedited transcript of an interview on March 31, 1971 in New York City between Hugh Ross, Director of the Schola Cantorum of New York, Richard Gaddes, Artistic Administrator of the Santa Fe Opera Company and Arminda Villa-Lobos which the Santa Fe Opera Association offered this writer for use.

About the latter Villa-Lobos writes that 'we got used to its banality' and about *Madame Butterfly* he remarks that Puccini only 'made concessions to the public to earn as much money as possible with his works' ([7]).

The aforementioned may explain why Villa-Lobos was neither particularly keen to finish his opera *Izaht* nor interested to have a dramatic work of his performed in Paris at that time, when the Opera Director approached him at the beginning of 1928. 'He didn't love opera, not too much, but when he wrote it, he loved it' ([6]). On the other hand, Villa-Lobos was eager to boast about his talent and ability to master all types of compositions, including stage writing which, in fact, he so much disliked then and until the end of his life. At any rate, the Opera Director must have assumed the existence of several other Villa-Lobos stage works besides *Izaht*. Because the composer had talked about several additional dramatic compositions of his which, besides *Izaht,* would include *Femina* and *Jesus* ([8]). *Femina* which allegedly was rehearsed but never performed by a Portuguese group in Rio de Janeiro's Teatro Trianon 'pour cause de faillite le jour même de la première représentation!' and the opera *Jesus* 'opéra biblique en trois actes, bâti sur des thèmes juifs dont le sujet, fort audacieux, n'a pas permis jusqu'ici la représentation' ([2]) remained as unperformed and untraceable as *Zoé* 'opéra en trois actes sur un livret brésilien de Renato Vianna (1894-1953)' ([2]) which should present 'l'histoire d'une femme fatale et du rôle de la danse dans la vie moderne' ([2]). From *Zoé* only exists one piece: *Dança Frenética* (Frenetic Danse) presumably from the first act, written in 1919 and first performed on March 7, 1922 at the Teatro Municipal in São Paulo under the auspieces of the Sociedade de Cultura Artística in an all-Villa-Lobos program which also included the *Izaht* overture. Occasionally *Dança Frenética* also appears as the second piece in the *Suite Indígena Brasileira* whose first piece is the orchestration of the piano composition *A Lenda da Caboclo* (The Legend of the Caboclo) which was composed in 1920 and first performed — as orchestral version — on June 13, 1921.

Likewise the opera *Malazarte* remained planned and projected and never was realized. However, Villa-Lobos declared that *Malazarte* 'ne fut de même pas joué pour des raisons de difficultés scéniques; il est entièrement construit sur des thèmes de folklore et met en scène un personnage symbolique de la race métisse, croisé d'Indiens, de nègre, d'Espagnol et de Portugais' ([2]). Such remarks are indeed phantastic and somewhat incredible since he had declared before — and again later — that opera writing was scarcely of interest to him. It is true, he did not feel too happy with dramatic compositions just as he did not feel at home

---

([7]) *Heitor Villa-Lobos, Leben und Werk des brasilianischen Komponisten* by Lisa M. Peppercorn, Zurich, 1972, page 35.

([8]) Kings, Jazz and David by Irving Schwerké, Paris 1927.

with symphonies or similar works which require a formal structure which lends itself less to his own compositorial expressions. Yet, he still felt that he had to prove himself 'pour prouver victorieusement ses capacités à ses détracteurs' (^{2}).

It is quite astonishing and a little difficult to understand why Villa-Lobos again turned to stage writing towards the end of his life. Perhaps the prospect of the scenic staging of his first opera *Izaht* in his native city sometime during 1958 animated him to try his hand once more on another dramatic work. Or, maybe, he was swept away by the thought that, as in 1955/56, when he was commissioned, in the United States, to write the music to Federico García Lorca's (1899-1936) play *Yerma,* he could again command a commissioned stage-work and was, therefore, unusually wrapped up in ideas to compose for the stage. At any rate, in early 1958, a Rio de Janeiro publication carried an extraordinary news-item under the title 'An Opera by Villa-Lobos at the Metropolitan' which says: 'For this year's season the Metropolitan Opera House of New York commissioned an opera by Villa-Lobos who invited the writer Lúcia Benedetti (^{9}) to write the libretto. *A Menina das Nuvens* — a work by two Brazilians — will have as female interpretor the Italian soprano Renata Tebaldi. The authors will receive US$ 500.000 from the Metropolitan without prejudicing their authors' performing rights. Maestro Villa-Lobos will rehearse and conduct his opera. Likewise La Scala in Milan, the Operas in Paris, Berlin and London will include in their season this year *A Menina das Nuvens*' (^{10}). This amazing story in a serious Rio de Janeiro publication sounded very much like having been inspired by the composer himself or someone near him, perhaps in the hope that such a trial-balloon might land Villa-Lobos a hoped-for or desired commission though probably with only a slice of the exorbitant fee mentioned. It is nevertheless, remarkable and somewhat bewildering that, at the age of seventy-one, Villa-Lobos felt that he had to resort to such publicity stunts because it seems highly unlikely that the contents of the newspaper story originated from other sources than the composer himself or from his entourage. Villa-Lobos was always known for his phantasy and whims and how, in visions, he unrealistically projected himself to far-off horizons or got himself unattainable objects. Such idealism may still be pardonable at the age of forty-two when Villa-Lobos's romantic imagination saw himself already conducting in all European capitals and the Unites States (^{11}) which, however, was, at that time, far from reality. Yet, at the age of seventy-one and physically very sick, but still at the height of his career as an internationally renown composer and guest conducting celebrity

---

(^{9}) Lúcia Mathias Benedetti Magalhaẽs (Mococa, São Paulo 1914), Brazilian writer and married to the writer Raimundo Magalhães Junior, published her first stories in the Brazilian press. She distinguished herself as dramatic writer for children including *A Menina das Nuvens.*

(^{10}) *O Globo,* March 27, 1958, Rio de Janeiro.

(^{11}) Letter from Villa-Lobos to Arnaldo Guinle, April 14, 1929, quoted in *Villa-Lobos, Leben und Werk des brasilianischen Komponisten* by Lisa M. Peppercorn, Zurich, 1972, page 82.

on both sides of the Atlantic, he woud have acted more appropriately — one would think — had he denied such press reports unless he loved it, had inspired it himself or felt it only added to his secret wishes and hopes which however did not realize — this time. At any rate, the Metropolitan Opera, in a reply to this writer's inquiry, stated 'that a leading executive of the Metropolitan in the late'50's knows nothing of any commission involving Villa-Lobos. He thinks that the story has no basis whatsoever. Even the correspondence of the management throws no light on the subject' ([12]).

Villa-Lobos finished *A Menina das Nuvens,* a two-act Musical Fantasy, in 1958, only one year prior to his death. The work was staged twice posthumously: on November 29, 1960 and in a matinée performance on Sunday morning on December 4, 1960 at Rio de Janeiro's Teatro Municipal with Edoardo di Guarnieri conducting. The work, based on a fairy tale, had merely a success d'estime. Perhaps the stage did not provide the proper medium after all because Villa-Lobos had envisaged this work rather for television on account of the story's action ([6]).

Villa-Lobos's most interesting stage work, *Yerma,* was also performed only posthumously, namely twelve years after the composer's death and was also played just twice (August 12 and 18, 1971) despite the fact that its Santa Fe Opera performances in New Mexico had a wide repercussion. Reviews appeared in the *Houston Chronicle* and *The Houston Post,* the *Los Angeles Times* and the *San Francisco Chronicle, The Christian Science Monitor* in Boston, as well as *The New York Times* and other U.S. publications, including *Newsweek.* All reported this world première at length. Even several Swiss newspapers and the Brazilian daily, *Jornal do Brasil,* in Rio de Janeiro gave the event space and due attention. This may have been as much due to the fact that it concerned the music of the most distinguished Brazilian composer of his time as that it was the play *Yerma* ([13]) by Federico García Lorca which was set to music.

The opera *Yerma* dates from Villa-Lobos's last period. The coming into being of *Yerma* may well have been the result of the sucess which Villa-Lobos enjoyed in the United States in the middle of the fifties. And it would also have been unthinkable had it not been for the friendships with leading personalities that he had formed in America ever since his U.S. debut in Los Angeles on November 26, 1944 when, for the first time, he conducted a program of his own works with the Werner Janssen Symphony Orchestra. Therefore, the birth of *Yerma* was only possible because Villa-Lobos moved in a circle of friends and

---

([12]) Letter from the Metropolitan Opera House Association, Inc., Lincoln Center, New York City, to Lisa M. Peppercorn, December 8, 1978.

([13]) The Spanish word yermo means barren and Lorca invented a feminine form of this word — Yerma — to name a woman who is barren.

artists who were far-sighted, well connected, influential and enterprising enough in sponsoring contemporary works and getting the required organizations to realize them. Had Villa-Lobos not resided again in the United States during the middle of the fifties, it may well be assumed, that he had not encountered then, for the first time, Basil Langton, the producer of the Empire State Music Festival which he had recently founded together with John Brownlee and Frank Forest. And without Langton, the composer would probably not have come in contact with José Arcadio Limón (1906-1972), the Mexican-born choreographer and dancer, who, later, choreographed *Yerma* in Santa Fe. Because it was Langton, who, in 1955, commissioned Villa-Lobos to write a ballet based on the play *The Emperor Jones* by Eugene O'Neill. This dance-drama was performed on July 12 (and 14), 1956 within the framework of the Empire State Music Festival in Ellenville, N.Y. under the conductorship of the composer, choreographed and danced by Limón and his group with the Symphony of the Air orchestra which originally was Arturo Toscanini's Radio Orchestra at NBC.

Langton had much taken to Villa-Lobos artistically since *The Emperor Jones* production. So he hoped to entice the composer, in 1955, to write another composition. This time, it should be an opera based on the Macbeth theme though the action should take place in Brazil. The composer made no comment, and there was no opera on the Macbeth story. The fact was that Villa-Lobos had already accepted, in 1955/1956, the commission offered by somebody else to write *Yerma* on García Lorca's play, which — so it turned out later — Basil Langton was to produce in Santa Fe with Limón as choreographer about fifteen years after it was composed. This opera was commissioned by John Blankenship who headed the Drama Department of Sarah Lawrence College at Bronxville, N.Y. where also his friend, Hugh Ross, conductor of the Schola Cantorum of New York, worked. Ross was an old friend of Villa-Lobos. They had first met in Paris in the late twenties and it was Ross who conducted the American first performance of the composer's *Chôros No. 10* in New York on January 15, 1930 with the Philharmonic-Symphony Orchestra at Carnegie Hall, long before Villa-Lobos's name was known in that country ([14]). Aware of this, Blankenship turned to Ross because 'he wanted Lorca's *Yerma* to be set to music. I (Ross) introduced him (Blankenship) to Villa-Lobos who was his (Blankenship's) favorite choice for composer for a further interesting reason, namely that he thought *Yerma* should be played by a black cast. And it was interesting that the first performance of excerpts in a private hearing at Dona Vasconcellos's (1910-1973) apartment in New York (with Villa-Lobos present) were sung by the famous

---

([14]) 'Villa-Lobos was one of my greatest friends, and it was the success of his *Chôros X* which finally established me as ranking conductor on the New York scene', from a letter by Hugh Ross to Lisa M. Peppercorn, New York, October 16, 1973.

black artists Adele Addison and Betty Allen with chorus supplied by Schola Cantorum singers' ([15]). 'Dora Vasconcellos was at that time Consul General of Brazil in New York and it's rather rare that you have a lady to be that, but she was very artistic and indeed she was a great friend of Villa-Lobos and she wanted to help Blankenship and all of us to get something of the opera known. So I got all these singers together, I got some of my chorus from Tanglewood who sang the chorus in the final scene, and also those two leads and the baritone to sing the parts. And, of course, Villa-Lobos was still here while we were doing it' ([6]).

After Villa-Lobos had accepted Blankenship's commission, it was arranged that 'Alastair Raid (born 1926), the British poet' — who also taught at Sarah Lawrence College at that time (1950-1955) — 'and I (Hugh Ross) were supposed to translate the play and give Villa-Lobos the English but Villa-Lobos didn't wait for that at all. He went out and bought a copy of the play in Spanish, and he started setting it in Spanish without waiting for us to do anything in English. By the time we ever saw anything, it was already done in Spanish' ([6]). The point was that Villa-Lobos knew no English then or at any other time. An English translation would have only presented problems for him. He prefered, therefore, to set the original Spanish play into music. 'I think I am succeeding in achieving what Lorca wanted', Villa-Lobos said ([6]).

The way Villa-Lobos composed *Yerma* 'was the same fascinating way of composing as Mozart or Wagner. One day in his apartment at the Alrae Hotel in New York, I (Hugh Ross) asked him: 'How is your composition of *Yerma* progressing?'. He answered: 'There is the score', pointing to a big sheaf of manuscript paper on his table. I opened it and discovered to my amazement page after page with all the clefs and bar lines with time signatures ruled, but no notes! So he had it all in his head, but he had not written it down yet' ([15]). The music, in fact, had again Puccini influences as the press reviews recorded. Maybe Villa-Lobos felt that a Puccini flavored opera was just what the public wanted. He did not live to the day to witness the Santa Fe performance under the then twenty-four-year-old Californian conductor Christopher Keene with the Spanish leading lady Mirna Lacambra, when the work played to a sellout audience. 'Being one of the only Spanish operas and a South American work as well, the management had to put in 500 extra seats for each performance to accomodate all the visitors from Chile, Brazil, Columbia, Venezuela, and Mexico' ([16]).

Notwithstanding, to get *Yerma* staged at all was no easy venture. 'Promoting *Yerma* has been difficult, not only because of legal complications between

([15]) From a letter by Hugh Ross to Lisa M. Peppercorn, New York City, October 16, 1973.

([16]) From a letter of Hugh Ross to Lisa M. Peppercorn, New York City, n.d., postmarked 17 April 1981.

the Lorca and Villa-Lobos estates ([17]), but above all because of my conviction that the opera should be performed in Spanish', Basil Langton remarks ([18]). Because after Hugh Ross had shown Langton the score in 1959, 'I (Langton) resolved to promote it. Both Covent Garden and Sadlers Wells expressed great interest when I showed them the score but they wanted the work performed in English, in (Continental) Europe it was wanted in German. I was resolved that the first performance should be in the language the composer had chosen for his text — Lorca's Spanish... It was this determination of mine... as much as anything else which delayed the first performance of *Yerma*' ([18]).

Eventually, it was again Hugh Ross who 'secured the world première of Villa-Lobos's posthumous opera *Yerma* at Santa Fe' ([19]). 'Due to the fact that I (Hugh Ross) was the only possessor of the full score and vocal score of *Yerma* other than those in the possession of Harold Stern, Villa-Lobos's legal executor, or copies in Brazil, it was only my copies that were available for presentation to prospective performing organizations. It was my friend Basil Langton who finally secured the interest of Gaddes, and with some aid from the Sullivan Foundation ([20]), which I direct, Santa Fe agreed to buy the rights from the organization *Music Now,* which at that time held the option on the first performance' ([15]). Since then the opera was not performed anywhere else ([21]), although 'the work appeals to the audience, judging from the heavy applaus... another advantage is its relatively easy staging without scenic changes. This may well help the opera to be represented in other places as well' ([22]).

Completely different is Villa-Lobos's stage work *Magdalena* whose background is the Magdalena river country near a great emerald mine. This two-act operetta, which Villa-Lobos called a Musical Adventure, was commissioned, in 1947, by Edwin Lester, the founder and president of The Los Angeles Civic Light Opera Association. *Magdalena* is based on the book by Frederick Hazlitt Brennan and Homer Curran. The latter who conceived the original idea of *Magdalena,* started working on the play and project in 1945. Curran 'created a basis story', Edwin Lester recalls, 'and our next task was to find a composer who could bring color and authenticity to match the locale. The

([17]) 'Hardly any of Villa-Lobos's works were played for ten years after his death because the performers and publishers didn't know to whom they should pay the performance rights. If they paid Arminda, they could be sued by Lucília, and maybe vice-versa. It finally became to ridiculous that the Brazilian government stepped in and decided that fees for works written prior to a certain date (I believe when Villa-Lobos left Lucília) should revert to her and fees for subsequent works should go to Arminda. This freed *Yerma*, and Basil Langton and I got its first and only really worth performance given at the Santa Fe Opera in 1971' (From a letter of Hugh Ross to Lisa M. Peppercorn, New York City, n.d. postmarked 17 April 1981).
([18]) Basil Langton in the Program Book to *Yerma,* Santa Fe Opera, Santa Fe, New Mexico, 1971.
([19]) From a letter by Hugh Ross to Lisa M. Peppercorn, New York City, September 14, 1973.
([20]) The William Matheus Sullivan Musical Foundation, Inc. 410 E. 57th Str., New York, N.Y. 10022.
([21]) 'There could be no performance in Europe, because Lorca's surviving sister obstinately believed that Franco had had her brother killed and that because of this, no money could go to the Spanish government as long as Franco was alive' (From a letter of Hugh Ross to Lisa M. Peppercorn, New York City, n.d., postmarked 17 April 1981).
([22]) *Neue Zürcher Zeitung,* Zürich, Switzerland, September 4, 1971.

perfect choice was the distinguished Brazilian Heitor Villa-Lobos, South America's foremost composer. We extended the invitation to Maestro Villa-Lobos with much more hope than confidence. The musical world was as amazed as we when Villa-Lobos accepted our proposal. It was part of our arrangement that (Robert) Wright and (George) Forrest (from the entertainment world) would write the lyrics and pattern the music to the requirements of the story... ([23]). Villa-Lobos was invited to come to New York City to discuss the story. He 'arrived in New York late in January 1947... By some unaccountable miracle, the basic score was finished in less than eight weeks and Villa-Lobos returned to South America... With the decision to premiere *Magdalena* as the closing event of the 1948 Season of the Los Angeles and San Francisco Civic Light Opera Association, the endless conferences between the collaborators, included the necessity for bringing Villa-Lobos to New York again (this time from Paris) for a final session with Wright and Forrest. It is of interest that the orchestrations were done by Villa-Lobos in Paris, New York and Rio' ([23]).

The operetta, premiered at Philharmonic Auditorium in Los Angeles on July 26, 1948, was directed by Jules Dassin, choreographed by Jack Cole, with the chorus directed by Robert Zeller and the musical direction in the hands of Arthur Kay. *Magdalena* was produced by Edwin Lester. '*Magdalena* had thirty-two performances in Los Angeles and thirty-two performances at the Curran Theatre in San Francisco during its 9th annual season of 1948 and somewhere around seventy performances in New York' ([24]) at the Ziegfeld Theatre. Villa-Lobos attended none of these performances due to ill-health. *Magdalena* was, in fact, one of his last compositions that he had finished before he succumbed to a very grave illness which obliged him to enter New York's Memorial Hospital on July 9, 1948 for a successfully performed cancer operation of the bladder which gave him another eleven years of life although his health was precarious since then. At the time of his operation Villa-Lobos's financial situation was not too good. He, therefore, needed and used his share of the box-office receipts

---

([23]) Edwin Lester in the *Magdalena* Souvenir Program Book, San Francisco, 1948.

([24]) From a letter by Edwin Lester to Lisa M. Peppercorn, Los Angeles, October 17, 1978: 'I do not recall the exact number in New York and have no records of it handy, but I would say, somewhere around seventy performances'. The Ziegfeld Theatre was unable to furnish any information as it was demolished in 1968 with no more records available now, according to a reply received, upon this writer's inquiry, from the new Ziegfeld (Cinema) in New York City, dated July 29, 1978 and signed by Ed Lapidus.

My article 'Villa-Lobos's Last Years', *The Music Review,* Cambridge, Nov. 1979, (Vol. 40 No. 4 p. 290) gives 15 November 1948 for the opening night at the Ziegfeld Theatre. This date, which meanwhile has shown to be erroneous, was taken in good faith from the Catalogue (p. 11 Item 89A) of a Villa-Lobos Exhibition, organized by the Brazilian Embassy in London from 19 February to 12 March 1964, because the Museum Villa-Lobos, Rio de Janeiro, which possesses all the relevant material, gave me no information and ignored my request to provide me with a photocopy of the program and reviews to check the correct date. Only recently was I able to consult *The New York Times* (microfilm) where a review of *Magdalena,* dated 21 September 1948, mentions 20 September as the opening night at the Ziegfeld Theatre. I regret my previous error.

from all *Magdalena* performances, with additional financial help from the Brazilian government, to meet his medical and hospital bills.

Despite his illness, Villa-Lobos continued to take a vital interest in everything that concerned his *Magdalena* performances. When 'Villa-Lobos discovered that they had changed the course of the show (in New York) — something about the bus not falling onto the stage — which resulted in considerable changes in his musical score, I (Hugh Ross) remember his saying angrily: 'At the first performance I shall stand up in my box and say: People of New York, this is not my music!' He did not actually do so, because most unfortunately he was in the hospital at the time' ([15]).

From this ninety-minute operetta Villa-Lobos made, at a later date, two Suites for orchestra, solo voices and mixed chorus, each lasting eight minutes which were premiered in Rio de Janeiro, at the Municipal Theatre with the composer conducting, on December 30, 1948. The first Suite consists of the numbers: My bus and I, Bon Soir Paris, and Food for Thought. The second Suite contains the numbers: The singing Tree, The Emerald and Vals d'España.

Revue Belge de Musicologie, **XXXVI–VIII**, 1982–84, 175–84

Corrigenda

p172 *FN3*:
For de read do
p179 *FN 17 line 3*:
For to read so
p181 *last line*:
For Vals read Valse

Menschen, Masken, Mythen
Heitor Villa-Lobos und die brasilianische Musik

Das Aufblühen der nationalen Schulen um die Mitte des neunzehnten Jahrhunderts markiert einen wichtigen Einschnitt in der Geschichte der abendländischen Kunstmusik. Es ist das Erwachen eines nationalen Selbstbewußtseins, das im Streben nach politischer Autonomie ebenso seinen Ausdruck fand wie in der Suche nach einer Künstlerischen Identität. Die Grundlage aller nationalen musikalischen Schulen war die folkloristische Quelle, die es möglichst getreu in die kunstmusikalische Komposition zu übernehmen galt. Das Bemühen um die Authentizität des Materials schuf Antipoden, sogar Feinde: das "Mächtige Häuflein" gegen Tschaikowsky, de Falla gegen Bizets *Carmen* und Sarasates *Spanische Tänze*, Bartók und Kodály gegen Liszts *Ungarische Rhapsodien* und Brahms' *Ungarische Tänze* – Original gegen Fälschung. Ähnliche Bewegungen lassen sich auch außerhalb Europas beobachten, Bewegungen, die eng mit herausragenden Komponistenpersönlichkeiten verknüpft sind. Zu diesen gehört auch Heitor Villa-Lobos (1887–1959), der "Vater der brasilianischen Musik", dessen Todestag sich am 17. November zum 25. Male jährt. Wie aber is Villa-Lobos zu seinem nationalen Stil gekommen? Die brasilianische Musikwissenschaftlerin Lisa M. Peppercorn, profunde Kennerin des Lebens und der Werke des Komponisten und Autorin einer grundlegenden Biographie (*Heiter Villa-Lobos*, Zürich, 1972), ist dieser Frage nachgegangen und hat die – zum Teil überraschenden – Quellen zahlreicher Werke identifizieren können.

Ich schreibe kein Potpourri von folkloristischen Melodien, erklärte Heitor Villa-Lobos am 17. Dezember 1944 — drei Wochen nach seinem Nordamerika-Debüt mit dem Janssen Symphony Orchestra of Los Angeles — gegenüber Olin Downes, dem damaligen Musikkritiker der *New York Times*. Dagegen habe er sehr gründlich brasilianische Quellen studiert: Geschichte, Kultur, Sitten, Gebräuche und das Leben der Menschen in Brasilien; der brasilianische Geist seiner Musik beruhe auf diesem Quellenstudium.

Anders als Béla Bartók hat Villa-Lobos nie selbst folkloristische Melodien gesammelt, sondern nur — zumeist
freilich in pseudo-folkloristischer Form — die von anderen gefundenen Melodien verarbeitet. Die Anfänge dieses
Quellenstudiums fallen in die Zeit zwischen seiner ersten
Europareise (1923/24), die ihm durch ein Staatsstipen-
dium ermöglicht worden war, und seinen zweiten Aufenthalt auf dem Kontinent (1927—1930); die Jahre 1924 bis
1927 verbrachte er in Brasilien, und hier fand er zu seinem
ausgeprägt persönlichen Stil.

Daß sich Villa-Lobos von Brasilien inspirieren ließ, war eine Konsequenz, die er aus seinem ersten Aufenthalt in Paris gezogen hatte. Irgendwelche europäischen oder speziell französischen Einflüsse lassen sich dagegen in keiner Weise feststellen. In Paris war er viel zu sehr damit beschäftigt gewesen, Konzerte vorzubereiten und nach einem potentiellen Verleger Ausschau zu halten, als daß ihn etwas anderes beschäftigt oder beeindruckt hätte. Er war nicht daran interessiert, Igor Strawinsky, Serge Diaghilew oder andere prominente Musikerpersönlichkeiten kennenzulernen, die damals in Paris lebten. Ebensowenig war ihm daran gelegen, in den literarischen Salon einer Gertrude Stein eingeladen zu werden, um mit der „Verlorenen Generation" in Berührung zu kommen — mit den im selbstgewählten Exil lebenden amerikanischen Schriftstellern und Dichtern —, und auch an der Bekanntschaft von Malern zeigte er kein Interesse. Er ging n kein Theater, und der Zauber des Pariser Lebens übte einerlei Faszination auf ihn aus — streng verschlossen gegenüber jeder Art von neuen Ideen, die er hätte absorbieren können. Das einzige, was Villa-Lobos interessierte, war die Frage: Was läßt sich am besten „verkaufen", und wie kann man sich in Paris einen Namen machen? Und die Antwort lautete: originell sein, anders als die anderen, und so auf sich aufmerksam machen.
Nach Brasilien zurückgekehrt ging Villa-Lobos daran, diese Antwort in die Tat umzusetzen. Originalität bedeutete für ihn, dem Publikum etwas typisch Brasilianisches anzubieten, und es gab nichts, was ihn davon hätte abbringen können. Gewiß, er hatte auch früher schon Werke mit brasilianischen Titeln komponiert, aber ihre musikalische Sprache war von europäischen Vorbildern beeinflußt und gänzlich unbrasilianisch gewesen.
Wie aber ging Villa-Lobos vor, um seiner Musik eine nationale Färbung zu geben? Nicht anders wie jeder Forscher es auf seinem Gebiet getan hätte — durch und durch intellektuell: er kaufte und las Bücher, konsultierte in Bibliotheken und Archiven alte Chroniken, Dokumente, Annalen und Überlieferungen, studierte Lithographien, Zeichnungen, Stiche und Fotografien, besuchte Museen, wo er die Instrumente der Eingeborenen erforschen konnte und hörte sich (von anderen gesammelte) Schallaufzeichnungen indianischer Musik an. Ein Studium nicht der Musik also, sondern der Tradition, der Geschichte und Kultur seiner Heimat, der Vergangenheit

und Gegenwart Brasiliens, seiner Sitten und Gebräuche, der Indianer, ihrer Sprachen und Legenden. Literatur und Ikonographie früherer wie zeitgenössischer Epochen boten dabei reichhaltige Anregungen. Was er wissen wollte, konnte sich Villa-Lobos selbst aneignen, und wo er nicht weiter wußte, da gaben die bedeutenden Werke der Vergangenheit Rat. Doch es gab ein Problem: wie ließen sich diese Elemente auf möglichst natürliche Weise assimilieren, wie konnte man sie mühelos der eigenen Ausdruckswelt anpassen?

Zunächst interessierte sich Villa-Lobos für brasilianische Legenden, von denen Gustavo Dodd Barroso (1888 — 1959) 1930 eine Auswahl auch in französischer Sprache veröffentlicht hatte. Einige dieser Legenden dienten dem Komponisten als Vorlage musikalischer Werke; *Erosão* zum Beispiel — 1950 im Auftrag des Louisville Orchestra komponiert — geht auf den *Ursprung des Amazonasstromes* zurück.

Fasziniert las Villa-Lobos alte Geschichtsbücher, darunter das erste Buch, das je über Brasilien geschrieben wurde: den in mehreren Sprachen erschienenen Bericht über die beiden Reisen (1548 und 1555) des deutschen Forschers Hans Staden (ca. 1525 — ca. 1576). Schon die Titelvignette der Erstausgabe (Marburg 1557), die sich motivisch auch in Barrosos *Mythes, Contes et Légendes des Indiens, Folklore Brésilien* (Paris 1930) wiederfindet, regte Villa-Lobos zu einer Komposition an: zu dem Stück *Idílio na Rêde* aus der *Suite Floral* op. 97.

Eine weitere Quelle bildete das Werk von Jean de Léry (1534 — 1613), eines calvinistischen Geistlichen, Reisenden und Schriftstellers; der Franzose hatte sich 1556 dem Admiral Nicolas Durand de Villega(i)gnon (1510 — 1575) angeschlossen, der in Brasilien eine Hugenottenkolonie gründen wollte. Lérys Erfahrungen und Erlebnisse während seines zehnmonatigen Aufenthalts faßte er in seiner berühmten, in mehreren Auflagen veröffentlichten *Histoire d'un voyage faiu en la terre du Brésil, autrement dite Amérique* zusammen. In der dritten Auflage dieses Buches (1585) finden sich fünf Melodien der Tupinambá-Indianer, von denen Villa-Lobos eine — *Canidé-Ioune* — in seinem Liederzyklus *Três Poemas Indígenas* von 1926 verwendet hat. Auch für die Komposition der Filmmusik zu *Descobrimento do Brasil* (1936 — 1940) lieferte Lérys Buch ihm Vorlagen.

Titelblatt der Erstausgabe eines Buches (Marburg 1557)

Ein weiteres Buch, das auf Villa-Lobos einen nachhaltigen Einfluß ausübte, war die Reise in Brasilien (München 1823), die der Zoologe Johann Baptist von Spix (1781 – 1826) und der Botaniker Carl Friedrich Philipp von Martius (1794 – 1865) im Anschluß an ihren knapp dreijährigen Aufenthalt in Brasilien veröffentlichten; hier findet sich eine überaus interessante *Musikbeilage von vierzehn*

brasilianischen Volksliedern und Indianischen Melodien,
auf die sich der Komponist berufen konnte. Anregungen
ganz anderer Art fand Villa-Lobos in der *Voyage pitto-*
resque et historique au Brésil ou Séjour d'un artiste français
au Brésil depuis 1816 jusqu'en 1831 inclusivement (Paris
1834 — 1839) von Jean Baptiste Debret (1768 — 1848). Der
französische Maler hatte sich einer Gruppe von Künstlern und Handwerkern angeschlossen, die 1816 unter der
Führung von Joachim Lebreton (1760 — 1819) nach Brasilien ging. Debret gehört zu den bedeutendsten Doku-
mentaristen der brasilianischen Kolonialzeit; sein Buch
umfaßt drei Bände mit einer vielseitigen und künstlerisch
hochstehenden Ikonographie über das Leben der Menschen in Brasilien: Tagesszenen, Landschaften, Sitten und
Gebräuche. Dem Studium Debrets konnte Villa-Lobos
zahlreiche Anregungen für seine Kompositionen entneh-
men, vor allem für die, die unter das Genre der Programm-
musik fallen. (Villa-Lobos hat vielen seiner Werke einen
erklärenden Text beigefügt; diese Texte sind in dem
Werkverzeichnis — *Villa-Lobos, Sua Obra,* Rio de Janeiro [2]1972 — veröffentlicht worden.) Villa-Lobos legte
größten Wert darauf, daß dem Hörer diese programmati-
schen Texte bekannt sind. Inwieweit sie sich in der Musik
wiederspiegeln, ist freilich eine andere Frage. Er jedenfalls
glaubte, seinen Werken damit ein brasilianisches Kolorit
zu geben. Hinzu kommt, daß er seinen Kompositionen
oft brasilianische Titel gab — etwa *Chôros* — obwohl
diese Stücke aller möglichen Gattungen auch ebensogut
irgendeinen traditionellen Titel hätten erhalten können.
Auch die Stiche des deutschen Malers (Johann) Moritz
Rugendas (1802 — 1858) boten Villa-Lobos zahlreiche
Anregungen; Rugendas hatte sich 1821 der Expedition
des Barons Georg Heinrich Landsdorff angeschlossen
und war bis 1825 in Brasilien geblieben. Seine *Malerische*
Reise in Brasilien erschien 1835 in Paris.
Natürlich beschäftigte sich Villa-Lobos auch mit der Musik der Indianer, aber er hat nie selbst den Urwald durch-
streift, wie er es oft behauptet hat. Einerseits amüsierte er
sich köstlich, wenn man ihm diese Expeditionen abnahm,
zum anderen schuf er damit einen Mythos, der seine
Originalität (und die seiner Quellen) betonen sollte.
Das Studium der indianischen Musik betrieb der Komponist vielmehr im Nationalmuseum von Rio de Janeiro,
wo er auch die *Nozani-ná*-Melodie (auf Schallplatte)

hörte, die er in seinem *Chôros Nr. 3* und im zweiten Lied
der *Chansons Typiques Brésiliennes* verwendete. Auch die
Teirú-Melodie, die sich im zweiten der *Três Poemas Indi-
genas* wiederfindet, hörte Villa-Lobos im Schallarchiv des
Nationalmuseums; er hat sie in ähnlicher Manier verar-
beitet, wie die *Canidé-Ioune*-Melodie im ersten Lied dieses
Zyklus.
Direktor dieses Museums war damals Edgard Roquette
Pinto (1884—1954), der an der Forschungsreise (1907/
08) des brasilianischen Offiziers Cândido Mariano da
Silva Rondon (1865—1958) im Nordosten von Mato
Grosso teilgenommen hatte und 1913 nach Goiás und
Amazonien, in die spärlich von Indianern bevölkerten
Gegenden vordrang, wo er Material über die Parecís-
Indianer sammelte und Schall- und Bildaufzeichnungen
machte, die die Basis seiner ethnologischen Studie *Rondo-
nia* bildeten, wo auch die Melodien abgedruckt sind. Au-
ßerdem konnte Villa-Lobos im Nationalmuseum auch
verschiedene Instrumente der Eingeborenen untersuchen.
Einige von ihnen verwendete er später in seinen Komposi-

TEIRU'
(INDIOS PARECÍS)

tionen, den Klang anderer versuchte er mit einem her-
kömmlichen Instrumentarium nachzuahmen, für die er
spezifische Anweisungen der Spieltechnik gab.

FONOGRAMA 14.597

(INDIOS PARECÍS)

Im Nationalmuseum von Rio de Janeiro studierte Villa-Lobos Tonauf-
nahmen indianischer Musik

Ebenso beschäftigte sich Villa-Lobos mit Landkarten, mit Masken — und immer wieder auch mit den Menschen, denen er begegnete: es waren nicht nur die Bewohner der Großstädte wie Rio de Janeiro oder São Paulo, die ihn faszinierten, sondern auch die, die in der Wildnis, im Sertão lebten, die Kaffeepflücker, Goldsucher, Diamantenjäger, Gummibaum-Zapfer, Viehtreiber des Südens, die Pflücker von Mate-Tee — kurz, alle, die eng mit der Erde und dem Land Brasilien verbunden sind. Das Wesen dieser Menschen und ihre Lebenswelt hoffte der Komponist in seiner Musik wiedergeben zu können. Wo es ihm nicht überzeugend gelungen zu sein schien, fügte er seinen Werken Titel oder Erklärungen hinzu, um sicher zu sein, daß der Hörer seinen Absichten folgte. Und es sind nicht zuletzt diese Erläuterungen, die Villa-Lobos' Musik ihren brasilianischen Charakter geben.

Neue Zeitschrift für Musik, September 1984, 8–11

Corrigenda

p185 *second paragraph line 2*:
For Dodd read Dodt
p185 *line 8 from bottom*:
For fait read faict
p186 *line 5*:
For 1865 read 1868

Villa-Lobos op 53-jarige leeftijd (1940).

hoe villa-lobos de vader werd van de braziliaanse muziek

Mens & Melodie, October 1984, 412–17

Op 17 november zal het vijf en twintig jaar geleden zijn dat Heitor Villa-Lobos, voor velen de enige representant van de Braziliaanse muziek, overleed. Hij was een kleurrijk mens, een hartelijke man die op zijn vele concertreizen in Europa en Noord- en Zuid-Amerika talloze vrienden maakte. Hij hield ervan overal de draak mee te steken maar hij vertelde óók over zichzelf de ongelooflijkste verhalen, wat menigeen in de war bracht omdat feiten en verzinsels moeilijk waren te scheiden. Lisa M. Peppercorn, een Braziliaanse musicologe die in Zwitserland woont, heeft heel wat artikelen over hem geschreven, ook een nu uitverkocht boek over zijn leven en werk. Weldra zal van haar hand een nieuw boek verschijnen over de wereld van Villa-

Lobos met veel tot nu toe niet gepubliceerd iconografisch en
documentair materiaal. In het volgende artikel herdenkt zij de
componist die zij bewonderde en die zij goed heeft gekend.

Villa-Lobos had weinig hobbies want zijn drang tot componeren was
zo sterk dat hij altijd en overal, onder welke omstandigheden dan
ook, muziek wilde scheppen. Ondanks zijn grote vriendenkring
waren er toch maar weinigen die van dat scheppingsproces getuigen
konden zijn. Een van die weinigen was de nu 82-jarige Walter Burle
Marx, de Braziliaanse componist-dirigent die sinds het begin van de
jaren vijftig in Philadelphia woont.

Burle Marx wilde zo'n dertig jaar geleden een werk van Villa-Lobos
uitvoeren op een jeugdconcert in Rio de Janeiro. De componist had
een speciale compositie in uitzicht gesteld maar de partituur kwam
maar niet en er moest gerepeteerd worden. "Ik had Villa-Lobos een
paar dagen tevoren in de vroege avond opgezocht", vertelt de
dirigent. "Villa-Lobos was net klaar met avondeten, de tafel was
afgeruimd en ik informeerde naar de inlossing van zijn belofte. Hij
antwoordde: "Ik zal het werk voor je jeugdconcert vrijdagmorgen 4
uur klaar hebben". Ik zei: "Mijn repetitie begint om 9 uur 's morgens.
Hoe zit je stuk in elkaar?" Antwoord: "De partijen doe ik zelf, met een
paar vrienden die mij willen helpen". "Accoord", reageerde ik, "dan
laat ik je nu alleen." "Waarom?", vroeg Villa-Lobos, "je stoort me
helemaal niet."

Terwijl de componist dat zei, liep hij naar zijn werktafel en ging verder
met de orkestratie van zijn stuk, met inkt schrijvend en tegelijk
pratend tegen mij. In de kamer ernaast speelde Vieira Brandâo, een
leerling die de naaste medewerker van Villa-Lobos was geworden,
het symfonische gedicht *Amazonas*. Al werkend luisterde Villa-Lobos
naar zijn andere werk in de andere kamer en riep Brandâo van tijd tot
tijd correcties toe."G-flat in de bassen!", klonk het bijvoorbeeld. Het
lijkt onwaarschijnlijk maar de nieuwe compositie voor het jeugdconcert was op de afgesproken tijd compleet in mijn bezit."

In een brief van 31 mei 1981 heeft Burle Marx mij dit voorval mee-
gedeeld. Het was geen unieke gebeurtenis in het leven van de
componist. Villa-Lobos kon componeren terwijl een stofzuiger door
zijn kamer raasde of terwijl de radio luid aanstond. Aldo Parisot, de
Braziliaanse cellist die nu verbonden is aan de muziekfaculteit van
de Universiteit van Yale, herinnert zich een soortgelijk voorval dat hij
beschreef in zijn brief aan mij, gedateerd 25 october 1983.
Parisot had Villa-Lobos gevraagd een celloconcert voor hem te
componeren. Ongeveer veertig jaar na het eerste zou dit het tweede
celloconcert van Villa-Lobos worden. De componist vroeg Parisot
naar een New-Yorks hotel te komen om bij het componeren tegenwoordig te zijn. "Inderdaad was hij er mee bezig toen ik arriveerde
maar al gauw bleek dat hij tegelijk aan een symfonie werkte en als het
ware tussen de beide werken heen en weer pendelde. Als ik het mij
goed herinner", schrijft Parisot, "was mijn concert in een week af".

Villa-Lobos op 69-jarige leeftijd, drie jaar voor zijn dood in 1959.

Natuurlijk had deze onwaarschijnlijke bekwaamheid om in alle situaties te kunnen componeren en van het ene werk-in-wording op het andere te kunnen overschakelen, ook zijn schaduwzijden. Lang niet altijd heeft Villa-Lobos voldoende tijd besteed aan de afwerking van zijn partituren. Burle Marx schreef me, dat hij op de Wereld-tentoonstelling van 1939 in New York de première dirigeerde van de *Bachianas Brasileiras no. 5* met de Braziliaanse, in de Verenigde Staten wonende sopraan Bidú Sayao en het New York Philharmonic Orchestra. "Toen ik later het mancuscript van het werk nog eens onder de ogen kreeg, viel het mij op dat er een herhalingsteken bij de eerste inleidende maat in 5/4 was toegevoegd. Ik vroeg Villa-Lobos waarom hij dat had gedaan. Hij antwoordde dat hij de introductie te kort vond, en toen ik daarna verder vroeg waarom hij niet meer had gecomponeerd, moest hij lachen, verklaarde dat hij daarvoor niet genoeg verbeeldingskracht bezat maar voegde er aarzelend aan toe: *Para dizer verdade, eu tive preguiça* (om de waarheid te zeggen, ik was er te lui voor).

Dit was ontegenzeglijk een van Villa-Lobos' fouten. Als een werk eenmaal af was, gebeurde het maar heel zelden dat hij het verbeterde, laat staan veranderde. De rijke fontein van zijn ideeën werkte zo gestaag dat hij soms te lui of te moe was om een werk te perfectioneren. Hieruit moet de buitenstaander nu ook weer geen verkeerde conclusie trekken, Villa-Lobos was consciëntieus en heel precies als hij wezenlijke gedachten en gevoelens wilde overbrengen. U las hierboven dat hij de cellist Parisot vroeg tegenwoordig te zijn bij het ontstaan van het tweede celloconcert dat hij voor hem maakte. In feite vroeg hij Parisot gedurende een week dagelijks een beetje te komen studeren in de hotelkamer waar Villa-Lobos werkte. "Hij vroeg me toonladders te spelen en ook passages uit études, sonates, concerten. Hij wilde naar mij luisteren en mijn spel in zich opnemen om een concert naar mijn maat te kunnen schrijven, een concert helemaal afgestemd op mijn techniek, op mijn speelstijl. "Terwijl hij werkte, liet hij mij gedeelten zien en vroeg me die te beproeven. Vaak onderbrak hij me en demonstreerde mij hoe hij ze gespeeld, in Rio de Janeiro, in een orkestje dat vaudevilles, films en me voor." Villa-Lobos kon dat want in zijn jeugd had hij cello gespeeld, in Rio de Janeiro, in een orkestje dat Vaudevilles, films en andere theatrale manifestaties begeleidde.

Villa-Lobos was een geweldig vruchtbaar componist. Zoals veel componisten moest hij zich door zelfstudie en door de praktijk bekwamen om in staat te zijn elk genre muziek te componeren na slechts enkele lessen over fundamentele beginselen. Hij werd bepaald niet op stel en sprong beroemd. Met een éénjarige studie-beurs van de regering kon hij in 1923/24 voor het eerst naar Parijs gaan om daar te ontdekken wat luisteraars aansprak en waarmee hij naam zou kunnen maken. Naar eigen zeggen wilde hij aandacht trekken door anders en origineel te zijn. Lof en succes begon langzaam aan te komen, op het eind van de jaren twintig in Parijs en pas op het eind van de laatste wereldoorlog in de Verenigde Staten. Daar tussenin ontstond er erkenning in zijn thuisland.

In Parijs had Villa-Lobos geleerd wat hem te doen stond. Hij was van nature een doorzetter en als hij ergens zijn zinnen op had gezet, kon niets hem van zijn doel afbrengen. Inderdaad bereikte hij dat luisteraars in zijn muziek getroffen worden door een typische melodievorm, een exotische klankkleur, een opmerkelijke ritmische structuur. Het is een veel verbreide maar toch helemaal verkeerde gedachte dat Villa-Lobos om zijn muziek een Braziliaans karakter te geven door de maagdelijke wouden van het Amazone-gebied trok, zich mengde onder de inboorlingen, folkloristisch materiaal verzamelde en dat in zijn composities verwerkte. In feite heeft Villa-Lobos zelf nooit inheemse muziek verzameld op de manier waarop Bartók en Kodály dat in Hongarije deden.

Hoe slaagde Villa-Lobos er dan toch in zijn muziek een karakter te geven dat als Braziliaans overkomt? Hij deed wat andere onderzoekers op andere terreinen ook doen: hij las boeken over het Brazilië van vroeger, maakte zich vertrouwd met het legendarische verleden van zijn vaderland, raadpleegde oude kronieken, bestudeerde in musea de inheemse muziekinstrumenten en luisterde naar grammofoon- en andere opnamen van folkloristische muziek die *anderen* hadden opgespoord en vastgelegd. Bij de een of andere gelegenheid, waarvan de datum mij niet bekend is, moet hij in eigen handschrift hebben verklaard "dat hij heeft geprobeerd zichzelf zo goed mogelijk te documenteren". Zijn geëngageerd onderzoek naar wat zich afspeelde in de vóór-Columbiaanse tijd, en naar alle tijdperken tot aan de dagen waarin hij zelf leefde, bewerkstelligde na verwerking in zijn geest en zijn ziel wat ervaren wordt als het Braziliaanse karakter van zijn werk: de sensualiteit van bepaalde melodische lijnen, de vrolijke of weemoedige klankcombinaties, de eigenaardige toonkleur, de typische ritmiek.

Oude Braziliaanse legenden hebben Villa-Lobos' fantasie inderdaad in gang gezet. In 1917, toen hij 30 jaar was, componeerde hij, uitgaande van zo'n legende, het symfonische gedicht *Uirapuru* dat ook als ballet wordt gegeven. Dit gebeurde met meer van zijn werken. Van zijn vader hoorde hij een Indiaans verhaal over de Amazone-rivier dat, ook in 1917, leidde tot het symfonische gedicht *Amazonas* dat in 1934 in Serge Lifars choreografie als ballet werd gepresenteerd. Lifar was in 1936 eveneens de choreograaf en de solodanser in *Jurupari*, gebaseerd op de in 1926 voor koor en orkest gecomponeerde *Chôrus No. 10*, een van zijn interessantste en persoonlijkste werken.

Het eerste buitenlandse boek dat ooit over Brazilië is geschreven, maakte op Villa-Lobos veel indruk. Het heet *Zwei Reisen nach Brasiliën* en werd geschreven door de Duitser Hans Staden. De titelpagina van de eerste uitgave, in Marburg verschenen in 1557, toont een afbeelding van een inboorling, rustend in een hangmat. Deze plaat kristalliseerde zich bij Villa-Lobos uit in *Idílio na Réde* (Idylle in een hangmat), een onderdeel van de *Suite Floral* voor piano.

Na intenção da verdade sobre o nosso folk-lore, procurei documentar-me, o mais que pude, com uma cuidadosa busca neste immenso manancial dos nossos factos e causas, desde a época pre-colombiana até os nossos dias

H. Villa-Lobos

Facsimile van Villa-Lobos' verklaring dat hij erop uit was "zich zo goed mogelijk te documenteren".

Ook het boek van de Franse calvinistische dominee Jean de Léry, die omstreeks 1570 tien maanden in Brazilië rondtrok, fascineerde Villa-Lobos. Léry's *Histoire d'un voyage faict en la terre du Brésil autrement dite Amérique* verscheen voor het eerst in 1578 en werd daarna in ettelijke edities en vertalingen herdrukt. De derde editie uit 1585, verzorgd door Antoine Chuppin in Genève, bevatte voor het eerst vijf melodieën van de Tupinambá Indianen waarvan Villa-Lobos gebruik maakte in zijn *Três Poemas Indígenas*. Het boek van Léry kwam de componist verder goed van pas bij het componeren van *Descobrimento do Brasil*, een suite over het ontstaan van Brazilië, waaraan hij van 1936 tot 1942 werkte.

Sterk gepakt werd Villa-Lobos ook door de *Reise in Brasilien* van Johann Baptist von Spix en Carl Friederich Philipp von Martius, twee Duitse wetenschappers die tussen 1817 en 1820 de fauna en de flora van het land bestudeerden en beschreven. Hun boek bevat een hoogst interessant muzikaal supplement met volksliederen en Indiaanse melodieën die voor de muziek van Villa-Lobos van onschatbare waarde zijn geweest.

Beeldende informatie en inspiratie vond de componist in de drie delen van de *Voyage pittoresque et historique au Brésil, ou séjour d'un artiste francais depuis 1816 jusqu'en 1831 inclusivement*, een boeiend document van wat de schilder Jean Baptiste Debret en collega-kunstenaars en ambachtslieden waarnamen. Door Johann Moritz Rugendas, een Duits artiest uit het begin van de vorige eeuw, en diens *Malerische Reise in Brasilien*, gepubliceerd in 1835, leerde Villa-Lobos veel over het landschap en het dagelijks leven in die dagen.

Met dat al was de allerbelangrijkste bron van inspiratie voor Villa-Lobos Rio de Janeiro's Nationale Museum in Quinta da Boa Vista dat hij vaak met zijn vrouw Lucilia bezocht. Daar hoorde hij de Nozaniná-melodie die hij toepaste in *Choros No. 3* en in zijn *Chansons Typiques Brésiliennes,* en ook de Teirú-melodie die hij verwerkte in zijn al eerder genoemde *Poemas Indígenas.* In het genoemde museum heeft de componist ook veel inheemse muziekinstrumenten kunnen bestuderen.

De titels die Villa-Lobos aan zijn composities gaf, hebben aanleiding gegeven tot misverstand. Aanvankelijk gebruikte hij de aanduidingen van muzikale vormen zoals internationaal gewoonte is: symfonie, kwartet, trio of iets dergelijks. Na zijn herhaald museumbezoek zag hij daarvan af en besloot alleen nog Braziliaanse titels te gebruiken zoals hij incidenteel al eerder had gedaan. Doordat zijn stukken veelal een pseudo-folkloristische opzet hebben maar niettemin onmiskenbaar de stijl van Villa-Lobos bezitten, ontstond er opnieuw misverstand. Bij zijn eerste bezoek aan New York moest hij nog eens uit-drukkelijk stellen: "Ik schrijf nooit potpourri's van volksliedjes". Nadat Villa-Lobos op het einde van de laatste wereldoorlog veel opdrachten kreeg van internationaal bekende kunstenaars zag hij weer af van de Braziliaanse titels en keerde terug naar de traditionele aanduidingen. Opportunist, zoals hij altijd was geweest, zal hij hebben aangevoeld dat de opdrachtgevers het meest voor traditionele titels voelden omdat die door een internationaal concertpubliek het gemakkelijkst werden geaccepteerd.

Mens & Melodie, October 1984, 412–17

Corrigenda

p194 *line 8*:
For Sayao read Sayão
p194 *line 16*:
For dizer verdade read dizer a verdade
p196 *second line*:
For 1570 read 1556
p197 *line 4*:
For Choros read Chôros
line 6:
For *Poemas Indígenas* read *Três Poemas Indígenas*

VILLA-LOBOS'S COMMISSIONED COMPOSITIONS

ON 26 November 1944 Heitor Villa-Lobos made his United States debut with the Janssen Symphony Orchestra in Los Angeles, followed during the ensuing weeks by appearances as composer-conductor in Boston, Chicago, and New York City (where he was also interviewed about his composing methods by Olin Downes, then music critic of *The New York Times*). All these events changed the composer's life completely: he was suddenly catapulted into the limelight, lionized and fêted by prominent persons from musical and cultural life at a reception at the Waldorf-Astoria Hotel. A long-sought dream had unexpectedly come true: international recognition as a composer and as Latin America's foremost musical figure of his generation.

These events were crowned by three commissions in 1945. One honour came from the Elizabeth Sprague Coolidge Foundation at the Library of Congress, Washington, D.C. He responded with a *Trio* for violin, viola, and cello and sent it together with the parts before 1 October 1945, ready for performance by the Albeneri Trio at the Founder's Day Concert on 30 October 1945 in the Coolidge Auditorium at the Library of Congress. Another invitation came from Ellen Ballon (1898-1969), the Canadian pianist of Russian parents, for a Piano Concerto, and a third request was received from the Koussevitzky Music Foundation. The composer answered with a work for orchestra called *Madona*, written in December 1945 and dedicated to Natalie (1882-1942), the first wife of Serge Koussevitzky (1874-1951), an old friend of his from their Parisian days. This was to be the beginning of a long series of commissions Villa-Lobos obtained during the last fifteen years of his life from institutions, orchestras, and virtuoso artists, through which he enriched the literature of music in all fields.

To these belong two stage works, a type of music which was not too much to his liking. *Magdalena*, a 'musical adventure', commissioned by Edwin Lester (b.1895), President of the Los Angeles Civic Light Opera Association, was written between January and March 1947 and premièred on 26 July 1948 at Philharmonic Hall in Los Angeles—but despite 32 performances each in that city and San Francisco and 72 presentations at New York's Ziegfeld Theatre (which brought several reviews in *The New York Times* from various angles), it was a flop. *Yerma*, on the other hand, commissioned in 1955 by his old friend Hugh Ross (b. 1898), the British-born director of the New York Schola Cantorum, and John Blankenship, then director of the drama department at Sarah Lawrence College, Bronxville, N.Y., was finished in 1956 and was written partly in New York, partly in Paris. The work, based on the play by Federico García Lorca, was well acclaimed by the American press when it was posthumously premièred at the Santa Fe Opera on 12 July

1971 and repeated two days later. It received favourable notices everywhere despite—or because of—its Puccinian flavour.

By 1949 Villa-Lobos had come to the United States practically every year since his American debut, and conducted his works with all the major orchestras; but he had also become a well-known figure in Europe, particularly in France—with the result that institutions and foundations approached him to compose special works for special occasions. Thus, in 1949, it was UNESCO (an organisation of which the composer was known to be distrustful) that tried to honour Villa-Lobos by commissioning him, as one of eleven composers who were to write a work each for a gala concert commemorating the centenary of Chopin's death. Villa-Lobos responded with a piano piece, dedicated to Irving Schwerké (1893-1975), the American writer who lived in Paris, and called it *Hommage à Chopin*. It was played upon that occasion by the Brazilian pianist Arnaldo Estrela (1908-1979).

A joint invitation from the Koussevitzky Music Foundation in the Library of Congress and the Boston Symphony Orchestra was sent on 29 October 1954 to Villa-Lobos as one in a number of leading composers of the United States, South America, and Europe—to compose a work celebrating the occasion of the 75th anniversary of that orchestra during 1955/56. Villa-Lobos accepted and composed his Symphony No. 11, premièred on 2/3 March 1956 in Boston.

Other American orchestras also besieged the composer and hoped to be granted a composition. Among them were the Louisville Orchestra, which commissioned him twice, after it had decided on the important policy of 'instead of engaging expensive soloists ... using the budget for soloists to commission composers of world renown to write pieces especially for the orchestra'. This decision was taken in the spring of 1948. Villa-Lobos was thus fortunate to be included in this new endeavour. The first Louisville commission occurred in 1950. He wrote *Erosão*, a symphonic poem on 'The Origin of the Amazon River', premièred on 7 and 8 November 1951 by the Louisville Orchestra conducted by Robert Whitney (b. 1904). With this work, as well as the subsequent one, Villa-Lobos deviated from a path he had principally followed after his debut in the United States and gave his work a title that recalled his compositions in the period in the 1920's when he emphatically stressed the Brazilian angle in the names that he gave to his compositions. The second work for the Louisville Orchestra was named *Alvorada na Floresta Tropical* (Dawn in a Tropical Forest): commissioned only three years after the first one, in 1953, it was performed in January 1954 by the orchestra for a commercial recording.

The other American orchestra trying to get Villa-Lobos's attention in 1958 and 1959, shortly before the composer's death, was in Pittsburgh. Two very interesting commissions reached him from Robert Austin Boudreau (b. 1927), founder and director of the American Wind Symphony Orchestra in Pittsburgh—interesting because the instrumental combinations which the Brazilian composer could chose here were very much the kind in which he excelled by creating tone colours of unusual beauty. Villa-Lobos wrote *Fantasia em tres Movimentos* and dedicated it to 'The Rivers of Pittsburgh'. It was premièred on 29 June 1958 in that city and the following year, just a few months before he died, he responded to the second commission, by sending the orchestra a *Concerto Grosso* for flute, oboe, clarinet, bassoon, and wind orchestra, first performed on 5 July 1959 with a repeat performance on 7 June 1981 on the occasion of the orchestra's Silver Jubilee Anniversary.

In the 1950's, Villa-Lobos's fame and popularity had reached such a point, particularly in the United States, that he was asked to write two ballets in short succession. The first commission was given him by Janet Collins (b. 1917), the American dancer who appeared in solo dances before becoming *première danseuse* at the Metropolitan Opera in New York from 1951-1954. In 1954 she asked Villa-Lobos to compose *Gênesis*, a symphonic poem and ballet, for which she provided the scenario and prepared the choreography, though she did not actually dance it. The première in the concert hall was in Rio de Janeiro on 21 November 1969.

To write a ballet of a completely different type was the commission he received from the British-born dancer, actor, theatre and opera director Basil Langton. In 1956 he asked Villa-Lobos to compose music based on Eugene O'Neill's play *The Emperor Jones*. It was premièred the same year (12 July 1956) during the Empire State Music Festival at Ellenville, N.Y., choreographed by the Mexican-born dancer and choreographer José Arcadia Limón (1908-1972).

But there were also his many friends, the virtuoso artists, who approached Villa-Lobos to enrich their literature with additional compositions which they planned to première soon after they received the music. These artists, of international fame, included Eugene List, Andres Segovia, Nicanor Zabaleta, John Sebastian, Aldo Parisot, Bernardo Segall, Felicja Blumenthal, and Ellen Ballon. Only a composer with such facility as Villa-Lobos—for whom it was, as he termed it himself, 'a physical necessity' to compose—could attend to all the demands made on him for so different instruments and musical genres.

To fulfil, in 1953, a commission by Eugene List (b. 1918), Villa-Lobos hit on a different idea. He composed and dedicated to the American pianist not a piece for piano solo but a *Fantasia Concertante* for piano, clarinet and bassoon, an instrumental combination much to the liking of the composer. The work was first performed on 19 November 1968 in the Sala Cecília Meirelles in Rio de Janeiro. The Concerto for Guitar, written in 1951, was premièred by Andres Segovia and the Houston Symphony Orchestra on 6 February 1956 with Villa-Lobos himself conducting. The Concerto for Harp, written in 1953, was premièred on 14, 15, and 17 January 1955 by the Philadelphia Orchestra with Nicanor Zabaleta and the composer conducting.

Also composed in 1953 was the Cello Concerto No. 2, commissioned by and dedicated to his countryman Aldo Parisot (b. 1918) who, since 1946, has lived in the United States and is presently on the faculty of the Yale School of Music. The work was first given by him with the New York Philharmonic Symphony Orchestra on 5 February 1955 under Walter Hendl (b. 1917) with Villa-Lobos present at the performance. Villa-Lobos himself was a cellist and as such played in his youth in vaudevilles, movies, and theatres, and more specifically as member of the concert and opera orchestra of Rio de Janeiro's Municipal Theatre. This may explain why he took particular care and special interest in the writing of this Concerto. For this reason he asked Parisot to 'go every day, for one week, to his hotel in New York and practise in his apartment. He asked me', Parisot wrote to the present writer on 25 October 1983, 'to play scales, etudes, sonatas, concertos, etc., so he could hear my playing and write a work that was tailor-made, so to speak. I remember that while he was writing passages of the Concerto he would show them to me and ask me to try them. Many times he would remark "no, try this way", and would pick up the cello and demonstrate to me how he wanted the passage played … If I remember correctly, he finished the Concerto in one week'.

Villa-Lobos fared differently with the commission he received from John Sebastian (1914-1980), the American self-taught harmonica virtuoso, and which produced the Concerto which the artist premièred with the Kol Israel Orchestra in Jerusalem on 27 October 1959. To familiarize the composer with the harmonica's potentialities, Sebastian made drawings for Villa-Lobos in order to demonstrate the possibilities of the instrument, revealing its unusually wide register and combinations. Sebastian's widow quoted, in a letter to the present writer dated 12 August 1981, an interesting comment on the Concerto for Harmonica by Glen Clugston, one-time accompanist of John Sebastian:

It was one of my joys to work with John and Villa-Lobos during the writing of the Concerto. The composer sat at a huge semi-circular desk with a pot of black thick coffee, several cigars in ashtrays all around, working on several compositions at once, while watching a TV at intervals. All the time wearing a hat ... When we played the first play-through, he rushed forward and embraced us. John wasn't at ease with the Cadenza, feeling it wasn't quite right and together they rewrote it. I think Villa-Lobos caught the spirit of the instrument very well in the first two movements. I believe it was nearly his last composition.

In his commissions for Piano Concertos Villa-Lobos again turned to classical titles, either in accordance with the artists' wishes or for greater acceptability on the concert circuit. Of the five Concertos for Piano and Orchestra, three were commissions: the First, Fourth and Fifth. No. 4 was written and dedicated in 1952 to his countryman Bernardo Segáll (b. 1911) who first performed it with the Pittsburgh Symphony Orchestra on 9 and 11 January 1953, with the composer conducting.

'All I remember of Villa-Lobos's correspondence on the Concerto', Bernardo Segáll wrote this writer on 6 May 1984, from his home near Los Angeles, where he is a member of the faculty of the University of Southern California,

were reports of its progress from Rio, then Paris, where he finished the second movement. He finished it in New York in 1952. I was then living in New York. He conducted my performance of the Concerto with the Pittsburgh and the Los Angeles Philharmonic which was performed at the Hollywood Bowl. I performed it with the New York Philharmonic under Leonard Bernstein. I also performed in Rio and São Paulo under Eleazar de Carvalho ...

No. 5, commissioned by and dedicated to Felicja Blumenthal (b. 1915), the Brazilian pianist of Polish origin who first played the work under Jean Martinon with the London Philharmonic Orchestra on 8 May 1955, has since been played again with the Vienna Philharmonic and other orchestras. The commission for the First Concerto for Piano and Orchestra was by Ellen Ballon, who premièred this work in Rio de Janeiro's Municipal Theatre on 11 October 1946 under the composer's direction only a year after she had given Villa-Lobos the commission. She also played the American first performance in Dallas (29 December 1946) under Antal Doráti (b. 1906), as well as the Canadian première under Désiré Defauw (1885-1960) on 28 October 1947 at Plateau Auditorium in Montréal, and a repeat performance with the Orchestre Symphonique de Montréal on 30/31 January 1951 under Ernest Ansermet, with whom she had also made a recording in 1949. The Canadian première was put on by the International Service of the Canadian Broadcasting Corporation before an invited audience, and the concert was also broadcast to South America by shortwave. 'The program was presented free of charge to any Canadian who wanted to hear it. And many did. Threequarters of an hour before the concert began, they were lined up outside the hall, standing there in spite of the thinly, spattering rain', as *The Gazette* in Montréal reported the day following the concert in an extensive review about the event. This was the first concert in Canada entirely given over to works of Villa-Lobos, not just the performance of his Concerto.

Whether it was Villa-Lobos's charm, his warm-hearted nature, his talent to make friends easily everywhere he went, or his smartness to entice others to commission him, or whether it was the unusual tone colours and instrumental combinations of his music that led to twenty commissions in a period of fifteen years, is difficult to say and really irrelevant. The fact remains that the music literature has been greatly enriched by these commissioned compositions of so varied a nature, listed here together for the first time in accordance with all available primary sources, on the occasion of the twenty-fifth anniversary of Villa-Lobos's death on 17 November 1959.

Tempo, (151), December 1984, 28–31

Corrigenda

p199 *line 5 from bottom*:
For tres read três
p200 *third paragraph fourth line*:
For Segall read Segáll

HEITOR VILLA-LOBOS: PROFILO DEL COMPOSITORE BRASILIANO

Era un uomo di media altezza, con i capelli neri pettinati all'indietro, portava abiti un po' sformati e sfoggiava camicie dai colori sgargianti. Fumava tutto il giorno, in continuazione, dei grossi sigari neri che erano come il suo marchio fino dalla adolescenza. Profondeva il suo fascino su tutti quelli che gli erano simpatici, affascinando chi voleva conquistare ai suoi progetti e alle sue idee, ma era reticente, quasi sospettoso, verso coloro che non stavano al passo con lui. Si dice che abbia prodotto circa mille composizioni durante i suoi settantadue anni di vita e ne esistono innumerevoli registrazioni nella interpretazione di artisti di ogni nazionalità. Divenne celebre di qua e di là dall'Atlantico dopo la seconda guerra mondiale e tale fama è dovuta principalmente agli Stati Uniti che lo catapultarono nel circuito dei direttori ospiti in tutti i maggiori paesi per farvi conoscere le sue opere.

Questo era Heitor Villa-Lobos (1887-1959), il piú notevole compositore brasiliano della prima metà di questo secolo, anzi il piú famoso che l'America Latina abbia avuto in tale epoca. Egli era nato a Rio de Janeiro quando il suo paese era ancora un impero sul modello britannico sotto l'imperatore Pedro II (1825-1891) e vigeva ancora la schiavitú che fu abolita soltanto un anno dopo la sua nascita, allorché la principessa Isabella (1846-1921), figlia e erede legittima dell'imperatore, il 13 maggio 1888 firmò il decreto di abolizione mentre suo padre si trovava in Europa. Villa-Lobos morí il 17 novembre 1959, cinque mesi prima che il Brasile, divenuto ormai da tempo una repubblica, spostasse la sua capitale per la terza volta. Capitale era stata per circa duecento anni, cioè dal 1763 al 1960, Rio de Janeiro sulla baia di Guanabara e il 21 aprile

1960 venne trasferita nell'interno, a Brasilia, città interamente costruita su un altopiano nello stato di Goias.

Villa-Lobos arrivò tardi sulla scena delle celebrità internazionali. Il 26 novembre 1944, all'età di 57 anni, fece il suo debutto statunitense a Los Angeles con la Werner Janssen Symphony Orchestra. L'interesse degli Stati Uniti per questo veemente compositore sudamericano fu dovuto in gran parte alla politica di buon vicinato di Franklin D. Roosevelt e al coordinatore di questa per gli affari interamericani, Nelson A. Rockefeller (1909-1979), valido aiuto nello scambio dei programmi culturali fra gli Stati Uniti e il Brasile. Fu così che molti studiosi, musicisti, solisti, direttori d'orchestra e orchestre si recarono in Brasile e resero omaggio al famoso compositore. Heitor Villa-Lobos non parlava inglese né lo parlò mai in vita sua eccetto le parole *strong, strong coffee* e *vanilla ice cream*, e i suoi ospiti molto probabilmente conoscevano poco o nulla del portoghese, la lingua del Brasile. Ciò nonostante Villa-Lobos e i suoi ospiti americani divennero ben presto grandi amici. Fu invitato a recarsi negli Stati Uniti come ambasciatore musicale del suo paese e gli furono promessi onori e opportunità di eseguire la sua musica e quella di altri compositori brasiliani, ma Villa-Lobos rifiutò cortesemente. Sarebbe andato soltanto alle proprie condizioni, senza alcun legame. Istintivamente sentiva che gli si presentava l'occasione imprevista di salire sulla scena concertistica dell'America, il paese tanto bramato da ogni artista, specialmente durante gli anni della guerra, quando l'Europa era preclusa.

Villa-Lobos era già stato fuori del suo paese, principalmente in Argentina e in Uruguay e anche in Europa, in particolare a Parigi dove aveva trascorso diverso tempo negli anni Venti. Non conosceva però il sistema di vita americano e aveva solo una vaga idea degli Stati Uniti da quanto gli avevano detto gli amici brasiliani e statunitensi. Sapeva ascoltare, era intelligente e anche opportunista. Da alcuni anni aveva un buon impiego in Brasile come sovrintendente all'istruzione musicale nella municipalità di Rio de Janeiro e non aveva fretta di lanciarsi in un'avventura ignota, su al Nord, in un paese per il quale non si sentiva ancora pronto. Essere pronto per lui significava saper adattarsi e seguire le usanze del paese ospite. Temeva tutto ciò che non gli era familiare, ma da furbo quale era studiava attentamente la situazione, analizzando quanto apprendeva dagli altri riguardo a quel grande paese dalle illimitate opportunità.

Infine decise che il suo ingresso nella repubblica sorella doves-se avvenire cosí: come ebbe a dire a chi scrive, in Brasile, egli si vedeva a New York in un lussuoso appartamento di Park Avenue, pronto a ritrarre musicalmente le sembianze dei suoi visitatori se-condo le linee del sistema di millimetrizzazione che aveva da poco inventato e su cui si basava la sua composizione del 1939 per pianoforte o orchestra *The New York Skyline*. La linea melodica era stata tracciata sul profilo fotografico di Manhattan per soddi-sfare la curiosità di un giornalista del «Time» che era venuto a informarsi sul sistema di millimetrizzazione usato dal compositore nella sua *Melodia della montagna*, un giuoco musicale per studen-ti. Villa-Lobos mi disse che avrebbe chiesto ai suoi visitatori a New York un prezzo esorbitante per il loro ritratto, che tuttavia riteneva equo e giustificato per la sua ingegnosa creazione. Inoltre voleva dimostrarsi un abile uomo di affari — come si raffigurava tutti gli americani — offrendo uno sconto del cinquanta per cento se piú di cinque visitatori si fossero presentati in un solo giorno. Per annunciare la sua disponibilità a questa straordinaria impresa del ritratto in musica, per il quale gli americani non avrebbero dovuto fare altro che mandargli la loro fotografia o quella dei loro parenti, Villa-Lobos avrebbe tenuto al suo arrivo a Manhattan una conferenza stampa allo scopo di informare i cittadini di New York, tramite i mass-media, che il grande maestro era a loro disposizione per ritrarre musicalmente chiunque lo desiderasse. Parlava seria-mente di questo progetto: non era un'idea momentanea o impulsi-va, perché me la ripropose diverse volte per mesi e anni. Natural-mente non realizzò mai questo sogno fantasioso, ma qui c'era tutto il tipico Villa-Lobos che credeva di conquistarsi gli amici con scherzi e iperboli per attrarre su di sé l'attenzione a ogni costo.

Per i suoi amici americani teneva pronta un'altra storia. Non era nuova di zecca nemmeno allora, essendo stata già raccontata molti anni prima, ma gli sembrava che si incastrasse perfettamente nello scenario del momento. Diceva che la sua intenzione di andare negli Stati Uniti datava da lungo tempo, ma che i piú strani avveni-menti gli avevano impedito di realizzarla nel passato. Per rendere attuale la vecchia storia, Villa-Lobos aggiungeva un nuovo argo-mento — l'interesse per il folclore — che era particolarmente in voga all'inizio degli anni Quaranta, e quindi l'episodio era cosí narrato: all'inizio di questo secolo, quando era ragazzo, si trovava già in viaggio per gli Stati Uniti, ma la nave non arrivò a destina-

zione perché disgraziatamente fece naufragio al largo dell'Isola
Barbados sulla quale, a suo dire, ebbe la fortuna di salvarsi. Là
osservò le danze negre i cui ritmi gli ricordavano quelli uditi nello
stato di Bahia nel Brasile settentrionale. Si era annotato quei motivi
e aveva iniziato a raccogliere materiale folcloristico che diceva di
aver poi usato nelle sue *Danças características africanas* composte
nel 1914-15. Già il 16 febbraio 1925, a 38 anni, aveva parlato di
questa sua improbabile avventura in una intervista rilasciata all'importante quotidiano «O Estado de S. Paulo». Tanto allora che poi
la storia fu ritenuta parto della sua vivida fantasia. Agli inizi degli
anni Quaranta ritenne opportuno ripeterla ai suoi amici americani
che la trovarono divertente, giudicandola parte delle risorse menta-
li dell'esuberante compositore per far colpo sulla gente.

Villa-Lobos poteva ben permettersi di abbandonarsi a queste
favole e rendersi simpatico al prossimo prendendosi giuoco degli
amici e dei nemici perché a quell'epoca aveva già composto un'e-
norme massa di musica meravigliosa e godeva di grande stima in
patria; e non era affatto sconosciuto neppure negli Stati Uniti.
Poco prima della seconda guerra mondiale, durante l'Esposizione
mondiale di New York del 1939, il suo compatriota Walter Burle-
Marx, nato nel 1902, che poi si stabilí a Filadelfia, diresse musica
brasiliana il 4 e il 9 maggio e i concerti inclusero musiche di Villa-
Lobos che furono notate da Olin Downes, allora critico del «New
York Times». A quella esposizione il governo brasiliano inviò
dischi di musica brasiliana che comprendevano naturalmente anche
opere del piú notevole compositore di quel paese. Un anno dopo,
dal 12 al 20 ottobre 1940, il Museo di arte moderna di New York
patrocinò un festival di musica brasiliana durante una mostra di
dipinti del pittore brasiliano Cândido Portinari (1903-1962) e fu
dedicata una serata esclusivamente alla musica di Villa-Lobos, in-
terpretata, per la maggior parte, dal pianista Arthur Rubinstein.
Perciò Villa-Lobos era già noto in certi ambienti americani prima
ancora della sua visita negli Stati Uniti su invito di Werner Janssen
che aveva a quel tempo la propria orchestra a Los Angeles. Villa-
Lobos e Janssen erano amici dai primi anni della guerra, quando il
musicista americano aveva diretto un paio di concerti a Rio de
Janeiro e aveva invitato il compositore brasiliano a andare in California a dirigervi la sua musica con la Werner Janssen Symphony
Orchestra.

Questa volta Villa-Lobos accettò e fece il suo ingresso sulla scena musicale americana non come molti artisti fanno, sulla costa orientale, ma su quella occidentale. Prima che egli dirigesse alcuni concerti nelle città dell'est: Boston, Chicago e New York, l'Occidental College di Los Angeles gli aveva conferito la laurea ad honorem. Dieci anni piú tardi, nel 1954, fu l'Università di Miami e quattro anni dopo, il 3 dicembre 1958, quella di New York a insignirlo del titolo di dottore honoris causa. Vennero anche altre onorificenze da vari paesi: la Légion d'Honneur a Parigi e la nomina a membro dell'Institut de France, nonché numerosi altri riconoscimenti dall'Argentina, dal Brasile, dall'Italia, dal Paraguay, dalla Spagna, ecc. Egli ricevette la maggior parte di questi titoli dopo la sua prima visita negli Stati Uniti, al termine della seconda guerra mondiale, e divenne una celebrità internazionale principalmente perché gli Stati Uniti gli avevano dato la possibilità di dirigere le sue composizioni con le maggiori orchestre del paese, convogliando cosí su di lui l'attenzione della stampa e procurandogli l'occasione di pubblicare alcuni suoi lavori e di incidere numerosi dischi in America.

Ne seguí una serie di commissioni da parte di vari artisti fra cui il suonatore di armonica John Sebastian, il grande chitarrista Andrés Segovia, il pianista americano Eugene List, il violoncellista brasiliano Aldo Parisot, i pianisti, pure brasiliani, Bernardo Segall e Felicja Blumenthal e molti altri. Gli furono richieste anche due opere liriche: una, nel 1947, da Edwin Lester, fondatore e presidente del Los Angeles Civic Light Opera, che Villa-Lobos chiamò *Magdalena* con il sottotitolo *Un'avventura musicale* e che ebbe per scenario la grande regione fluviale colombiana. Se ne ebbero trentadue rappresentazioni tanto a Los Angeles che a San Francisco e circa settanta allo Ziegfeld Theatre di New York nel 1948. Quando il compositore scoprí che per la rappresentazione a New York si progettavano alcuni cambiamenti che avrebbero alterato sensibilmente la partitura, si incollerí e disse al fedele amico Hugh Ross, direttore della Schola Cantorum di New York e suo ammiratore e interprete: «Alla prima rappresentazione mi alzerò in piedi nel mio palco e dirò: "Pubblico di New York, questa non è la mia musica"», come Ross stesso mi riferí il 16 ottobre 1973. Tuttavia Villa-Lobos non pose in atto la sua divertente intenzione perché purtroppo al momento si trovava al Memorial Hospital di New York per essere operato di cancro alle vescica. L'operazione ebbe successo e il compositore fu poi sottoposto a cure mediche per il resto della sua vita tanto che poté vivere per altri undici anni.

La seconda opera lirica gli fu commissionata da John Blankenship che dirigeva allora la sezione teatrale del Sarah Lawrence College di Bronxville, N.Y., dove lavorava anche Hugh Ross. Blankenship cercava un compositore per musicare il dramma *Yerma* di
Federico Garcia Lorca e metterlo in scena con un cast negro; per
questo si rivolse a Ross che lo presentò a Villa-Lobos, il quale
accettò e musicò il testo originale spagnolo, sebbene si fosse pensato di fornirgliene una traduzione in inglese. Furono eseguiti per la
prima volta alcuni brani di *Yerma* in udienza privata a New York
nell'appartamento di Dora Vasconcellos, allora console generale
del Brasile a New York, presente Villa-Lobos, ad opera delle famose cantanti negre Adela Addision e Betty Allen con il coro di
elementi della Schola Cantorum, come appresi poi da Hugh Ross.
La prima rappresentazione ebbe luogo in seguito, dopo la morte
del compositore, a Santa Fe, New Mexico, il 12 agosto 1971 sotto
la direzione di Christopher Keene, protagonista la cantante spagnola Mirna Lacambra. Ancora una volta furono gli Stati Uniti a
promuovere la prima rappresentazione di un'opera che è indubbia-
mente la piú importante delle quattro opere teatrali portate a com-
pimento da Villa-Lobos, ma furono necessarie alcune segrete ma-
novre prima che l'opera potesse raggiungere le scene.

Hugh Ross mi scrisse:

Per il fatto di essere l'unico possessore dalla partitura completa di *Yerma*, eccet-
tuate quelle in possesso di Harold Stern, esecutore legale di Villa-Lobos, o copie
esistenti in Brasile, solo la mia poteva essere messa a disposizione di chi aveva
intenzione di eseguirla in teatro. Fu il mio amico Basil Langton che alla fine
sollevò l'interesse di Richard Gaddes, direttore artistico della Santa Fe Opera
Company.

In precedenza Langton si era rivolto invano a teatri d'opera
europei che non avevano accettato il suo desiderio di fare eseguire
l'opera nella lingua originale spagnola. In Inghilterra tanto il Covent Garden che il Sadler's Wells avevano espresso grande interesse
ma volevano l'esecuzione in inglese, mentre sul continente la ri-
chiedevano in tedesco. Scriveva Ross:

Finalmente, con l'aiuto della Sullivan Foundation di cui sono direttore, la Santa
Fe accettò di acquistare i diritti dall'organizzazione Music Now che a quell'epoca deteneva i diritti di opzione per la prima rappresentazione.

Prima di *Yerma*, a Villa-Lobos era stato chiesto, sempre negli
Stati Uniti, di scrivere un balletto sul dramma di Eugene O'Neill

L'Imperatore Jones. Langton, che era il produttore dell'Empire State Music Festival da lui fondato poco prima con John Brownlee e Frank Forest, si rivolse all'illustre compositore brasiliano e gli commissionò il lavoro per la stagione 1955-56. Questo balletto, con la coreografia dell'oriundo messicano José Arcadio Limón (1906-1972), andò in scena per la prima volta il 12 luglio 1956 e fu ripetuto il 14 nel programma di manifestazioni dell'Empire State Music Festival a Ellenville, N.Y., sotto la direzione del compositore, con la Symphony of the Air Orchestra che era in origine l'Orchestra della NBC diretta da Toscanini.

Villa-Lobos era un genio musicale, autodidatta eccetto poche nozioni rudimentali ricevute da giovane in Brasile. Scriveva ogni tipo di musica e avendo un grande senso dell'opportunità adattava la sua produzione e modellava il carattere delle composizioni secondo l'occasione. In Francia, dove risiedette per qualche tempo durante gli anni Venti, prima con una sovvenzione del governo brasiliano (1923-24) e poi (1927-30) finanziato da due industriali e filantropi brasiliani, i fratelli Arnaldo (1884-1964) e Carlos Guinle (1883-1969), prontamente comprese che, se voleva aver successo in un mondo musicale competitivo, doveva fare quello che andava per la maggiore in quel momento, cioè scrivere musica su base folcloristica, e così fece. Scelse titoli inconsueti per la sua musica, come *Chôros*, per darle un carattere più brasiliano. In seguito chiamò *Chôros* tutto un miscuglio di pezzi, alcuni per un solo strumento, altri per complessi strumentali vari, come pure musica per orchestra con o senza la partecipazione del coro. Per dare un'impronta ancora più brasiliana alla propria personalità, forní una varietà di spiegazioni riguardo alla parola *Chôros*, sebbene in questo caso si trattasse di un titolo qualsiasi e niente più e quella musica avrebbe potuto avere un nome diverso. Comunque ciò lo aiutò a attrarre su di sé l'attenzione e aiutò anche il suo cocciuto desiderio di essere originale e diverso dagli altri.

Negli Stati Uniti Villa-Lobos usò un metodo simile ma su un tono diverso. In primo luogo voleva essere riconosciuto per quel grande compositore brasiliano che fu realmente per un certo periodo, ma al tempo stesso gli piaceva atteggiarsi a clown. Aveva un forte senso dell'umorismo e prendeva gusto a smascherare quelli che si prendevano troppo sul serio. Di conseguenza, subito dopo il suo arrivo a Los Angeles nel tardo autunno del 1944, quando gli era stata appena conferita una laurea, pronunziò un discorsetto d'occasione che fu tradotto dal famoso scrittore brasiliano Érico Veríssimo, che si trovava là avendo appena terminato un ciclo di conferenze sulla letteratura brasiliana alla University of California di Berkeley. Villa-Lobos disse al distinto pubblico «che egli era un figlio della natura e che aveva appreso il linguaggio della libertà con gli uccelli nella giungla brasiliana». Non si sa ciò che i presenti pensarono di questa enigmatica confessione. Il giorno seguente, durante un sontuoso ricevimento offerto da un grande magnate dell'industria cinematografica, presente tutta la gente che conta nel mondo del cinema oltre alle socie di un club femminile, Villa-Lobos fu informato che non aveva alcuna importanza il fatto che non conoscesse una parola d'inglese e che lí erano state ricevute altre persone famose. Attraverso l'interprete Villa-Lobos rispose: «Dica a questa signora che non sono un pappagallo e nemmeno un pagliaccio da circo», come riferí poi Érico Veríssimo. Invece di parlare, Villa-Lobos propose di eseguire della musica per i presenti, ma si lagnò che il pianoforte era «cosí stonato da sembrare l'organetto di un mendicante cieco». L'interprete, che si vergognava dello strano comportamento del compositore, salvò la situazione dicendo cortesi parole di sua invenzione invece di tradurre quelle osservazioni piuttosto sgarbate.

L'antipatia di Villa-Lobos per coloro con cui non aveva niente in comune, a causa del diverso livello sociale o intellettuale, o perché ignoravano la sua musica, e un'assoluta sfiducia in certe istituzioni, inclusa l'UNESCO, lo rendevano agli occhi di alcuni una persona stizzosa e arrogante. Tutte le istituzioni culturali appartenevano a quel regno al quale Villa-Lobos guardava con diffidenza e rancore. Quando fu invitato dalla University of California di Los Angeles per una conferenza al principio degli anni Cinquanta, il compositore si fece beffe del pubblico composto di sole trenta persone. In piedi sul palco, con a fianco l'interprete Lucas Foss, compositore, pianista e musicologo, cominciò a parlare tenendo un grosso sigaro fra le mani. Era certamente la prima volta che un conferenziere, specialmente in una università, fumava mentre si rivolgeva agli ascoltatori. Ma non tenne una conferenza, raccontò invece un aneddoto dopo l'altro e una quantità di barzellette. Comunque il pubblico sembrò divertirsi, ma chi si divertí di piú fu lui stesso. Comportarsi da buffone per far colpo sugli ascoltatori in un istituto di cultura è piuttosto strano. Certi scherzi hanno un limite nel buon gusto e possono essere considerati indegni di un compositore sessantenne che cerca di essere preso sul serio. Eppure la reputazione di Villa-Lobos aumentò continuamente e lo stesso può dirsi della sua produzione musicale che tuttavia durante gli ultimi anni della sua vita rimase allo stesso livello e non ebbe uno sviluppo stilistico, come ci si poteva aspettare. Probabilmente questo fu in parte dovuto all'età e al deterioramento delle condizioni fisiche.

Negli Stati Uniti, dove ogni anno trascorse molti mesi dal 1944 al 1959, Villa-Lobos diresse tutte le maggiori orchestre da un punto all'altro del paese. Il 5 marzo 1957, per il suo settantesimo compleanno, il «New York Times» pubblicò un articolo di fondo in suo onore. Alla City Hall, Abe Stark, presidente del City Council, consegnò a Villa-Lobos una pergamena firmata dall'allora sindaco Robert F. Wagner, Jr., per «i notevoli e eccezionali servizi resi nella promozione dei rapporti culturali fra i popoli delle due Americhe». Villa-Lobos comparve anche nel programma televisivo della NBC *Tonight: After Dark*.

Alla sua morte, il 17 novembre 1959, la stazione radio WQXR del «New York Times» cambiò il programma della serata per trasmettere musiche di Villa-Lobos. Poco dopo, all'inizio del 1960, la New York Public Library gli dedicò una mostra con partiture, libri e fotografie. L'anno seguente, in occasione della ricorrenza della sua nascita, ci fu un concerto alla Carnegie Hall, organizzato da The Universal Symphony Orchestra e dal Music Institute alla presenza dei piú eminenti rappresentanti del mondo sociale e culturale americano e brasiliano. Non c'è dubbio che erano stati gli Stati Uniti a lanciarlo e renderlo famoso e che di là il compositore aveva preso il volo alla conquista dell'Europa e di Israele.

Durante il suo soggiorno a Parigi si installò all'Hotel Bedford in Rue de l'Arcade 17, nell'ottavo *arrondissement*, vicino alla Madeleine e non lontano dall'editore delle sue opere, le Editions Max Eschig, al 48 di Rue de Rome. Non fu questa tuttavia la ragione del suo alloggio in quell'albergo, bensí perché in quel luogo era vissuto l'ultimo imperatore del Brasile, Dom Pedro II, che dopo la proclamazione della repubblica, il 15 novembre 1889, era andato in esilio con la famiglia e aveva trascorso lí gli ultimi anni della sua vita. Villa-Lobos, conscio di avere un posto nella storia, scelse questo albergo nel 1952 e, nelle stesse stanze in cui aveva abitato il suo grande compatriota, Villa-Lobos visse e scrisse musica per diversi mesi ogni anno fino alla morte. Nel 1971, nell'ottantaquattresimo anniversario della sua nascita, fu scoperta una lapide in sua memoria sulla facciata dell'albergo sotto a quella che ricorda il soggiorno dell'imperatore Pedro II.

La Francia ha onorato Villa-Lobos in molti modi: le Editions Max Eschig hanno pubblicato le sue opere, si è eseguita la sua musica e se ne sono incisi dischi. Da Parigi il compositore andò in altre città europee. Il resto del tempo lo trascorse a Rio de Janeiro, in un modesto appartamento di tre stanze nel centro della città a pochi passi dal Teatro municipale dove si eseguivano opere e concerti prima della costruzione della Sala Cecilia Meireles.

Villa-Lobos visse sempre modestamente e fu un indefesso lavoratore fino alla morte. Per lui il comporre e dirigere musica era la gioia della vita. Non aveva bisogno di essere in un particolare stato d'animo o calato in un'atmosfera speciale per creare le sue opere. Componeva con la radio accesa a tutto volume o ascoltando le trasmissioni di melodrammatici romanzi a puntate.

Hugh Ross riteneva che Villa-Lobos avesse la stessa affascinante maniera di comporre di Mozart o Wagner. Un giorno Ross disse a chi scrive queste righe:

All'Hotel Alrae di New York gli chiesi «Come progredisce la tua composizione di *Yerma*»? Villa-Lobos rispose: «Ecco là la partitura» e indicò un grosso fascio di carta manoscritta sul suo tavolo. Lo sfogliai e scoprii con sorpresa che sulle pagine erano segnate tutte le chiavi e le divisioni di battuta con le indicazione del tempo, ma non una nota! Così aveva tutto il lavoro in testa, ma non l'aveva ancora messo sulla carta.

Usava lo stesso procedimento quando riscriveva materiale andato perduto. Una volta mi disse dove potevano trovarsi certi lavori che affermava di avere scritto ma che erano introvabili e assicurava che erano esistiti senza dubbio: dovevano essere andati smarriti e lui li avrebbe riscritti. Se poi lo facesse veramente usando la memoria, dove pretendeva che fosse immagazzinata tutta la sua musica fino all'ultimo dettaglio come in un computer, nessuno lo può sapere. Eppure quasi sempre, quando alla fine si metteva a scrivere queste opere "perdute", componeva la musica proprio nello stile dell'epoca in cui affermava che fossero state scritte in origine. Questo processo di riscrittura, o forse si trattava in effetti di cose nuove, avveniva di solito quando riceveva una commissione o gli si presentava l'occasione di eseguire un lavoro nuovo in un momento in cui era troppo occupato per concepire un'opera originale. Poiché generalmente eseguiva i suoi lavori subito dopo averli composti, è improbabile che si trattasse veramente di un'operazione di riscrittura perché i cosiddetti lavori perduti non erano stati mai eseguiti prima. Forse in origine aveva buttato giú degli appunti ma probabilmente questo era tutto. Comunque quelle storie sul fatto di riscrivere le opere perdute certamente accrescevano quel particolare aroma della sua personalità che tanto gli piaceva spargere intorno a sé.

Anche a Parigi Villa-Lobos era in vena di scherzi e questo negli anni Venti, quando ancora non era un compositore affermato. Ebbe la fortuna di essere finanziato da Carlos e Arnaldo Guinle che gli permisero di vivere comodamente al n. 11 di Place St. Michel dal gennaio 1927 fino alla fine di maggio del 1930 con sua moglie Lucília Guimarães (1886-1966). Là riceveva amici, colleghi e alcune delle celebrità che vivevano a Parigi nei ruggenti anni Venti. Per rendersi gradito ai francesi e attirare l'attenzione su un brasiliano a Parigi, Villa-Lobos raccontò a René Dumesnil una storiella comicissima che nel 1930 fu pubblicata in *La musique contemporaine en France*. Eccola: catturato dai selvaggi, Villa-Lobos fu testimone per tre giorni di cerimonie funebri celebrate in suo onore perché i selvaggi si preparavano a mangiarlo. In un'altra occasione ricorse a un nuovo racconto. Piú morto che vivo rimase in uno stato di semi-incoscienza che gli permise tuttavia di memorizzare gli accenti degli officianti. Liberato dai bianchi, fece ritorno da questa terribile avventura con una grande scorta di ritmi e modulazioni che da allora ha usato a profusione nelle sue composizioni. Questa storiella andò a finire nel n. 12 di «Le Monde Musical» del 31 dicembre 1927, poco dopo che Villa-Lobos aveva dato il secondo di due concerti (24 ottobre e 5 dicembre) che gli assicurarono una posizione nella società parigina. Alla fine di maggio 1930 tornò in Brasile da Parigi, che avrebbe rivisto solo dopo la fine della seconda guerra mondiale, e il 6 giugno fu pubblicata un'altra storia delle sue avventure brasiliane nella parigina «Guide du Concert». Può sorprendere che il compositore, a quarantatre anni, dovesse ancora ricorrere a storielle strabilianti e incredibili per attirarsi l'attenzione pubblica. Il suo racconto veniva cosí riportato:

Nel corso di una delle mie spedizioni avevo portato con me un grammofono e dei dischi. Ebbi un'idea diabolica: volevo vedere quale effetto avesse sugli indigeni la musica europea. Arrivato presso una certa tribú che, ne ero certo, non era stata ancora raggiunta dai benefici della civiltà, installai la mia macchina e le feci suonare qualcosa che ritenevo adatto per loro. Gli indigeni si misero a urlare e a picchiare la divinità meccanica che riuscii a stento a proteggere dal loro furore. Ma no, non era cosí, non avevano paura della mia scatola di Pandora, ma della musica stessa. La prova? Tornata la calma misi un disco di musica indigena registrata presso un'altra tribú con la quale essi non potevano avere avuto alcun contatto. I buoni selvaggi passarono da un estremo all'altro e cominciarono a urlare, cantare e ballare e dar segni di religioso rispetto verso il grammofono. Quando furono sufficientemente eccitati, volli fare un esperimento suonando di nuovo il primo disco. Ci fu un momento di stupore, poi, un attimo dopo, la povera macchina non era altro che un mucchio di pezzetti di legno e rottami metallici [...] Come il selvaggio della favola, questi non potevano sopportare l'idea che dalla stessa bocca uscisse ora il fuoco, ora il gelo [...] Ripetei spesso questo esperimento e le reazioni furono sempre le stesse anche se non altrettanto violente [...] Ciò mi è costato parecchi grammofoni e anche qualche chitarra perché a volte usai questo strumento. Una sequenza di accordi armonici suonati sulla chitarra veniva recepita in modo scoraggiante, mentre le mie improvvisazioni su ritmi indigeni suscitavano l'entusiasmo degli Indios. Questo fu uno dei successi piú belli della mia carriera di musicista.

I brasiliani non si divertirono molto alle storielle parigine di Villa-Lobos perché avevano l'impressione di essere stati messi in ridicolo, ma egli ignorò i rimproveri. A queste storie non credeva neppure lui ma le riteneva buona pubblicità e senza dubbio era il migliore agente pubblicitario di se stesso. A suo giudizio i francesi sapevano a quel tempo pochissimo sulla sua patria e pensava che alcuni di loro credessero che i serpenti strisciavano ancora per le strade principali delle grandi città e cosí cercava di riparare la loro ignoranza prendendosi gioco di loro, ed era felice quando i suoi scherzi trovavano posto nella stampa.

Incontrai Villa-Lobos per la prima volta in Brasile negli anni Trenta, ed egli cercò subito di darmi una vivida impressione del suo enorme coraggio e del suo spirito d'avventura. Si vantò dei suoi numerosi viaggi nell'interno del Brasile, delle peregrinazioni in ogni direzione attraverso quell'immenso paese e alla fine sortí fuori con una storia che in sostanza era il racconto dei suoi viaggi fatti con due amici lungo tutti gli affluenti del Rio delle Amazzoni in un piccolo battello di sua fabbricazione. Viaggi di questo genere, che ancor oggi richiederebbero un'accurata programmazione e una lunga preparazione, erano assai meno attuabili all'inizio del secolo. Quando chiesi conferma di questi viaggi a sua moglie Lucilia, dalla quale il compositore si separò nel maggio 1936, essa mi assicurò che Villa-Lobos amava prendere in giro la gente con storielle di pura fantasia, specialmente se tali da sfuggire al controllo della loro autenticità. Amava circondare la propria persona di un alone di storie fiabesche e stravolgere il suo stile musicale per giustificare a se stesso e agli altri la ragione per cui solo piuttosto tardi aveva avuto il riconoscimento del proprio paese.

Se non fosse stato per i fratelli Guinle che finanziarono i suoi primi concerti a Parigi e le prime pubblicazioni dei suoi lavori presso le Editions Max Eschig, Villa-Lobos non avrebbe fatto progressi fuori della sua patria. Fu il pianista Arthur Rubinstein che attirò l'attenzione dei Guinle su questo compositore di talento dopo averlo conosciuto nel 1918 dietro suggerimento del direttore d'orchestra svizzero Ernest Ansermet che aveva sentito parlare di Villa-Lobos quando questi faceva ancora parte della orchestra del Teatro municipale di Rio de Janeiro come violoncellista. Ansermet si trovava allora in Brasile per una tournée nell'America Latina quale direttore dei Balletti Russi di Serge Diaghilew. Rubinstein incitò i fratelli Guinle, Carlos in particolare, a mandare questo musicista di talento in Europa a ampliare le sue conoscenze. Carlos Guinle mi disse che, con suo fratello Arnaldo, fece tutto il possibile per realizzare quella proposta. I due fratelli vissero abbastanza da vedere il frutto del loro investimento nel talento di Villa-Lobos dopo che questi era divenuto uno stimato compositore di fama internazionale.

Tuttavia, nonostante l'aiuto dei Guinle, Villa-Lobos non godette di sicurezza finanziaria per la maggior parte della vita. Suo padre, Raúl Villa-Lobos (1862-1899), un bibliotecario della Biblioteca nazionale di Rio de Janeiro, discendeva da genitori spagnoli. Raúl fu uno scrittore prolifico e violoncellista dilettante, con una intelligenza versatile e interessi in molti campi culturali, e seguí attentamente il talento musicale del figlio. Dopo la sua morte prematura, a soli 37 anni, la vedova, che viveva di una piccola pensione e del suo lavoro di lavandaia, non poté permettersi di dare a Heitor l'istruzione che presumibilmente suo marito aveva progettato per il maggiore dei suoi molti figli. Heitor entrò ben presto in ambienti bohémiens ove suonava la chitarra di cui il padre gli aveva dato un ottimo insegnamento e, non appena possibile, cercò di guardagnare qualcosa suonando il violoncello nei caffè, nei cinema e in altri luoghi di divertimento. Entrò poi a far parte di alcune compagnie girovaghe di vaudeville. Giovanissimo cominciò a comporre musica chiedendo occasionalmente il consiglio di professori dell'Istituto nazionale di musica di Rio. Soltanto all'età di 28 anni, nel 1915, ebbe l'occasione di presentare la sua musica al pubblico per la prima volta. Da allora fu un regolare esecutore delle sue composizioni, aiutato dalla moglie e da altri artisti. La stampa parlò di lui ma il successo tardàva a venire. Malgrado ciò, con straordinaria energia, riuscí a farsi strada vivendo con poco, perché gli mancò qualsiasi fonte di guadagno regolare fino al suo ritorno da Parigi alla fine di maggio 1930. Desiderava sempre tornare nella capitale francese e sperava che i Guinle continuassero a finanziarlo, ma non lo fecero e furono irremovibili: anche la generosità ha un limite. Pensavano che Villa-Lobos, a 43 anni, fosse abbastanza adulto da poter fare da solo.

I cambiamenti che poi si verificarono in Brasile offrirono al compositore l'occasione di sistemarsi finanziariamente. Dopo la rivoluzione dell'ottobre 1930 e l'avvento sulla scena politica di Getúlio Dornelles Vargas (1883-1954) quale presidente della Repubblica, con il diffondersi di tendenze nazionalistiche in ogni campo, Villa-Lobos, sempre camaleontico e pronto ad adattarsi a qualsiasi circostanza da cui trarre vantaggio, fu ancora l'opportunista che era sempre stato. Con abili sondaggi accoppiati all'entusiasmo e all'energia che lo distinguevano, si assicurò un impiego nella Municipalità di Rio de Janeiro con la nomina a sovrintendente della istruzione musicale, carica che piú tardi esercitò per l'intero Brasile. Cosí, nel 1932, a 45 anni, aveva per la prima volta un impiego stabile con un regolare stipendio mensile, impiego che era stato creato appositamente per lui.

Qui sconfisse anche i suoi nemici e avversari piú accaniti che ritenevano assurdo che una persona come lui, senza alcun precedente tirocinio amministrativo o pedagogico, dovesse guidare gli altri in questo settore, ma il suo incredibile talento lo trasformò nel piú grande fenomeno didattico. Istruí e addestrò gli altri a divenire insegnanti di musica, organizzò cori e concerti, creò un nuovo e ingegnoso sistema didattico, dette dimostrazioni con cori composti da 10.000 fino a 35.000 scolari e si rivelò un amministratore oculato del proprio dominio. Le sue doti non tardarono a essere riconosciute in patria ma anche all'estero da esperti di fama internazionale, come il grande pedagogo Leo Kestenberg (1882-1962) che invitò Villa-Lobos a Praga nel 1936 e in Israele nel 1952 per esporre il suo metodo a congressi di educazione musicale. In quegli anni compose e arrangiò musiche per i suoi cori brasiliani, fondò un'Accademia brasiliana di musica alla quale tuttora appartengono compositori, artisti e musicologi, trovando anche il tempo per comporre alcune delle sue musiche piú deliziose, molte delle quali divennero le piú note eseguite della sua produzione e anche registrate su dischi, come le *Bachianas Brasileiras*. Eppure, senza la seconda guerra mondiale e il programma di scambi culturali fra gli Stati Uniti e il Sud America, Villa-Lobos sarebbe probabilmente rimasto in patria un semplice impiegato fino al termine della sua vita. Non avrebbe forse affascinato i molti amici di ogni nazione con le sue stravaganze, né gli ascoltatori di qua e di là dall'Atlantico avrebbero avuto la possibilità di godere della sua musica. Energia, fede nelle proprie capacità, enorme forza di volontà e lavoro indefesso con un pizzico di fortuna possono cambiare di colpo la vita di una persona. Questo accadde per Villa-Lobos e gli Stati Uniti vi contribuirono non poco.

(traduzione dall'inglese di Lelia Berretti)

Nuova Rivista Musicale Italiana, **XIX**(2), April/June 1985, 254–67

Corrigenda

p208 *line 12*:
For Addision read Addison
p213 *second paragraph, line 6*:
For Lucilla read Lucília

H. Villa-Lobos in Paris

On November 17, 1985, it will be twenty-
six years since Heitor Villa-Lobos (1887–1959), the Brazilian composer,
died at this home at the Rua Araújo Pôrto Alegre 56, Apto. 54 in Rio
de Janeiro due to kidney congestion, which had slowly developed after
a cancerous bladder operation had been successfully performed eleven
years before at New York's Memorial Hospital. Fifteen years before his
death, on November 26, 1944, Villa-Lobos had made his debut in the
United States with the Janssen Symphony Orchestra in Los Angeles.
This was followed by performances of his own music he conducted in
New York City, Chicago, and Boston early in 1945. Before returning to
Brazil he was feted at New York's Waldorf Astoria Hotel at a reception
accorded him by celebrities from the world of music and culture. His
entry into the American musical scene was to be the beginning of many
ensuing successful years as composer-conductor on both sides of the Atlantic; it was the realization of a dream: the recognition as a composer
for which he had fought so long, the opportunity to present his works,
and commissions to write new ones, as well as compose many more
whenever he found time.

Villa-Lobos still kept his home in Rio de Janeiro. A modest three-
room downtown apartment, it was not far from his office, where he
worked as head of the School Music Department of Rio de Janeiro's
Municipality, and only a short walk from the Municipal Theatre, where
operas, symphony concerts, and recitals were given.

In Europe, where he traveled a great deal soon after the end of World
War II, Villa-Lobos chose Paris as his headquarters. This was not the
first time that he had lived there; in fact, it was his third and longest
sojourn in the French capital. The first time he went to Paris was in
1923 on a one-year Brazilian government grant to perform not only his
own music—of which he did rather little—but principally to organize
and play Brazilian music. This was quite a novelty in those days in

France. He remained in Paris about one year, with short trips to Belgium and Portugal.

His second sojourn was considerably more extensive. Villa-Lobos was fortunate enough to be able to remain in Paris three and a half years because this time his stay was financed by two Brazilian industrialists and philanthropists, the brothers Arnaldo and Carlos Guinle. They had decided to give Villa-Lobos an opportunity to savor all that France and Paris could offer and to try to get his music performed. They even helped him financially to have his first works published outside of Brazil with Editions Max Eschig. These grants proved to be successful, Villa-Lobos being able to arrange quite a few concerts in Paris and get the attention of the musical press, particularly that of the music critic of the influential daily newspaper *Le Temps*, Florent Schmitt (1870–1958), who turned into a great admirer and close friend of Villa-Lobos. It was a friendship which lasted until the death of Schmitt shortly before that of the Brazilian composer. The Guinle brothers, especially Carlos, had acted on the advice of Arthur Rubinstein, the American pianist of Polish origin, who had met Villa-Lobos in Rio de Janeiro around 1918. The two artists became friends and the Brazilian implored the virtuoso pianist to help him get to Paris because he felt that his own country was slow in recognizing his talents. Rubinstein obliged and in turn asked his Brazilian friend, Carlos Guinle, to give Villa-Lobos a chance. This he did, nine years later. Thus, in early 1927, Villa-Lobos could embark for Paris, where he remained until the summer of 1930.

After he had returned to Rio de Janeiro much happened that prevented Villa-Lobos from going back to Paris as he had planned to do after a short Brazilian vacation. On the one hand, the Guinle brothers felt that he was now old enough—at age forty-three— to stand on his own feet. They were unwilling to provide any further support. On the other hand, the revolution in Brazil and its ensuing developments offered Villa-Lobos an opportunity to obtain a civil servant position which, for the first time in his life, enabled him to get a salaried job as head of the School Music Department in Rio de Janeiro's Municipality. Here he unfolded into a musical pedagogue when he formed and conducted mass choruses of thirty thousand school children, an unprecedented event at that time in Brazil that was to have a wide repercussion in the musical-educational field in Brazil. With the outbreak of World War II in 1939 Europe was closed to travelers, so Villa-Lobos stayed in Brazil until his debut in the United States toward the end of the war.

Not long thereafter Villa-Lobos visited Europe once more and eventually in 1952 decided to make Paris his European headquarters. This it remained until his death in 1959. Villa-Lobos loved Paris and the Parisian life. Here he felt completely at home. However, he did not

move into an apartment as he had done during the twenties, when he
had settled at Place St. Michell, 11. There every second Sunday afternoon he had held—on the advice of his sponsor Carlos Guinle—his *jour
fixe* where his new-won friends gathered. This time, in the fifties, Villa-
Lobos preferred to live in a hotel; because of his incessant travels he felt
this to be more convenient.

I do not know if it was his idea to reside at the Bedford Hotel at 17
Rue de l'Arcade, near the Madeleine. The last emperor of Brazil, Dom
Pedro II (1825–1891) had lived out his remaining years at the Bedford
Hotel after his dethronement in 1889, when the Republic was proclaimed.
Legend has it that Villa-Lobos was given the same suite in which the
emperor had lived and was allowed to use the emperor's writing desk.
On the hotel's façade is affixed a memorial plaque in memory of Dom
Pedro II. On the posthumous occasion of Villa-Lobos' eighty-fourth
birthday, at the initiative of the consul general, Minister Helio Scara-
botolo, and the Brazilian ambassador, General Aurélio de Lyra Tavares,
a memorial tablet was placed above that of Dom Pedro II upon which
was engraved: ''The Brazilian composer Heitor Villa-Lobos, great interpreter of the spirit of his country, stayed at this Hotel from 1952–
1959.''

Opposite the Bedford Hotel was the L'Acropole Restaurant. Villa-
Lobos used to take his meals there in the company of friends or visitors.
Only occasionally did he lunch somewhere else, as for instance on his
birthday in 1948, just a few months before he fell ill with cancer. Still,
in the early spring days of that year, when he turned sixty-one, Brazilian
friends who happened to be in Paris at the time feted him at La Maison
de l'Amérique Latine. Only one non-Brazilian was invited to join the
party: Villa-Lobos' great admirer and friend Florent Schmitt.

In order to honor Florent Schmitt and show his gratitude for Schmitt's
endeavors and early recognition of his talents, Villa-Lobos tried to persuade the French composer and music critic to come to Brazil. Thus, the
following year, in September 1949, Florent Schmitt sailed for Rio de
Janeiro on the invitation of the Brazilian Academy of Music, founded
by Villa-Lobos in 1945, and the Conservatório Nacional de Canto Orfeônico, which Villa-Lobos also had brought into being. A reception
was held and concerts were organized with the almost eighty-year-old
Florent Schmitt conducting some of his works.

To my knowledge there is just one letter presently available testifying
to the great friendship between Villa-Lobos and Florent Schmitt, written
from Rio de Janeiro on 25 September 1951 and signed by Arminda and
Heitor Villa-Lobos.

The only place in Paris of which Villa-Lobos was distrustful and reticent was the Unesco, although much had been done there to honor him.

In 1949 he was one of twelve composers commissioned to write works for a gala concert commemorating the centenary of Chopin's death. Villa-Lobos responded with *Hommage à Chopin* for piano, about which he corresponded with Irving Schwerké (1893–1975), the American writer who lived in Paris for many years and became a great friend of the Brazilian composer. On November 3, 1958, Unesco again tried to honor Villa-Lobos by performing his *Bendita Sabedoria*, a composition to words of the Bible for unaccompanied chorus written at the suggestion of Carleton Sprague Smith, former chief of the Music Division of the New York Public Library and then with New York University. Unesco performed the music on the occasion of the opening of the new Unesco building at Place Fontenoy in Paris. René Alix conducted the chorus of Radiodiffusion Française. The composer was conspicuously absent. Still, Villa-Lobos did not warm up to this cultural organization, although he was a member of the Brazilian Unesco Commission. Notwithstanding his indifference, Villa-Lobos paid a visit to Unesco on June 15, 1956, which is recorded in some photos.

Villa-Lobos' publisher, Editions Max Eschig, and its directors, who had shown much faith in his talents when first he appeared in Paris at the beginning of his career, remained his principal publisher and lifelong friends. He was represented in the United States by Associated Music Publishers in New York City, though gradually other firms in the United States and other countries began to publish music of the Brazilian composer.

Memorial plate at the Bedford Hotel.

General Aurélio de Lyra Tavares (b. 1905), Brazilian soldier and diplomat.

Villa-Lobos is seen here in front of the Bedford Hotel surrounded by young friends. From right to left: Marietta de Plater Syberg (Polish), Margaret Smith (English), Maria Cecilia de Azevedo, daughter of the Brazilian musicologist Luiz Heitor Corrêa de Azevedo (b. 1905), and Maria Louise Marty (French). The photograph is reproduced here by permission of Luiz Heitor Corrêa de Azevedo, who took the picture on May 18, 1955.

Villa-Lobos standing in front of the L'Acropole Restaurant enjoying an after-lunch cigar. The photograph is reproduced here by permission of Luiz Heitor Corrêa de Azevedo, who took the photograph on May 18, 1955.

Num restaurante situado do outro lado da rua, bem defronte do hotel, chamado l'**Acropole** e cujo proprietário era um grego de nome Papainac, vulgo Papa, ele fazia suas refeições e convidava amiude os amigos. Eram os seus momentos de folga, de pausa, pelo menos aparente, da atividade criadora. No cardápio do restaurante se achava inscrito um certo **Café Villa-Lobos**, mais caro que o ordinário, ultra-forte, destinado a satisfazer o gosto exigente do compositor, para o qual os outros eram **mijo de gato** e que, onde quer que fosse, ensinava os **maitres d'hôtel** a preparar uma infusão à brasileira, digna do nome de café.

Luiz Heitor Corrêa de Azevedo comments on Heitor Villa-Lobos and the L'Acropole Restaurant (Presença de Villa-Lobos, Vol. 10 MEC/ DAS/MVL, Rio de Janeiro, 1977).

After a delicious meal at which the Brazilian national dish of *feijoada*—
black beans and rice—was served, the party gathered outside the build-
ing and Luiz Heitor Corrêa de Azevedo recorded the event in a photograph (published here by his permission). The photograph was taken on
March 5, 1948. First row from right to left: Arminda Villa-Lobos, Hei-
tor Villa-Lobos, Luíza Bailley from the Brazilian Embassy in Paris,
Florent Schmitt, Cristina Maristany (b. 1918), Brazilian soprano of
Portuguese origin. Second row from right to left: Violeta Corrêa de
Azevedo (b. 1913) wife of Luiz Heitor Corrêa de Azevedo, Mariuccia
Iacovina (b. 1912), violinist and wife of Arnaldo Estrella, Brazilian
pianist Arnaldo Estrella (1908–1979), and Brazilian cellist Iberê Gomes
Grosso (b. 1905).

Festival Florent Schimitt

(Sinfônico e Coral)

Organização da A.B.M. e do C.N.C.O.

Segunda-feira, 31 de Outubro de 1949, às 21 horas

Teatro Municipal

Sob o patrocínio de SS.EE. o Ministro da Educação e Saúde
Dr. Clemente Mariani Bittencourt e o Prefeito do Distrito Federal
General Angelo Mendes de Moraes

Participantes:

Orquestra e Corpo Coral do Teatro Municipal do Rio de Janeiro

Orfeão de Professôres do Conservatório Nacional de Canto Orfeônico

Côro Feminino da Associação de Canto Coral

Solista: soprano CRISTINA MARISTANY
Organista: Martinez Gráu

Sob a regência dos maestros:

FLORENT SCHMITT

VILLA - LOBOS

Santiago Guerra

Programs of the concert and reception given in honor of Florent Schmitt during his stay in Rio de Janeiro (courtesy Biblioteca Nacional, Rio de Janeiro).

PROGRAMA

I — LA TRAGÉDIE DE SALOMÉ — para orquestra (1907)

(segundo um poema de Robert d'Humières).

Regente: O AUTOR.

II — SIX CHOEURS — para vozes femininas e orquestra (1930):

n° 3 — «Si la lune rose» (L'âme en borgeon), de Cécile Sauvage.

n° 5 — «L'amoureuse» (Ballades françaises), de Paul Fort.

n° 2 — «Marionnettes» (Tourbillons), de Charle Auvrey.

Pelo Côro du Associação de Canto Coral.

III — IN MEMORIAM (à GABRIEL FAURÉ) — para orquestra (1935).

IV — RONDE BURLÈSQUE — para orquestra (1929).

Regente: VILLA-LOBOS.

V — PSAUME XLVII (vuigata XLVI) — op. 38 — Roma. 1905 — para orquestra, orgão, coros e solo de soprano.

Solista: CRISTINA MARISTANY.

Ao orgão: Martinez Gróu.

Regente: O AUTOR.

(Cores): Santiago Guerra.

Outras Homenagens a Florent Schmitt

A Academia Brasileira de Música realiará em 1 de Novembro, às 17 horas, no audítório da Associação Brasileira de Imprensa, com entrada franca, a Sessão Pública em recepção a FLORENT SCHMITT. — A saudação será feita pelo acadêmico JOÃO ITIBERÊ DA CUNHA, seguindo-se a execução de um programa composto de obras corais do PADRE JOSÉ MAURÍCIO, pelo côro homônimo sob a regência do prof. MAXIMILIANO HELLMANN (tendo ao piano o maestro AFONSO MARTINEZ GRÁU). — Por último, serão executadas as «Três Rapsódias» (Francesa, Polonesa e Vienense), para dois pianos, do homenageado, sendo intérpretes os pianistas ERMANO SOARES DE SÁ e WANDA SOARES DE OLIVEIRA.

No auditório do Ministério da Educação e Saúde, em 4 de Novembro do corrente, às 21 horas, com entrada franca, haverá o «FESTIVAL DE MÚSICA DE CÂMARA FLORENT SCHMITT», cujo programa, organizado pela A.B.M. e a C.N.C.O., é o seguinte:

1. — QUARTETO DE FLAUTAS, op. 106.

   Intérpretes: Ary Ferreira — Antonio F. Faria — Sebastião Vianna — Radamés Lasson.

2. — QUATRE POÈMES DE RONSARD, op. 98 (canto e piano).

   Intérpretes: soprano CRISTINA MARISTANY.
   pianista Alceu Bocchino.

3. — ANDANTE DO QUINTETO, op. 51 (piano e quarteto de cordas).

   Intérpretes: O AUTOR (ao piano)
   Quarteto Haydn (do D.N.C. de São Paulo).

4. — TROIS DANSES, op. 86 (solos de piano).

   Intérprete: JOSÉ VIEIRA BRANDÃO.

5. — TROIS RAPSÓDIES, op. 53 (para dois pianos).

   Intérpretes: ERMANO SOARES DE SÁ.

   WANDA SOARES DE OLIVEIRA.

H. VILLA·LOBOS
R. ARAUJO PORTO ALEGRE, 56 · APT.º 54
RIO DE JANEIRO
BRASIL

Rio, 25 Septembre, 1951

Chèrs Amis:

C'était pour nous une grande joie recevoir votre lettre, toujours bienvenue.

Nous étions déjà inquiets sans rien de nouvelle de vous deux.Nous ne savons pas pourquoi les lettres n'arrivent pas.

Nous sommes très content de savoir de les éxecutions des œuvres de nôtre cher Florent, et qu'elles ont beaucoup de succèss comme meriten.

Merci beaucoup pour la lettre si gentil de notre cher Florent.Nous esperons être ensemble en février, et c'est domage que nous ne pouvons pas monter le Pão de Assucar avec vous deux.

Tous les amis d'ici ont rappelent toujours de vous, et ils vous envoyent les affectueux souvenirs.

Il y a longtemps que je ne vois pas Jean Français. Nous avons été beaucoup de fois avec Mme.Mineur, charmante, si gentil avec nous, et qui/parlé beaucoup de vous.

Dans l'espoir de vous revoir bientôt, nous vous embrassons cordiellement.

Aminda *×* Heitor

H.Villa-Lobos

Mr.Florent Schmitt
44 Quai du Passy
Paris - France

Facsimile of the letter of Arminda and Heitor Villa-Lobos to Florent Schmitt, dated September 25, 1951. The original is in the Bibliothèque Nationale, Paris, and is reproduced here by courtesy of François Lesure, curator of the Music Department. Mme (Gabrielle) Mineur, who is mentioned in the letter, was cultural attaché at the French Embassy in Rio de Janeiro.

Villa-Lobos, himself a member of the national Brazilian commission of Unesco, is seen here with Luiz Heitor Corrêa de Azevedo at Unesco (courtesy Unesco, Paris).

Heitor Villa-Lobos with Luiz Heitor Corrêa de Azevedo (left), chief of the Section for Cooperation with the International Cultural Organizations at the Department of Cultural Activities at Unesco, and John Evarts, executive joint secretary of the International Music Council (courtesy Unesco/R. Lesage, Paris).

Two photos of Heitor Villa-Lobos during his visit to Unesco, June 15, 1956 (courtesy Unesco by M. Weissmann).

Latin American Music Review, **6**(2), Fall/Winter 1985, 235–48

The Villa-Lobos Family

The centenary of the birth of Heitor Villa-Lobos (1887–1959), which fell on 5th March, 1987, was observed and celebrated world-wide. The year 1987 was proclaimed "Villa-Lobos Year" at the suggestion of the Brazilian composer Marlos Nobre (b. 1939), who, in 1987, was President of the International Music Council (IMC/UNESCO). The IMC member-countries were requested to include a Villa-Lobos work in their concert, radio and television programmes on 1st October, 1987, the day that the IMC had called "International Day of Villa-Lobos's Music".

Reference books and biographies, journals and encyclopaedias in many countries list and document the works and life of the colourful personality that was Villa-Lobos. To the legends that surround him the composer often contributed a great deal himself by telling many most amusing stories about his own person. These handicapped researchers and scholars in separating the facts from the fictions that conspired to cloud Villa-Lobos's life all along. Nothing essential, however, has hitherto been published in the English language about Villa-Lobos's family. Here are presented, therefore, for the first time in English, particulars of the composer's family, with all available details based upon all the accessible source-material.

Villa-Lobos's father was of neither Brazilian nor Portuguese origin but was the son of Spanish parents. The name of the composer's paternal grandmother was Maria Carolina Serzedelo Villa-Lobos; his grandfather was called Francisco da Silveira Villa-Lobos. According to the composer, his father spelt his last name originally without a hyphen, in the Spanish way: Villalobos. In accessible historical records the name already appears in the Brazilian spelling: Raúl Villa-Lobos. He was born on 7th January, 1862 in Rio de Janeiro and died there of malaria, at the age of 37, on 18th July, 1899. Raúl was raised in a modest family. An intellectual, an amateur musician and a writer and translator of scholarly books, Raúl wanted to become a medical doctor. Lack of sufficient financial funds, however, forced him to abandon his medical studies after only two years, when he had to look for a salaried post. At the age of 28 he found work at Rio de Janeiro's National Library. This work was, in fact, more compatible with his natural talents. Six years later—in 1896—and three years before his death, Raúl was commissioned to reorganize the library of the Senate in Rio de Janeiro (at the time, the capital of Brazil). Raúl's literary work appeared partly under the pseudonym Epaminondas Villalba, which his composer-son also used occasionally, adding merely the word "filho" ("son"). Raúl practised chamber music at his home, was open-minded towards new tendencies and trends in literature and other arts, had many-sided interests and exercised strong literary and musical influences on his eldest son, Heitor.

In 1884, six years before he found work as a clerk at the National Library in Rio de Janerio, the 22-year-old Raúl, then a teacher, married Noêmia Umbelina Santos Monteiro, who was his senior by three years. Born on 25th February, 1859 in Rio de Janeiro, she died there, aged 87, on 13th March, 1946.

The composer's maternal grandmother was Domitildes Costa Santos Monteiro; the grandfather's name was Antônio Santos Monteiro. He was known as a pianist at social dance-gatherings. He also composed quadrilles and other dances of the kinds

SERVIÇO PÚBLICO FEDERAL ,
FUNDAÇÃO NACIONAL-PRÓ-MEMORIA
BIBLIOTECA NACIONAL-S. DE REFERÊNCIA

RAUL VILLALOBOS

NOMEADO PARA TRABALHAR NA BIBLIOTECA NACIONAL, POR PORTARIA DE 13.10.1890. TOMOU POSSE NO DIA 16 E COMPARECEU O RESTO DO MES, COMO OFICIAL AMANUENSE, GANHANDO O ORDENADO DE 86$021 E GRATIFICAÇÃO DE 43$011.
TRANSFERIDO POR PORTARIA DE 2/8/1892 PARA A SECRETARIA DOS MINISTERIOS DA INSTRUÇÃO PUBLICA.ATÉ O DIA 13/11/1892
NOMEADO POR DECRETO DE 6/10/1892, PARA A BN, COMO 1º OFICIAL. TOMOU POSSE NO DIA 14/11/1892.
SUSPENSO POR PORTARIA DE 26/11/1892 ARTIGO 70 PARAGRAFO 4º E ARTIGO 71, SEGUNDO O DECRETO 5659 DE 6/6/1874.
SUSPENSO DE 26/11/1892 ATÉ 17/9/1893, POR NÃO TER ASSUMIDO AS SUAS FUNÇÕES NA BIBLIOTECA NACIONAL
REASUMIU NO DIA 18/9/1893 ATÉ O DIA 12/7/1899, FICANDO DOENTE, ONDE VEIA A FALECER NO DIA 18/7/1899, GANHANDO 120$430 E DE GRATIFICAÇÃO 25$806.

Document of the National Library, Rio de Janeiro recording Raúl Villa-Lobos's appointment and promotions
(Courtesy of Biblioteca nacional, Rio de Janeiro)

that were popular and fashionable at that time. According to legend, Raúl and Noêmia had eight children, but only four survived. Only the composer was musical: his two sisters and one brother, just like their mother Noêmia, had no interest in music.

A year after Raúl and Noêmia had married, their first child was born—on 3rd November, 1885—and called Bertha, but she became better known under her pet name "Lulucha". She died in 1976, at the advanced age of 91, in Belo Horizonte in the State of Minas Gerais. Bertha never took up any employment but was a dedicated housewife, having married Romeu Augusto Borman de Borges. The couple had three children: Clélia (born 11th September, 1908), Haygara (b. 10th May, 1917) and Paulo Emygidio (b. 10th October, 1922).

Two years after Bertha was born, on 5th March, 1887, there came into the world Heitor Villa-Lobos, whose fame was to carry the Villa-Lobos name far beyond Brazil's frontiers. His father, who died when Heitor was only 12 years old, was destined never to know of his son's celebrity. But his mother witnessed her son's becoming an internationally known composer.

The next surviving child was called Carmen (with the pet name "Bilita"). She was the composer's junior by approximately eighteen months. Born on 10th October, 1888 in Rio de Janeiro, she died in her 82nd year, on 20th April, 1970, in

Cruzeiro in the State of São Paulo. Carmen was a teacher and married Danton Condorcet da Silva Jardim. They had one daughter, Haygara Yacyra (b. 26th August, 1933). Othon, the youngest member of the Villa-Lobos family, was born on 23rd June, 1897, just two years before his father, Raúl, passed away on 18th July, 1899. Othon's life also was short: at the age of 21, he passed away on 27th July, 1918, not long after he had married Octavia, who herself had died in the meanwhile. Othon was an electrician, interested in football but with no inclination for music.

The year of Heitor Villa-Lobos's birth seemed, for a long time, to be ambiguous and uncertain, his several identity cards giving as many birth-dates as there were personal documents. No birth certificate for the composer is available—at least, up to the present, none can be found anywhere. This is not surprising, because in Brazil, between 1881 and 1891, birth registration was not compulsory. Hence, the births of many Brazilians born during that period were not recorded. The only available document that mentions Villa-Lobos's year of birth is the baptism certificate, which states that Villa-Lobos was born on 5th March, 1887. His baptism took place on 17th January, 1889 in São José Church in Rio de Janeiro, together with that of his younger sister, Carmen. Godmother was the paternal grandmother, Maria Carolina Serzedelo Villa-Lobos. The baptism certificate, which the Brazilian diplomat and musicologist Vasco Mariz (b. 1921) discovered in the 1940s, is now generally recognized and accepted as the official document asserting the date and the year of the composer's birth. There occurred, however, an interesting incident worth recording, since even Villa-Lobos's mother, so it seems, was uncertain as to the date of her son's birth:

> . . . when Villa-Lobos was married at the registrar office on November 12, 1913, a birth certificate or anything stating the year of his birth was apparently not available, for this writer found at the registrar's office that Villa-Lobos's Mother made a statement (dated 24 October, 1913) which was attached to the marriage documents, to be found at the Eighth Civil Registrar in Rio de Janeiro, in which she declared that her son was born in the [then] Federal Capital in 1886. (The Marriage registration, however, says that Villa-Lobos was twenty-eight years old.)[1]

On 1st November, 1912 Heitor Villa-Lobos met the concert pianist and teacher Lucilia Guimarães (26th May, 1886—25th May, 1966), who later performed many of his piano works. They were married on 12th November, 1913 in Rio de Janeiro and separated, after a childless marriage, on 28th May, 1936. Divorce did not exist in Brazil at that time. Lucilia died six and a half years after the composer. Arminda Neves d'Almeida (26th July, 1912—5th August, 1985), Villa-Lobos's companion during his last twenty-three years, then changed her name by deedpoll to Villa-Lobos. After the composer had passed away on 17th November, 1959, Arminda d'Almeida Villa-Lobos was nominated Director of the Museu Villa-Lobos in Rio de Janeiro, which was founded on 22nd June, 1960 ". . . to preserve the

---

[1] Lisa M. Peppercorn. "The History of Villa-Lobos's Birth Date", *Monthly Musical Record*. Vol. 78 No. 898 (July—August, 1948). p. 155.

Conego Dr. Benedicto Marinho de Oliveira

Vigario da Freguezia de S. José

do Arcebispado de Rio de Janeiro

Certifico que no livro 18 de termos de bafismos desta
freguesia, á folhas 55, consta o seguinte:

- H e i t o r -

"A dezessete de janeiro de mil oitocentos e oitenta e
nove, batizei solenemente HEITOR, nascido a cinco de março de
mil oitocentos e oitenta e sete, filho legitimo de Raul Villa
Lobos e Noemia Villa Lobos, foram padrinhos José Jorge Rangel
e Maria Carolina Villa Lobos. Conego R. P. dos Santos Lemos,
Parocho Encomendado. - À MARGEM LE-SE: Casou-se com Lucilia
Guimarães em 12 de novembro de 1913. O Vigario Conego Dr. B.
Marinho. - NADA MAIS CONSTA. ITA IN FIDE PAROCHI.

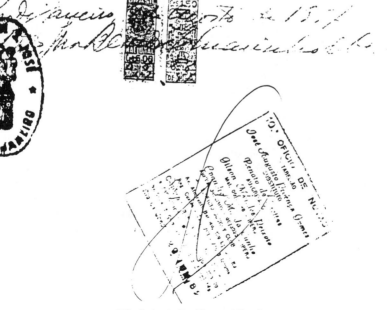

Villa-Lobos's Certificate of Baptism

Villa-Lobos's father, Raúl Villa-Lobos
(Courtesy of Museu Villa-Lobos, Rio de
Janeiro)

Villa-Lobos's mother, Noêmia Umbelina
Santos Monteiro
(Courtesy of Museu Villa-Lobos, Rio de
Janeiro)

Earliest known picture of Villa-Lobos (aged
18), taken in November, 1905 and dedicated
to one of his sisters
(Courtesy of Museu Villa-Lobos, Rio de
Janeiro)

Villa-Lobos's elder sister, Bertha Borman de
Borges
(Courtesy of Oldemar Guimarães, the com-
poser's brother-in-law)

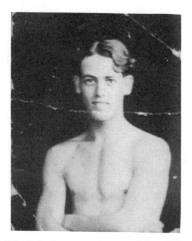

Villa-Lobos's younger sister, Carmen Condorcet da Silva Jardim
(Courtesy of Oldemar Guimarães, the composer's brother-in-law)

Villa-Lobos's younger brother, Othon Villa-
Lobos
(Courtesy of Oldemar Guimarães, the com-
poser's brother-in-law)

Outside and inside views of São José Church, Rio de Janeiro, where the composer and his sister Carmen
were baptized
(Courtesy of São José Church)

memory of Heitor Villa-Lobos and disseminate his work". She held the post until her death. The annual concert festivals, publication of books and recordings, lectures and international competitions that she had initiated and admirably organized and administered continually helped to spread the composer's name in many countries.*

---

* Little is known of Villa-Lobos's family or of his own childhood. and much that has come down to us about his early years is of a legendary nature. Amongst the family photographs presented with this article are some—those of the composer's brother and two sisters—that are now being published for the first time. These. kindly made available to Mrs. Peppercorn by Oldemar Guimarães. the composer's brother-in-law. form part of her recently completed but as yet unpublished book entitled *The World of Villa-Lobos in Pictures and Documents.* [Ed.]

The Music Review, **49**(2), May 1988, 134–7

Tempo, (169), June 1989, 42–5

Villa-Lobos in Israel

Heitor Villa-Lobos's sole visit to Israel, in 1952, was significant in several ways. During a stay of a few days, he presented himself as conductor of his own works, lectured on his pedagogical ideas by explaining and demonstrating his manosolfa system, and was inspired to compose a symphonic poem based on his impressions of Israel, which he dedicated to that country. Seven years later, in 1959, it was in Israel that Villa-Lobos's *Concerto for Harmonica and Orchestra*, a work commissioned by John Sebastian, the American virtuoso harmonica player, was first performed.

Reports about the length of Villa-Lobos's 1952 visit vary. Bathya Bayer (b. 1928), the former chief of the music division of the Jewish National and University Library in Jerusalem, informed me that according to musicians she had consulted, Villa-Lobos remained in Israel only three days, from 17–19 June.[1] *The New York Times*, on the other hand, published on 14 September 1952 an article by its Israel music correspondent, according to whom 'Villa-Lobos stayed in Israel six days'. Certainly on 18 June 1952 Villa-Lobos conducted the Israel Philharmonic Orchestra and performed works of his own which showed his talents from various angles. The concert opened with Corelli's *Concerto grosso No.8*, followed by Bach's Prelude and Fugue for organ in C minor, No.6 in Villa-Lobos's orchestral arrangements of Bach. The concert finished with two of the Brazilian composer's larger works: the Piano Concerto No.2 (composed in 1948, first performed 21 April 1950 in Rio de Janeiro)[2] with the soloist Maxim Shapiro, and *Chôros No.6*, a work begun in 1926 but only completed shortly before its world première on 18 July 1942 in Rio de Janeiro.

On the invitation of Villa-Lobos's old friend Leo Kestenberg (1882-1962) whom he had met for the first time in 1936 at the Prague First International Congress for Musical Education,

Villa-Lobos held a lecture at Tel Aviv's Music Teachers Training College. Kestenberg, the eminent Israeli music educator of Hungarian origin, had lived in Germany until, in 1933, he moved to Prague; in 1938 he settled finally in Israel, where he was Music Director of the Palestine (now Israel) Philharmonic Orchestra from 1939-1945. After his retirement, he founded the First Music Teachers Training College of Israel in 1945. Kestenberg had invited Villa-Lobos to demonstrate, for the teachers and students of the College, his 'Manosolfa' methods, which Villa-Lobos had invented in Brazil and very successfully applied in Brazilian schools. In order to fulfill Kestenberg's request, Villa-Lobos arranged an *ad hoc* chorus with the College's teachers and students, and gave a practical demonstration of his system.[3]

Villa-Lobos's impressions of Israel and her people inspired him to write a symphonic work which he composed the following year and called *Odisséia de uma Raça* (The Odyssey of a Race). The original idea for this work came from Peter Gradenwitz (b.1910), the Israeli musicologist of Berlin origin, who, in 1936, settled in Israel after periods in Prague and London. Gradenwitz was a lecturer at Tel Aviv University, which added a musicological division in 1966. He was also co-founder of the Israeli Section of the International Society of Contemporary Music and Director of Israeli Music Publications. Thus, it was natural that Gradenwitz should come to know Villa-Lobos during the latter's visit to Israel in 1952. On this

---

[1] Letter of 28 December 1972.

[2] Not 1953, as listed in the catalogue of the Museu Villa-Lobos (*Villa-Lobos - sua Obra*, 2nd ed., Rio de Janeiro, 1972, p.42).

[3] Personal communication from the late Käthe Jacob, a long-time collaborator of Kestenberg in both Berlin and Israel, who was present at this demonstration. (Letter of 2 January 1973).

Villa-Lobos lecturing at the Tel Aviv Teachers Training College, June 1952, about his 'Manosolfa' System. At his left is Leo Kestenberg, and at his right the music teacher and composer Yariv Eerach (b.1905)

occasion Gradenwitz suggested to the Brazilian composer that he should write a work reflecting his impressions of the country. Gradenwitz recalled the circumstances for me in a letter dated 5 April 1984:

You yourself will remember that the work was composed at my personal suggestion, abroad, and was arranged to be delivered to Israel, and that I visited Villa-Lobos in the summer of 1953, the year of its completion, in his New York hotel. He was working, simultaneously, on three scores that lay on the desk before him - one was (I think) a Harp Concerto and one the *Odisséia*. He promised the score for December, and it arrived punctually in December at Tel Aviv.[4]

The world première of Villa-Lobos's symphonic poem took place on 30 May 1954: the work was the opening item in the First Symphony Concert of the 28th Festival of the International Society

of Contemporary Music, held from 30 May to 8 June in Haifa, Israel. M⁻hael Taube (1980-1972), an Israeli conductor of Polish origin who had been resident in Israel since 1934, conducted the first half of this concert, including the Villa-Lobos work.

Two years later the American harmonica virtuoso John Sebastian (1914-80) commissioned Villa-Lobos to write a work for him. Sebastian was a self-taught harmonica player who had studied law in Philadelphia and 17th and 18th-century literature in Rome and Florence. During his career he gave over 600 performances throughout the USA and Canada, and played with most of the world's important orchestras. Villa-Lobos was only one of many composers who wrote and dedicated compositions to him: his work was the Harmonica Concerto, which he composed between 1955 and 1956. The world première of this concerto took place in Jerusalem on 27 October 1959, with the Kol Israel Orchestra conducted by George Singer.[5] A review of the work and Sebastian's interpre-

---

[4] 'Sie erinnern sich bestimmt, dass das Werk auf meine persönliche Anregung hin komponiert und Israel zur Verfügung gestellt worden ist, und dass ich Villa-Lobos im Sommer 1953 in seinem New Yorker Hotel im Jahre der Fertigstellung besucht habe - er war an der Arbeit, gleichzeitig, an drei Partituren, die vor ihm auf seinem Schreibtisch lagen, eine war (glaube ich) ein *Harfenkonzert* und eine die *Odisséia*. Er versprach die Partitur für Dezember und pünktlich im Dezember kam sie in Tel Aviv an'.

VILLA-LOBOS CONCERTO
CADENZA by JOHN SEBASTIAN

EMI
music academy manuscript

tation of it appeared in the *Jerusalem Post* on 1 November.

John Sebastian, the Harmonica virtuoso, had already given a most impressive account of his technical and musical abilities in his interpretation of the Tscherepnin Concerto with the same orchestra and conductor the week before in Tel Aviv. Here again, he proved the great value of cooperation between a performing artist and a composer in the creation of new works. Villa-Lobos seems to have written this

concerto not only for Sebastian, but actually together with him: although this is a fine opus in its own right, the possibilities of the harmonica were exploited to

[5] David P. Appleby, in *Heitor Villa-Lobos, A Bio-Bibliography* (Greenwood Press, 1988), p.117, W 524, states that the première took place with the US Air Force Orchestra, John Sebastian (harmonica), Guillermo Espinoza (conductor), no date. This information is erroneous, and transcribed from *Villa-Lobos - sua Obra*, p.47. See further my review of the Appleby volume in *Tempo* No.166.

EML
music academy manuscript

the maximum extent, enabling Sebastian to display his sweet *cantilena* as well as his breath-taking aerobatics (especially in the *cadenza* of the third movement) to the best advantage of player and work alike. [...]

Perhaps the most fascinating first-hand comment about this work is contained in a letter from the soloist's widow, Nadia Sebastian, from her home in St Vicent de Cosse, France, because it includes the following remarks about the Harmonica Concerto by Glen Clugston, John Sebastian's erstwhile accompanist:

It was one of my joys to work with John and Villa-Lobos during the writing of the Concerto. The composer sat at a huge semi-circular desk with a pot of black thick coffee, several cigars and ashtrays all around working on several compositions at once, while watching a TV at intervals. All the time wearing a hat... When we played the first play-through, he rushed forward and embraced us. John wasn't at ease with the Cadenza, feeling it wasn't right, and together they rewrote it. I think Villa-Lobos caught the spirit of the instrument very well in the first two movements. I believe it was nearly his last composition.[6]

The Cadenza mentioned in this letter, jointly worked out by John Sebastian Villa-Lobos, was

transcribed by John M. Ferguson and is here reproduced in facsimile[7] - for the first time, to our knowledge. Despite the fact that Villa-Lobos was personally in Israel only for a short time, this fleeting contact (chronicled here for the first time from primary sources) was certainly significant for him as composer, conductor and musical educator.

[6] Letter to the author dated 12 August 1981.

[7] Kindly made available by John M. Ferguson and reproduced by his permission in a letter dated 21 September 1982.

Tempo, 169, June 1989, 42–5

Corrigenda

p240 *second column, line 2*:
For 1980 read 1890
p243 *first column, last line*:
For John Sebastian Villa-Lobos read John Sebastian and Villa-Lobos

Villa–Lobos 'ben trovato'

Heitor Villa-Lobos's musical output is very comprehensive. Nevertheless, he thought it useful or necessary, at some later stage, to incorporate certain pieces – in their original form or in transcription – into other compositions, apparently for lack of time to write a completely new work, or sheer laziness. Or, he found delight in teasing his listeners, friends and admirers, unless they discovered his hoax. The Brazilian composer–conductor Walter Burle-Marx (b. 1902), in a letter to me of 31 May 1981 from Caracas, Venezuela (and reproduced here by his kind permission), commented on this characteristic of Villa-Lobos:

A typical example of Villa-Lobos's temperament and way of thinking concerns the *Bachianas Brasileiras # 5*. I did the U.S premiere in New York at the World's Fair on May 4th, 1939 with the New York Philharmonic and Bidú Sayão, using the manuscript of Villa-Lobos. Later on, when I saw the manuscript again, there was a repeat sign on the first introductory measure in 5/4. I asked him why he did that and he replied that he felt that the introduction was too short. I asked why he didn't compose two different measures – he who had so much imagination – and he smiled and said: 'To tell the truth, I felt lazy'. This was one of his faults; once a work was finished, he very rarely went back to polish it much less to change it.

The opposite is the case with the First String Quartet. The Villa-Lobos catalogue, 2nd Edition, 1972, published by the Museu Villa-Lobos (MVL) in Rio de Janeiro, states (p.84) that the work was written in Friburgo, Brazil in 1915 and first performed on 3 February 1915 in 'the residence of the Brazilian composer Homero Barreto'. (Homero de Sá Barreto, 1884–1924, was a composer, pianist and teacher.) The third edition of the MVL catalogue, 1989, mentions (p.108) 3 December 1915 as premiere. About 50 years ago, in Rio de Janeiro, the present writer had an opportunity to consult the manuscript in question. She found a string quartet of small dimensions. The title of this work, which dates from 5 March 1915, was *Suíte Graciosa* and it was dedicated to the Quarteto de Friburgo, which is not mentioned in the two MVL catalogues. It consisted of three movements: *Cantilena, Cançonetinha Grega* and *Brinquedo* (Toy). A manuscript copy of the work had the following title: *Suíte de Quartetos de Corda: Suíte Graciosa* (Andante, Allegretto and *Grega Cançonette*). When the official First String Quartet, with the date of composition also as 5 March 1915, was performed by the Iacovino Quartet on 7 August 1946 in Rio de Janeiro, this writer concluded that, while *based* on the *Suíte Graciosa*, this work was most probably written just before the performance given by the Iacovino Quartet. The respective movements bear the headings: *Cantilena, Brincadeira* (Joke), *Canto lírico, Cançoneta, Melancolia* and *Saltando como um Saci* (skipping like a *Saci* – a Brazilian legendary figure). The composer wrote on the manuscript: 'First performance in the home of the family of Homero Barreto in the town of Friburgo (1915), copied 1946'[1].

Many of Villa-Lobos's works, particularly those written between 1940 and 1946, prove that he was always able to imitate the style of any of the stages of his development and that he was, so to speak, an ingenious plagiarist of his own compositions. In fact, a whole series of the works which date from a much earlier period but were supposed to have been mysteriously lost, were written during those years. The truth is therefore, probably, that they were composed years later in the style of the time in which they allegedly originated, but had progressed no further than the title and the occasional sketch. In every catalogue of his work, and in whatever else may have appeared about him in print, these compositions are shown as completed during the early period, with the corresponding date of origin.

[1] Lisa M. Peppercorn, *Heitor Villa-Lobos, Leben und Werk des brasilianischen Komponisten* (Zurich: Atlantis, 1972) p.37.

This kind of self–delusion was also a characteristic feature of Villa-Lobos's desire to appear original – though he seems to have overlooked this time that the public could not share in this because even the Brazilian press believed in the sudden resurrection of these works.[2]

The music critic of Rio de Janeiro's *Jornal do Comércio*, on 14 August 1946, however, had his doubts when he commented on the première of the First String Quartet and wrote:

...the third part [of the concert] was the novelty on this programme, a first performance in Rio de Janeiro, a first performance – even for the composer: the *First String Quartet*, composed by Villa-Lobos 1915 in Friburgo, thirty–one years earlier! Its young composer (I am referring to the Villa-Lobos of today) must have heard this youthful work with mixed feelings... .

When I questioned Villa-Lobos about the manuscript in the early 1940s in Rio de Janeiro, he repeatedly told me that it had been lost. Éditions Max Eschig published the Second and Third Quartets but the First was never mentioned, nor had it even been performed publicly. The composer, who saw to it that all his works received public performances, would certainly have had this work performed earlier if it had existed.[3] The First String Quartet was eventually published by Peer–Southern in New York, whom the composer came to know after his first visit to the United States in 1944.

Alegria na Horta (Gaiety in the vegetable garden) for piano solo, the last of three pieces from the *Suíte Floral* (Floral Suite) op.97, was composed in 1919 and premièred by Arthur Rubinstein as an encore during his Rio de Janeiro recital of 5 July 1922. The original manuscript of *Alegria na Horta* contains the note 'Impressions of various racial characters during an outburst of happiness'. On publication, this note was replaced by 'Impressions of a garden party'[4] Almost 20 years after the completion of this piece, in 1937, the composer orchestrated and incorporated it in the *First Suite* of the film music *Descobrimento do Brasil* (Discovery of Brazil – this

First Suite was also included on 12 July 1959 in Villa-Lobos's last concert of his life, at the Empire State Music Festival in the United States). The original *Alegria na Horta* composition is hardly related to *Descobrimento do Brasil*, and lacks any context in Villa-Lobos's elaborate text supplied for this latter work which, he says, is based on a historical document: the letter which Pero Vaz de Caminha, secretary of the fleet of Pedro Álvares Cabral, the discoverer of Brazil, had sent to King Manoel on 1 May 1500 from Pôrto Seguro on the Island of Vera Cruz, reporting Brazil's discovery. Did Villa-Lobos really think listeners would not notice his musical wile and take this textual explanation serious? Did nobody ever question him about it?

A striking example of Villa-Lobos's re-use of solo pieces in orchestral transcription, to form a wholly different composition, and attaching some textual explanation to fit this transform-ation, is *Bachianas Brasileiras* No.2 for chamber orchestra which was premièred on 5 September 1938 during the Sixth International Festival for Contemporary Music in Venice, held from 5–13 September 1938[5]. Guido M. Gatti called this work, 'quelques curieux mélanges folklore-bachien de Villa-Lobos' in his review in *La Revue Musicale*, Paris, September 1938, No.186, p.173. In fact, *Bachianas Brasileiras No.2* is an orchestration

---

[2] *Villa-Lobos, The Illustrated Lives of the Great Composers* by Lisa Peppercorn (London: Omnibus Press, 1989). p.95.

[3] Peppercorn, *op. cit.* p.99, footnote 8.

[4] A review of Rubinstein's recital appeared in Rio de Janeiro's *Jornal do Comercio* on 9 July 1922. The date 21 October 1922 is quoted as premiere in the Villa-Lobos catalogue, issued by the Museu Villa-Lobos (MVL) in Rio de Janeiro under the title: *Villa-Lobos – Sua Obra*, 2nd Ed. p.165 and 3rd Ed. p.144. This date is copied in the *Bio-Bibliography* by David P. Appleby, p.34, item W117. This information is incorrect.

[5] Peppercorn *op. cit.*, p.106. The MVL catalogue, 2nd Edition p.28 mentions 3 September 1938 and the Second Festival. Appleby *op. cit*, p.64 item W247 states 3 September 1934, which is also mentioned in the MVL catalogue, third edition. p.41. Adhemar Nóbrega's *As Bachianas Brasileiras de Villa-Lobos*, Rio de Janeiro, 1971, p.37 gives the date 1934 and says it was the second Festival. My most recent research reveals that Venice's Second International Biennale Art Exhibition was held in 1932 (not 1934), in tandem with a Festival of the ISCM which presented, in a concert of South American music, four of Villa-Lobos's *Chansons Typiques Brasiliennes* (not the *Bachianas Brasileiras No.2*). The Third International Biennale was held in Venice in 1934, and the musical part of the Festival performed no Villa-Lobos work at all. (Source: *La Revue Musicale*, September 1932 and September 1934).

of three pieces for violoncello and piano and one piece for piano solo, all composed in São Paulo in 1930. The cello pieces are: O Canto do Capadócio (The song of the pompous ass)[6], O Canto da Nossa Terra (The song of our land), O Trenzinho do Caipira (The little train of the smallholder) with the subtitle Uma Suggestão de uma viagem num trenzinho de interior (An impression of a journey in a little train of the hinterland), and for piano solo Lembrança do Sertão (Memory of the Brazilian backwoods). O Canto do Capadócio was originally subtitled No.3 of the Suíte Típica while O Canto da Nossa Terra already bore the title Bachianas Brasileiras.

Villa-Lobos's decision to transcribe these four pieces for chamber orchestra, presumably for lack of time to write a new orchestral work, made him seek an adequate title for the orchestrated version. Influenced by the neo-classical trend during his recent stay in Paris (1927–1930), he attempted to lean on this new European tendency (as he so often in his life adjusted himself to current drifts anywhere). Obviously he endeavoured at the same time to attach to it his own original label. He thus hit on the idea of calling this, as well as a number of subsequent works, written after his return to Brazil in the summer of 1930, Bachianas Brasileiras. And he thought it convenient, therefore, to adapt some recently composed solo pieces for this particular purpose although there is no connexion amongst nor within the four pieces, nor were they in any way 'bachian' in spirit or style when originally composed. Yet, all Villa-Lobos did was merely to add pre-classical names to the orchestrated version of the solo pieces, and to call this as well as subsequent works Bachianas Brasileiras. Eventually there were nine altogether. They were written during his years in Brazil from 1930–1945 before he accommodated himself to North American requirements after his debut in Los Angeles on 26 November 1944 and turned away from this type of music, towards international standard forms like symphonies, concertos and the like. The words Bachianas Brasileiras, in this writer's opinion, are artificially invented titles given to a versatile set of compositions, in order to demonstrate a contribution to Europe's neo-classical trend by a Brazilian composer

seeking to appear original. But despite the Brazilianized–baroqueian name, this music mostly lacks baroque substance, except what has been artificially added.

One of the most grotesque reshuffles is Villa-Lobos's composition A Mariposa na Luz (The butterfly in the light), composed in July 1917[7], the last movement of a three-part work for violin and piano entitled O Martírio dos Insectos (The martyrdom of the Insects), which – without the first two parts – was premièred on 17 November 1917 in Rio de Janeiro. A few years later, Villa-Lobos had in mind to write a piece for violin and orchestra, which he called Fantasia de Movimentos Mixtos (Phantasy of Mixed Movements). The second movement, Serenidade (Serenity), was written in 1920, the first Alma Convulsa (Tortured Soul), the following year, in 1921. But when this work was premièred on 15 December 1922[8] Serenidade was performed as first movement, and as second movement Villa-Lobos presented A Mariposa na Luz with the piano part orchestrated. This set of arrangements was played until a concert in Paris on 7 May 1930, when A Mariposa na Luz was substituted with Alma Convulsa. (Further reshuffles of the Fantasia de Movimentos Mixtos are described in my biography of Villa-Lobos, op.cit. p.183).

A Mariposa na Luz was yet to enter into another Villa-Lobos composition, which however was never performed, and only planned in 1932 according to the MVL catalogues. Perhaps stimulated by Diaghilev's Russian Ballets in Paris when he himself lived there, Villa-Lobos – who always desired to participate in whatever trend was current at the time, wherever he lived, to show that he, too, could do as well as others –

[6] The MVL catalogue 2nd Ed. p.178 erroneously states that O Canto do Capadócio, written in 1930, was premiered fifteen years before (!) on 29 January 1915 at the Teatro D. Eugenia in Friburgo, Brazil; which Appleby copied, op. cit., p.64 item W251. He also writes that the four pieces 'were transcribed from Bachianas Brasileiras No.2' while just the opposite is correct, namely the solo pieces existed first and were later orchestrated. The MVL catalogue, 3rd Ed. p.123, gives the first performance date as 23 January 1931.

[7] Peppercorn, op. cit. p.42. The MVL catalogue, 2nd Ed. states the composition dates from 1925, Appleby op. cit. p.55, item W214 mentions 1916, and so do others.

The programme of the concert in which Villa-Lobos's 'Fantasia de Movimentos Mixtos' was premiered; and, r., the announcement of this concert with altered dates.

H. VILLA-LOBOS

THEATRO MUNICIPAL

⊁ PROGRAMMA ⊱

DO 4.ᵒ CONCERTO SYMPHONICO
EM HOMENAGEM
Ao Snr. Dr. Arnaldo Guinle

1.ª PARTE

1 —(1922)—**Phantasia de movimentos mixtos** — violino e orchestra
    A) — Andante — (Serenidade)
(1915)—B) — Allegro — (A mariposa na luz)
      Senhorinha Paulina d'Ambrosio
2 —(1920)—Dois **Epigrammas ironicos sentimentaes** canto e orchestra — poesia de Ronald de Carvalho
      Senhorita Maria Emma
    A) — Epigrammas
    B) — Noite de Junho
3 —(1919)—A **Guerra** — 1.ª Symphonia do Tricyclico Symbolico — (orchestra e banda)
    A)—Allegro quasi justo —(A vida e o labôr)
    B)—Movimento vivo — Como um scherzo —(Intrigas e cochichos
    C)—Allegro — A batalha

2.ª PARTE

4 —(1919) —A **Victoria** — 2.ª Symphonia do Tricyclico Symbolico.
    A)—Allegro impetuoso
    B)—Andantino
    C)—Lento com Allegro

FIM

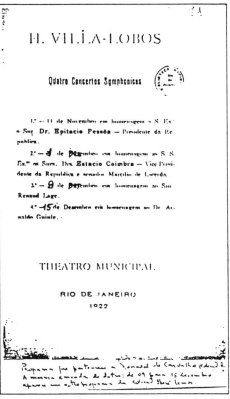

H. VILLA-LOBOS

Quatro Concertos Symphonicos

1.ᵒ — 11 de Novembro em homenagem a S. Ex.ª Snr Dr. Epitacio Pessôa — Presidente da Republica.

2.ᵒ — 4 de Dezembro em homenagem a S. S. Ex.ᵃˢ os Snrs. Drs. Estacio Coimbra — Vice-Presidente da Republica e senador Marcilio de Lacerda.

3.ᵒ — 9 de Dezembro em homenagem ao Snr Renand Lage.

4.ᵒ — 15 de Dezembro em homenagem ao Dr. Arnaldo Guinle.

THEATRO MUNICIPAL

RIO DE JANEIRO
1922

Programa foi patrocinado a Ronald de Carvalho (rdc.) ? A musica emenda de datas: de 09 p——— 15 dezembro ——— ———————————

decided to write a ballet. But, as before and afterwards, when he lacked time or was too lazy to compose a new work, he planned to use pieces from previously completed compositions, grouped them together and gave the new work a new name. With Lindbergh's solo flight across the Atlantic in 1927, airflights became a topic. Thus Villa-Lobos decided to entitle some projected ballet music: *Evolucão dos Aeroplanos* (Evolution of Airplanes). And what did he do? He intended to use pieces from earlier compositions. For the first part of the ballet he planned to use *Música Inquieta* (Disquiet Music), the third piece from the *Suíte Característica* for strings, composed 1912/1913 and premièred on 31 July 1915 in Rio de Janeiro. For the second movement should serve the orchestrated version of *Valsa Mística* (Mystic Waltz), the first of the three-piece piano work *Simples Coletânea* (Simples Anthology), begun on 18

November 1917, finished in 1919 and first performed on 12 November 1919. And to round off the ballet *A Mariposa na Luz* had to fill in here again.[9]

[8] Peppercorn, op. cit. p.183. The MVL catalogue, 2nd and 3rd editions, list the première in orchestrated form as 9 December 1922, copied by Appleby *op. cit.* p.46 item W174. Luiz Guimarães in *Villa-Lobos, Visto da Platéia e na Intimidade 1912/ 1935,* (Rio de Janeiro, n.d.), p.89 states the date 12 December 1922. Upon my request to verify the correct date, Thereza Aguiar Cunha, Deputy Chief of the Music Division of the National Library in Rio de Janeiro, provided me on 11 February 1988 with a copy of the programme and the *rectified* date of the concert announcement, herewith reproduced by courtesy of the National Library. In Cunha's handwriting is added at the bottom: 'Programme belonged to Ronald de Carvalho [Brazilian poet 1893-1935] Collection Ronald de Carvalho. The same change of date – 9-15 – December appears in another programme in the collection of Iberê Lemos'. [Arthur de Iberê Lemos. (1901-1967). Brazilian composer, pianist and critic].

This is not the only composition that used pieces written earlier in orchestral form under a new title. *Mômoprecóce* (Precocious Carnival King) for piano and orchestra is but the orchestration of the eight piano pieces called *Carnaval das Crianças Brasileiras* (Carnival of Brazilian Children), written in 1919/20 and premièred on 22 September 1925[10]. In 1929 the Brazilian pianist Magdalena Tagliaferro (1893?–1986) who mostly lived in Paris, commissioned Villa–Lobos to write a piano concerto for her. Lacking time, or being too lazy, Villa–Lobos, while vacationing in Brazil during his Paris sojourn, orchestrated the *Carnaval das Criancas Brasileiras* and retitled it *Mômoprecóce*, which Tagliaferro premièred in Paris on 23 February 1930[11] under the conductor Enrique Fernandez Árbos (1863–1939).

Only three years before his death in 1956 Villa–Lobos – so it seems – resorted again to using pieces he had written before when he was commissioned by Basil Langton (b.1912) to write the music for a ballet based on Eugene O'Neill's drama *The Emperor Jones*. Langton, the British-born actor, dancer, theatre and opera director, who lives in the United States, communicated his suspicions and ideas regarding this matter to me in a letter, dated 22 July 1988, reproduced here by his kind permission:

As co-founder with John Brownlee [1901–1969] of The Empire State Music Festival for which I was executive director and stage director....we were now planning our second [season] and I was in search of ideas. One evening I was invited to a dinner party and some young man said to me: 'I always thought *The Emperor Jones* would make a wonderful ballet'. I don't know who that fellow was, but he lit a spark of an idea. That night I saw the possibility of commissioning a dance work for José Limón [Mexican–born dancer and choreographer, 1908–1972] to music by Villa–Lobos. The following day, I made inquiries & found Villa-Lobos was in New York. I went to see him at his hotel and he said 'yes'. I went to see my friend Limón & he said 'yes'. A few weeks later Villa–Lobos sent word the work was finished. With Limón I went over to his hotel to hear it. To my amusement, the very thing I assumed the composer would latch on to is the dramatic device in the play of the jungle drum beats beginning & accelerating to the end, which is what drives the Emperor Jones to madness. The composer had totally ignored this. I found myself wondering if he had read

the Spanish script of the play I had given him. I looked at Limón who seemed equally surprised, and I then asked Villa–Lobos why he had ignored this very dramatic & musical device. He looked at us both and then said to Limón in Spanish: 'Does he think he's Diaghilev?' He made no change and we produced the work as he wrote it. Limón made it a success, but my own feeling is that the composer really strung together music he already had in his head or on his desk, and that it had very little to do with the O'Neill theme of *The Emperor Jones*.

Such remarks are characteristic of Villa–Lobos when he felt trapped and tried to cover up some weakness of his. *The New York Times*, on 13 July 1956, one day after the première of Villa–Lobos's ballet *The Emperor Jones* at Ellenville, observed the same: 'one rather wondered why O'Neill's specification of gradually accelerating drum beats, which he asked to be heard throughout the play, were ignored'.

Perhaps the most bizarre example of Villa–Lobos presenting to the public a composition with a date of years gone by, though having written it most likely very many years later and then having forgotten about what he did in the past, is the *Sexteto Místico*. This work, published by Editions Max Eschig in 1957, was premièred, according to the MVL catalogues, on 16 November 1962 in Rio de Janeiro, and written, as is also indicated on the published score, in 1917. In 1939, while living in Rio de Janeiro, I saw a sketch of this Sextet which did not go further than six bars. With the publication date only a couple of years before Villa–Lobos's death, and a première only three years after he had died, it may not be too far off to assume that the work was written, not in 1917, but only shortly before its publication. But even so, the composer

---

[9] Peppercorn *op. cit.* p.216 and the MVL catalogue, second ed. p.110. The third edition of the MVL catalogue, p.90, states 'adaption of *Martírio dos Insectos*'.

[10] Peppercorn *op. cit.* p.117. The MVL catalogues, 2nd Ed (p.152), and third ed. (p.129) date the première to 1? September, as does Appleby *op. cit.* item 157; but C *Imperial*, the Brazilian publication, on 24 September 1925 refers to the concert in a review as 'the day before yesterday' (quoted in Luis Guimarães, *op. cit.* p.114–116).

[11] The MVL catalogues, 2nd and 3rd editions, state a première: 1929 Amsterdam with Magdalena Tagliaferro a soloist and Pierre Montreux as conductor.

seemed to have forgotten that in 1921, and *not* in 1917, had he begun to write this work and intended to dedicate it to [José Pereira da] Graça Aranha (1868-1931), the Brazilian poet, an admirer and supporter of Villa–Lobos in the early 1920s. The sketch here reproduced, which appeared in the São Paulo publication of *Klaxon*, has no affinity with the published work, nor is the composition date indentical. Thus, the true composition date of the *Sexteto Místico* may well remain 'mystical'. It all goes to show that Villa–Lobos's composition dates on published works or on manuscripts should be taken with a grain of salt, and that the titles and explanations he so fancied adding to compositions, have often little or no bearing on the work – indeed, some of them may well be written off as occasional ballyhoo.

This is also true of the often publicized tales and the many published stories that Villa–Lobos roamed through Brazil's interior and its jungles to collect folklore material. If he really ever did so, where is this material, published or unpublished? Nor has his music any such folktunes as he was supposed to have collected himself. But this supposed folktune collecting always gave good

Villa-Lobos's original sketch of the 'Sexteto Místico', composed in 1921, reproduced from the São Paulo publication 'Klaxon' No. 8–9, 1922, p.16. Opposite page: the opening of the published 'Sexteto Místico', reproduced by kind permission of Editions Max Eschig, Paris.

H. VILLA-LOBOS
(Rio, 1917)

© Copyright 1957 by EDITIONS MAX ESCHIG   TOUS DROITS D'EXÉCUTION ET DE REPRO-
         48, rue de Rome - PARIS   DUCTION RÉSERVÉS POUR TOUS PAYS

publicity copy for the composer, who most likely invented and spread these stories himself.

And does anybody really believe his glorious tale that he was shipwrecked on the island of Barbados and there had nothing more urgent to do than busy himself with the folklore of this country? Why then is this legend retold and printed so often and believed in all seriousness? Does really nobody think of this, as well as of his other folklore stories:

Se non è vero
è ben trovato?

Tempo, (177), June 1991, 32–9

Corrigenda

p244 *paragraph 3, line 11*:
For premiere read première
p245 *second column, line 3 from bottom*:
For bachien read bachiens
p246 *FN 6, line 2*:
For premiered read premièred
FN 7 line 2:
For 1925 read 1916
p248 FN 10 last line:
For Luis read Luiz

Acknowledgements

Reprint permission was kindly granted by the editors and/or publishers of the publications mentioned below.

Américas, Washington, D.C.
Bimonthly magazine, published in English, Portuguese and Spanish by the General Secretariat of the Organization of American States. The photos are reprinted by courtesy of OAS, The Museum Villa-Lobos, Rio de Janeiro and Lisa M. Peppercorn, Zürich.
'Villa-Lobos: Father and Son', (English, Spanish, Portuguese) **24**(4), April 1972, 19–24 in all language issues.
'The Villa-Lobos Museum', (English and Spanish), **25**(11/12), November/December 1973, 18–23 in both language issues.

Bulletin of the Pan American Union, Washington, D.C.
'Musical Education in Brazil', **74**(10), October, 1940, 689–93.

Ibero-Amerikanisches Archiv, West Berlin
'Foreign Influences in Villa-Lobos's Music', NF, **3**(1), 1977, 37–51.
'The Fifteen-Year-Periods in Villa-Lobos's Life', NF, **5**(2), 1979, 179–97.

International Cyclopedia of Music and Musicians, Dodd, Mead & Company, New York
'Heitor Villa-Lobos (b. Rio de Janeiro, March 5, 1887 – d. there, Nov. 17, 1959)', 10th edn 1975, and 11th edn 1985, 2363–71

Journal of Musicological Research, New York/London/Paris
Copyright © Gordon and Breach Science Publishers, reprinted by permission.
'The Paris Bibliothèque Nationale's autograph letter of Villa-Lobos to his sponsor', **3**(3/4), 1981, 423–33.

Latin American Music Review, University of Texas Press, Austin, Texas
'A Villa-Lobos Autograph Letter at the Bibliothèque Nationale (Paris)', (Addressee: Florent Schmitt), **1**(2), Fall/Winter 1980, 253–64, reproduced by permission.
'H. Villa-Lobos in Paris', **6**(2), Fall/Winter 1985, 235–48. The material and illustration first appeared in the *Latin American Music Review*, and is re-used in this book by permission of the University of Texas Press, Austin, Texas, and courtesy of the other copyright holders.

Mens & Melodie
'Heitor Villa-Lobos en zijn Familie', September 1980, 457–60, The Spectrum, De Meern, Netherlands.

'Hoe villa-Lobos de vader werd van de braziliaanse muziek', October 1984, 412–17, Libricom, Frits Knuf, Buren, Netherlands.

Monthly Musical Record, The, London
'The History of Villa-Lobos's Birth-Date', **78**(898), July/August 1948, 153–5.

Music and Letters, Oxford University Press, Oxford
'Correspondence between Heitor Villa-Lobos and his wife Lucília', **61**(3/4), July/October 1980, p. 284–92.

Music Review, The, Cambridge, England
'Some Aspects of Villa-Lobos' Principles of Composition', **4**(1), February 1943, 28–34.
'Villa-Lobos's Last Years', **40**(4), November 1979, 285–99.
'The Villa-Lobos Family', **49**(2), May 1988, 134–7.

Musica Viva, Rio de Janeiro
'Uma Opera de H. Villa-Lobos', **I**(3), July 1940, 6–7.

The Musical Times, London
'Villa-Lobos's Brazilian excursions', **113**(1549), March 1972, 263–5.

Neue Zeitschrift für Musik, B. Schott's Söhne, Mainz
'Menschen, Masken, Mythen: Heitor Villa-Lobos und die brasilianische Musik', September 1984, 8–11.

Neue Zürcher Zeitung, Zürich
'Heitor Villa-Lobos: Festanlässe zum Todestag des brasilianischen Komponisten', (489), 19 November 1974, 39.

New York Times, New York
'A Villa-Lobos Opera', 28 April 1940, IX, 8.
'Violin Concerto by Villa-Lobos', 8 June 1941, IX, 5.
'New Villa-Lobos Works', 11 October 1942, VIII, 6.
Copyright © 1940/41/42 by The New York Times Company, reprinted by permission.

Nuova Rivista Musicale Italiana, Rome
'Le Influenze del Folklore Brasiliano nella Musica di Villa-Lobos', **X**(2), April/June, 1976, p. 179–84.
'Heitor Villa-Lobos: Il Burlone', **XIV**, (3), July/September 1980, 378–92.
'Heitor Villa-Lobos: Profilo del Compositore Brasiliano', **XIX**(2), April/June 1985, 254–67.

Revue Belge de Musicologie, Brussels
'Villa-Lobos's Stage Works', **XXXVI–VIII**, 1982–84, 175–84.

Studi Musicali, Accademia Nazionale di Santa Cecilia, Rome
'A Letter of Villa-Lobos to Arnaldo Guinle', **X**(1), 1981, 171–9.

Tempo, Boosey & Hawkes Music Publishers Ltd., London
'Villa-Lobos's Commissioned Compositions', (151), December 1984, 28–31.
'Villa-Lobos in Israel', (169), June 1989, 42–45.
'Villa-Lobos "ben trovato"' (177), June 1991, 32–9.

Name index

Index of works mentioned